Verse by Verse Commentary on the Book of

GENESIS

Enduring Word Commentary Series
By David Guzik

*The grass withers, the flower fades,
but the word of our God stands forever.*
Isaiah 40:8

Commentary on Genesis

Copyright ©2018 by David Guzik

Printed in the United States of America or in the United Kingdom

Print Edition ISBN: 978-1-939466-42-6

Enduring Word

5662 Calle Real #184

Goleta, CA 93117

Electronic Mail: ewm@enduringword.com

Internet Home Page: www.enduringword.com

All rights reserved. No portion of this book may be reproduced in any form (except for quotations in reviews) without the written permission of the publisher.

Scripture references, unless noted, are from the New King James Version of the Bible, copyright ©1979, 1980, 1982, Thomas Nelson, Inc., Publisher.

Contents

Genesis 1 – The Account of God's Creation 7
Genesis 2 – Creation Completed; Adam in the Garden of Eden 35
Genesis 3 – Man's Temptation and Fall 46
Genesis 4 – Cain and Abel 66
Genesis 5 – The Descendants of Adam 74
Genesis 6 – Man's Wickedness; God Calls Noah 79
Genesis 7 – God Destroys the World with a Flood 88
Genesis 8 – Noah and His Family Leave the Ark 93
Genesis 9 – God's Covenant with Noah and Creation 99
Genesis 10 – The Table of Nations 107
Genesis 11 – Mankind after the Flood; the Tower of Babel 112
Genesis 12 – God's Call of Abram; Abram in Egypt 118
Genesis 13 – God Promises Abram the Land Again 126
Genesis 14 – Abram Rescues Lot and Meets Melchizedek 131
Genesis 15 – God Confirms the Covenant with Abram 137
Genesis 16 – Hagar and the Birth of Ishmael 146
Genesis 17 – God Reaffirms the Covenant 155
Genesis 18 – The Promise of Isaac Confirmed 163
Genesis 19 – The Destruction of Sodom and Gomorrah 171
Genesis 20 – Abraham Lies About Sarah Again 181
Genesis 21 – The Birth of Isaac 185
Genesis 22 – Abraham Is Willing to Offer Isaac 192
Genesis 23 – Sarah Dies and Is Buried 202
Genesis 24 – A Bride for Isaac 205
Genesis 25 – Abraham's Death; Jacob and Esau Born to Isaac 216
Genesis 26 – Isaac Sins Like Abraham 224
Genesis 27 – Jacob Deceptively Gains the Blessing of Isaac 232
Genesis 28 – Jacob Flees from Esau 241

Genesis 29 – Jacob's Marriages and Children ... 247
Genesis 30 – The Children Born to Jacob ... 256
Genesis 31 – Jacob Flees from Laban to Canaan ... 265
Genesis 32 – Jacob Prepares to Meet Esau ... 275
Genesis 33 – The Meeting of Jacob and Esau ... 286
Genesis 34 – Simeon and Levi Massacre the Men of Shechem ... 290
Genesis 35 – Revival in Jacob's Life ... 298
Genesis 36 – The Family of Esau ... 306
Genesis 37 – Joseph Is Sold into Slavery ... 310
Genesis 38 – Tamar and the Sin of Judah ... 322
Genesis 39 – Joseph in Potiphar's House ... 327
Genesis 40 – Joseph Interprets Dreams in Prison ... 337
Genesis 41 – Joseph Interprets Pharaoh's Dream, Rises to Power ... 343
Genesis 42 – Joseph Meets His Brothers in Egypt ... 353
Genesis 43 – Joseph Meets His Brothers a Second Time ... 365
Genesis 44 – Joseph Tests His Brothers ... 372
Genesis 45 – Joseph is Reunited With His Brothers ... 379
Genesis 46 – The Family of Jacob Comes to Egypt ... 384
Genesis 47 – Jacob Meets Pharaoh; the Family Settles in Egypt ... 389
Genesis 48 – Jacob Blesses Joseph's Sons ... 394
Genesis 49 – The Blessing of the Sons of Jacob ... 402
Genesis 50 – The Burial of Jacob; the Death of Joseph ... 413

Bibliography - 421
Personal Remarks from the Author - 423

Genesis 1 – The Account of God's Creation

A. Thoughts to begin with as we study the Bible.

1. We come to the Bible knowing there is a God.

   a. There are many good and strong philosophical and logical reasons to believe in God. Yet the Bible does not make elaborate arguments for the existence of God. However, it does tell us how we can know God exists.

   b. The Bible tells us we can know God exists because of what we see in the created world.

   > i. Psalm 19:1-4 explains this: *The heavens declare the glory of God; and the firmament shows His handiwork. Day unto day utters speech, and night unto night reveals knowledge. There is no speech nor language where their voice is not heard. Their line has gone out through all the earth, and their words to the end of the world.*

   > ii. Romans 1:20 also explains: *For since the creation of the world His invisible attributes are clearly seen, being understood by the things that are made, even His eternal power and Godhead, so that they are without excuse.*

   c. This is an example of the *teleological* argument for the existence of God. It is the understanding that there must be a purposeful intelligence that created this world because the world shows both purpose and intelligence. In the view of many (including the author), this argument from purpose and design remains unanswered by the atheist or the agnostic.

2. We come to the Bible believing it is the place where God has spoken to man, perfectly and comprehensively.

   a. We believe what is written in 2 Timothy 3:16-17: *All Scripture is given by inspiration of God, and is profitable for doctrine, for reproof, for correction, for instruction in righteousness, that the man of God may be complete, thoroughly equipped for every good work.*

i. We can study God, but we can't put Him under a microscope or test Him in a laboratory. We can only confidently know about Him what He chooses to reveal to us. We are also confident that what He chooses to tell us is profitable and useful for us.

b. We believe the Bible must be understood *literally*, that is, as straightforward and true according to its *literary* context.

i. The Bible is much more than a book; it is a library of books, and books written in different literary forms. Some portions of the Bible give a historical account, others are poetic, and some are prophetic.

ii. We must understand the Bible literally according to its literary context. For example, when David wrote in Psalm 6:6: *All night I make my bed swim; I drench my couch with my tears…* he used a poetic literary form. We understand he didn't *literally* mean he cried so much that he flooded his room and set his bed afloat.

iii. Psalm 119:128 says: *All Your precepts concerning all things I consider to be right.* The Psalmist confidently proclaimed the inerrancy of God's Word. It was *right*, not wrong; and it was right *concerning all things*.

- When the Bible gives us history, it is *right* and true; the events actually happened as described.
- When the Bible gives us poetry, it is *right* and true; the feeling and experiences were real for the writer and ring true to human experience.
- When the Bible gives us prophecy, it is *right* and true; the events described will come to pass, just as it is written.
- When the Bible gives us instruction, it is *right* and true; it truly does tell us the will of God and the best way of life.
- When the Bible tells us of God, it is *right* and true; it reveals to us what the nature and heart and mind of God are, as much as we can comprehend.

iv. If we *don't* approach the Bible this way, then we can only come to it with how we feel about the text, and we decide what is true or false about the text – making ourselves greater than the text itself. Though the teachings of the Bible have many applications, they only have one true interpretation. Sometimes the interpretation is easy to discern and sometimes not, but God meant *something* with the text revealed to us.

v. "The only proper way to interpret Genesis 1 is not to 'interpret' it at all. That is, we accept the fact that it was meant to say exactly what it says." (Morris)

c. We believe the Bible is not a book of science; yet where it touches science, it speaks the truth. After all, if the Bible is false in regard to science or other things that we *can* prove, then we cannot regard it as reliable in regard to spiritual matters that we *cannot* objectively prove.

3. We come to the Bible knowing the copies we have in our hands are *reliable* duplicates (though not perfect duplicates) of the exact writings, which God perfectly inspired.

a. We can know this about the Old Testament by seeing the incredible care and reliability of the ancient Jewish scribes, demonstrated by the Dead Sea Scroll discoveries.

b. We can know this about the New Testament by knowing that because of earlier manuscripts, and a greater number of ancient manuscripts, the New Testament is by far the most reliable and exhaustively crosschecked ancient document we possess. Really, no more than one one-thousandth of the New Testament text is in question.

4. We come to the Bible knowing the unique place of the Book of Genesis.

a. The Bible would be incomplete and perhaps incomprehensible without the Book of Genesis. It sets the stage for the entire drama of redemption, which unfolds in the rest of the book.

b. Almost all of the important doctrines and teachings of the Bible have their foundation in of Genesis.

   i. Genesis gives the foundation for the doctrines of:
   - Sin, the fall, redemption, justification.
   - The promise of the Messiah and Jesus Christ.
   - The personality and personhood of God.
   - The kingdom of God.

   ii. Genesis shows us the origin of:
   - The universe.
   - Order and complexity.
   - The solar system.
   - The atmosphere and hydrosphere.
   - Life, man, marriage.
   - Good and evil.
   - Language, government, culture, nations, religion.

iii. It is precisely because people have abandoned the truth of Genesis that society is in such disarray.

c. Genesis is important to the New Testament. There are at least 165 passages in Genesis either directly quoted or clearly referred to in the New Testament; many of these are quoted more than once, so there are at least 200 quotations or allusions to Genesis in the New Testament.

i. In John 5:46-47, Jesus spoke of the importance of believing what Moses wrote: *For if you believed Moses, you would believe Me; for he wrote about Me. But if you do not believe his writings, how will you believe My words?* We can't truthfully and consistently say we believe in Jesus if we don't believe in the Book of Genesis.

ii. Martin Luther wrote: "I beg and faithfully warn every pious Christian not to stumble at the simplicity of the language and stories that will often meet him there [in Genesis]. He should not doubt that, however simple they may seem, these are the very words, works, judgments, and deeds of the high majesty, power, and wisdom of God" (cited in Boice).

5. According to the New Testament, Moses wrote the Book of Genesis (Luke 24:27 and 24:44). We can surmise that he did this with help from actual written records from the past God had preserved.

a. There are indicators of where these records begin and end. Note the phrasing of Genesis 2:4, 5:1, 6:9, 10:1, 11:10, 11:27, 25:12, 25:19, 36:1, 36:9, and 37:2.

b. In these passages phrases such as "this is the history" and "this is the book" and "this is the genealogy" may indicate the start or end of the records Moses collected.

i. "Thus it is probable that the Book of Genesis was written originally by actual eyewitnesses of the events reported therein. Probably the original narratives were recorded on tables of stone or clay, in common practice of early times, and then handed down from father to son, finally coming into the possession of Moses. Moses perhaps selected the appropriate sections for compilation, inserted his own editorial additions and comments, and provided smooth transitions from one document to the next, with the final result being the Book of Genesis as we have received it." (Morris)

B. The first five days of creation.

1. The philosophical importance of knowing God as creator.

a. The philosopher Jean-Paul Sartre and many others have stated the essential problem of philosophy: that there is something, instead of nothing. *Why?* Everything else in our life flows from the answer to this question.

> i. If everything around us, including ourselves, is the result of random, meaningless occurrences apart from the work of a creating God, then it says something about who I am, and where I, and the whole universe, are going. If that is the case then the only dignity or honor we bestow upon men is pure sentimentality, because we don't have any more significance than an amoeba and there is no greater law in the universe than survival of the fittest.

b. Some 100 years ago, there was a great German philosopher named Arthur Schopenhauer. By habit, he usually dressed like a vagrant, and one day he sat on a park bench in Berlin, deep in thought. His appearance made a policeman suspicious, so the policeman asked the philosopher "Who are you?" Schopenhauer answered, "I would to God I knew."

> i. The only way we can ever really find out who we are is from God. The best place to find out begins in Genesis.

c. There are many possible answers to the question of how everything came into being. Some say, once there was absolutely nothing and now there is something. Others (including the Bible) say before there was anything created, there was a Personal Being.

d. There is a story saying that one day, students in a great physics professor's class – someone like Albert Einstein – said that they had decided there was no God. The professor asked them how much of all the knowledge in the world they had among themselves collectively, as a class. The students discussed it for a while and decided they had 5% of all human knowledge among themselves. The professor thought their estimate was a little generous, but he asked them: "Is it possible God exists in the 95% you don't know?"

2. (1) A simple factual statement regarding God's work as Creator.

In the beginning God created the heavens and the earth.

> a. **God created**: This summary statement will be detailed in the following verses, but the Bible simply and straightforwardly declares the world did not create itself or come about by chance. It was created by God who, by definition, is eternal and has always been.
>
>> i. "It is no accident that *God* is the subject of the first sentence of the Bible, for this word dominates the whole chapter and catches the eye at every point of the page: it is used some thirty-five times in as many verses of the story." (Kidner)

ii. If you believe Genesis 1:1, you really have no problem believing the rest of the Bible. The God big enough to have **created the heavens and the earth** is big enough to do all the rest the Bible says that He did and does.

b. **God**: This is the ancient Hebrew word *Elohim*. Grammatically it is a plural word used as if it were singular. The verbs and pronouns used with *Elohim* should be in the plural, but when *Elohim* refers to the LORD God the verbs and pronouns are in the singular.

i. Adam Clarke quoted Rabbi Simeon ben Joachi, commenting on the word *Elohim*: "Come and see the mystery of the word Elohim; there are *three degrees*, and each degree by itself *alone*, and yet notwithstanding they are all *one*, and *joined together* in *one*, and are not divided from each other." Clarke adds: "He must be strangely prejudiced indeed who cannot see that the doctrine of a Trinity, and of a Trinity in unity, is expressed in the above words."

ii. Luther on *Elohim*: "But we have clear testimony that Moses aimed to indicate the Trinity or the three persons in the one divine nature" (cited in Leupold).

c. **God created the heavens**: The simple fact of God's creation is even more amazing when we consider the greatness of God's universe.

i. A typical galaxy contains billions of individual stars; our galaxy alone (the Milky Way) contains 200 billion stars. Our galaxy is shaped like a giant spiral, rotating in space, with arms reaching out like a pinwheel, and our sun is one star on one arm of the pinwheel. It would take 250 million years for the pinwheel to make one full rotation. But this is only our galaxy; there are many other galaxies with many other shapes, including spirals, spherical clusters, and flat pancakes. The average distance between one galaxy and another is about 20 million trillion miles. Our closest galaxy is the Andromeda Galaxy, about 12 million trillion miles away.

ii. For every patch of sky the size of the moon, if you could look very deep, you would see about a million galaxies.

iii. But God did all this Himself: *Indeed My hand has laid the foundation of the earth, and My right hand has stretched out the heavens; when I call to them, they stand up together* (Isaiah 48:13).

iv. But God is bigger and greater than all His creation: *Who has measured the waters in the hollow of His hand, measured heaven with a span and calculated the dust of the earth in a measure?* (Isaiah 40:12).

d. **God created the heavens and the earth**: If **God** created the heavens and the earth, then we must forever put away the idea that anything *happens* by chance. "Chance" merely describes the statistical probability of something happening. *Chance* itself can neither do or perform anything.

i. Some intelligent people may fall into this delusion. Jacques Monod, a biochemist, wrote: "Chance *alone* is at the source of every innovation, of all creation in the biosphere. Pure chance, absolutely free but blind, at the very root of the stupendous edifice of evolution."

ii. But assigning such power to *chance* doesn't make sense. Chance has no power. For example, when a coin is flipped, the chance it will land heads is 50%; however, *chance* does not make it land heads. Whether or not it lands heads or tails is due to the strength with which the coin is flipped, the strength of air currents and air pressure as it flies through the air, where it is caught, and if it is flipped over once it is caught. *Chance* doesn't *do* anything but describe a probability.

iii. Many years ago a scientist named Carl Sagan petitioned the U.S. government for a grant to fund the search for intelligent life in outer space. He hoped to find evidence of life by using a super-sensitive instrument to pick up radio signals from distant space. When he received those radio signals, he looked for *order* and *pattern*, which demonstrated the signals were transmitted by intelligent life. In the same way, the order and pattern of the whole universe demonstrate that it was fashioned by intelligent life, not by *chance*. Scientists detect chance in the radio signals constantly (in the form of static with no pattern), but it tells them *nothing*.

iv. Therefore, when someone says the universe or anything else came about by *chance*, one may say that despite their expertise or skill in other areas, when it comes to this subject they are ignorant, superstitious, or simply repeating a tired theory said and disproved before, yet unthinkingly accepted.

e. **God created**: Inherent in the idea of God is that He is an *intelligent designer*. Only an intelligent designer could create a just-right universe, not chance. Our universe is a just-right universe. According to Hugh Ross in his book *The Fingerprint of God*:

i. The universe has a just-right gravitational force.

- *If it were larger*, the stars would be too hot and would burn up too quickly and too unevenly to support life.
- *If it were smaller*, the stars would remain so cool, nuclear fusion would never ignite, and there would be no heat and light.

ii. The universe has a just-right speed of light.

- *If it were larger*, stars would send out too much light.
- *If it were smaller*, stars would not send out enough light.

iii. The universe has a just-right average distance between the stars.

- *If it were larger*, the heavy element density would be too thin for rocky planets to form, and there would only be gaseous planets.
- *If it were smaller*, planetary orbits would become destabilized because of the gravitational pull from other stars.

iv. The universe has a just-right polarity of the water molecule.

- *If it were greater*, the heat of fusion and vaporization would be too great for life to exist.
- *If it were smaller*, the heat of fusion and vaporization would be too small for life's existence, liquid water would become too inferior a solvent for life chemistry to proceed, ice would not float, leading to a runaway freeze-up.

v. We could conclude that there is *no chance* that such a universe could create itself, apart from an intelligent designer.

f. **In the beginning God created the heavens and the earth**: This tells us that God used no pre-existing material to create the earth. The ancient Hebrew word *bara* (**created**) is specific. It means *to create out of nothing*, showing that God created the world out of nothing, not out of Himself. God is separate from His creation. Unlike Eastern and pantheistic perceptions of god, the Bible teaches the universe could perish yet He would remain.

i. Men cannot *create* in the sense the term is used in Genesis 1:1. We can only *fashion* or *form* things out of existing material. The closest we come to creating is in reproducing ourselves sexually. This is perhaps one reason why Satan wants to pervert and destroy God's plan and standard for sexuality; it is deeply connected to our being made in the image of God.

ii. Louis Ginzberg relayed a fascinating legend on how the 22 letters of the Hebrew alphabet all wanted to begin the Bible, but in the end, the letter "*bet*" was allowed, because he said, "O Lord of the world! May it be Thy will to create Thy world through me, seeing that all the dwellers of the world give praise daily unto Thee through me, as it is said, **B**lessed be the Lord forever. Amen, and Amen." For this reason (according to the legend), the Hebrew Book of Genesis begins, "**B**ereshit God created the heaven and the earth."

3. The Bible's clear teaching of God's creation and the uncertainty of modern science.

   a. Some scientists often act certain in their knowledge about the origin of the universe, but their continually revolutionary discoveries prove they are, in some way, feeling their way along in the dark. *Honest* scientists, those who resist pride or arrogance, appreciate how little they do know, and hold their present discoveries with a sense of humility.

   b. Some scientists may be overly sure when it comes to what can be known of the universe, but we do not have to accept such arrogance. The constantly changing scene of science is illustrated by a sidebar to a science article many years ago in the *Los Angeles Times* titled, "The Big Bang and What Followed It":

   > In the beginning, there was light – but also quarks and electrons. The Big Bang spewed out energy that condensed into radiation and particles. The quarks joined into protons and careened wildly about in a hot, dense, glowing goop as opaque as a star.
   >
   > Time (300,000 years or so) passed. Space expanded. Matter cooled. The electrons and protons, electrically irresistible to each other, merged into neutral hydrogen, and from this marriage, the first atoms were born. Space between atoms became as transparent as crystal – pretty much the way it looks today.
   >
   > The rest, as they say, is history. Atoms merged to form dust clouds, which grew into stars and galaxies and clusters. Stars used up their nuclear fuel, collapsed and exploded in recurring cycles, fusing elements in the process.
   >
   > Occasionally, a stable planet condensed around a second-generation star, where carbon-based life forms grew into, among other things, cosmologists, the better to contemplate it all.

   c. In 1913, an astronomer in Arizona discovered that stars appeared to be moving away from the earth at tremendous speeds, up to two million miles an hour. In 1919, another American astronomer named Edwin Hubble used this information to develop a theory of an expanding universe, which is the foundation of the "Big Bang" idea. Early on, other scientists discovered background radiation from all parts of the universe, which they suppose is the leftover "noise" from the first great explosion. But scientists are really not much closer at all to knowing anything about this instant beginning to the universe.

   d. In fact, the more they find out, the more they discover how much they *don't* know. There was a time when astrophysicists were faced with another challenge: trying to figure out what "dark matter" is. Dark matter is a term some scientists use to explain an enormous apparent excess of gravity in the universe. Dark matter may make up 99.9% of everything in the universe, but no one knows what it is. Though suggestions are offered, they are only suggestions. David O. Caldwell of the University of California at Santa Barbara said, "When it comes to dark matter, the only thing that we are convinced of at the moment is that it's there." But actually, scientists cannot even agree on that! Michael S. Turner, an astrophysics professor at the University of Chicago, said: "It's very humbling. The origin, composition, energy and mass of the most common matter in the entire universe is unknown."

e. This uncertainty is shown in a March 6, 1995, front-page article in the *Los Angeles Times* headlined, "Rethinking Cosmic Questions":

> Ever since people first stood up amid the tall grasses and looked about the world in wonder, religion, mythology and science all have struggled to explain how the world came to be. But when it comes to creation stories, few can hold a candle to the tale cooked up by modern cosmologists.
>
> Dialing back the cosmic clock about 15 billion years, they depict a time before time, a place before space existed. Out of nothing and nowhere, all the energy and matter in the universe exploded into existence in an event that came to be called... the Big Bang.
>
> While masterfully spinning ideas out of faith and equations, cosmologists were pitifully short on data. They could not see or measure the phenomena they were trying to explain. "Twenty-five years ago, cosmology was very close to religion," said physicist Roberto Peccei of UCLA.
>
> Experimental cosmologist Chris Stubbs of the University of Washington, "You've got these things that are ridiculously far away and ridiculously faint, and... you've got to make sense out of it."
>
> "At times, I miss the old days when I could just work in my office and not worry that someone would disprove my theory in a few weeks," said Rocky Kold of the Fermi National Accelerator Laboratory in Illinois.
>
> "Many of us who have worked in this field for decades still worry that the whole house of cards is going to collapse," said Princeton cosmologist David Wilkinson.

Recent observations, for example, suggest that the universe is younger than its oldest stars – an enigma that has astronomers scrambling for explanations.

The biggest mystery, however, strikes even scientists as so astonishing as to be absurd: 99% of the universe, according to some estimates, is made of totally unfamiliar stuff. Commonly known as dark matter, it is actually mostly transparent; it neither shines nor casts a shadow. Whatever it is, it is not like us... According to some theories, it also is the glue that holds the universe together, and keeps it from expanding forever into endless space.

f. "The study of human origins seems to be a field in which each discovery raises the debate to a more sophisticated level of uncertainty." (Christopher Stringer of the Natural Museum of London)

4. One may doubt the ability of many modern scientists to answer the question of origins. But that does not automatically give us confidence in the answer found in the Book of Genesis. Some believe that Genesis only records a creation myth, meant only to show the greatness of God in poetic grandeur. Though there are poetic elements to the account, we believe it was still written to record a historical reality. Other Scriptures, in their approach to Genesis 1, demonstrate this.

a. Psalm 136 connects the Genesis account of creation with the rest of Israel's history in a seamless fabric. The creation account is not put in a category of historical fiction.

b. Jesus quoted Genesis as if it were a purely historical record (Matthew 19:4-6 and 23:35).

c. C.S. Lewis wrote that when he heard a Biblical scholar claim the Genesis creation account was a myth, he didn't want to know about the man's credentials as a Biblical scholar. He wanted to know how many myths the man had read. Myths were Lewis' business as a literary scholar, and he could see the Biblical account of creation was unlike mythical accounts.

d. It is true that Genesis was not written primarily as a scientific document. But if God gave us a truly scientific, detailed account of creation, written in scientific language, there would be no one who could understand it and no end to the length of such an account. Even if it were written in simple, 20th-century scientific language, it would have made no sense to all previous generations and no sense to future generations either.

e. *It is the glory of God to conceal a matter, but the glory of kings is to search out a matter* (Proverbs 25:2). Scientific inquiry is the glory of man; yet it must all be done with utmost humility, realizing God *conceals* these matters for man to search out.

5. God did all this **in the beginning**, yet there was much before the **beginning**.

   a. **In the beginning, God**: God Himself was before the beginning: *Your throne is established from of old; You are from everlasting* (Psalm 93:2). Some are troubled by the questions, "Where did God come from?" and "Who created God?" The answer is found in the definition of God – that God is the uncreated Being, eternal – without beginning or end.

   i. This is demonstrated in several passages of Scripture. *LORD, You have been our dwelling place in all generations. Before the mountains were brought forth, or ever You had formed the earth and the world, even from everlasting to everlasting, You are God* (Psalm 90:1-2).

   ii. J. Edwin Orr used a memorable definition of God, which was thoroughly Biblical: *God is the only infinite, eternal, and unchangeable spirit, the perfect being in whom all things begin, and continue, and end.*

   b. **In the beginning, God**: God was in three Persons before the beginning, and the Persons shared a relationship of love and fellowship: "*O Father, glorify Me together with Yourself, with the glory which I had with You before the world was... for You loved Me before the foundation of the world*" (John 17:5, 17:24).

   c. **In the beginning, God**: Before the beginning, there was an *eternal purpose* in the heart of God (Ephesians 3:11) to *gather together in one all things in Christ* (Ephesians 1:10). God's purpose was to "resolve" or "sum up" all things in Jesus as if Jesus Himself were the answer to a great and complex problem God wrote out on the "blackboard" of the universe.

   d. **In the beginning, God**: Before the beginning, God had a specific plan to fulfill this eternal purpose, with many different aspects revealed to us:

   i. The mission of Jesus was foreordained before the foundation of the world: *He indeed was foreordained before the foundation of the world, but was manifest in these last times for you* (1 Peter 1:20).

   ii. Eternal life was promised before time began: *in hope of eternal life which God, who cannot lie, promised before time began* (Titus 1:2).

   iii. The mystery of the gospel (the cross) was foreordained before the ages: *But we speak the wisdom of God in a mystery, the hidden wisdom which God ordained before the ages for our glory* (1 Corinthians 2:7).

   iv. The grace given unto us was given before the world began: *who has saved us and called us with a holy calling, not according to our works, but according to His own purpose and grace which was given to us in Christ Jesus before time began* (2 Timothy 1:9).

v. Believers in Jesus Christ were chosen in Him before the foundation of the world: *just as He chose us in Him before the foundation of the world, that we should be holy and without blame before Him in love* (Ephesians 1:4).

e. **In the beginning, God**: At some time before the beginning, God created the angels, because they witnessed the creation of the heavens and the earth (Job 38:7).

6. (2) The state of the earth before God organized creation.

The earth was without form, and void; and darkness *was* on the face of the deep. And the Spirit of God was hovering over the face of the waters.

a. **The earth was without form, and void**: Some translate the idea in this verse as **the earth *became* without form and void**. Their thinking is the earth was originally created *not* **without form and void**, but it *became* **without form and void** through the destructive work of Satan. However, this is not the plain grammatical sense of the ancient Hebrew.

i. Those who follow this idea look to Isaiah 45:18: *For thus says the LORD, Who created the heavens, Who is God, Who formed the earth and made it, Who has established it, Who did not create it in vain, Who formed it to be inhabited: "I am the LORD, and there is no other."* The idea, here, is God says He did *not* create the world *in vain* (the Hebrew word is the same as the word for *void* in Genesis 1:1).

ii. Based on these ideas, some have advanced what has been called the "Gap Theory." It is the idea that there was a long and indefinite chronological gap between Genesis 1:1 and 1:2. Most gap theory advocates use the theory to explain the fossil record, assigning old and extinct fossils to this indefinite gap.

iii. Whatever merit the gap theory may have, it cannot explain the extinction and fossilization of ancient animals. The Bible says plainly death came by Adam (Romans 5:12), and since fossils are the result of death, they could not have happened before Adam's time.

b. **Darkness was on the face of the deep**: This may describe a sense of resistance to the moving of the Holy Spirit on the earth. Some speculate this was because Satan was cast down to the earth (Isaiah 14:12; Ezekiel 28:16) and resisted God's plan, though his resistance was futile.

c. **The Spirit of God was hovering over the face of the waters**: When God began to transform the earth into something beautiful and compatible with His great plan, He started with the work of **the Spirit of God**. The Holy Spirit begins every work of creation or re-creation.

i. "The first divine act in fitting up this planet for the habitation of man was for the Spirit of God to move upon the face of the waters. Till that time, all was formless, empty, out of order, and in confusion. In a word, it was chaos; and to make it into that thing of beauty which the world is at the present moment, even though it is a fallen world, it was needful that the movement of the Spirit of God should take place upon it." (Spurgeon)

ii. Leupold on **the Spirit of God was hovering**: "The verb… signifies a vibrant moving, a protective hovering… His was the preparatory work for leading over from the inorganic to the organic."

ii. **Hovering**: "Any impression of Olympian detachment which the rest of the chapter might have conveyed is forestalled by the simile of the mother-bird 'hovering' (Moffatt) or fluttering by her brood. The verb reappears in Deuteronomy 32:11 to describe the eagle's movements in stirring its young into flight." (Kidner)

d. **The earth was without form, and void**: When God created the earth, He quite likely built an "old" earth, creating things in the midst of a time sequence, with either apparent or manufactured age built into creation.

i. For example, Adam was already of mature age when he was created; there was age purposefully built in. Likewise, the trees in the Garden of Eden had rings in them, and there were undoubtedly canyons and sandy beaches in Adam's world.

7. (3-5) The first day of creation: light is created and divided from the darkness.

Then God said, "Let there be light"; and there was light. And God saw the light, that *it was* good; and God divided the light from the darkness. God called the light Day, and the darkness He called Night. So the evening and the morning were the first day.

a. **Let there be light**: The first step from chaos to order is to bring light. This is also the way God works in our life.

i. Paul wrote about the light brought to us by the gospel: *But even if our gospel is veiled, it is veiled to those who are perishing, whose minds the god of this age has blinded, who do not believe, lest the light of the gospel of the glory of Christ, who is the image of God, should shine on them. For we do not preach ourselves, but Christ Jesus the Lord, and ourselves your bondservants for Jesus' sake. For it is the God who commanded light to shine out of darkness, who has shone in our hearts to give the light of the knowledge of the glory of God in the face of Jesus Christ* (2 Corinthians 4:3-6).

b. **Then God said**: God did not have to fashion light with His hands. It was enough for God to merely speak the words, *Light be!* And there was light.

> i. "I must have you notice that this light came instantaneously. The Hebrew suggests this far better than our translation–it is sublimely brief. 'Light be: light was.'" (Spurgeon)
>
> ii. Because God created things by speaking them into existence, some have said we can operate on the same principle, speaking things into existence by faith. This is often based on a wrong understanding of Hebrews 11:3 (*by faith we understand that the worlds were framed by the word of God*), which is taken to say, God Himself *used* faith in creating the world. Instead, it says it is by faith *we understand* God created the world.
>
> iii. Also, some have a wrong understanding of Mark 11:22 which is taken to literally mean "have God's faith" as if we are to have the same faith God has. But the words *Jesus answered and said to them, "Have faith in God"* cannot mean this, because faith, as Hebrews 11:1 tells us, *is the substance of things hoped for, the evidence of things not seen*. What does God hope for? What does He not see? An omnipotent, omniscient Being certainly does not need faith. He is the *object* of faith as well as the source of faith (Ephesians 2:8).

c. **There was light**: Genesis tells us that light, day, and night each existed before the sun and the moon were created on the fourth day (Genesis 1:14-19). This shows us that light is more than a physical substance; it also has a supernatural aspect. In the new heavens and the new earth, there won't be any sun or moon. God Himself will be the light (Revelation 22:5).

> ii. The darkness God later sent upon the Egyptians (Exodus 10:21) had a tangible quality to it, far beyond what we usually think of as being associated with darkness; it could be *felt*. This demonstrates a certain supernatural element, which can be related to light and darkness.

d. **So the evening and the morning were the first day**: Many wonder if this was a literal day (in the sense we think of a day) or if it was a geological age. Some say that God created the world in six days, and others say He created it in six vast geological ages. Though there is disagreement among Christians on this, the plainest and simplest meaning of the text is that He created in six days *as we think of days*.

i. "If the *days* were not days at all, would God have countenanced the word? Does He trade in inaccuracies, however edifying? The question hinges on the proper use of language." (Kidner)

ii. "There ought to be no need of refuting the idea that *yom* means period. Reputable dictionaries… know nothing of this notion. Hebrew dictionaries are our primary source of reliable information concerning Hebrew words." (Leupold)

iii. "This is, no doubt, a literal and accurate account of God's first day's work in the creation of the world." (Spurgeon)

8. (6-8) The second day of creation: God makes an atmospheric division.

Then God said, "Let there be a firmament in the midst of the waters, and let it divide the waters from the waters." Thus God made the firmament, and divided the waters which *were* under the firmament from the waters which *were* above the firmament; and it was so. And God called the firmament Heaven. So the evening and the morning were the second day.

a. **Let there be a firmament**: The idea of a **firmament** is of an *expanse* (NIV, NAS) or *space* (NLT). The waters of the land are separated from the water vapor in the sky.

b. **The waters which were above the firmament**: Some commentators and scientists believe that here the Bible recognizes the existence of significant water vapor in the sky. Such a vapor blanket would change the ecology of the earth, and Henry Morris suggests several effects of a vapor blanket:

i. "The *waters above the firmament* thus probably constituted a vast blanket of water vapor above the troposphere and possibly above the stratosphere as well, in the high temperature region now known as the ionosphere, and extending far into space." (Morris)

ii. It would serve as a global greenhouse, maintaining an essentially uniform, pleasant temperature all over the world.

iii. Without great temperature variations, there would be no significant winds, and the water-rain cycle could not form. There would be no rain, as we know it today.

iv. There would be lush, tropical-like vegetation all over the world, fed not by rain, but by a rich evaporation and condensation cycle, resulting in heavy dew or ground-fog.

v. The vapor blanket would filter out ultraviolet radiation, cosmic rays, and other destructive energies bombarding the planet. These are known to be the cause of mutations, which decrease human longevity. Human and animal lifespans would be greatly increased.

vi. A vapor blanket would provide the necessary reservoir for a potential worldwide flood.

9. (9-13) The third day of creation: the land is divided from the sea; plants and all types of vegetation are created.

Then God said, "Let the waters under the heavens be gathered together into one place, and let the dry *land* appear"; and it was so. And God called the dry *land* Earth, and the gathering together of the waters He called Seas. And God saw that *it was* good. Then God said, "Let the earth bring forth grass, the herb *that* yields seed, *and* the fruit tree *that* yields fruit according to its kind, whose seed *is* in itself, on the earth"; and it was so. And the earth brought forth grass, the herb *that* yields seed according to its kind, and the tree *that* yields fruit, whose seed *is* in itself according to its kind. And God saw that *it was* good. So the evening and the morning were the third day.

a. **Let the waters under the heavens be gathered together**: The idea is that before this, the earth was covered with water. Now the waters are **gathered together into one place**, and dry land appears.

b. **Let the earth bring forth grass**: All this happened before the creation of the Sun (the fourth day of creation, Genesis 1:14-19). This means the plants must have had sufficient nourishment because of the light God had created before the sun and the moon (in Genesis 1:3).

i. Those who propose these days of creation were not literal days, but successive ages of slow, evolutionary development have a real problem here. It is hard to explain how plants and all vegetation could grow and thrive eons before the sun and the moon. No modern evolutionist would argue plant life is older than the sun or the moon, but this is what the Genesis record tells us.

ii. Many wonder how the sun, moon, and stars were created on the fourth day when light (including day and night) was created on the first day. Many have suggested the problem is solved by saying these heavenly bodies were created on the first day, but were not specifically visible, or not finally formed, until the fourth. But Revelation tells us of a coming day when we won't need the sun, moon, and stars any longer (Revelation 21:23). There's no reason why God couldn't have started creation in the same way He will end it.

b. **And it was so**: This is the beginning of life on planet earth, directly created by God, not slowly evolving over millions of years.

i. Some scientists now say life on earth began when immense meteorites carrying amino acids impacted earth at a time when the sun was cooler and the earth was a watery ball covered with ice up to 1,000 feet thick. The idea is that a meteor hit the ice, broke through, and "seeded" the water underneath with the building blocks of life, which assembled into an "organic soup." However the process was triggered, the scientists said life on earth began in "a geological instant." But by an instant, they mean 10 million years or less. In the opinion of the author, it takes more faith to believe this than to believe in Genesis.

ii. The fossil evidence is more consistent with the idea that life exploded into existence on earth, instead of slowly evolving.

c. **The earth brought forth grass, the herb that yields seed… and the tree that yields fruit, whose seed is in itself**: The plants were created not as seeds, but as full-grown plants each bearing seeds. They were thus created as mature plants, having the appearance of age. The chicken really did come before the egg.

d. **According to its kind**: This phrase appears ten times in Genesis chapter 1. It means God allows variation within a **kind**, but something of one **kind** will never develop into something of another **kind**.

e. **And God saw that it was good**: God knows what is **good**. He is not some vague moral neutral. He knows what is **good** and organizes His creation to result in something **good**.

i. God does not call the earth **good** until it has become habitable, a place where man can live.

f. **Let the earth bring forth… every herb that yields seed… the herb that yields seed according to its kind… And God saw that it was good**: Some use this passage to justify the use of drugs (especially marijuana) because **grass** and **every herb** came forth at God's command. But certainly, not every herb is good for every purpose. Hemlock is natural, but not good.

i. In fact, the use of drugs in this manner is nowhere approved and is always condemned in the Bible. The wrong use of drugs is often associated with sorcery and the occult.

ii. Sorcery is universally condemned in the Bible (Exodus 22:18, Deuteronomy 18:10, 2 Chronicles 33:6, Revelation 21:8 and 22:15). In both the Old and New Testaments, the word *sorcery* was connected with the making and taking of drugs.

10. (14-19) The fourth day of creation: the sun, moon, and stars.

Then God said, "Let there be lights in the firmament of the heavens to divide the day from the night; and let them be for signs and seasons, and for days and years; and let them be for lights in the firmament of the heavens to give light on the earth"; and it was so. Then God made two great lights: the greater light to rule the day, and the lesser light to rule the night. *He made* **the stars also. God set them in the firmament of the heavens to give light on the earth, and to rule over the day and over the night, and to divide the light from the darkness. And God saw that** *it was* **good. So the evening and the morning were the fourth day.**

a. **Let them be for signs and seasons**: God made the sun and the moon – these **lights in the firmament of the heavens** to be for **signs and seasons**. Since the beginning, man has used God's provision of the sun, moon, and stars to mark and measure time and direction.

b. **God set them in the firmament of the heavens**: God knew exactly how far to set the sun from the earth. A few million miles more or less and life as we know it would be impossible.

i. The intricate balance of our ecosystem argues strongly for the existence of a Creator. We live in a very complex world.

ii. Ginzberg quotes a Jewish legend connecting the movement of the sun to the praise of God (as in Psalms 113:3, 50:1, and 148:3): "The progress of the sun in his circuit is an uninterrupted song of praise to God. And this song alone makes his motion possible. Therefore, when Joshua wanted to bid the sun stand still, he had to command him to be silent. His song of praise hushed, the sun stood still."

c. **Let them be for signs and seasons**: When God set the **lights in the heavens** to be **for signs**, it probably includes what we commonly call the constellations, but was called by the ancient Hebrews the *Mazzaroth* (Job 38:31-32).

i. Significantly, the sequence of the zodiac is the same in every language and culture, even if the specific names of the constellations change. Also, we know the figures of the constellations suggested to us don't look like those things at all, and, they never did. Yet the names for the figures of the constellations are the same in all cultures. This points to a common, pre-Babel beginning for all these things before the truth of the constellations was corrupted.

ii. Luke 1:70 and Acts 3:21 speak of *holy prophets since the world began*. These *prophets* may be the stars themselves. Psalm 147:4 and Isaiah 40:26 tell us God has the stars all numbered and God has a *name* for them all. Psalm 19:1-6 tells us the heavens contain a message from God.

iii. Astrology is a satanic corruption of God's original message in the stars, a message outlining His plan of redemption. Because astrology is a corruption, it is to be avoided always by man (Isaiah 47:12-15).

d. **He made the stars also**: With all the other stars in our universe, we often wonder if there is life on other planets.

i. When you take into account all that is necessary for the sustenance of life, as we know it, there are few planets able to support life. Taking into account factors such as our galaxy type, star location, star age, star mass, star color, distance from stars, axis tilt, rotation period, surface gravity, tidal force, magnetic field, oxygen quantity in atmosphere, atmospheric pressure, and 20 other important factors, the probability of all 33 occurrences happening on any one planet is one in 10 to the 42nd power. The total number of possible planets in the universe is 10 to the 22nd power.

ii. At one time the U.S. government spent $100 million a year looking for extraterrestrial intelligence. It might have been wiser to spend the money cultivating intelligent life in Washington or other centers of government.

11. (20-23) The fifth day of creation: birds and sea creatures are created.

Then God said, "Let the waters abound with an abundance of living creatures, and let birds fly above the earth across the face of the firmament of the heavens." So God created great sea creatures and every living thing that moves, with which the waters abounded, according to their kind, and every winged bird according to its kind. And God saw that *it was* good. And God blessed them, saying, "Be fruitful and multiply, and fill the waters in the seas, and let birds multiply on the earth." So the evening and the morning were the fifth day.

a. **Let the waters abound with an abundance of living creatures**: We see the great variety of birds and sea creatures were created at the same time, not evolving slowly over millions of years. Even though plant life was created before animal life, animal life was not created out of plant life.

i. Among the diversity of animals, many share similar structures: birds, reptiles, mammals, and so forth. This argues at least as persuasively for a common Designer as it does for a common life source. All life did not come from the same primordial cell, but it did all come from the same Designer.

b. **According to their kind**: Again, all animal life is created **according to its kind**. God deliberately structured plenty of variation within a kind, but one "kind" does not become another.

> i. For example, structure among dogs is diverse. The teacup poodle is very different from the Great Dane, but they are both dogs. However, they won't become mice, no matter how much breeding is done.

> ii. Evolutionists often give convincing examples of *microevolution*, the variation of a kind within its kind, adapting to the environment. For example, the ratio of black to white peppered moths may increase when pollution makes it easier for dark moths to escape detection; or finches may develop different beaks in response to their distinctive environment. But the moths are still moths, and the finches are still finches. There has been no change outside of the kind. *Micro*evolution *does not* prove *macro*evolution.

12. Doesn't the fossil record show these creatures slowly evolved into existence, instead of suddenly appearing?

> a. Most people are unaware that Darwin's strongest opponents were not clergymen, but fossil experts. Darwin admitted the state of the fossil evidence was "the most obvious and gravest objection which can be urged against my theory," and because of the fossil evidence, "all the most eminent paleontologists… and all our greatest geologists… have unanimously, often vehemently, maintained" that the species do not change.

> b. The fossil record is marked by two great principles: first, *stasis*, which means most species are unchanged in all their documented history. The way they look when they first appear in the fossil record is the way they look when last appearing in the fossil record. They have not changed. Second, *sudden appearance*, which means in any local area, a species does not arise gradually, but appears all at once and "fully formed."

>> i. Philip Johnson: "If evolution means the gradual change of one kind of organism into another kind, the outstanding characteristic of the fossil record is the absence of evidence for evolution."

> c. The Bighorn Basin in Wyoming contains a continuous record of fossil deposits for what geologists say is five million years. Because this record is so complete, paleontologists assumed a positive trail of evolution could be found. Instead, "the fossil record does not convincingly document a single transition from one species to another" (Johnson).

>> i. Evolutionist Nile Eldredge wrote: "We paleontologists have said that the history of life [in the fossil record] supports [the story of gradual evolution], all the while knowing that it does not" (Johnson).

d. Either evolution happened slowly, with each tiny change building on the last, over billions of years; or the changes came as quick leaps: something like a mouse coming out of a snake's egg.

> i. The fossil record totally rejects the idea of millions of tiny changes; the quick leaps are a way of attributing miraculous power to "chance" or "nature" instead of God. While admiring the faith of those who believe in such hopeful monsters, it seems far more rational to believe in a wise, creating, designing God.

C. The sixth day of creation: the creation of man.

1. (24-25) God makes land animals.

Then God said, "Let the earth bring forth the living creature according to its kind: cattle and creeping thing and beast of the earth, *each* **according to its kind"; and it was so. And God made the beast of the earth according to its kind, cattle according to its kind, and everything that creeps on the earth according to its kind. And God saw that** *it was* **good.**

a. **Let the earth bring forth the living creature**: On the fifth day of creation, God made birds and sea animals, but now God turned His creative attention towards land animals of various types.

b. **God made the beast of the earth according to its kind**: When we look at the infinite variety of the animal kingdom (both living and extinct), we must be impressed with God's creative power, as well as His sense of humor. Any Being who makes the giraffe, the platypus, and the peacock is a God of joy and humor.

> i. To a peahen, the most attractive peacocks are the ones with the biggest fans, but the big fan on the tail makes it difficult to escape a predator. Therefore, the peahen rewards the peacock with the least chance of survival. This is one example of a natural phenomenon that presents a great problem for the idea of survival of the fittest.

c. **According to its kind**: Again, this important phrase is emphasized. God allows tremendous variation within a **kind**, but one kind will never become another kind.

2. (26) God plans to make man in His image.

Then God said, "Let Us make man in Our image, according to Our likeness; let them have dominion over the fish of the sea, over the birds of the air, and over the cattle, over all the earth and over every creeping thing that creeps on the earth."

a. **Let Us make man in Our image**: The repeated use of the plural (**Let Us... in Our image, according to Our likeness**) is consistent with the idea that there is One God in three Persons, what we know as the Trinity.

   i. Leupold does a good job showing that the plurality of **let Us make** cannot be merely the plurality of royalty, nor can it be God speaking with and to the angels. It is an indicator of the Trinity, though not clearly spelled out.

b. **In Our image**: An understanding of who man is begins with knowing we are made in the image of God. Man is different from every other order of created being because He has a created consistency with God.

   i. This means there is an unbridgeable gap between human life and animal life. Though we are biologically similar to certain animals, we are distinct in our moral, intellectual, and spiritual capabilities.

   ii. This means there is also an unbridgeable gap between human life and angelic life. Nowhere are we told the angels are made in the **image** of God. Angels cannot have the same kind of relationship of love and fellowship with God we can have.

   iii. This means the incarnation was truly possible. God (in the second Person of the Trinity) could really become man because although deity and humanity are not the same, they are compatible.

   iv. This means human life has intrinsic value, quite apart from the "quality of life" experienced by any individual, because human life is made in the **image** of God.

c. **In Our image**: There are several specific things in man that show him to be made in the **image** of God.

   - Mankind alone has a natural countenance looking upward.
   - Mankind alone has such a variety of facial expressions.
   - Mankind alone has a sense of shame expressing itself in a blush.
   - Mankind alone speaks.
   - Mankind alone possesses *personality*, *morality*, and *spirituality*.

d. **In Our image**: There are at least three aspects to the idea that we are made in the **image** of God.

   - It means humans possess *personality*: knowledge, feelings, and a will. This sets man apart from all animals and plants.
   - It means humans possess *morality*: we are able to make moral judgments and have a conscience.

- It means humans possess *spirituality*: man is made for communion with God. It is on the level of spirit we communicate with God.

e. **In Our image**: This does not mean that God has a physical or human body. God is Spirit (John 4:24). Though God does not have a physical body, He designed man so his physical body could do many of the things God does: see, hear, smell, touch, speak, think, plan, and so forth.

i. "It will hardly be safe to say that the body of man is patterned after God, because God, being an incorporeal spirit, cannot have what we term a material body. Yet the body of man must at least be regarded as the fittest receptacle for the man's spirit and so must bear at least an analogy that is so close that God and His angels choose to appear in human form when they appear to men." (Leupold)

f. **In Our image, according to Our likeness**: The terms for **image** and **likeness** are slightly different. **Image** has more to do with appearance, and **likeness** has more to do with an abstract similarity, but they both essentially mean the same thing here in this context.

g. **Let them have dominion**: Before God ever created man, He decreed that man would **have dominion over** the earth. Man's pre-eminence of the created order and his ability to affect his environment is no accident; it is part of God's plan for man and the earth.

i. In this sense, it is sin if man does not use this dominion responsibly, in the sense of a proper regard for stewardship on this earth.

3. (27-31) God's creation of man and initial commission to Adam.

So God created man in His *own* image; in the image of God He created him; male and female He created them. Then God blessed them, and God said to them, "Be fruitful and multiply; fill the earth and subdue it; have dominion over the fish of the sea, over the birds of the air, and over every living thing that moves on the earth." And God said, "See, I have given you every herb *that* yields seed which *is* on the face of all the earth, and every tree whose fruit yields seed; to you it shall be for food. Also, to every beast of the earth, to every bird of the air, and to everything that creeps on the earth, in which *there is* life, *I have given* every green herb for food"; and it was so. Then God saw everything that He had made, and indeed *it was* very good. So the evening and the morning were the sixth day.

a. **So God created man in His own image**: God created man according to His plan as described in Genesis 1:26. The concept of man being created **in the image of God** is repeated to give emphasis to the idea.

i. We are plainly told God created man fully formed, and created him in one day, not gradually over millions of years of progressive evolution. The idea that a slow, progressive evolution could produce a complex mechanism like the human body just doesn't hold up.

ii. It is said there would be at least 40 different stages of evolution required to form an eye. What possible benefit could there be for the first 39 stages? The mathematician D.S. Ulam argues it was highly improbable for the eye to evolve by the accumulation of small mutations because the number of mutations must be so large and the time available was not nearly long enough for them to appear. Evolutionist Ernst Mayr commented: "Somehow or other by adjusting these figures we will come out all right. We are comforted by the fact that evolution has occurred." Johnson observes: "Darwinism to them was not a theory open to refutation but a fact to be accounted for" (Johnson).

iii. Darwin wrote: "If it could be demonstrated that any complex organ existed which could not possibly have been formed by numerous, successive, slight modifications, my theory would absolutely break down." Professor Richard Goldschmidt, a geneticist at the University of California at Berkley, listed a series of complex structures (from the hair of mammals to hemoglobin) he thought could not have been produced by thousands of years of small mutations. "The Darwinists met this fantastic suggestion with savage ridicule. As Goldschmidt put it, 'This time I was not only crazy but almost a criminal'… To suppose that such a random event could reconstruct even a single complex organ like a liver or kidney is about as reasonable as to suppose that an improved watch can be designed by throwing an old one against the wall" (Johnson).

b. **Male and female He created them**: This does not mean Adam was originally some type of androgynous being, being both male and female. This passage of Genesis gives us an overview of God's creation of man, and Genesis 2 will explain how exactly God created male and female.

i. In our day, many say there is no real difference between men and women. This makes sense if we are the result of mindless evolution, but not if it is true that **male and female He created them**. To God, the differences between men and women are not accidents. Since He created them, the differences are good and meaningful.

ii. Men are not women, and women are not men. One of the saddest signs of our culture's depravity is the amount and the degree of gender confusion today.

iii. It is vain to wonder if men or women are superior to the other. A man is absolutely superior at being a man. A woman is absolutely superior at being a woman. But when a man tries to be a woman or a woman tries to be a man, you have something inferior.

c. **Then God blessed them**: the first thing God did for man was to bless him. Without the goodness of God's blessing, human life would be not only unbearable but also impossible.

d. **Be fruitful and multiply; fill the earth and subdue it; have dominion**: God also gives man a job to do: fulfill God's intention of man's exercise of dominion over the earth. Inherent in this command is that man should **be fruitful and multiply** and **fill the earth**. Man cannot fulfill God's plan for him on the earth unless he populates it.

   i. Additionally, God gave mankind a desire for sex, which would make the populating of the earth quick and likely.

   ii. However, many have thought that being fruitful and multiplying was God's only or main purpose for sex, but this isn't the case. The primary reason God created sex was to contribute to the bonding of a one-flesh relationship.

   iii. Animals have sexual relations only for reproduction, but human sexual response is different from animal sexual response in many ways. Human ovulation has no outward sign; humans have sex in private; humans have secondary sexual characteristics (only in humans do females develop breasts *before* the first birth). Only humans demonstrate a constant availability for and interest in sex, as opposed to a "heat" season in animals. In humans, the duration of the sexual interlude is longer and the intensity of the pleasure of sex is stronger, and only humans continue to have intercourse after the end of fertility. None of these specifically human dimensions of sex are required for reproduction, but all of them are useful for sex as a tool of bonding.

e. **To you it shall be for food**: God gave man dominion over the whole earth, but only vegetation is specifically mentioned as being **for food**. Seemingly, before the flood, the human race was vegetarian, but after the flood, man was given permission to eat the flesh of animals (Genesis 9:3).

f. **God saw everything that He had made, and indeed it was very good**: God's final analysis of His work of creation is that it was **very good**. God was pleased with His creation, and so are we!

   i. When God pronounced the creation **good**, He really meant it. At the time, it was entirely **good**; there was no death or decay on earth at all.

4. The fossil discoveries of our so-called human ancestors such as *Australopithecus afarensis*, *Australopithecus africanus*, *Homo habilis*, and *Homo erectus* show that the search for our human ancestors has been one filled with dishonest science and wishful thinking.

   a. Quoting Johnson: "The psychological atmosphere that surrounds the viewing of hominid fossils is uncannily reminiscent of the veneration of relics at a medieval shrine." In 1984, the American Museum of Natural History held an unprecedented showing of original fossils said to depict human evolution titled *Ancestors*.

   b. From Johnson: "The 'priceless and fragile relics' were carried by anxious curators in first-class airplane seats and brought to the Museum in a VIP motorcade of limousines with police escort. Inside the Museum, the relics were placed behind bullet-proof glass to be admired by a select preview audience of anthropologists, who spoke in hushed voices because 'It was like discussing theology in a cathedral.' A sociologist observing this ritual of the anthropologist tribe remarked, 'Sounds like ancestor worship to me.'"

   c. Solly Zuckerman is a committed evolutionist and one of Britain's most influential scientists. He also regards much of the fossil evidence for human evolution as nonsense. Zuckerman has subjected key fossils to years of biometric testing and declares that the idea that they walked and ran upright is flimsy wishful thinking. He remarked that the record of reckless speculation in the field of human origins "is so astonishing that it is legitimate to ask whether much science is yet to be found in this field at all" (Johnson).

   d. "The story of human descent from apes is not merely a scientific hypothesis; it is the secular equivalent of the story of Adam and Eve, and a matter of immense cultural importance. Propagating the story requires illustrations, museum exhibits, and television reenactments. It also requires a priesthood, in the form of thousands of researchers, teachers, and artists who provide realistic and imaginative detail and carry the story out to the general public... The scientific priesthood that has authority to interpret the official creation story gains immense cultural influence thereby, which it might lose if the story were called into question. The experts therefore have a vested interest in protecting the story, and in imposing rules of reasoning that make it invulnerable. When critics ask, 'Is your theory really true?' we should not be satisfied to be answered that 'it is good science, as we define science.'" (Johnson)

   e. Evolutionists are not interested in testing if their theory is true. They simply believe once you ignore the creating hand of God, it is the only explanation available, so their job is to figure out *how* it works, not *if* it is true.

5. Why is the theory of evolution so universally believed today?

a. In the 1920's, a former substitute teacher in a Tennessee school volunteered to be the defendant in a case meant to challenge a state law prohibiting the teaching of evolution in the public schools. The teacher wasn't even sure he had taught evolution, but the trial went ahead.

b. Prosecuting the case was William Jennings Bryan, former Secretary of State under Woodrow Wilson, and a three-time Democratic candidate for President. Bryan believed in the Bible, but not literally. He thought the "days" of Genesis referred not to 24-hour days, but to historical ages of indefinite duration. Leading the defense was Clarence Darrow, a famous criminal lawyer, and agnostic lecturer. Darrow maneuvered Bryan to take the stand as an expert witness on the Bible, and he humiliated Bryan in a devastating cross-examination. Once that purpose was accomplished, Darrow pleaded guilty on behalf of his client and paid a $100 fine.

c. The trial was therefore inconclusive, but the "Scopes Monkey Trial" was presented to the world by sarcastic journalist H.L. Mencken, Broadway, and Hollywood, and was a huge public relations triumph for Darwinism. People who believed in God's creation came to be thought of as fools and hicks, and evolution was given the veneer of respectability. Combine this with a strong anti-supernaturalism on the part of many scientists and educators, and today's acceptance of evolution is understandable.

d. The same attitude is used to squelch debate and questions about evolution today. "When outsiders question whether the theory of evolution is as secure as we have been led to believe, we are firmly told that such questions are out of order. The arguments among the experts are said to be about matters of detail, such as the precise time scale and the mechanism of evolutionary transformations. These disagreements are signs not of crisis but of healthy creative ferment within the field, and in any case there is no room for doubt whatever about something called the 'fact' of evolution" (Johnson).

Genesis 2 – Creation Completed; Adam in the Garden of Eden

A. The completion of creation.

1. (1-3) The seventh day of creation.

Thus the heavens and the earth, and all the host of them, were finished. And on the seventh day God ended His work which He had done, and He rested on the seventh day from all His work which He had done. Then God blessed the seventh day and sanctified it, because in it He rested from all His work which God had created and made.

> a. **And He rested on the seventh day**: God did not need rest on the seventh day because He was tired. He **rested** to show His creating work was done, to give a pattern to man regarding the structure of time (in seven-day weeks), and to give an example of the blessing of rest to man on the seventh day.
>
>> i. The seven-day week is permanently ingrained in man. Though some through history tried to change the seven-day week (a ten-day week was attempted during the French Revolution), those attempts have come to nothing. We are on a seven-day cycle because *God* is on a seven-day cycle.
>
> b. **God blessed the seventh day and sanctified it**: God **sanctified** the seventh day because it was a gift to man for rest and replenishment, and most of all because the Sabbath is a shadow of the rest available through the person and work of Jesus Christ.
>
>> i. Colossians 2:16-17 and Galatians 4:9-11 tell us Christians are not under obligation to observe the Sabbath today because Jesus fulfilled the purpose and plan of the Sabbath for us and in us (Hebrews 4:9-11). Yet Christians do not lose the Sabbath; *every day* is a day of rest in the finished work of Christ. Every day is specially set apart to God.

ii. Though we are free from the legal obligation of the Sabbath, we dare not ignore the importance of a day of rest. God has built us so we *need* one. But we are also commanded to work six days. "He who idles his time away in the *six* days is equally culpable in the sight of God as he who works on the *seventh*" (Clarke). In our modern world of four or five-day workweeks and generous vacation time, surely more "leisure time" can be given to the work of the LORD.

c. **In it He rested from all His work**: Though God rested on the seventh day of creation, He did not institute the Sabbath or show us His rest for His own sake. God does not take the Sabbath off. Jesus Himself said, *My Father has been working until now, and I have been working* (John 5:17). God does not need a day off, but man needs to see the rest of God and know he can enter into it by the finished work of Jesus.

i. The description of each other day of creation ended with the phrase, *so the evening and the morning were the... day.* However, this seventh day of creation does not have that phrase. This is because God's rest for us isn't confined to one literal day. In Jesus, God has an *eternal* Sabbath rest for His people (Hebrews 4:9-11).

ii. "God, having completed His work of creation, rests, as if to say, 'This is the destiny of those who are My people; to rest as I rest, to rest in Me.'" (Boice)

2. (4-7) The history of the heavens and the earth.

This *is* the history of the heavens and the earth when they were created, in the day that the LORD God made the earth and the heavens, before any plant of the field was in the earth and before any herb of the field had grown. For the LORD God had not caused it to rain on the earth, and *there was* no man to till the ground; but a mist went up from the earth and watered the whole face of the ground. And the LORD God formed man *of* the dust of the ground, and breathed into his nostrils the breath of life; and man became a living being.

a. **This is the history of the heavens and the earth**: This probably ends the "genealogy" of **the heavens and the earth**, a history given directly by God to either Moses or Adam, recording the history of God's seven-day creation. This was something no human was present to witness.

b. **In the day that the LORD God made the earth and the heavens**: This is the first use of **LORD** (Yahweh) in the Bible. Our English word *Lord* comes from the Anglo-Saxon word for *bread* (as does our word *loaf*) because ancient English men of high stature would keep a continual open house, where all could come and get bread to eat. They gained the honorable title of *lords*, meaning "dispensers of bread."

c. **Before any plant of the field was in the earth**: This history begins before there was any vegetation on the earth at all (back to Genesis 1:1), a time when there were only space and a watery globe we know as the earth.

d. **The LORD God had not caused it to rain on the earth**: When God first created vegetation (on the third day of creation, Genesis 1:11-13), man had not yet been created to care for the vegetation of the earth, and there was no rain. The thick blanket of water vapor in the outer atmosphere created on the second day of creation (Genesis 1:6-8) made for no rain cycle (as we know it) but for a rich system of evaporation and condensation, resulting in heavy dew or ground-fog.

e. **The LORD God formed man of the dust of the ground**: When God created man He made him out of the most basic elements, **the dust of the ground**. There is nothing "spectacular" in what man is made of, only in the way those basic things are organized.

i. When the Bible uses **dust** in a figurative or symbolic sense, it means something of little worth, associated with lowliness and humility (Genesis 18:27; 1 Samuel 2:8; 1 Kings 16:2). In the Bible, **dust** isn't evil and it isn't nothing; but it is *next* to nothing.

f. **And breathed into his nostrils the breath of life; and man became a living being**: With this Divine breath, man became **a living being**, like other forms of animal life (the term *chay nephesh* is used in Genesis 1:20-21 and here). Yet only man is a **living being** made in the **image of God** (Genesis 1:26-27).

i. The word for **breath** in Hebrew is *ruach* – the word imitates the very sound of breath – is the same word for *Spirit*, as is the case in both ancient Greek (*pneuma*) and Latin (*spiritus*). God created man by putting His *breath*, His *Spirit*, within him.

ii. "The implication, readily seen by any Hebrew reader, [is] that man was specially created by God's breathing some of His own breath into him." (Boice)

iii. The King James Version reads: *man became a living soul*. This makes some wonder if man *is* a soul, or if man *has* a soul. This passage seems to indicate that man *is* a soul, while passages like 1 Thessalonians 5:23 and Hebrews 4:12 seem to indicate that man *has* a soul. It seems that the Scripture speaks in both ways, and uses the term in different ways and in different contexts.

B. Adam in the Garden of Eden.

1. (8-9) Two trees in the Garden of Eden.

The LORD God planted a garden eastward in Eden, and there He put the man whom He had formed. And out of the ground the LORD God made every tree grow that is pleasant to the sight and good for food. The tree of life *was* also in the midst of the garden, and the tree of the knowledge of good and evil.

a. **The LORD God planted a garden eastward in Eden**: Eden was a **garden** specifically **planted** by God; it was a place God made to be a perfect habitation for Adam (and later, Eve).

b. **There he put the man whom He had formed**: The details in the creation of Adam and Eve teach us something. After reading Genesis 1, we might have assumed that man and woman were made at the same time, but the text doesn't specifically say so. We assume it. We don't know the details about man's creation until Genesis 2.

c. **Out of the ground the LORD God made every tree grow**: The rest of Genesis chapter 2 does not present a different or contradictory account of creation. Rather, it is probably the history of creation from Adam's perspective. This is Adam's experience of creation, which does not contradict the account of Genesis 1:1-2:7 – it fills it out.

i. In Matthew 19:4-5, Jesus referred to events in Genesis 1 and to events in Genesis 2 as one harmonious account.

d. **The tree of life… the tree of the knowledge of good and evil**: These two trees were among all the other trees God created and put in the Garden of Eden.

i. The **tree of life** was to grant (or to sustain) eternal life (Genesis 3:22). God still has a tree of life available to the His people (Revelation 2:7), which is in heaven (Revelation 22:2).

ii. The **tree of the knowledge of good and evil** was the "temptation" tree. Eating the fruit of this tree would give Adam an experiential knowledge of good *and* evil. Or, it is possible that it is called **the tree of the knowledge of good and evil** not so *man* would know good and evil, but so *God* could test good and evil in man.

2. (10-14) Rivers in the Garden.

Now a river went out of Eden to water the garden, and from there it parted and became four riverheads. The name of the first is Pishon; it is the one which skirts the whole land of Havilah, where *there* is gold. And the gold of that land is good. Bdellium and the onyx stone are there.

The name of the second river *is* Gihon; it *is* the one which goes around the whole land of Cush. The name of the third river *is* Hiddekel; it *is* the one which goes toward the east of Assyria. The fourth river *is* the Euphrates.

a. **Now a river went out of Eden**: The whole feel of this account gives the sense that it was written by an actual eyewitness of the rivers and surroundings. Adam probably wrote this himself.

b. **The name of the first is Pishon**: These rivers are given specific names which answer to names of rivers known in either their modern or ancient world. However, the names of these rivers can't be used to determine the place of the Garden of Eden because the flood dramatically changed the earth's landscape and "erased" these rivers.

i. We know modern rivers today such as the **Tigris** or **Euphrates** because Noah and his sons named some rivers in the post-flood world after familiar pre-flood rivers.

3. (15-17) God's command to Adam.

Then the LORD God took the man and put him in the garden of Eden to tend and keep it. And the LORD God commanded the man, saying, "Of every tree of the garden you may freely eat; but of the tree of the knowledge of good and evil you shall not eat, for in the day that you eat of it you shall surely die."

a. **Put him in the garden of Eden to tend and keep it**: God put Adam into the most spectacular paradise the world has seen, but God put Adam there to do *work* (**to tend and keep it**). Work is something good for man and was part of Adam's perfect existence before the fall.

i. "The ideal state of sinless man is not one of indolence without responsibility. Work and duty belong to the perfect state." (Leupold)

b. **Of the tree of the knowledge of good and evil you shall not eat**: The presence of this tree – the presence of a choice for Adam – was good because for Adam to be a creature of free will, there had to be a *choice*, some opportunity to rebel against God. If there is never a command or never something forbidden there can then never be choice. God wants our love and obedience to Him to be the love and obedience of *choice*.

i. Considering all that, look at Adam's advantages. He only had *one way* he could sin and we have countless ways. There are many trees of temptation in our lives, but Adam had only one.

ii. God made this command originally to Adam, not to Eve; God had not yet brought woman out of man.

c. **In the day that you eat of it you shall surely die**: God not only made His command clear to Adam, but He also clearly explained the consequences for disobedience.

C. God creates the first woman.

1. (18) God declares He will make **a helper comparable** to Adam.

And the LORD God said, "*It is* not good that man should be alone; I will make him a helper comparable to him."

a. **It is not good that man should be alone**: For the first time, God saw something that was **not good** – the aloneness of man. God never intended for man to be alone, either in the marital or social sense.

i. Marriage, in particular, has a blessed civilizing influence on man. The wildest, most violent, sociopathic men in history have always been single, never under the plan God gave to influence men for good. For society as a whole, this is **not good**.

b. **I will make him a helper comparable to him**: God's "blueprint" for creating this companion to Adam was to make a **helper comparable** to Adam.

i. Different versions of the Bible translate this idea in a variety of ways, but the idea is essentially the same in each of them:

- *Helper meet (suitable, adapted, completing)* (Amplified).
- *A companion... a helper suited to his needs* (Living).
- *A helper such as he needs* (Beck).
- *A helper correspondent to himself* (Septuagint Bible).
- *A helper suitable* (NIV, NASB).
- *A help meet for him* (KJV).

c. **A helper comparable**: In reference to the marriage relationship, God created woman to be a perfectly suitable helper to the man. This means God gave the plan and agenda to Adam, and he and the woman together work to fulfill it.

i. The phrase "in reference to the marriage relationship" is used because God has not ordained women to be helpers to men in authority (instead of being in authority themselves), except in marriage and in the church (1 Timothy 2:12-13).

ii. God gives to man the responsibility (and the accountability) to be the leader in the home and gives to the woman the responsibility and the accountability to help him.

iii. This does not mean there is to be no help from the man to the woman (though in many cases this is sadly true). It means when God looks down from heaven upon the family, He sees a man in leadership, good or bad, faithful or not, to the calling of leadership. A true leader will, of course, help those helping him.

iv. We only see "helping" as a position of inferiority when we think like the world thinks. God considers positions of service as most important in His sight (Matthew 20:25-28).

d. **A helper comparable**: Not only was the woman to be a **helper** but also she was made **comparable** to the man. She should be considered and honored as such. A woman or wife cannot be regarded as a mere tool or worker, but as an equal partner in God's grace and an equal human being.

2. (19-20) No helper was found comparable for Adam among the animals.

Out of the ground the LORD God formed every beast of the field and every bird of the air, and brought *them* to Adam to see what he would call them. And whatever Adam called each living creature, that was its name. So Adam gave names to all cattle, to the birds of the air, and to every beast of the field. But for Adam there was not found a helper comparable to him.

a. **Brought them to Adam to see what he would call them**: Since Adam had the capability to intelligently name all the animals, it shows he was a brilliant man. Because at this time Adam's intellect had not yet suffered from the fall, he was probably the most brilliant man who ever lived. Adam was the first and greatest of all biologists and botanists.

b. **So Adam gave names**: Adam did not name any other animal after himself, calling any other animal "man" or "human." By this, we see he understood that he was essentially different from all the animals. They were not made in the image of God.

i. Mark Twain had a joke where he described Adam coming home to Eve after naming all the animals. Eve looked at an elephant and said, "What did you name that big animal?" Adam replied, "I called it an elephant." Eve asked, "Why did you call it an elephant?" Adam answered, "Because it looked like an elephant!"

c. **But for Adam there was not found a helper**: It was obvious to Adam that the animals came in pairs and he had no mate. Since God deliberately had Adam name the animals after seeing his need for a partner (Genesis 2:18), God used this to prepare Adam to receive the gift of woman.

3. (21-22) God makes the first woman from Adam's side.

And the Lord God caused a deep sleep to fall on Adam, and he slept; and He took one of his ribs, and closed up the flesh in its place. Then the rib which the Lord God had taken from man He made into a woman, and He brought her to the man.

> a. **God caused a deep sleep to fall on Adam**: This is the first surgery recorded in history. God even used a proper anesthetic on Adam.
>
> b. **The rib which the Lord God had taken from man He made into a woman**: God used Adam's own body to create Eve to forever remind him of their essential oneness. As Adam came to know Eve he would see many ways that they were different, but he must never forget that they are essentially one and that they are made of the same substance. They are more alike than they are different.
>
>> i. We don't really know *exactly* what God took from Adam's side to make Eve, and it doesn't really matter. Modern research into cloning and genetic replication shows every cell in our body contains the body's entire genetic blueprint. God took some of Adam's cells and changed their genetic blueprint in the creation of Eve. Nevertheless, the story that women have one more rib than men because of the way Eve was created is a myth.
>>
>> ii. We also know the Bride of Christ comes from the wound made in the side of the second Adam, Jesus Christ.
>>
>> iii. There is a beautiful Jewish tradition saying God made woman, not out of man's foot to be under him, nor out of his head to be over him, but "She was taken from under his arm that he might protect her and from next to his heart that he might love her" (Barnhouse).
>
> c. **He made into a woman**: It is important to realize that there are not two beginnings to the human race, one in Adam and one in Eve. There was one beginning of the human race in Adam.
>
> d. **And He brought her to the man**: God brought Eve to Adam and created Eve out of Adam. He was first – the source and the head. She was created to be a helper perfectly suited to him. Thus the subordinate relationship of wives to husbands is found *before* the curse, not only after it.

4. (23) Adam's brilliant understanding of who Eve is and her connection to him.

And Adam said:

**"This is now bone of my bones
And flesh of my flesh;
She shall be called Woman,
Because she was taken out of Man."**

a. **This is now bone of my bones**: Adam recognized that Eve was both like him (**bone of my bones and flesh of my flesh**) and not like him (**woman… taken out of man**). They were one, but they were not the same.

b. **Flesh of my flesh**: Adam understood the essential *oneness* in his relationship with Eve. This point is so important that it is referred to several times in the New Testament, including the great marriage passage in Ephesians 5:28-29: *So husbands ought to love their own wives as their own bodies; he who loves his wife loves himself. For no one ever hated his own flesh, but nourishes and cherishes it.*

> i. No one walks into a room and seeks the most uncomfortable seat. The natural concern we have for ourselves causes us to take care of ourselves. In a healthy marriage relationship, the husband realizes the essential union he has with his wife, and that he cannot bless her without blessing himself and he cannot mistreat or neglect her without mistreating or neglecting himself.

c. **She was taken out of Man**: Adam recognized that though he and Eve were one, she was not the same as him. He understood that two different people were becoming one. 1 Peter 3:7 tells husbands to recognize that they are one with someone different, someone whom they must understand: *Likewise, you husbands, dwell with them with understanding, giving honor to the wife, as to the weaker vessel.*

> i. If men and women are different, are they equal? Elisabeth Elliot said: "In what sense is red equal to blue? They are equal only in the sense that both are colors in the spectrum. Apart from that they are different. In what sense is hot equal to cold? They are both temperatures, but beyond this it is almost meaningless to talk about equality" (cited in Boice).

> ii. **She shall be called woman**: "*Woman* has been defined by many as compounded for *wo* and *man*, as if called *man's wo* because she tempted him to eat the forbidden fruit; but this is *no* meaning of the original word, nor could it be intended, as the transgression was not then committed." (Clarke)

5. (24-25) The marriage of Adam and Eve.

Therefore a man shall leave his father and mother and be joined to his wife, and they shall become one flesh. And they were both naked, the man and his wife, and were not ashamed.

> a. **They shall become one flesh**: The marriage principle stated here is based on the dynamic of oneness yet distinction. A man and wife can truly come together in a **one-flesh** relationship, yet they must **be joined**. It is a

spiritual fact, but the benefits of that oneness are not gained by accident or by chance.

b. **They shall become one flesh**: This passage forms the foundation for the Bible's understanding of marriage and family. Both Jesus (Matthew 19: 5) and Paul (Ephesians 5:31) quoted it in reference to marriage.

i. "The institution of monogamous marriage, home, and family as the basic medium for the propagation of the race and the training of the young is so common to human history that people seldom pause to reflect on how or why such a custom came into being." (Morris)

ii. Many want to believe that the monogamous, two-parent family was invented in the 1950's by American television icons Ozzie and Harriet, but Adam and Eve are the original family. This is God's ideal family. This isn't polygamy. This isn't having a concubine. This isn't the keeping of mistresses. This isn't adultery. This isn't homosexual cohabitation. This isn't promiscuity. This isn't living together outside the marriage bond. This isn't serial marriage. This is God's ideal for the family, and even when we don't live up to it, it is still important to set it forth as God's ideal.

c. **One flesh**: The idea of **one flesh** is taken by many to be mainly a way of expressing sexual union. While sexual union is certainly related to the idea of **one flesh**, it is only one part of what it means to be **one flesh**. There are also important spiritual dimensions to **one flesh**.

i. Paul makes it clear the sexual union has **one flesh** implications even when we don't intend so, as when a man has sex with a prostitute (1 Corinthians 6:16). Husband and wife become **one flesh** under God's blessing. In extramarital sex, the partners become "one flesh" under God's curse.

ii. In this sense, there is no such thing as "casual sex." Every sexual relationship at least begins a one-flesh bond. The bond will either be something beautiful (like the beautiful dancing of Fred Astaire and Ginger Rogers) or it will be something grotesque (like Siamese twins).

iii. It depends on whether the bonding takes place in a relationship with the right conditions: committed love, demonstrated by the marriage commitment, and a pursuit of true intimacy. Just because sex is taking place in marriage doesn't mean it is truly fulfilling God's purpose of bonding together a *one-flesh* relationship.

d. **They shall become one flesh**: Though an initial bond in a one-flesh relationship can be formed at the first sexual relationship a couple has, the fullness of what God wants to do in the **one flesh** relationship takes time. It has to **become**.

e. **They were both naked, the man and his wife, and were not ashamed**: Before the fall, Adam and Eve were both **naked... and not ashamed**. The idea of "nakedness" is far more than mere nudity. It has the sense of being totally open and exposed as a person before God and man. To be **naked... and not ashamed** means you have no sin, nothing to be rightly ashamed of, and nothing to hide.

> i. Adam and Eve knew they were physically naked – nude – before the fall. What they did not know was a sinful, fallen condition, because they were not in that condition before their rebellion.

> ii. We often feel uncomfortable when someone stares at us. This is because we associate staring with prying, and we don't want people to pry into our lives. We want to remain hidden and only reveal to other people what we want to reveal.

> iii. When we want to be most attractive to someone else, we do the most to change our normal appearance. We have the thought, "If I really want to impress this person, I have to fix myself up." None of this feeling was present with Adam and Eve when they were **naked... and not ashamed**.

Genesis 3 – Man's Temptation and Fall

A. The temptation from the serpent.

1. (1) The serpent begins his temptation.

Now the serpent was more cunning than any beast of the field which the LORD God had made. And he said to the woman, "Has God indeed said, 'You shall not eat of every tree of the garden'?"

> a. **The serpent**: The text here does not, by itself alone, clearly identify the **serpent** as Satan, but the rest of the Bible makes it clear this is Satan appearing as a serpent.
>
>> i. In Ezekiel 28:13-19 tells us that Satan was in Eden. Many other passages associate a serpent or a snake-like creature with Satan (such as Job 26:13 and Isaiah 51:9). Revelation 12:9 and 20:2 speak of *the dragon, that serpent of old, who is the Devil and Satan.*
>>
>> ii. The representation of Satan as a serpent makes the idea of Moses saving Israel by lifting up a bronze serpent all the more provocative (Numbers 21:8-9), especially when Jesus identifies *Himself* with that very serpent (John 3:14). This is because, in this picture, the serpent (a personification of sin and rebellion) is made of *bronze* (a metal associated with judgment, since it is made with fire). The lifting of a bronze serpent is the lifting up of sin judged, in the form of a cross.
>>
>> iii. Ezekiel 28 tells us Satan, before his fall, was an angel of the highest rank and prominence, even something of a leader of worship in heaven. Isaiah 14 tells us Satan's fall had to do with his desire to be equal to or greater than God, to set his will against God's will.
>>
>> iv. We may not understand everything involved in the way Satan used the body of a serpent, but we can know it was true and this is no mere fable. "It is idle to call the narrative of the Fall a mere allegory; one had better say at once that he does not believe the Book… There was a real

serpent, as there was a real paradise; there was a real Adam and Eve, who stood at the head of our race, and they really sinned, and our race is really fallen. Believe this" (Spurgeon).

b. **The serpent was more cunning than any beast**: Satan's effectiveness is often found in His cunning, crafty ways. We can't outsmart Satan, but we can overcome him with the power of Jesus.

i. It was the craftiness of Satan that made him successful against Eve: *as the serpent deceived Eve by his craftiness* (2 Corinthians 11:3).

ii. "Man has, perhaps, far more cunning than any mere creature… but Satan has more of cunning within him than any other creature that the Lord God hath made, man included." (Spurgeon)

c. **And he said to the woman**: Apparently, before the curse pronounced in Genesis 3:14-15, the serpent was different than what we know today as a serpent. This creature didn't *start* as a snake as we know it, it *became* one.

i. "In all probability the reptile called the serpent was a nobler creature before the Fall than now. The words of our text, so far as they literally concern the serpent, threaten that a change would be wrought in him. It has been a sort of speculative opinion that the creature either had wings, or was able to move without creeping upon the earth as it now does." (Spurgeon)

ii. Demonic spirits evidently have the ability, under certain circumstances, to indwell human or animal bodies (Luke 8:33). On this occasion, Satan chose to indwell the body of a pre-curse serpent. "An immaterial spirit must be invisible; and therefore he must embody himself in some way or other before he can be seen. That Satan has power to enter into living bodies is clear, for he did so upon a very large scale with regard to men in the days of Christ… Being compelled to have an embodiment, the master evil spirit perceived the serpent to be at that time among the most subtle of all creatures; and therefore he entered into the serpent as feeling that he would be most at home in that animal" (Spurgeon).

iii. Poole says the woman wasn't surprised at the serpent's speaking because Adam and Eve had free conversation with angelic beings that often appeared in the form of men. If this is true, it wasn't so strange to Eve that an angelic being might appear to her in the form of a beautiful pre-curse serpent.

iv. Perhaps Satan made the voice supernaturally seem to come forth from the serpent, or perhaps Satan communicated this to Eve in her thoughts. *What* Satan said is more important than *how* he said it.

d. **To the woman**: Satan brought his temptation against the woman because he perceived she was more vulnerable to attack. This is because she did not receive the command to not eat of the tree of the knowledge of good and evil directly from God but through Adam (Genesis 2:15-17).

> i. Perhaps Satan knew by observation Adam didn't do an effective job of communicating to Eve what the LORD told him. This failure on Adam's part made Eve more vulnerable to temptation.
>
> ii. Satan will often attack a chain at its weakest link, so he gets at Adam by tempting Eve. The stronger ones in a "chain" must expect an attack against weaker links and support them against those attacks.
>
> iii. It was also in God's plan to allow Satan to tempt Eve this way. If Adam would have sinned first, and if he had then given the fruit to Eve, she might have a partial excuse before God: "I was simply obeying the head of our home. When he gave me the fruit, I ate of it."

e. **Has God indeed said**: Satan's first attack was leveled against the Word of God. If he could make Eve confused about what God said, or to doubt what God said, then his battle was partially won.

> i. From the beginning, Satan has tried to undermine God's people by undermining God's Word. He can undermine just as effectively by getting us to *neglect* God's Word as by getting us to doubt it.

f. **Has God indeed said, "You shall not eat of every tree of the garden"?** Satan took God's positive command in Genesis 2:16-17 (*Of every tree of the garden you may freely eat; but of the tree of the knowledge of good and evil you shall not eat*) and rephrased it in a purely negative way: "God won't let you eat of every tree."

2. (2-3) Eve's reply to the serpent.

And the woman said to the serpent, "We may eat the fruit of the trees of the garden; but of the fruit of the tree which is in the midst of the garden, God has said, 'You shall not eat it, nor shall you touch it, lest you die.'"

> a. **And the woman said to the serpent**: Eve's first mistake was in even carrying on a discussion with the serpent. We are called to talk to the devil, but never to have a discussion with him. We simply and strongly tell him, "*The Lord rebuke you!*" (Jude 9).
>
> b. **We may eat of the fruit of the trees of the garden**: Eve's knowledge of what she should not do is partially correct, but what she doesn't seem to know makes her all the more vulnerable to deception.

i. Eve does not seem to know the *name* of this tree; she only calls it **the tree in the midst of the garden**, instead of *the tree of the knowledge of good and evil* (Genesis 2:17).

ii. Eve misquoted God's command to Adam. Her words, **you shall not eat it** and **lest you die** are close enough, but she added to the command and put words in God's mouth when she said, **nor shall you touch it**. Of course, it was a good idea to completely avoid the temptation; no good could come from massaging the fruit you're not supposed to eat. But it is a dangerous thing to teach the doctrines of man as if they are the commandments of God (Matthew 15:9).

iii. Clarke on **nor shall you touch it**: "Some Jewish writers... state that as soon as the woman had asserted this, the serpent pushed her against the tree and said, 'See, you have *touched* it, and are still alive; you may therefore safely *eat* of the fruit, for surely you shall not die.'"

c. **God has said**: Eve's ignorance of exactly what God said was really Adam's responsibility. He did a poor job of relating to his wife the word God gave him.

i. We can almost picture Adam telling Eve, "See that tree in the middle of the garden? Don't touch it or God says we'll die!" While this is better than saying nothing, what Adam *didn't* explain made a vulnerable place where Satan could attack.

d. **Lest you die**: This may seem like a small thing to hinge the destiny of the human race and all creation on. But the tree was nothing more than a restraint on Adam and Eve. It reminded them *they* were not God, that God had a legitimate claim to their obedience, and that they were responsible to Him.

3. (4-5) Satan's direct challenge to God's Word.

Then the serpent said to the woman, "You will not surely die. For God knows that in the day you eat of it your eyes will be opened, and you will be like God, knowing good and evil."

a. **You will not surely die**: Satan effectively laid the groundwork. He drew Eve into a discussion with him and planted the seed of doubt about God's Word, and he exposed Eve's incomplete understanding of God's Word. Now he moves in for the kill, with an outright contradiction of what God said.

i. Satan can only effectively work when he has established a foothold. No one falls like Adam and Eve will fall, "all of a sudden." A foundation has been laid.

ii. This is why we are called to never *give place to the devil* (Ephesians 4:27). This shows how remarkable it is that Jesus could say, "Satan *has nothing in Me*" (John 14:30).

b. **You will not surely die**: Satan first wanted Eve to forget all about what God said about the consequences of sin. When we know and remember the consequences of sin, we are more likely to give up the *passing pleasures of sin* (Hebrews 11:25).

i. In Satan's direct challenge, he tries to get Eve to doubt the *goodness of God*. If God lies to her, how can He be good?

ii. In Satan's direct challenge, he tries to get Eve to doubt the *badness of sin*. If this fruit is something good for her, why doesn't God want her to have it?

iii. Satan wants us to see sin as something good that a bad God doesn't want us to have. His main lie is "sin is not bad, and God is not good."

iv. "Satan and the flesh will present a thousand reasons to show how good it would be to disobey His command." (Barnhouse)

c. **In the day you eat of it your eyes will be opened**: Satan's temptation was all the more powerful because there was *truth* in it. It was true **your eyes will be opened**, and this was fulfilled (Genesis 3:7). But their eyes were instantly opened to their own sin and rebellion.

i. It is as if a deaf person was promised to be able to hear again, but all they could hear was screaming.

ii. Their eyes were opened, they did know good and evil, but not as *gods*. A complete lie is rarely effective in temptation. If Satan doesn't couple it with some truth, there is little power in his temptation.

d. **You will be like God, knowing good and evil**: The final enticement was the most powerful because it was how Satan himself fell, wanting to be equal with God. Eve tried to become a god by rebelling against God.

i. Jewish rabbis embellished on Satan's temptation to Eve: "Nothing but malice has prompted God's command, because as soon as you eat of it, you will be as God. As He creates and destroys worlds, so will you have the power to create and destroy. As He does kill and revive, so will you have the power to kill and revive. God Himself ate first of the fruit of the tree, and then He created the world. Therefore, He forbids you to eat of it, lest you create other worlds... Hurry now and eat the fruit of the tree in the midst of the garden, and become independent of God, lest He bring forth still other creatures that will rule over you" (Ginzberg).

ii. The goal of becoming God is the center of so many non-Christian religions, including Mormonism. But in our desire to be gods, we become like Satan. It was Satan who said, *I will ascend into heaven, I will exalt my throne above the stars of God... I will be like the Most High* (Isaiah 14:13-14). In contrast, we should be like Jesus, who came as a servant (Matthew 20:28).

iii. The New Age movement and the desire to be "god" are just as strong as ever. According to a 1992 survey, as many as 12 million Americans can be considered active participants in the New Age movement, and another 30 million are avidly interested. If all these people were brought together in a church-like organization, it would be the third largest religious denomination in America. More than 90% of the subscribers to New Age Magazine are college graduates, compared to half the general population.

iv. In 1995, New Age influence made it all the way to the White House. New Age author Marianne Williamson (author of *A Return to Love: Reflections on the Principles of A Course in Miracles*), guru to many of Hollywood's spiritual seekers, spent a night at the White House as the personal guest of Hillary Clinton. Anthony Robbins, motivational guru and king of late-night infomercials, consulted with President Clinton at Camp David. Robbins is also recognized as a leader in the New Age movement.

B. The sin of Adam and Eve and the fall of the human race.

1. (6) Adam and Eve both disobey God in their own way.

So when the woman saw that the tree was good for food, that it was pleasant to the eyes, and a tree desirable to make *one* wise, she took of its fruit and ate. She also gave to her husband with her, and he ate.

a. **So when the woman saw**: Eve surrendered to this temptation in exactly the way John describes in 1 John 2:16. First, she gave in to the lust of the flesh (**saw that it was good for food**), then she gave in to the lust of the eyes (**pleasant to the eyes**), then she gave in to the pride of life (**desirable to make one wise**).

i. Jesus was tempted in the same three-fold way: an appeal to the physical appetites, an appeal to covetous and emotional desires, and an appeal to pride (Matthew 4:1-11).

b. **The woman saw that the tree was good for food**: Eve's perceptions were partially true and partially false. The tree was *not* really **good for food**, though Eve was deceived into thinking it was so. The fruit probably was

pleasant to the eyes, though that shouldn't mean much. And it was only true in Eve's *mind* that the tree was **desirable to make one wise**.

> i. We can see the precise truth of Paul's statement in 1 Timothy 2:14, that Eve was *deceived* when she sinned. In her mind, she thought she was doing something good for herself.

c. **She took of its fruit and ate**: Satan could tempt Eve, but she didn't have to take it. The taking was all her doing. Satan couldn't cram the fruit down her throat. Eve was responsible. She couldn't rightly say, "the devil made me do it."

> i. As with every temptation, God had made for Eve a *way of escape* (1 Corinthians 10:13). She could have simply run from Satan and the tree, but Eve didn't take God's way of escape.

d. **She also gave to her husband with her**: Not only did Eve sin, but also she became the agent of temptation for Adam. But when Adam ate, he was not deceived as Eve was. Adam sinned with his eyes wide open, in open rebellion against God.

> i. Therefore, it is Adam and not Eve who bears the responsibility for the fall of the human race and for the introduction of death into the created order (Romans 5:12, 1 Corinthians 15:22). Eve was tricked into sinning; Adam knew exactly what he was doing (1 Timothy 2:14).

> ii. Many have speculated that Adam sinned because he didn't want Eve to be alone in the fall, and he ate of the fruit out of a romantic impulse. This may well be true, but it makes Adam's sin not one bit less rebellious. Rebellion against God is not "better" when motivated by a romantic impulse.

> iii. "Take and eat" will one day become verbs of salvation, but only after Jesus had lived in the world of Adam's curse and surrendered to death.

2. (7) The nakedness of Adam and Eve.

Then the eyes of both of them were opened, and they knew that they *were* naked; and they sewed fig leaves together and made themselves coverings.

a. **Then the eyes of both of them were opened**: Seemingly, it was only after the sin of Adam that they knew of their sinful state. They knew they were **naked**, in the sense of having their shame exposed to all creation.

b. **They knew that they were naked**: Both Psalm 104:2 and Matthew 17:2 suggest that light can be a garment for the righteous. It may be that Adam and Eve were previously clothed in God's glorious light, and the immediate loss of this covering of light left them feeling exposed and **naked**.

>i. "It is more than probable that they were clothed in light before the fall, and when they sinned the light went out." (Barnhouse)

c. **The eyes of both of them were opened**: The way they saw themselves changed, but also the way they saw the entire world was now different. After the fall, everything looked worse.

>i. When Adam and Eve saw their nakedness and felt terrible about it, it didn't feel good but it was good. It is good to feel guilty when you have done something wrong, and having no sense of guilt or shame is worse.

d. **They sewed fig leaves together**: Their own attempt to cover themselves took much ingenuity, but not much wisdom. Fig leaves have something of a prickly quality, which would make for some pretty itchy coverings.

>i. Every attempt to cover our own nakedness before God is just as foolish. We need to let Jesus cover us (Revelation 3:5, 18), and put on Jesus Himself as our covering garment (Galatians 3:27). God has a covering for His people (Isaiah 61:10), and the exhortation from Jesus is for us: *Behold, I am coming as a thief. Blessed is he who watches, and keeps his garments, lest he walk naked and they see his shame* (Revelation 16:15).

>ii. Obviously, they covered their genital areas. In virtually all cultures, adults cover their genital areas, even though other parts of the human body may be more or less exposed from culture to culture.

>iii. This is not because there is something intrinsically unclean in our sexuality, but because we have both received our fallenness and pass it on genetically through sexual reproduction. Because of this, God has implanted it in the minds of men that more modesty is appropriate for these areas of our body.

e. **Made themselves coverings**: After making their **coverings**, Adam and Eve waited. It would not be until *the cool of the day* (Genesis 3:8) when God would normally come to them. With anxiety and perhaps a bit of agony they waited until God patiently came to them.

>i. "Their hearts must have been sorely perplexed within them while they were waiting to see what God would do to them as a punishment for the great sin they had committed." (Spurgeon)

3. (8-9) Adam and Eve hide from God; God calls out to them.

And they heard the sound of the LORD God walking in the garden in the cool of the day, and Adam and his wife hid themselves from the presence of the LORD God among the trees of the garden. Then the LORD God called to Adam and said to him, "Where are you?"

a. **They heard the sound of the LORD God walking in the garden in the cool of the day**: Adam and Eve knew that when they heard the LORD coming, He would want to be with them. This was how the LORD had fellowship with Adam and Eve, in a very natural, close, intimate way.

> i. Leupold on **walking in the garden in the cool of the day**: "The almost casual way in which this is remarked indicates that this did not occur for the first time just then... There is extreme likelihood that the Almighty assumed some form analogous to the human form which was made in His image."
>
> ii. We can assume this is God, in the Person of Jesus Christ, appearing to Adam and Eve before His incarnation and birth at Bethlehem, because of God the Father it is said, "*No one has seen God at any time. The only begotten Son, who is in the bosom of the Father, He has declared Him*" (John 1:18); and no man has ever seen God in the Person of the Father (1 Timothy 6:16).
>
> iii. **Cool of the day** is literally "the breeze of the day." From Hebrew geography and culture, we might guess this means late afternoon or early evening. Charles Spurgeon thought the sense was, "in the wind of the evening," when the evening breeze was blowing through the garden.
>
> iv. "Not in the dead of night when the natural glooms of darkness might have increased the terrors of the criminal, not in the heat of the day, lest he should imagine that God come in the heat of passion; not in the early morning, as if in haste to slay, but at the close of the day, for God is long-suffering, slow to anger, and of great mercy." (Spurgeon)

b. **Adam and his wife hid themselves**: This shows that Adam and Eve knew that their attempt to cover themselves failed. They didn't proudly show off their fig-leaf outfits; they knew their own covering was completely inadequate, and they were embarrassed before God.

c. **Where are you?** This was not the interrogation of an angry commanding officer, but the heartfelt cry of an anguished father. God obviously knew where they were but He also knew a gulf had been made between Him and man, a gulf that He Himself would have to bridge.

- The question was meant to arouse Adam's sense of being lost.
- The question was meant to lead Adam to confess his sin.

- The question was meant to express God's sorrow over man's lost condition.
- The question was meant to show that seeks after lost man.
- The question was meant to express the accountability man had before God.

   i. God's question demanded an answer. They couldn't *refuse* to answer God the way a criminal might keep silent when questioned. "In our courts of law, we do not require men to answer questions which would incriminate them, but God does; and, at the last great day, the ungodly will be condemned on their own confession of guilt" (Spurgeon).

   ii. The way God came to Adam and Eve is a model of how He comes to lost and fallen humanity ever since.

   - God came to them patiently, waiting for the cool of the day – the evening time.
   - God came to them with care, coming before the darkness of night.
   - God came to them personally, addressing Adam and Eve directly.
   - God came to them with truth, showing them their lost condition.

C. God confronts Adam and Eve with their sin.

1. (10-12) Adam tries to explain his sin.

So he said, "I heard Your voice in the garden, and I was afraid because I was naked; and I hid myself." And He said, "Who told you that you *were* naked? Have you eaten from the tree of which I commanded you that you should not eat?" Then the man said, "The woman whom You gave *to be* with me, she gave me of the tree, and I ate."

   a. **I heard Your voice in the garden, and I was afraid**: Sin made Adam afraid of God's presence and afraid of God's voice. Ever since Adam, men run from God's presence and don't want to listen to His Word.

   i. We are still made in God's image, so we *want* to be in the presence of God and hear His voice, while at the same time, we are afraid of Him.

   b. **Who told you that you were naked?** God knew the answer to this question. He asked it because He allowed Adam to make the best of a bad situation by repenting right then and there, but Adam didn't come clean and repent before God.

   i. We all sin, but when we sin, we can still give glory to God by openly confessing without shifting the blame onto others (Joshua 7:19-20).

ii. There is often nothing you can do about yesterday's sin (though in some cases you may be able to make restitution). Yet you can do what is right before God right now by confessing and repenting.

c. **Have you eaten from the tree of which I commanded you that you should not eat?** God confronted Adam's problem squarely. This wasn't primarily a wardrobe problem or a fear problem or a self-esteem problem. This was a *sin* problem and Adam's wardrobe, fear or self-understanding could not be addressed until the sin problem was addressed.

d. **Then the man said**: Notice that to this point, God has not addressed Eve at all. Adam, being the head, is the problem here.

e. **The woman whom You gave to be with me, she gave me of the tree, and I ate**: Adam's attempt to blame Eve is completely consistent with human nature. Few of us are willing to simply say as David did, *I have sinned against the LORD* (2 Samuel 12:13).

i. Significantly, if there is any blame, it is on Adam, not Eve. Not only does Adam unjustly accuse Eve, but also he refused to accept proper responsibility for his part in her sin.

ii. By saying **the woman whom You gave to be with me**, Adam essentially blamed God for the sin saying, "*You* gave me the woman, and *she* is the problem." Adam wasn't content to blame Eve; he had to blame God also.

iii. "He was guilty of unkindness to his wife and of blasphemy against his maker, in seeking to escape from confessing the sin which he had committed. It is an ill sign with men when they cannot be brought frankly to acknowledge their wrong-doing." (Spurgeon)

2. (13) Eve's reply to God.

And the LORD God said to the woman, "What is this you have done?" The woman said, "The serpent deceived me, and I ate."

a. **The serpent deceived me, and I ate**: When confronted by God, Eve didn't necessarily shift the blame when she admitted the serpent deceived her and then she ate. This much was true: she had been deceived, and she did eat.

b. **Deceived me**: The problem comes when we fail to see that being deceived is sin in itself. It is sin to *exchange the truth of God for the lie* (Romans 1:25).

D. The curse and its aftermath.

1. (14-15) God's curse upon the serpent.

So the LORD God said to the serpent:

"Because you have done this,
You *are* cursed more than all cattle,
And more than every beast of the field;
On your belly you shall go,
And you shall eat dust
All the days of your life.
And I will put enmity
Between you and the woman,
And between your seed and her Seed;
He shall bruise your head,
And you shall bruise His heel."

a. **And the Lord God said to the serpent**: When God spoke to Adam and to Eve, He questioned each of them. God didn't ask Satan (the being animating the serpent) any questions because there was nothing to teach him.

i. "The Lord God did not ask the serpent anything, for he knew that he was a liar, but he at once pronounced sentence upon him." (Spurgeon)

b. **You are cursed more than all cattle**: The first part of the curse is directed at the animal that Satan used to bring the temptation. God commanded the serpent to slither on the ground instead of walking on legs like any other animal.

i. "The creature that tempted Eve became a serpent as a result of God's judgment on it, and it went slithering away into the bushes." (Boice)

ii. Adam and Eve must have been terrified as this once-beautiful creature called a serpent was transformed into the creeping, slithering, hissing snake we know today. They must have thought, "It's our turn next!"

iii. **I will put enmity between you and the woman**: In addition, there is a natural aversion between mankind and serpents, especially on the part of women.

c. **On your belly you shall go**: Whatever noble bearing the creation known as the serpent had before the fall and the curse, that nobility was gone. Now the creature Satan used to tempt Eve would be a low, groveling creature.

i. "Beings engaged in evil designs have no other way of going, but with tricks, devices, concealments, double meanings. When men deny the Scriptures and the truth of God, they always go to work in an underhand, mean, and serpentine style: 'Upon thy belly shalt thou go.' If guilty man begins to plot for his own advantage, scheme for his own glory, and aim at perverting the truth, you will notice that he never takes a bold, open, manly stand, but he dodges, he conceals, he twists and shifts: 'Upon thy belly shalt thou go.' Sin is a mean and despicable thing. The greatest potentate of evil was here doomed to cringe and crawl, and his seed have never forgotten their father's posture." (Spurgeon)

d. **You shall eat dust all the days of your life**: This was true of the serpent as an animal, but it is also true of Satan. To **eat dust** has the idea of *total defeat* (Isaiah 65:25, Micah 7:17). God's judgment on Satan is for him to always know defeat. He will always reach for victory but always fall short of it.

i. Satan was, in his own thinking, majestic and triumphant over Jesus on the cross, but he failed. In attacking Jesus, Satan made his own doom certain.

ii. In Jesus, we share in the victory over Satan: *And the God of peace will crush Satan under your feet shortly* (Romans 16:20).

e. **Enmity between you and the woman, and between your seed and her Seed**: The second part of the curse is directed against Satan himself. God placed a natural animosity between Satan and mankind. **Enmity** has the idea of ill will, hatred, and a mutual antagonism. Satan's hatred of Eve was nothing new; it was already present – but now man will, generally speaking, have antagonism towards Satan.

i. The friendship Eve and the serpent seemed to enjoy earlier in the chapter is finished. There is now a natural fear of Satan in the heart of man.

ii. If we are born naturally rebellious against God, we are also born cautious and afraid of Satan. One must be hardened to willingly and knowingly serve Satan. Instinctively, we don't serve God or Satan; we serve ourselves (which is fine with Satan).

f. **He shall bruise your head, and you shall bruise His heel**: In this, God prophesies the doom of Satan, showing that the real battle is between Satan and the **Seed** of the Woman.

i. There is no doubt this is a prophecy of Jesus' ultimate defeat of Satan. God announced that Satan would wound the Messiah (**you shall bruise His heel**), but the Messiah would crush Satan with a mortal wound (**He shall bruise your head**). It was as if God could not wait to announce His plan of salvation, to bring deliverance through the one known as **the Seed** of the woman.

ii. The **heel** is the part within the serpent's reach. Jesus, in taking on humanity, brought Himself near to Satan's domain so Satan could strike Him. "That bruised heel is painful enough. Behold our Lord in his human nature sore bruised: he was betrayed, bound, accused, buffeted, scourged, spit upon. He was nailed to the cross; he hung there in thirst and fever, and darkness and desertion" (Spurgeon).

iii. This prophecy also gives the first hint of the virgin birth, declaring the Messiah – the Deliverer – would be the Seed of the Woman, but not of the man.

iv. Genesis 3:15 has been called the *proto-evangelium*, the first gospel. Martin Luther said of this verse: "This text embraces and comprehends within itself everything noble and glorious that is to be found anywhere in the Scriptures" (Leupold).

v. "This is the first gospel sermon that was ever delivered upon the surface of this earth. It was a memorable discourse indeed, with Jehovah himself for the preacher, and the whole human race and the prince of darkness for the audience." (Spurgeon)

g. **He shall bruise your head**: For God to see the defeat of Satan at Satan's first flush of victory shows God knew what He was doing all along. God's plan wasn't defeated when Adam and Eve sinned because God's plan was to bring forth something greater than man in the innocence of Eden. God wanted more than *innocent* man; His plan is to bring forth *redeemed* man.

i. Redeemed man – this being who is greater than innocent man – is only possible because man had something to be redeemed from.

2. (16) God's curse upon the woman.

To the woman He said:

"I will greatly multiply your sorrow and your conception;
In pain you shall bring forth children;
Your desire *shall be* for your husband,
And he shall rule over you."

a. **I will greatly multiply your sorrow**: God first cursed the woman with multiplied sorrow. Men and women have each known sorrow throughout history, yet the unique sorrow of women is well known.

i. Under Jesus, some of the effects of the curse are relieved, and it has been the Christianizing of society that brought rights and dignity to women.

ii. "It is difficult for women in Christian lands to realize the miseries of their hundreds of millions of sisters in pagan lands, where the lot of women is little above that of cattle. Where the gospel has gone, the load has been lifted, and woman in Christ has become the reflection of the redeemed Church, the bride of Christ." (Barnhouse)

b. **Your sorrow and your conception; in pain you shall bring forth children**: The first curse upon women is a broad one. It has the idea that women would experience pain in regard to their children in general, not just in the act of giving birth. God ordained that the pain with which women bring children into this world be an example of the pain they experience more generally in life.

i. It has been observed that women bring forth children with more pain than just about any other creature.

c. **Your desire shall be for your husband**: This is true of women in a way that it is not true for men. Barnhouse explained: "This verse will be understood better when it is realized that the desire of man toward his wife alone is solely by God's grace and not by nature."

d. **Your desire shall be for your husband, and he shall rule over you**: The idea is to contrast the woman's **desire** and the husband's **rule over** her. This speaks of an inherent challenge in embracing the husband's role as leader of the home and family.

i. This same word for **desire** is used in Genesis 4:7 of the *desire* of sin to master over Cain. Because of the curse, Eve would have to fight a desire to master her husband, a desire that works against God's ordained order for the home.

ii. The principle of Adam's headship as a husband was established before the fall (see Genesis 2:18 and 2:22). Now the curse on Eve makes it much harder for her to submit and flow with God's institution of male headship in the home.

iii. "As a result of the fall, man no longer rules easily; he must fight from his headship. Sin has corrupted both the willing submission of the wife and the loving headship of the husband. The woman's desire is to control her husband (to usurp his divinely appointed headship), and he must master her, if he can. So the rule of love founded in paradise is replaced by struggle, tyranny and domination." (Susan T. Foh, cited in Boice)

3. (17-19) God's curse upon the man.

Then to Adam He said, "Because you have heeded the voice of your wife, and have eaten from the tree of which I commanded you, saying, 'You shall not eat of it':

"Cursed *is* the ground for your sake;
In toil you shall eat *of* it
All the days of your life.
Both thorns and thistles it shall bring forth for you,
And you shall eat the herb of the field.
In the sweat of your face you shall eat bread
Till you return to the ground,
For out of it you were taken;
For dust you *are*,
And to dust you shall return."

    a. **Because you have heeded the voice of your wife**: It wasn't just as if Adam took Eve's advice. He chose to be with Eve instead of obeying God. There is a sense in which *idolatry of Eve* was an aspect of Adam's disobedience against God.

    b. **Cursed is the ground**: Because of Adam, there is a curse upon all creation. Before the curse on man, the ground only produced good. After the curse, it still produced good, but **thorns and thistles** will come faster and easier than good fruit.

        i. The curse promised **thorns and thistles**, and we remember that Jesus was crowned with thorns (Matthew 27:29). In this vivid way, Jesus bore the curse for us. "This curse of the earth was on his head, and wounded him full sore. Was he crowned with thorns, and do you wonder that they grow up around your feet? Rather bless him that ever he should have consecrated the thorns by wearing them for his diadem" (Spurgeon).

    c. **In toil you shall eat of it**: Adam worked before the curse, but it was all joy. Now work has a cursed element to it, with pain and weariness a part of work. *Is there not a time of hard service for man on earth? Are not his days also like the days of a hired man? Like a servant who earnestly desires the shade, and like a hired man who eagerly looks for his wages* (Job 7:1-2).

        i. "Although the sentence took away from Adam the luscious fruits of paradise, yet it secured him a livelihood. He was to live; the ground was to bring forth enough of the herb of the field for him to continue to exist. Albeit that henceforth all he ate was to be with the sweat of his face, yet still he was to have enough to eat, and he was to live on." (Spurgeon)

    d. **Dust you are, and to dust you shall return**: The final curse upon man promised there would be an end of his toil and labor on the earth – but it was an end of *death*, not an end of *deliverance*.

i. The curse of death shows that the result of Adam's sin extended to the entire human race. Because of Adam:

- Sin entered the world (Romans 5:12).
- Death came to all mankind (Romans 5:15, 1 Corinthians 15:22).
- Death reigned over man and creation (Romans 5:17)
- All men were condemned (Romans 5:18).
- All men were made sinners (Romans 5:19).

ii. The principle of Galatians 3:13 is established as we consider that Jesus bore each aspect of the curse upon Adam and Eve in its totality: *Christ has redeemed us from the curse of the law, having become a curse for us.*

- Sin brought pain to childbirth, and no one knew more pain than Jesus did when He, through His suffering, brought many sons to glory (Hebrews 2:10).
- Sin brought conflict, and Jesus endured great conflict to bring our salvation (Hebrews 12:3).
- Thorns came with sin and the fall, and Jesus endured a crown of thorns to bring our salvation (John 19:2).
- Sin brought sweat, and Jesus sweat, as it were, great drops of blood to win our salvation (Luke 22:44).
- Sin brought sorrow, and Jesus became a man of sorrows, acquainted with grief, to save us (Isaiah 53:3).
- Sin brought death, and Jesus tasted death for everyone that we might be saved (Hebrews 2:9).

4. (20) The naming of Eve.

And Adam called his wife's name Eve, because she was the mother of all living.

a. **Adam called his wife's name Eve**: Up to Genesis 3:20, the woman has never been called Eve. We are so used to saying "Adam and Eve" that we assume she already had her name. But to this point, she was called a *female* (Genesis 1:27), a *helper comparable* (Genesis 2:18), a *woman* (Genesis 2:22, 23), and a *wife* (Genesis 2:24, 25; 3:8). This does not mean God did not have a name for Eve, but we are told what the name is in Genesis 5:2: *He called them Mankind.*

i. The idea that the woman takes her name from the husband, and the idea that both genders are encompassed in terms like *mankind, humanity,* and *chairman*. Our use of these terms is not merely cultural, it is Biblical.

ii. A woman gains more of her identity from her husband than the man does from the wife. For this reason, women should take special care in which man they marry.

b. **Because she was the mother of all living**: Adam named her **Eve**, even though she was not a mother at all at the time. She was not even pregnant yet. Adam named her in faith, trusting God would bring forth a deliverer from the woman because God said He would defeat Satan through the *Seed of the woman* (Genesis 3:15).

i. "She was not a mother at all, but as the life was to come through her by virtue of the promised seed, Adam marks his full conviction of the truth of the promise though at the time the woman had borne no children." (Spurgeon)

5. (21) God clothes Adam and Eve in the skins of animals.

Also for Adam and his wife the Lord God made tunics of skin, and clothed them.

a. **The Lord God made tunics of skin, and clothed them**: God wanted Adam and Eve clothed, not naked. If nudity represented a higher, freer life, then God would have let them remain naked – but He **clothed them**.

i. "God gave His approval of the sense of shame which had led our first parents to cover their nakedness." (Leupold)

b. **Tunics of skin**: In order for Adam and Eve to be clothed, a sacrifice had to be made. An animal had to die. *Without shedding of blood there is no remission* (Hebrews 9:22).

i. "Some creature had to die in order to provide them with garments, and you know who it is that died in order that we might be robed in his spotless righteousness. The Lamb of God has made for us a garment which covers our nakedness so that we are not afraid to stand even before the bar of God." (Spurgeon)

ii. There are only two religions; there is the religion of fig leaves and there is the religion of God's perfect provision through Jesus. Covering ourselves with our good works is like Adam and Eve trying to cover themselves with fig leaves. Our good works are like monopoly money – great for monopoly, but not legal tender. Your good works are essential to what it takes to live out your life, but they are not legal tender before God.

iii. Adam and Eve were clothed with a garment that was purchased with the life of another. We are clothed with a garment of righteousness that was purchased with the life of another, Jesus Christ.

c. **And clothed them**: This, together with the expression of faith in God's promise indicated in the naming of Eve (Genesis 3:20), indicates that Adam and Eve were rescued from their sinful condition. Adam had faith in God's promise of a Savior, and God provided a covering for them through a sacrifice. We will see Adam and Eve in heaven.

6. (22-24) God sets cherubim to guard the Tree of Life.

Then the LORD God said, "Behold, the man has become like one of Us, to know good and evil. And now, lest he put out his hand and take also of the tree of life, and eat, and live forever"; therefore the LORD God sent him out of the garden of Eden to till the ground from which he was taken. So He drove out the man; and He placed cherubim at the east of the garden of Eden, and a flaming sword which turned every way, to guard the way to the tree of life.

a. **Behold, the man has become like one of Us, to know good and evil**: The idea behind this phrase is difficult to understand. Perhaps there is a note of sarcasm by God here (as Elijah used in 1 Kings 18:27), regarding Satan's empty promise to become like gods. Or, perhaps the idea focuses on man's greater knowledge (though in a bad sense) now that he has the experiential knowledge of evil.

b. **And take also of the tree of life, and eat, and live forever**: In mercy, God protected Adam and Eve from the horrible fate of having to live forever as sinners by preventing them from eating from the tree of life.

c. **The LORD God sent him out of the garden of Eden**: We don't know if Adam and Eve *wanted* to stay in the garden of Eden. Perhaps they felt if they left the garden, they might never see God again because it was the only place where they met Him.

d. **He drove out the man; and He placed cherubim at the east of the garden of Eden**: Cherubim are always associated with the presence and glory of God (Ezekiel 10, Isaiah 6, Revelation 4). When cherubim are represented on earth (such as in the tabernacle, Exodus 25:10-22), they mark a *meeting place* with God. Though Adam and Eve and their descendants were prevented from eating the fruit of the tree of life (by God's mercy), they could still come there to meet God. This was their "holy of holies." Therefore, it was important to send cherubim and **a flaming sword** to **guard the way to the tree of life**.

i. "Any angel of the lowest rank could have dealt with Adam. The flaming sword was pointed against Satan to keep him from destroying the way of access to the altar, which God had set up." (Barnhouse)

ii. This is the last historical mention of the garden of Eden in the Bible. We can speculate that God did not destroy it, but left it to the effects of the curse and suppose that it generally deteriorated from its original condition, blending into the surrounding geography.

Genesis 4 – Cain and Abel

A. Cain's murder of Abel.

1. (1) The birth of Cain.

Now Adam knew Eve his wife, and she conceived and bore Cain, and said, "I have acquired a man from the LORD."

a. **Now Adam knew Eve his wife**: This is the first specific mention of sex in the Bible. The term **knew** or "to know" is a polite way of saying they had sexual relations and the term is used often in the Bible in this sense (Genesis 4:17, 4:25, 38:26, Judges 11:39, 1 Samuel 1:19).

i. This is a powerful way to describe sex. It shows the high, interpersonal terms in which the Bible sees the sexual relationship. Most terms and phrases people use for sex today are either coarse or violent, but the Bible sees sex as a means of *knowing* one another in a committed relationship. **Knew** indicates an act that contributes to the bond of unity and the building up of a one-flesh relationship.

ii. We have no reason to believe Adam and Eve did not have sex before this. Adam and Eve were certainly capable of sexual relations before the fall, because there is nothing inherently impure or unclean in sex itself, only in its misuse.

b. **And bore Cain, and said, "I have acquired a man from the LORD"**: The name **Cain** basically meant, *I've got him* or *Here he is*. It is likely Eve thought that Cain was the seed that God promised, the deliverer who would come from Eve (Genesis 3:15). There is a sense in which Eve said, "I have *the* man from the LORD."

i. Under normal circumstances, parents want good things for their children. They wonder if their children are destined for greatness. Adam, and especially Eve, had these expectations for Cain, but it went farther than normal parental hopes and expectations. Adam and Eve expected Cain to be the Messiah God promised.

ii. Eve thought she held in her arms the Messiah, the Savior of the whole world, but she really held in her arms a murderer.

c. **A man from the Lord**: Eve had faith to believe that the little baby she held would become a man. No baby had ever been born before. It is possible Adam and Eve wondered if their descendants would come forth fully mature, as they did.

2. (2-5) The birth of Abel and the offerings of Cain and Abel.

Then she bore again, this time his brother Abel. Now Abel was a keeper of sheep, but Cain was a tiller of the ground. And in the process of time it came to pass that Cain brought an offering of the fruit of the ground to the Lord. Abel also brought of the firstborn of his flock and of their fat. And the Lord respected Abel and his offering, but He did not respect Cain and his offering. And Cain was very angry, and his countenance fell.

a. **Abel was a keeper of sheep, but Cain was a tiller of the ground**: Agriculture and the domestication of animals were practiced among the earliest humans. Adam and his descendants did not spend tens of thousands of years living as hunter-gatherer cave dwellers.

b. **Cain brought an offering of the fruit of the ground to the Lord**: We can surmise that Cain brought his offering to the tree of life because cherubim guarded the way to the tree of life (Genesis 3:24), and cherubim are always associated with the dwelling place or meeting place with God (Exodus 25:10-22). It's possible that Cain, Abel and later others met with God at the tree of life, where the cherubim guarded access to the tree and prevented any from eating its fruit.

c. **The Lord respected Abel and his offering, but He did not respect Cain and his offering**: Abel brought an offering of blood (**the firstborn of his flock**) and Cain brought an offering of vegetation (**the fruit of the ground**). Many assume that *this* was the difference between their offerings, but grain offerings were acceptable before God (as seen in Leviticus 2), though not as an atonement for sin.

i. "The word for offering, *minchah*, is used in its broadest sense, covering any type of gift man may bring… Neither of the two sacrifices is made specifically for sin. Nothing in the account points in this direction." (Leupold)

ii. The writer to the Hebrews clearly explained why the offering of Abel was accepted and the offering of Cain was rejected: *By faith Abel offered up a more excellent sacrifice than Cain* (Hebrews 11:4). Cain's offering was the effort of dead religion, while Abel's offering was made in faith, in a desire to worship God in spirit and in truth.

d. **Abel also brought of the firstborn of his flock and of their fat**: This shows Abel's offering was extra special. The **fat** of the animal was prized as its "luxury" and was to be given to God when the animal was sacrificed (Leviticus 3:16-17 and 7:23-25). The burning of fat in sacrifice before God is called *a sweet aroma to the* L ORD (Leviticus 17:6).

> i. The offering of Cain was no doubt more aesthetically pleasing; Abel's would have been a bloody mess. But God was more concerned with faith in the heart than with artistic beauty.
>
> ii. Here, it was one lamb for a man. Later, at the Passover, it will be one lamb for a family. Then, at the Day of Atonement, it was one lamb for the nation. Finally, with Jesus, there was one Lamb who took away the sin of the whole world (John 1:29).

e. **Respected… did not respect**: We don't precisely know how Can and Abel knew their sacrifices were accepted or not accepted. Seemingly, there was some outward evidence making it obvious.

> i. There are Biblical examples of having an acceptable sacrifice consumed by fire from God (Judges 6:21; 1 Kings 18:38; 1 Chronicles 21:26; 2 Chronicles 7:1). Perhaps an acceptable sacrifice, brought to the cherubim at the tree of life, was consumed by fire from heaven or from the flaming swords of the cherubim (Genesis 3:24).

f. **Cain was very angry, and his countenance fell**: Cain's anger was undoubtedly rooted in pride. He couldn't bear that his brother was accepted before God and he was not. It is even possible that this was public knowledge if God consuming the sacrifice with fire indicated acceptance.

> i. The epidemic of sin quickly became worse. Cain now committed the relatively sophisticated sins of spiritual pride and hypocrisy.

3. (6-7) God's warning to Cain.

So the L ORD said to Cain, "Why are you angry? And why has your countenance fallen? If you do well, will you not be accepted? And if you do not do well, sin lies at the door. And its desire is for you, but you should rule over it."

> a. **Why are you angry? And why has your countenance fallen?** God dealt with Cain in terms of loving confrontation instead of automatic affirmation. God made it clear that Cain would be accepted *if* he did well.

> i. God knew the answers to the questions He asked, but He wanted Cain to know and to resist the pull toward violence and anger within.

b. **If you do not do well, sin lies at the door**: God warned Cain about the destructive power of sin. Cain could resist sin and find blessing, or he could give in to sin and be devoured.

c. **And its desire is for you, but you should rule over it**: We prevent sin from ruling over us by allowing God to master us first. Without God as our master, we will be slaves to sin.

4. (8) Cain murders Abel.

Now Cain talked with Abel his brother; and it came to pass, when they were in the field, that Cain rose up against Abel his brother and killed him.

> a. **Now Cain talked with Abel his brother**: The sense is that Cain planned to catch Abel by surprise, lulling him with pleasant conversation. This shows Cain committed *premeditated* murder, and therefore clearly ignored God's way of escape.

> b. **Cain rose up against Abel his brother and killed him**: No human had ever died or been killed before, but Cain saw how animals were being killed for sacrifice. He extinguished Abel's life in the same way.

>> i. The downward course of sin among the young human race progressed quickly. Now the hoped-for redeemer was found to be a murderer, and the second son was the victim of murder. Sin wasn't stopped at the root or man's moral condition quickly improved. Sin could not be contained.

B. God confronts Cain.

1. (9) God questions Cain.

Then the LORD said to Cain, "Where is Abel your brother?" He said, "I do not know. *Am* I my brother's keeper?"

> a. **Where is Abel your brother**: God knew the answer to this question. He asked Cain because He wanted to give him the opportunity to confess his sin and start to do right after having done wrong.

>> i. How futile it was for Cain to lie to God! It was madness for him to think God didn't know where Abel was, or that he could actually hide his sin from God.

> b. **Am I my brother's keeper?** This reply of Cain is famous. The fact of the matter is that he *was* supposed to be his **brother's keeper**, but was instead his brother's murderer, and he murdered him for the lowest of reasons.

Able had not injured Cain in any way. Cain's murderous rage was inspired purely by a spiritual jealousy.

> i. Spurgeon was shocked at the way Cain replied to God: "The cool impudence of Cain is an indication of the state of heart which led up to his murdering his brother; and it was also a part of the result of his having committed that terrible crime. He would not have proceeded to the cruel deed of bloodshed if he had not first cast off the fear of God and been ready to defy his Maker."

> ii. Jude 11 warns of the *way of Cain*, which is unbelief, empty religion leading to jealousy, persecution of the godly, and murderous anger.

> iii. There is no greater curse on the earth than empty, vain religion; those who *have a form of godliness but deny the power of God* (2 Timothy 3:5). Many are afraid of secular humanism or atheism, but dead religion sends more people to hell than anything else.

2. (10-12) God's curse upon Cain.

And He said, "What have you done? The voice of your brother's blood cries out to Me from the ground. So now you are cursed from the earth, which has opened its mouth to receive your brother's blood from your hand. When you till the ground, it shall no longer yield its strength to you. A fugitive and a vagabond you shall be on the earth."

> a. **The voice of your brother's blood cries out to Me from the ground**: The idea of blood crying out to God from the ground is later repeated in the Bible. Numbers 35:29-34 describes how the blood of unpunished murderers defiles the land.

>> i. The blood of Abel spoke, and it spoke of judgment. The blood of Jesus also speaks, but of better things, of grace and of sin having been judged (Hebrews 12:24).

> b. **So now you are cursed from the earth**: The curse upon Cain was that Adam's curse would be amplified in regard to him. If bringing forth food from the earth would be hard for Adam (Genesis 3:17-18), it would be impossible for Cain (who was a farmer). If Adam were driven from Eden (Genesis 3:24), Cain would find no resting-place on all the earth (**a fugitive and a vagabond you shall be on the earth**).

3. (13-15) Cain complains of the severity of God's judgment.

And Cain said to the LORD, "My punishment is greater than I can bear! Surely You have driven me out this day from the face of the ground; I shall be hidden from Your face; I shall be a fugitive and a vagabond on the earth, and it will happen *that* anyone who finds me will kill me."

And the LORD said to him, "Therefore, whoever kills Cain, vengeance shall be taken on him sevenfold." And the LORD set a mark on Cain, lest anyone finding him should kill him.

a. **My punishment is greater than I can bear!** Cain didn't feel bad about his sin, but only about his punishment. This attitude did not end with Can; like him, many people feel only bad about their punishment, not their sin.

i. "One of the clearest marks of sin is our almost innate desire to excuse ourselves and complain if we are judged in any way." (Boice)

ii. "One of the consequences of sin is that it makes the sinner pity himself instead of causing him to turn to God. One of the first signs of new life is that the individual takes sides with God against himself." (Barnhouse)

b. **Whoever kills Cain, vengeance shall be taken on him sevenfold**: As significant as God's judgment against Cain was, God did not want Cain killed by others. This is possibly because the population of the earth was precariously low anyway.

c. **The LORD set a mark on Cain**: Therefore, God set an identifying and protective mark upon Cain. Despite the speculation of some, nobody really knows what this mark upon Cain was.

C. Cain and his descendants.

1. (16-17) Cain moves away and marries.

Then Cain went out from the presence of the LORD and dwelt in the land of Nod on the east of Eden. And Cain knew his wife, and she conceived and bore Enoch. And he built a city, and called the name of the city after the name of his son—Enoch.

a. **And Cain knew his wife**: Genesis 5:4 says Adam had other sons and daughters. Cain obviously married his sister. Though marrying a sister was against the law of God according to Leviticus 18:9, 18:11, 20:17, and Deuteronomy 27:22 (which even prohibits the marrying of a half-sister), this was long before God spoke that law to Moses and the world.

i. Here, necessity demanded that Adam's sons marry his daughters. And at this point, the gene pool of humanity was pure enough to allow close marriage without harm of inbreeding. But as a stream can get more polluted the further it flows from the source, there came a time when God decreed there no longer be marriage between close relatives because of the danger of inbreeding.

ii. Even Abraham married his half-sister Sarah (Genesis 20:12). God did not prohibit such marriages until the time of Moses (Leviticus 18:9). Marrying a brother or sister was not forbidden until God forbade it.

b. **And he built a city**: Here we see the beginning of industry and of urbanization. From this beginning, it was strongly man-centered (**and called the name of the city after the name of his son**), not God-centered. The fall of the human race continued and even increased.

2. (18-22) The generations following Cain.

To Enoch was born Irad; and Irad begot Mehujael, and Mehujael begot Methushael, and Methushael begot Lamech. Then Lamech took for himself two wives: the name of one was Adah, and the name of the second was Zillah. And Adah bore Jabal. He was the father of those who dwell in tents and have livestock. His brother's name was Jubal. He was the father of all those who play the harp and flute. And as for Zillah, she also bore Tubal-Cain, an instructor of every craftsman in bronze and iron. And the sister of Tubal-Cain was Naamah.

a. **To Enoch was born Irad**: The picture is one of rapid advancement. Succeeding generations quickly made progress in areas such as the founding of a city (Genesis 4:17), home building (**the father of those who dwell in tents**), music and the arts (**the father of all those who play the harp and flute**), and metalworking (**an instructor of every craftsman in bronze and iron**).

i. The idea that mankind actually advanced very quickly goes against most modern theories, but archaeology can only evaluate on the basis of what is preserved, and thus is somewhat speculative.

b. **Methushael begot Lamech**: The name **Lamech** may mean, *conqueror*. He was the seventh from Adam on Cain's side. Lamech's arrogance (Genesis 4:23-24) is a contrast to Enoch, who was the seventh from Adam on Seth's line (Jude 14).

c. **Lamech took for himself two wives**: Lamech was the first bigamist in history, going against God's original plan for one man and one woman to become one flesh (Genesis 2:24, Matthew 19:4-8). The names of his wives and daughter show the emphasis in his heart: **Adah** means, "pleasure, ornament, or beauty." **Zillah** means, "shade" probably referring to a luxurious covering of hair. His daughter's name was **Naamah**, which means, "loveliness." Lamech's culture was committed to physical and outward beauty.

3. (23-24) Lamech's arrogant boast.

Then Lamech said to his wives:
"Adah and Zillah, hear my voice;
Wives of Lamech, listen to my speech!
For I have killed a man for wounding me,
Even a young man for hurting me.
If Cain shall be avenged sevenfold,
Then Lamech seventy-sevenfold."

> a. **I have killed a man for wounding me**: The way Lamech boasted about his murder of another, and the way he believed he could promise a greater retribution than God, shows a progressive degeneracy among humanity. Things quickly became worse with the human race, a true devolution.
>
> b. **If Cain shall be avenged sevenfold, then Lamech seventy-sevenfold**: This is all a representation of humanism, a man-centered perspective. The city was Cain's city; the focus of Lamech was his beautiful wives and his own perceived strength. But for all of Lamech's boasting, neither he nor his descendants are ever heard of again in the Bible. He came to nothing.

4. (25-26) Seth is born to Adam and Eve.

And Adam knew his wife again, and she bore a son and named him Seth, "For God has appointed another seed for me instead of Abel, whom Cain killed." And as for Seth, to him also a son was born; and he named him Enosh. Then *men* began to call on the name of the LORD.

> a. **And Adam knew his wife again, and she bore a son**: Adam and Eve had many children who were not specifically named in the Biblical record, but Seth was worthy of mention because he in some sense replaced Abel and was the one to whom the promise of a deliverer from the seed of the woman (Genesis 3:15) would be passed.
>
> b. **Then men began to call on the name of the LORD**: Even in those wicked days, the worship of God was not unknown. Some have called Genesis 4:26 the first revival, because it was the first indication of a spiritual resurgence after a clear decline.

Genesis 5 – The Descendants of Adam

A. Introduction to the genealogy.

1. (1-2) Adam's signature.

This is the book of the genealogy of Adam. In the day that God created man, He made him in the likeness of God. He created them male and female, and blessed them and called them Mankind in the day they were created.

   a. **This is the book of the genealogy of Adam**: There is good reason to believe this is the end of Adam's direct account, which was preserved and passed down to Moses who acted as an editor.

      i. The **history of the heaven and earth** comprises the things regarding creation that no man witnessed, (and was given by revelation to either Adam or Moses). This **history** ended at Genesis 2:4 and from there to this point is the account or record of Adam.

   b. **And called them Mankind**: The human race – **Mankind** – was given the name "man" by God from the beginning. It is not sexist or gender-biased to call the human race by the general heading **Mankind** because God does this.

2. Thoughts on genealogies.

   a. One can arrange the following genealogies in a sequential manner and chart out a time line. However, one cannot establish an absolutely reliable timeline with this method, because Biblical genealogies are not always complete. Sometimes generations are skipped over.

   b. If one takes the genealogies as being without omission, the time of Adam comes to be some 4,000 to 5,000 years before Jesus Christ. Even with omissions, it is hard to imagine that the time of Adam was significantly more than perhaps 10,000 years before Jesus.

i. This puts the Biblical record at incredible variance with the findings and assertions of modern science. Yet there are good reasons to believe God created the earth with apparent age built into it, even as Adam and the trees of Eden had apparent age built into them.

c. We are also confronted with the problem of extremely long lifespans. In this chapter, no one lived less than 365 years (and this was Enoch, who was a special case). Methuselah lived a total of 969 years. Several explanations of these long lifespans have been offered.

i. Some have thought the ages are figurative, or they count months as years. Yet on this basis, it would mean that Enoch fathered Methuselah when he was five and one-half years old.

ii. It is more likely that people did live much longer in the era before the flood. This is because the degenerative effects of the fall on the human gene pool had not yet accumulated greatly and because the environment in the pre-flood world was so different, with the blanket of water vapors surrounding the earth (Genesis 1:6-8). In the post-flood world, lifespans quickly came down to the lifespans we are familiar with today.

d. During this era, the world would be populated quickly. One writer has estimated that if Adam, during his lifetime, saw only half the children he could have fathered grow up, and if only half of those got married, and if only half of those who got married had children, then even at these conservative rates, Adam would have seen more than a million of his own descendants.

i. Using these calculations, we can say that by the time of the flood, there could have been seven billion people on the earth.

e. Genealogies can be very instructive. They speak to us of both the absolutely *historical* character of the Scriptures and are a powerful testimony to the end of every person on this earth.

i. "Have you never heard of one who heard read, as the lesson for the Sabbath-day, that long chapter of names, wherein it is written that each patriarch lived so many hundred years, 'and he died'? Thus it ends the notice of the long life of Methuselah with 'and he died,' The repetition of the words, 'and he died,' woke the thoughtless hearer to a sense of his mortality, and led to his coming to the Savior." (Spurgeon, *The Word a Sword*)

B. The descendants of Adam through Seth.

1. (3-5) Adam.

And Adam lived one hundred and thirty years, and begot *a son* **in his own likeness, after his image, and named him Seth. After he begot Seth, the days of Adam were eight hundred years; and he had sons and daughters. So all the days that Adam lived were nine hundred and thirty years; and he died.**

a. **And begot a son in his own likeness, after his image, and named him Seth**: Even as Seth was in Adam's fallen **image** and **likeness**, so also is every one of us. We are all sons and daughters of Adam, born fallen even as Adam was fallen. It would be redundant to say it, but every other person has been born in Adam's **image** and **likeness** except Jesus.

b. **And he had sons and daughters**: This tells us that Adam had many other sons and daughters who are not specifically named in the Biblical record. These **daughters** became the wives for the **sons** of Adam.

2. (6-17) From Seth to Mahalalel.

Seth lived one hundred and five years, and begot Enosh. After he begot Enosh, Seth lived eight hundred and seven years, and had sons and daughters. So all the days of Seth were nine hundred and twelve years; and he died. Enosh lived ninety years, and begot Cainan. After he begot Cainan, Enosh lived eight hundred and fifteen years, and had sons and daughters. So all the days of Enosh were nine hundred and five years; and he died. Cainan lived seventy years, and begot Mahalalel. After he begot Mahalalel, Cainan lived eight hundred and forty years, and had sons and daughters. So all the days of Cainan were nine hundred and ten years; and he died. Mahalalel lived sixty-five years, and begot Jared. After he begot Jared, Mahalalel lived eight hundred and thirty years, and had sons and daughters. So all the days of Mahalalel were eight hundred and ninety-five years; and he died.

3. (18-27) From Jared to Methuselah.

Jared lived one hundred and sixty-two years, and begot Enoch. After he begot Enoch, Jared lived eight hundred years, and had sons and daughters. So all the days of Jared were nine hundred and sixty-two years; and he died. Enoch lived sixty-five years, and begot Methuselah. After he begot Methuselah, Enoch walked with God three hundred years, and had sons and daughters. So all the days of Enoch were three hundred and sixty-five years. And Enoch walked with God; and he *was* **not, for God took him. Methuselah lived one hundred and eighty-seven years, and begot Lamech. After he begot Lamech, Methuselah lived seven hundred and eighty-two years, and had sons and daughters. So all the days of Methuselah were nine hundred and sixty-nine years; and he died.**

a. **Enoch walked with God; and he was not, for God took him**: Enoch, the son of Jared, was carried away to God in a miraculous way. **Walked with God** speaks of a true, deep relationship.

> i. "You cannot consciously walk with a person whose existence is not known to you. When we walk with a man, we know that he is there, we hear his footfall if we cannot see his face; we have some very clear perception that there is such a person at our side." (Spurgeon)

> ii. "If I wished to find a man's most familiar friend it would surely be one with whom he daily walked… In walking, friends become communicative — one tells his trouble, and the other strives to console him under it, and then imparts to him his own secret in return." (Spurgeon)

b. **Enoch walked with God**: Walking with God means walking by faith (2 Corinthians 5:7), walking in the light (1 John 1:5-7), and walking in agreement with God (Amos 3:3). After walking like this with God, it was as if one day God told Enoch, "You don't need to walk home. Why don't you just come home with Me?"

> i. **God took him**: "A very remarkable expression. Perhaps he did it in some visible manner. I should not wonder. Perhaps the whole of the patriarchs saw him depart even as the apostles were present when our Lord was taken up. However that may be, there was some special rapture, some distinct taking up of this choice one to the throne of the Most High." (Spurgeon)

> ii. Hebrews 11:5 tells us the foundation of Enoch's walk with God: *By faith Enoch was taken away so that he did not see death, "and was not found, because God had taken him"; for before he was taken he had this testimony, that he pleased God.* You can't walk with God or please God apart from faith.

> iii. "If men walk contrary to God, he will not walk with them, but contrary to them. Walking together implies amity, friendship, intimacy, love, and these cannot exist between God and the soul unless the man is acceptable unto the Lord." (Spurgeon)

> iv. "Enoch's life has no adventures; is it not adventure enough for a man to walk with God? What ambition can crave a nobler existence than abiding in fellowship with the Eternal?" (Spurgeon)

c. **After he begot Methuselah, Enoch walked with God**: It seems Enoch began to walk with God in a special way after the birth of **Methuselah**. The name Methuselah means, *when he is dead, it shall come*. At the birth of Methuselah, Enoch had a special awareness from God that judgment was coming, and this was one of the things that got him closer in his walk with God.

> i. Jude 14 also tells us Enoch was a prophet; even from his vantage point long ago, he could see the second coming of Jesus (*Behold, the Lord comes with ten thousands of His saints, to execute judgment on all, to convict all who are ungodly*).

d. **So all the days of Methuselah were nine hundred and sixty-nine years; and he died**: Methuselah's long life was no accident. It was because of the grace of God. When Methuselah died, the flood came. God kept him alive longer than anybody to give people as long as possible to repent.

4. (28-32) From Lamech to Noah.

Lamech lived one hundred and eighty-two years, and had a son. And he called his name Noah, saying, "This *one* will comfort us concerning our work and the toil of our hands, because of the ground which the LORD has cursed." After he begot Noah, Lamech lived five hundred and ninety-five years, and had sons and daughters. So all the days of Lamech were seven hundred and seventy-seven years; and he died. And Noah was five hundred years old, and Noah begot Shem, Ham, and Japheth.

a. **Lamech lived one hundred and eighty-two years, and had a son. And he called his name Noah**: If these genealogies are consecutive, Noah was born only 14 years after the death of Seth, Adam's son (Genesis 5:7-8). Seth died in year 1042 from creation and Noah was born in year 1056 from creation, if the genealogies are consecutive and without gaps.

> i. It's remarkable to think that Noah could have known and spoken with Adam's grandson Enosh and his other grandchildren. Since Adam and Eve had sons and daughters after Cain, Abel, and Seth (Genesis 5:3-4), it is possible or even likely that Noah spoke with one of the unnamed sons or daughters of Adam and Eve.

b. **And he died**: The overwhelming emphasis of Genesis 5 is that all these men *died*. They were all under sin and all subject to death. Some of them – many of them – were great men, but none of them was the deliverer God had promised.

> i. "This is the greatest glory of the primitive world, that it had so many good, wise, and holy men at the same time. We must not think that these are ordinary names of plain people; but next to Christ and John the Baptist, they were the most outstanding heroes this world has ever produced. And on the Last Day we shall behold and admire their grandeur." (Luther, cited in Boice)

Genesis 6 – Man's Wickedness; God Calls Noah

A. The wickedness of man in the days of Noah.

1. (1-2) Intermarriage between the **sons of God** and the **daughters of men**.

Now it came to pass, when men began to multiply on the face of the earth, and daughters were born to them, that the sons of God saw the daughters of men, that they *were* beautiful; and they took wives for themselves of all whom they chose.

> a. **When men began to multiply on the face of the earth**: During these days of rapid population expansion (especially because of long lifespans in the pre-flood world), there was a problem with ungodly intermarriage between the **sons of God** and the **daughters of men**.
>
> b. **The sons of God saw the daughters of men**: Many have believed the **sons of God** were those from the line of Seth, and the **daughters of men** were from the line of Cain, and this describes an intermarriage between the godly and the ungodly, something God specifically prohibits (Deuteronomy 7:1-4, 2 Corinthians 6:14).
>
>> i. But this approach leaves many unanswered questions: Why did this make God angry enough to wipe out almost all the earth's population? Why was there something unusual about the offspring of these unions (Genesis 6:4)? The idea that these were believers marrying unbelievers doesn't seem to fit the record of the text.
>
> c. **The sons of God saw the daughters of men**: It is more accurate to see the **sons of God** as either demons (angels in rebellion against God) or uniquely demon-possessed men, and the **daughters of men** as human women.
>
>> i. The phrase **sons of God** clearly refers to angelic creatures when it is used the three other times in the Old Testament (Job 1:6, 2:1, and 38:7). The translators of the Septuagint translated **sons of God** as

angels. Those ancient translators clearly thought **sons of God** referred to angelic beings, not to people descended from Seth.

ii. Jude 6 tells us of the *angels who did not keep their proper domain, but left their own habitation*. Jude goes on (Jude 7) to tell us they sinned *in a similar manner to these, having given themselves over to sexual immorality and gone after strange flesh*. Here in Genesis 6, as in Sodom and Gomorrah, there was an unnatural sexual union.

iii. It is useless to speculate on the nature of this union. Whether it was brought about by something like demon possession, or whether these angelic beings had power permanently to assume the form of men is not revealed. But we should understand the occult is filled with sexual associations with the demonic, and there are those today who actively pursue such associations.

iv. Jude 6 also makes it clear what God did with these wicked angels. They are *reserved in everlasting chains under darkness for the judgment of the great day* for not keeping their proper place. Their sinful pursuit of freedom has put them in bondage.

v. 1 Peter 3:19-20 tells us Jesus went to these disobedient spirits in their prison and proclaimed His victory on the cross over them.

vi. An objection offered to this understanding is found in Matthew 22:30, where Jesus said angels *neither marry nor are given in marriage*; but Jesus never said angels were sexless, and He was also speaking about faithful angelic beings (*angels of God in heaven*), not rebellious ones.

vii. From the book of 1 Enoch, which is not inspired scripture, but may still contain some accurate accounts: "And it came to pass that the children of men had multiplied that in those days were born unto them beautiful and comely daughters. And the angels, the children of heaven, saw and lusted after them, and said to one another: 'Come, let us choose us wives from among the children of men and beget us children...' [They] took unto themselves wives, and each chose for himself one, and they began to go unto them and to defile themselves with them, and they taught them charms and enchantments... And they became pregnant, and they bare great giants... And there arose much godlessness, and they committed fornication, and they were led astray, and became corrupt in all their ways."

d. **And they took wives for themselves of all whom they chose**: We can deduce *why* Satan sent his angels to intermarry (either directly or indirectly) with human women. Satan tried to pollute the genetic pool of mankind with a satanic corruption, to put something like a genetic virus to make the human race unfit for bringing forth the *Seed of the woman* – the Messiah – promised in Genesis 3:15.

> i. "The Savior could not be born of a demon-possessed mother. So if Satan could succeed in infecting the entire race, the deliverer could not come." (Boice)

> ii. And Satan *almost* succeeded. The race was so polluted that God found it necessary to start again with Noah and his sons, and to imprison the demons that did this so they could never do this again.

2. (3-4) God's response to this great wickedness.

And the Lord said, "My Spirit shall not strive with man forever, for he *is* indeed flesh; yet his days shall be one hundred and twenty years." There were giants on the earth in those days, and also afterward, when the sons of God came in to the daughters of men and they bore *children* to them. Those *were* the mighty men who *were* of old, men of renown.

> a. **My Spirit shall not strive with man forever**: God did not allow the human race to stay in this rebellious place forever. This means there is a point of no return in our rejection of God. God will not woo us forever; there is a point where He will say "no more."

>> i. All the more reason for us to say *today* is the day we will respond to Jesus instead of waiting for another day. We have no promise God will draw us some other day.

> b. **Yet his days will be one hundred and twenty years**: This is not the outside lifespan of man but the time left until the judgment of the flood. The flood happened 120 years after this announcement.

> c. **Giants on the earth in those days**: This refers to the unnatural offspring of the union between the **sons of God** and the **daughters of men**, though there were people of unusual size on the earth both before and after the flood (**and also afterward**). These ones before the flood were unique because of the demonic element of their parentage. They were the **mighty men of old, men of renown**.

3. (5-8) The great wickedness of man in Noah's day.

Then the Lord saw that the wickedness of man *was* great in the earth, and *that* every intent of the thoughts of his heart was only evil continually. And the Lord was sorry that He had made man on the earth, and He was grieved in His heart. So the Lord said, "I will destroy man whom I have created from the face of the earth, both man and beast, creeping thing and birds of the air, for I am sorry that I have made them." But Noah found grace in the eyes of the Lord.

a. **Every intent of the thoughts of his heart was only evil continually**: This says a lot. It means there was no aspect of man's nature not corrupted by sin.

> i. "A more emphatic statement of the wickedness of the human heart is hardly conceivable." (Vriezen, quoted in Kidner)
>
> ii. Jesus said, *as the days of Noah were, so also will the coming of the Son of Man be* (Matthew 24:37). In other words, the conditions of the world before the coming of Jesus will be like the conditions of the world before the flood:
>
> - Exploding population (Genesis 6:1).
> - Sexual perversion (Genesis 6:2).
> - Demonic activity (Genesis 6:2).
> - Constant evil in the heart of man (Genesis 6:5).
> - Widespread corruption and violence (Genesis 6:11).

b. **The LORD was sorry that He had made man... He was grieved in His heart**: God's sorrow at man, and the grief in His heart are striking. This does not mean that creation was out of control, nor does it mean that God hoped for something better but was unable to achieve it. God knew all along that this was how things would turn out, but our text clearly tells us that as God sees His plan for the ages unfold, it affects Him. God is not unfeeling in the face of human sin and rebellion.

c. **But Noah found grace in the eyes of the LORD**: While God commanded all the earth to be cleansed of this pollution, He found one man with whom to begin again: **Noah**, who **found grace in the eyes of the LORD**. Noah didn't *earn* grace; he *found* it. No one earns grace, but we can all *find* it.

> i. It was true then, and it is true today: *But where sin abounded, grace abounded much more* (Romans 5:20).

B. God calls Noah to build the Ark.

1. (9-10) Noah and his sons.

This is the genealogy of Noah. Noah was a just man, perfect in his generations. Noah walked with God. And Noah begot three sons: Shem, Ham, and Japheth.

a. **Noah was a just man, perfect in his generations**: This description of Noah – unique to him – not only refers to the righteous life of Noah, but also to the fact he was yet uncorrupted by Satan's attempt to sow something like a virus among the genetic pool of mankind. We could translate **perfect in his generations** as, "Noah was pure in his genetic profile."

i. "Did Noah live a perfect life? No, speaking popularly, and as the Scripture often speaks, we may say that Noah's character was a righteous one. There must have been flaws in it; and, certainly, after this time, there was one great sad flaw, of which it is not necessary now to speak more particularly, still, God regarded him as righteous." (Spurgeon)

ii. Spurgeon pointed out that we can know that Noah had the righteousness that is of faith because as soon as the floodwaters had dried up and he left the ark, he offered sacrifices (Genesis 8:20).

b. **Noah begot three sons: Shem, Ham, and Japheth**: Noah's three sons will figure into the account in a significant way. God will use them as a foundation for the rest of the human race.

2. (11-13) The corruption of the earth and the grace of God.

The earth also was corrupt before God, and the earth was filled with violence. So God looked upon the earth, and indeed it was corrupt; for all flesh had corrupted their way on the earth. And God said to Noah, "The end of all flesh has come before Me, for the earth is filled with violence through them; and behold, I will destroy them with the earth.

a. **The earth also was corrupt... and the earth was filled with violence**: Because of the corruption and violence on the earth, and the extent of the corruption, God told Noah that He would judge the wicked along with the earth.

b. **I will destroy them with the earth**: Some wonder if this is too harsh a judgment, or if this shows God to be cruel or a monster. However, since the fall in Genesis 3, every human being has a death sentence. The timing and method of that death are completely in the hands of God.

i. "On what grounds would God be told that He can bring death to millions of people at the end of a 'normal' lifespan, but that He may not do it in any other way?" (Barnhouse)

ii. In addition, it points to a deep and serious problem in the world at that time, something far beyond the problem of believers marrying those who do not believe.

c. **And God said to Noah**: God told all of this to Noah with the intention of saving Noah and his family. In the midst of such corruption and judgment, there is also grace. Instead of wiping out the entire race, God preserved a remnant.

3. (14-16) God tells Noah to build an ark.

"Make yourself an ark of gopherwood; make rooms in the ark, and cover it inside and outside with pitch. And this is how you shall make

it: **The length of the ark** *shall be* **three hundred cubits, its width fifty cubits, and its height thirty cubits. You shall make a window for the ark, and you shall finish it to a cubit from above; and set the door of the ark in its side. You shall make it** *with* **lower, second, and third** *decks*.**"**

a. **Make yourself**: This means this was Noah's project. He was not to simply contract it out to someone else.

b. **This is how you shall make it**: The ark was as long as a 30-story building is high (about 450 feet or 150 meters), and it was about 75 feet (25 meters) wide and 45 feet (15 meters) high. What is described is not really a boat, but a well-ventilated barge meant only to float and not to sail anywhere. After all, an **ark** is a chest, not a ship; this refers to the shoebox shape of the vessel.

i. The ark, roughly the shape of a shoebox, was plenty large enough (about the size of the Titanic), and had a cubit-wide opening (18 inches, one-half meter) all the way around the top.

ii. It was not until 1858 that a boat bigger than the ark was built. The ark was certainly big enough to do the job. If the ark carried two of every *family* of animals, there were around 700 pairs of animals; but if the ark carried two of every *species* of animals, there were around 35,000 pairs of animals.

iii. The average size of a land animal is smaller than a sheep. The ark could carry 136,560 sheep in *half* of its capacity, leaving plenty of room for people, food, water, and whatever other provisions were needed.

c. **You shall make it**: God had not yet told Noah *why* he must build an ark. At this point, all Noah knew was that God will judge the earth, and he was supposed to build a big barge. Since it had not rained yet on the earth, it is reasonable to suppose Noah didn't know what God was meant yet.

d. **You shall make it**: And Noah *did* make it. Beyond the Bible, there is rich historical evidence for the reality of Noah's Ark.

i. In 275 B.C., Berosus, a Babylonian historian, wrote: "But of this ship that grounded in Armenia some part still remains in the mountains... and some get pitch from the ship by scraping it off."

ii. Around A.D. 75, Josephus said the locals collected relics from the ark and showed them off to this very day. He also said all the ancient historians he knew of wrote about the ark.

iii. In A.D. 180, Theophilus of Antioch wrote: "the remains [of the ark] are to this day to be seen... in the mountains."

iv. An elderly Armenian man in America said that as a boy, he visited the ark with his father and three atheistic scientists in 1856. Their goal was to disprove the ark's existence, but they found it and became so enraged they tried to destroy it, but could not because it was too big and had petrified. In 1918 one of the atheistic scientists (an Englishman) admitted on his deathbed the whole story was true.

iv. In 1876 a distinguished British statesman and author, Viscount James Bryce, climbed Ararat and reported finding a four-foot long piece of hand-tooled timber at an altitude of more than 13,000 feet (4,300 meters).

vi. Six Turkish soldiers claimed to see the ark in 1916.

vii. In the early part of this century, a Russian aviator named Vladimire Rokovitsky claimed the discovery of Noah's ark. He was stationed in southern Russia near the Turkish border and Mount Ararat. As he tested a plane he and his co-pilot flew over Ararat and discovered on the edge of a glacier what he described as a boat the size of a battleship. He said it was partially submerged in a lake, and he could see there was an opening for a door nearly 20 feet (7 meters) square, but the door was missing. Rokovitsky told his commanding officer and an expedition was dispatched to find the ark and photograph it. The report was forwarded to the Czar, who was soon overthrown and the photos and the report perished.

viii. In 1936 a young British archaeologist named Hardwicke Knight hiked across Ararat and discovered interlocking hand-tooled timbers at a height of 14,000 feet (4,600 meters).

ix. During World War II two pilots saw and photographed something they believed was the ark on Mount Ararat.

x. There have been many more recent attempts to find and document the ark, but they have been hindered by politics and surrounded by controversy.

e. **Cover it inside and outside with pitch**: The **pitch** worked to waterproof the wood. God told Noah to cover it with pitch **inside and outside**, which makes it possible that the ark was preserved for a long time. It is possible God still has a purpose for the ark, to use it to remind the world of a past judgment shortly before a future judgment.

i. Peter, in 2 Peter 3:1-7, relates the future judgment to the judgment of the flood saying, unbelievers *willfully forget... the world that then existed perished being flooded with water*. Perhaps, before Jesus returns,

God will make it even more necessary for people to *willfully forget* these things.

ii. Because of this mention of **pitch** (a petroleum product) in what most people think is the Middle East, it is said that John D. Rockefeller looked for (and found) oil in that region based on this verse.

4. (17-21) Why the ark must be built and what Noah must do.

"And behold, I Myself am bringing floodwaters on the earth, to destroy from under heaven all flesh in which is the breath of life; everything that is on the earth shall die. But I will establish My covenant with you; and you shall go into the ark; you, your sons, your wife, and your sons' wives with you. And of every living thing of all flesh you shall bring two of every *sort* into the ark, to keep *them* alive with you; they shall be male and female. Of the birds after their kind, of animals after their kind, and of every creeping thing of the earth after its kind, two of every *kind* will come to you to keep *them* alive. And you shall take for yourself of all food that is eaten, and you shall gather it to yourself; and it shall be food for you and for them."

a. **Everything that is on the earth shall die**: We can only wonder what Noah felt when he heard this remarkable announcement from God. God called Noah to an essential role in the greatest judgment – and greatest salvation – the world had seen.

b. **But I will establish My covenant with you; and you shall go into the ark**: Despite the dramatic judgment coming, God will make a covenant with Noah, and he and his family will be saved. God will also use Noah to save a remnant of each animal so the earth could be populated with people and animals after the flood.

c. **Take for yourself of all food that is eaten, and you shall gather it to yourself**: God also commanded Noah to take all the food he could. There must be a lot of food for Noah and all the animals.

5. (22) Noah's obedience.

Thus Noah did; according to all that God commanded him, so he did.

a. **Thus Noah did**: When given this staggering job to do, Noah did it. We don't hear of him complaining or rebelling; he simply obeyed.

i. The words, **so he did** cover an awful lot of material and years; yet Noah did not shrink from what God told him to do.

b. **According to all that God commanded him, so he did**: The Bible presents Noah as a great hero of God. He was an outstanding example of righteousness (Ezekiel 14:14), a preacher of righteousness (2 Peter 2:5), and Noah condemned the world by offering salvation in the ark that the whole world rejected (Hebrews 11:7).

i. Noah was a *preacher of righteousness* (2 Peter 2:5), yet in his 120-year ministry, it seems that no one was saved.

ii. "The work of building the ark was laborious, costly, tedious, dangerous, and seemingly foolish and ridiculous; especially when all things continued in the same posture and safety for so many scores of years together; whereby Noah, without doubt, was all that while the song of the drunkards, and the sport of the wits of that age. So it is not strange that this is mentioned as an heroic act of faith." (Poole)

Genesis 7 – God Destroys the World with a Flood

A. The final preparations of Moses for the flood.

1. (1) God invites Noah into the ark.

Then the LORD **said to Noah, "Come into the ark, you and all your household, because I have seen that you are righteous before Me in this generation.**

> a. **Come into the ark**: The idea is that God was in the ark and would be with Noah in the ark, so He called Noah to **come into the ark** with Him.
>
>> i. "Notice that the Lord did not say to Noah, 'Go into the ark,' but 'Come,' plainly implying that God was himself in the ark, waiting to receive Noah and his family into the big ship that was to be their place of refuge while all the other people on the face of the earth were drowned." (Spurgeon)
>
> b. **I have seen that you are righteous**: Noah spent the years before the flood in active obedience. He not only believed God would send the flood; he obeyed what God told him to do in preparation for it.

2. (2-9) Noah gathers all the animals and his family.

"You shall take with you seven each of every clean animal, a male and his female; two each of animals that are unclean, a male and his female; also seven each of birds of the air, male and female, to keep the species alive on the face of all the earth. For after seven more days I will cause it to rain on the earth forty days and forty nights, and I will destroy from the face of the earth all living things that I have made." And Noah did according to all that the LORD **commanded him. Noah** *was* **six hundred years old when the floodwaters were on the earth. So Noah, with his sons, his wife, and his sons' wives, went into the ark because of the waters of the flood. Of clean animals, of animals that are unclean, of**

birds, and of everything that creeps on the earth, two by two they went into the ark to Noah, male and female, as God had commanded Noah.

>   a. **You shall take with you**: Some wonder how the animals came to Noah or how Noah got them. In Genesis 6:20 God said the animals would *come to* Noah by migration. In some animals, God has created a migratory instinct (which can operate in an amazing manner). It is no difficulty for Him to miraculously place an urge to migrate to the ark in each pair of animals He planned to be preserved in the ark.
>
>   > i. "This largest and most complete menagerie that was ever gathered together was not collected by human skill; divine power alone could have accomplished such a task as that." (Spurgeon)
>
>   b. **Two by two they went into the ark to Noah**: God never has a problem getting the animals to do what He wants. Only man is more stupid than the animals. *The ox knows its owner and the donkey its master's crib; but Israel does not know, My people do not consider* (Isaiah 1:3).

3. (10-12) God brings the waters upon the earth.

And it came to pass after seven days that the waters of the flood were on the earth. In the six hundredth year of Noah's life, in the second month, the seventeenth day of the month, on that day all the fountains of the great deep were broken up, and the windows of heaven were opened. And the rain was on the earth forty days and forty nights.

>   a. **After seven days that the waters of the flood were on the earth**: Noah, the animals, and his family had to wait in the ark seven days for the rain to come. They had never seen rain up to this time. This was a real test of faith – to wait a week after more than 100 years of preparation.
>
>   b. **The windows of heaven were opened**: This is when the heavens containing the great *waters that were above the firmament* (Genesis 1:7) opened up. These waters formed the huge so-called blanket of water in the upper part of the earth's atmosphere since creation.
>
>   c. **The fountains of the great deep that were broken up**: Waters came up from under the earth also, no doubt accompanied by great geological catastrophe.
>
>   d. **Forty days and forty nights**: The number 40 becomes associated with testing and purification, especially before entering into something new and significant. This is seen in:
>
>   - Moses' time on Mount Sinai (Exodus 24:18, Deuteronomy 9:25).
>   - The spies' trip to Canaan (Numbers 13:25).
>   - Israel's time in the wilderness (Numbers 14:33, 32:13).

- Elijah's miraculous journey to Sinai (1 Kings 19:8).
- Jesus' temptation in the wilderness (Mark 1:13).

4. (13-16) All enter the ark and the door is shut.

On the very same day Noah and Noah's sons, Shem, Ham, and Japheth, and Noah's wife and the three wives of his sons with them, entered the ark– they and every beast after its kind, all cattle after their kind, every creeping thing that creeps on the earth after its kind, and every bird after its kind, every bird of every sort. And they went into the ark to Noah, two by two, of all flesh in which is the breath of life. So those that entered, male and female of all flesh, went in as God had commanded him; and the LORD shut him in.

a. **Went in as God had commanded him**: This summary statement describes how everything was fulfilled exactly as the LORD had spoken. All things were ready for the flood God would bring upon the earth.

b. **And the LORD shut him in**: Noah did not have to shut the door on anyone's salvation; God did it. After the same pattern, it is never our job to disqualify people from salvation. If the door is to be shut, let God shut the door.

i. God kept the door open until the last possible minute, but there came a time when the door had to shut. When the door is open, it is open, but when it is shut, it is shut. Jesus is *He who opens and no one shuts, and shuts and no one opens* (Revelation 3:7).

ii. The ark was salvation for Noah, but condemnation for the world. There were no second chances for those left out. "Yea, when the one hundred and twenty years were over, and God's Spirit would no longer strive with men, there stood the great ark with its vast door wide open, and still Noah continued to preach and to declare that all who would pass within that open portal into the ark of safety should be preserved from the coming destruction. Outside that door death would reign universally, but all would be peace within" (Spurgeon).

B. Noah in the ark during the flood.

1. (17-23) The flood described.

Now the flood was on the earth forty days. The waters increased and lifted up the ark, and it rose high above the earth. The waters prevailed and greatly increased on the earth, and the ark moved about on the surface of the waters. And the waters prevailed exceedingly on the earth, and all the high hills under the whole heaven were covered. The waters prevailed fifteen cubits upward, and the mountains were covered. And

all flesh died that moved on the earth: birds and cattle and beasts and every creeping thing that creeps on the earth, and every man. All in whose nostrils *was* the breath of the spirit of life, all that *was* on the dry *land*, died. So He destroyed all living things which were on the face of the ground: both man and cattle, creeping thing and bird of the air. They were destroyed from the earth. Only Noah and those who *were* with him in the ark remained *alive*.

>a. **The waters prevailed and greatly increased on the earth**: The description of the flood in this passage is so complete and specific that it is impossible to reconcile a local flood with the Biblical record. Despite the claims of some, this is the description of a global deluge.
>
>>i. If this were not a global flood, then the ark itself would be unnecessary. If this were only a local flood, then God's promise to never again bring such a flood is false. If this were only a local flood, the Bible is wrong when it traces all of humanity back to Noah's sons and other passages that speak of a universal flood (such as Psalm 104:5-9 and 2 Peter 3:5-6).
>>
>>ii. Literally, hundreds of people groups have their own accounts and legends of the flood. One of the most remarkable is the Babylonian account, which is similar to the Genesis account in many ways and is clearly drawn from it. Since all mankind came from Noah's sons, all mankind remembers the flood.
>>
>>iii. Boice specifically cites the legends of the Samo-Kubo tribe of New Guinea, the Athapascan Indians of America, the Papago Indians of Arizona, Brazilian tribes, Peruvian Indians, African Hottentots, natives of Greenland, native Hawaiian islanders, Hindus, Chinese, Egyptians, Greeks, Persians, Australian natives, the Welsh, Celts, Druids, Siberians, and Lithuanians.
>>
>>iv. Of the more than 200 cultures that have their own account of the flood the following aspects of the story are common:
>>
>>- 88% describe a favored family.
>>- 70% attribute survival to a boat.
>>- 95% say the sole cause of the catastrophe is a flood.
>>- 66% say that the disaster is due to man's wickedness.
>>- 67% record that animals are also saved.
>>- 57% describe that the survivors end up on a mountain.
>>- Many of the accounts also specifically mention birds being sent out, a rainbow, and eight persons being saved.

b. **And the mountains were covered**: This took a lot of water, but there is plenty of water on the earth today to do this – but because of the topography of the earth, the water is collected into oceans. If the earth were a perfect sphere, the oceans would cover the land to a depth of two-and-a-half to three miles. Before the cataclysmic flood, the earth may have been much nearer to a perfect sphere.

> i. "If Moses had meant to describe a partial deluge upon only a small part of the earth, he used very misleading language; but if he meant to teach was that the deluge was universal, he used the very word which we might have expected that he would use." (Spurgeon)

c. **All in whose nostrils was the breath of the spirit of life, all that was on the dry land, died**: In the Scopes Monkey Trial (in America, 1925), Clarence Darrow humiliated William Jennings Bryan by asking him if he believed every word in the Bible. When Bryan said he did, Darrow asked him how the fish drowned in the flood. Bryan didn't know the answer, gave a long and confused speech, and died the next day. If only he would have known the Bible better, he would have known it says this about the **breath of the spirit of life**. The fish did not die in the flood; only animals with the **breath** of life in them died, the animals on dry land.

> i. God did just as He said. Virtually all of Noah's contemporaries did not believe God would do just as He said. Though it took 120 years, God demonstrated that He keeps His promises and is totally faithful.

2. (24) The flood lasted 150 days without receding.

And the waters prevailed on the earth one hundred and fifty days.

a. **One hundred and fifty days**: Some suggest that God put some or many of these animals into a period of hibernation for this period, meaning that less food, space, and supervision was be needed.

> i. God provides many animals today with an amazing instinct for hibernation. It would be no difficulty for Him to miraculously impart a unique instinct for these particular animals.

b. **One hundred and fifty days**: Safe in the ark, God sustained Noah and his family through this time of catastrophe and judgment. Shut in and sheltered from the storm and flood, they were safe.

> i. "Noah underwent burial to all the old things that he might come out into a new world, and even so we die in Christ that we may live with him." (Spurgeon)

Genesis 8 – Noah and His Family Leave the Ark

A. God remembers Noah.

1. (1) God focuses His attention on Noah again.

Then God remembered Noah, and every living thing, and all the animals that *were* with him in the ark. And God made a wind to pass over the earth, and the waters subsided.

> a. **God remembered Noah**: This is an *anthropomorphism* (a non-literal picture of God in human terms we can understand). Certainly, God never *forgot* Noah, sustaining him every day on the ark. But at this point, God again turned His active attention towards Noah. It was truly as if He **remembered Noah** again.
>
>> i. "Noah had been shut up in the ark for many a day, and at the right time God thought of him, practically thought of him, and came to visit him. Dear heart, you have been shut out from the world now for many days, but God has not forgotten you. God remembered Noah, and he remembers you." (Spurgeon)
>
> b. **God made a wind to pass over the earth**: God knew how to make the waters subside. Even a big problem like this was not a big problem to God. The God who created the heavens and the earth (Genesis 1:1) could also do this.

2. (2-5) As the floodwaters recede, the ark rests on Mount Ararat.

The fountains of the deep and the windows of heaven were also stopped, and the rain from heaven was restrained. And the waters receded continually from the earth. At the end of the hundred and fifty days the waters decreased. Then the ark rested in the seventh month, the seventeenth day of the month, on the mountains of Ararat. And the waters decreased continually until the tenth month. In the tenth *month*, on the first *day* of the month, the tops of the mountains were seen.

a. **The fountains of the deep and the windows of heaven were also stopped**: The rain that began in Genesis 7:11-12 was now **stopped**. God was in control of when waters began, and when they stopped.

b. **On the mountains of Ararat**: In one way of thinking, Mount Ararat was not a good place to leave the ark. Leaving the ark at a high altitude and mountainous terrain meant a difficult departure for everyone and everything in the ark. However, if God's purpose was to put the ark in a place where it might be preserved for thousands of years, He chose an excellent place for it.

c. **The tops of the mountains were seen**: This is another indication in the Biblical record that this was a worldwide flood. It was so significant that for a time **the tops of the mountains** were covered, and now they **were seen** again as the waters **decreased continually**.

3. (6-12) Birds are used to test the condition of the earth.

So it came to pass, at the end of forty days, that Noah opened the window of the ark which he had made. Then he sent out a raven, which kept going to and fro until the waters had dried up from the earth. He also sent out from himself a dove, to see if the waters had receded from the face of the ground. But the dove found no resting place for the sole of her foot, and she returned into the ark to him, for the waters *were* on the face of the whole earth. So he put out his hand and took her, and drew her into the ark to himself. And he waited yet another seven days, and again he sent the dove out from the ark. Then the dove came to him in the evening, and behold, a freshly plucked olive leaf *was* in her mouth; and Noah knew that the waters had receded from the earth. So he waited yet another seven days and sent out the dove, which did not return again to him anymore.

a. **At the end of forty days**: This was counted from the time when the rain and other water sources began (Genesis 7:11-12).

i. "God told Noah when to go into the ark, but he did not tell him when he should come out again. The Lord told Noah when to go in, for it was necessary for him to know that; but he did not tell him when he should come out, for it was unnecessary that he should know that. God always lets his people know what is practically for their good." (Spurgeon)

b. **Noah opened the window of the ark which he had made**: Genesis 6:16 describes the window that was to be made in the upper portion of the ark. The **window** was also made with some kind of covering that could be closed and **opened**.

i. "Because he believed in God, therefore he removed the covering of the ark, and looked abroad, expecting by-and-by to see not only the tops of the mountains, but also a dry and green earth once more. True faith often goes to the window. If your faith turns her face to the wall, and expects nothing, I do not think it is genuine faith." (Spurgeon)

c. **He sent out a raven, which kept going to and fro**: Apparently the **raven** did not return to the ark. Perhaps this was because the **raven** is a scavenger, and might rest and feed upon dead, floating carcasses.

d. **The dove found no resting place… she returned into the ark**: Being a clean, non-scavenging bird, the **dove** would not land upon the earth until there was a dry, suitable place to land. When the dove **returned into the ark**, Noah knew that the waters had not yet drained enough to leave the ark.

i. Charles Spurgeon made a spiritual point from the idea that **the dove found no resting place**. He explained that like the dove, the believer finds no true resting place in this world. "The world is said to be progressing, advancing, improving; but we cannot discover it. The same sin, the same filthiness, the same universally abounding unbelief, that our fathers complained of, we are obliged to complain of still; and we are weary with the world, weary with the nineteenth century, and all its boasted civilization. There is nothing upon which the sole of our foot can rest."

e. **The dove came to him… a freshly plucked olive leaf was in her mouth**: The raven never returned, but the **dove** came back with evidence that the terrible season of judgment through the flood was over and God had begun to renew plant life on the earth. Since this, a **dove** with an **olive leaf** has been a symbol of peace and goodness.

i. "Perhaps you have seen a picture of the dove carrying an olive branch in its mouth, which, in the first place, a dove could not pluck out of the tree, and in the second place, a dove could not carry an olive branch even if she could pluck it off. It was an olive leaf, that is all. Why cannot people keep to the words of Scripture? If the Bible mentions a leaf, they make it a bough; and if the Bible says it is a bough, they make it a leaf." (Spurgeon)

f. **The dove, which did not return again to him anymore**: The departure of the dove proved that the earth was habitable again.

4. (13-19) Noah, his family, and all the animals leave the ark.

And it came to pass in the six hundred and first year, in the first *month*, the first *day* of the month, that the waters were dried up from the earth;

and Noah removed the covering of the ark and looked, and indeed the surface of the ground was dry. And in the second month, on the twenty-seventh day of the month, the earth was dried. Then God spoke to Noah, saying, "Go out of the ark, you and your wife, and your sons and your sons' wives with you. Bring out with you every living thing of all flesh that is with you: birds and cattle and every creeping thing that creeps on the earth, so that they may abound on the earth, and be fruitful and multiply on the earth." So Noah went out, and his sons and his wife and his sons' wives with him. Every animal, every creeping thing, every bird, and whatever creeps on the earth, according to their families, went out of the ark.

a. **In the six hundred and first year**: Genesis 7:11-13 says that Noah entered the ark on the seventeenth day of the second month of the six hundredth year of his life. This is almost a full year later, and in the **second month** of his six hundred and first year Noah left the ark. It seems he was in the ark a full calendar year.

b. **Bring out with you every living thing**: Just as the ark was loaded with animals before the flood, it was then unloaded. We don't read of any animals that died in the year on the ark.

c. **That they may abound on the earth and be fruitful and multiply**: Living things from the ark would once again repopulate the earth.

i. "Noah came out of the ark — no longer cooped up and penned within its narrow limits, he walked abroad, and the whole world was before him where to choose. Was not that a picture of the freedom of the believer who has been 'buried with Christ,' and enjoys the possession of God's free Spirit?" (Spurgeon)

B. God's covenant with Noah.

1. (20) Noah builds an altar and offers a sacrifice.

Then Noah built an altar to the LORD**, and took of every clean animal and of every clean bird, and offered burnt offerings on the altar.**

a. **Then Noah built an altar**: Noah's first act after leaving the ark was to worship God through sacrifice. His gratitude and admiration of God's greatness led him to worship God.

b. **Took of every clean animal and every clean bird**: As is the nature of true sacrifice, this was a costly offering unto God. With only seven of each animal on the ark, Noah risked extinction by sacrificing some of these animals. But costly sacrifice is pleasing to God.

i. "Common sense would have said, 'Spare them, for you will want every one of them.' But grace said, 'Slay them, for they belong to God. Give Jehovah his due.'" (Spurgeon)

ii. The sacrifices we offer to God should also cost us something. We should present our bodies as a living sacrifice to God (Romans 12:1), the giving of our resources is a sacrifice (Philippians 4:18), and we should give the sacrifice of praise to God (Hebrews 13:15).

iii. Costly sacrifice pleases God, not because God is greedy and wants to get as much from us as He can but because God Himself sacrificed at great cost (Ephesians 5:2 and Hebrews 9:26, 10:12). God wants costly sacrifice from us because it shows we are being conformed into the image of Jesus, who was the greatest display of costly sacrifice. As Paul wrote in Ephesians 5:2, we should be like Jesus in this regard: *And walk in love, as Christ also has loved us and given Himself for us, an offering and a sacrifice to God for a sweet-smelling aroma.*

iv. May we think like David, who said he would never offer to God *that which costs me nothing* (2 Samuel 24:24).

2. (21-22) God's promise to Noah and to all mankind.

And the Lord smelled a soothing aroma. Then the Lord said in His heart, "I will never again curse the ground for man's sake, although the imagination of man's heart is evil from his youth; nor will I again destroy every living thing as I have done.

While the earth remains,
Seedtime and harvest,
Cold and heat,
Winter and summer,
And day and night
Shall not cease."

a. **The Lord smelled a soothing aroma**: Noah's costly sacrifice pleased God. It was as if God smelled the great aroma of the roasting meat (indicating that God loves the smell of grilling or burning meat), and He then made this wonderful promise to Noah and to man.

i. Of course, the Bible speaks anthropomorphically here – using a human analogy of a divine action or attribute. More pleasing to God than the smell of the sacrifice was the *heart* of Noah in his sacrifice.

b. **I will never again curse the ground for man's sake**: God promised to never again visit the earth with judgment by a flood on this scale, to **destroy every living thing**. God did this understanding that **the imagination of man's heart is evil from his youth**. This was a promise full of mercy.

i. We may observe a strange combination of truths; first, that **the imagination of man's heart is evil from his youth** and second, God's promise to **never again curse the ground for man's sake**. It would seem that man's evil would invite God's curse, not put it away. The strange combination is accounted for by Noah's altar and sacrifice, and God's pleasure in the sacrifice (**the LORD smelled a soothing aroma**).

ii. "The sacrifice is the turning-point. Without a sacrifice sin clamours for vengeance, and God sends a destroying food; but the sacrifice presented by Noah was typical of the coming sacrifice of God's only begotten Son, and of the effectual atonement therein provided for human sin." (Spurgeon)

iii. We can say that after the flood, Noah's story illustrated many things relevant to the life of the believer.

- Noah showed the believer's freedom.
- Noah showed the believer's faith (in sacrifice).
- Noah showed the believer's heart (by sacrifice).
- Noah showed the believer's covenant of mercy (in light of sacrifice).

c. Cold and heat, winter and summer: God promised that after the flood, the earth would have established seasons. This speaks of the profound climatic and ecological changes in the earth since the covering of water vapors covering the earth was emptied. Now, there would be seasonal and temperature variations.

i. "As there should be no more a general deluge, so should there be no more a serious disarrangement of the course of the seasons and the temperature appropriate thereto. Seed-time and harvest, and cold and heat, and summer and winter, and day and night, are to succeed each other in their perpetually unchanging change, so long as the present reign of forbearance shall last." (Spurgeon)

ii. The result of this change is found in the rapidly decreasing lifespans. There will never be 900-year-old men after the flood. The mass extinction of animals revealed in the fossil record (such as dinosaurs and other such creatures) probably took place shortly after the flood, when the earth changed so dramatically and plunged into an ice age.

iii. "How faithfully God fulfils his covenant with the earth! How truly will he keep his covenant with every believing sinner! Oh, trust ye in him, for his promise will stand fast for ever!" (Spurgeon)

Genesis 9 – God's Covenant with Noah and Creation

A. God's covenant and instructions to Noah.

1. (1-4) Instructions for living in a new world.

So God blessed Noah and his sons, and said to them: "Be fruitful and multiply, and fill the earth. And the fear of you and the dread of you shall be on every beast of the earth, on every bird of the air, on all that move on the earth, and on all the fish of the sea. They are given into your hand. Every moving thing that lives shall be food for you. I have given you all things, even as the green herbs. But you shall not eat flesh with its life, *that is***, its blood."**

a. **Be fruitful and multiply**: The world Noah entered from the ark was significantly different from the world he knew before. God gave Noah the same kind of mandate He gave Adam in the beginning of creation (Genesis 1:28) since Noah essentially began all over again.

b. **Every moving thing that lives shall be food for you**: Even as Adam received instructions for eating (Genesis 1:29, 2:15-17), so did Noah. Yet now, Noah received specific permission to eat animals, permission Adam was not given (as far as we know).

i. Perhaps this was because the earth was less productive agriculturally after the flood, because of the ecological changes mentioned in Genesis 9:1-3 and 8:22. Therefore God gave man permission to eat meat.

c. **The fear of you and the dread of you shall be on every beast of the earth**: If man now could and would eat animals, then God would help the animals. For their protection, God put in them a fear of mankind.

i. Again, presumably before the flood, man had a different relationship with the animals. God did not put this fear in animals because man did not look to them as food.

ii. "Did the horse know his own strength, and the weakness of the miserable wretch who unmercifully rides, drives, whips, goads, and oppresses him, would he not with one stroke of his hoof destroy his tyrant possessor? But while God hides these things from him he impresses his mind with the fear of his owner, so that... he is trained up for, and employed in, the most useful and important purposes." (Clarke)

d. **But you shall not eat flesh with its life, that is, its blood**: God also commanded Noah that if animals were killed and eaten, there must be a proper respect for the **blood**, which represents the life principle in the animal (Leviticus 17:11, 17:14 and Deuteronomy 12:23).

i. The importance of the idea of **blood** in the Bible is shown by how often the word is used. It is used 424 times in 357 separate verses (in the New King James Version).

ii. The respect for blood isn't based on mysticism or superstition, but simply because **blood** represents the **life** of the being, whether animal or human. When **blood** is poured out, **life** is poured out.

- Blood was the sign of mercy for Israel at the first Passover (Exodus 12:13).
- Blood sealed God's covenant with Israel (Exodus 24:8).
- Blood sanctified the altar (Exodus 29:12).
- Blood set aside the priests (Exodus 29:20).
- Blood made atonement for God's people (Exodus 30:10).
- Blood sealed the new covenant (Matthew 26:28).
- Blood justifies us (Romans 5:9).
- Blood brings redemption (Ephesians 1:7).
- Blood brings peace with God (Colossians 1:20).
- Blood cleanses us (Hebrews 9:14 and 1 John 1:7).
- Blood gives entrance to God's holy place (Hebrews 10:19).
- Blood sanctifies us (Hebrews 13:12).
- Blood enables us to overcome Satan (Revelation 12:11).

2. (5-7) God gives to man the right and responsibility of capital punishment.

"Surely for your lifeblood I will demand *a reckoning*; from the hand of every beast I will require it, and from the hand of man. From the hand of every man's brother I will require the life of man.

Whoever sheds man's blood,
By man his blood shall be shed;
For in the image of God
He made man.
And as for you, be fruitful and multiply;
Bring forth abundantly in the earth
And multiply in it."

    a. **Surely for your lifeblood I will demand a reckoning**: According to God's command, when a man's blood is shed there must be an accounting for it because **in the image of God He made man**. Because man is made in the image of God, his life is inherently precious and cannot be taken without giving account to God.

        i. **By man his blood shall be shed** means because life is valuable; when murder is committed the death penalty is in order.

        ii. In its original languages, the Bible makes a distinction between *killing* and *murder*. Not all killing is murder because there are cases where there is just cause for killing (self-defense, capital punishment with due process of law, killing in a just war). There are other instances where killing is accidental. This is killing, but not *murder*.

        iii. The Bible also consistently teaches that the punishment of the guilty is the role of human government (Romans 13:1-4) to restrain man's depravity. It also teaches that the guilt of unpunished murder defiles a land (Numbers 35:31-34). As Luther said, "God establishes government and gives it the sword to hold wantonness in check, lest violence and other sins proceed without limit" (cited in Boice).

    b. **From the hand of every beast I will require it**: To see the strength of God's command, He even requires a reckoning for the life of man from **every beast**. God does not condone the unlawful killing of any kind.

    c. **Be fruitful and multiply**: This point was repeated because it needed emphasis. The earth badly needed repopulating.

3. (8-11) God makes a covenant with man and with all of creation.

Then God spoke to Noah and to his sons with him, saying: "And as for Me, behold, I establish My covenant with you and with your descendants after you, and with every living creature that is with you: the birds, the cattle, and every beast of the earth with you, of all that go out of the ark, every beast of the earth. Thus I establish My covenant with you: Never again shall all flesh be cut off by the waters of the flood; never again shall there be a flood to destroy the earth."

a. **I establish My covenant**: This covenant was made with mankind (**you and your descendants after you**), and even with the animals (**every living creature that is with you**). God promised He would never again destroy all with a flood or cover the earth with a flood. This was a repetition and clarification of the promise God made in Genesis 8:21-22.

> i. "It cheered my heart, when thinking this matter over, to remember that although I depend upon covenant faithfulness, I am not alone in that dependence, for every living thing upon the face of the earth lives by virtue of the immutable covenant of God. Covenant engagements preserve the world from flood; were it not for that covenant, the tops of the mountains might be covered to-morrow." (Spurgeon)

b. **Never again shall there be a flood to destroy the earth**: God did not believe He did something wrong or too harsh in the flood. He made the promise because He did things in the post-flood world to guarantee that the exact evil conditions of the pre-flood world would never be precisely duplicated. These things included the imprisonment of the angels who sinned with human women (Jude 6) and shortening the lifespan of man.

> i. However, when things again become *similar* to the days of Noah (Matthew 24:37), God will destroy the earth – but by fire, not by flood (2 Peter 3:1-7).

4. (12-17) The sign of God's covenant.

And God said: "This is the sign of the covenant which I make between Me and you, and every living creature that is with you, for perpetual generations: I set My rainbow in the cloud, and it shall be for the sign of the covenant between Me and the earth. It shall be, when I bring a cloud over the earth, that the rainbow shall be seen in the cloud; and I will remember My covenant which is between Me and you and every living creature of all flesh; the waters shall never again become a flood to destroy all flesh. The rainbow shall be in the cloud, and I will look on it to remember the everlasting covenant between God and every living creature of all flesh that is on the earth." And God said to Noah, "This is the sign of the covenant which I have established between Me and all flesh that is on the earth."

> a. **This is the sign of the covenant which I make between Me and you, and every living creature… the covenant between me and the earth**: This impressive covenant was made not only between God and humanity, but God made the promise to all creation, including the animals and the **earth** itself.

b. **I set My rainbow in the cloud**: Because the blanket of water vapors was released in the flood and the water cycle of the earth changed after the flood, this may be the first occurrence of a **rainbow**. God used the rainbow as a sign to Noah and all generations that He would be faithful to His covenant.

c. **It shall be for the sign of the covenant between Me and the earth**: Every time we see a rainbow, we should remember the faithfulness of God and every one of His promises. He even says His covenant of peace with us is just as sure as His covenant with Noah and all generations.

> i. *For this is like the waters of Noah to Me; for as I have sworn that the waters of Noah would no longer cover the earth, so have I sworn that I would not be angry with you, nor rebuke you. For the mountains shall depart and the hills be removed, but My kindness shall not depart from you, nor shall My covenant of peace be removed, says the* L<small>ORD</small>, *who has mercy on you* (Isaiah 54:9-10).

d. **I will look on it to remember the everlasting covenant**: The other mentions of a **rainbow** in the Bible are set in the context of God's enthroned glory (Ezekiel 1:28; Revelation 4:3). If God set a rainbow around his throne, it is impressive that He set so close to Himself a reminder of His promise to man.

> i. God does not only look at the rainbow on earth and remember the covenant; He also looks at the rainbow that surrounds His throne. God is committed to remaining faithful to His covenant.

> ii. One the same principle, the believer *glories* in the sovereignty of God, because he knows God's sovereignty is *on his side*. It means no good purpose of God relating to the believer will ever be left undone.

B. Noah and his sons.

1. (18-19) The sons of Noah.

Now the sons of Noah who went out of the ark were Shem, Ham, and Japheth. And Ham was the father of Canaan. These three *were* the sons of Noah, and from these the whole earth was populated.

a. **The sons of Noah who went out of the ark were Shem, Ham, and Japheth**: Noah's three sons emerged from the catastrophe of the flood into a completely new world.

b. **The whole earth was populated**: From these three sons of Noah came the nations, as we know them. The descendants of these three sons are listed in the table of nations provided in Genesis 10.

2. (20-23) The sin of Ham, Noah's son.

And Noah began *to be* **a farmer, and he planted a vineyard. Then he drank of the wine and was drunk, and became uncovered in his tent. And Ham, the father of Canaan, saw the nakedness of his father, and told his two brothers outside. But Shem and Japheth took a garment, laid it on both their shoulders, and went backward and covered the nakedness of their father. Their faces** *were* **turned away, and they did not see their father's nakedness.**

a. **Noah began to be a farmer**: Making his way into the new world after the flood, Noah began to provide for himself and his family. He probably planted many things, among them **a vineyard**.

b. **He drank of the wine and was drunk**: This is the first mention of drunkenness in the Bible. Some think it was only after the flood that man made (or was able to make) intoxicating drink.

i. Noah's own sinful and shameful actions show the foolishness of drunkenness. Well do the Proverbs say, *Wine is a mocker, strong drink is a brawler, and whoever is led astray by it is not wise... Who has woe? Who has sorrow? Who has contentions? Who has complaints? Who has wounds without cause? Who has redness of eyes? Those who linger long at the wine, those who go in search of mixed wine. Do not look on the wine when it is red, when it sparkles in the cup, when it swirls around smoothly; at the last it bites like a serpent, and stings like a viper. Your eyes will see strange things, and your heart will utter perverse things* (Proverbs 20:1, 23:29-33).

ii. It also shows the foolishness of those who claim God's desire is to make people "drunk in the spirit" through the work of a "Holy Ghost Bartender." When Ephesians 5:18 says, *do not be drunk with wine, in which is dissipation; but be filled with the Spirit*, it makes a contrast of the work of the Spirit with the effects of drunkenness.

iii. Alcohol is a depressant. It loosens people because it depresses their self-control, their wisdom, their balance, and judgment. The filling of the Holy Spirit has an exactly opposite effect. He is a stimulant, and He influences every aspect of our being to better and more perfect performance.

c. **And became uncovered in his tent**: It may be Noah was abused sexually by one of his sons or relatives. The phrase **became uncovered** and the idea of **nakedness** is sometimes associated with sexual relations (Leviticus 18:6-20).

i. This is repulsive, but not terribly surprising. Many people who get drunk become victims of abuse, sexual and otherwise. A large majority of the men and women involved in date-rape situations were drinking or taking drugs just before the attack. According to some statistics, half of all rapes involve alcohol.

ii. There are more costs to drunkenness. In the 1990s it was recorded that in the United States 100,000 people died each year in alcohol-related deaths, while alcohol abuse cost the nation hundreds of billions of dollars each year.

d. **Saw the nakedness of his father**: Others think Ham's only sin here was in seeing Noah's drunken, uncovered state, and that he made fun of him, mocking him as a father and as a man of God.

i. Literally, the ancient Hebrew says that Ham "told with delight" what he saw in his father's tent. He determined to mock his father and was undermining his authority as a man of God.

3. (24-27) Noah's curse upon Canaan.

So Noah awoke from his wine, and knew what his younger son had done to him. Then he said:

"Cursed be Canaan;
A servant of servants
He shall be to his brethren."

And he said:

"Blessed *be* the Lord,
The God of Shem,
And may Canaan be his servant.
May God enlarge Japheth,
And may he dwell in the tents of Shem;
And may Canaan be his servant."

a. **Knew what his younger son had done to him**: This seems to indicate that whatever happened to Noah, it was more than one of his sons or grandsons seeing his nudity. This explains the strength of the curse.

b. **Cursed be Canaan**: It seems strange that if Ham sinned against Noah, that **Canaan** (Ham's son) was cursed. Perhaps Canaan was also involved in this sin against Noah in a way not mentioned in the text. Perhaps the strongest punishment against Ham was for Noah to prophetically reveal the destiny of his son Canaan.

i. We can trust God is not punishing the son (Canaan) for the sin of the father (Ham). This goes against the heart and justice of God

(Ezekiel 18:2-3). However, through Noah's prophecy, God told Ham what *would happen* to his son.

c. **May Canaan be his servant**: In earlier generations, prejudiced people regarded the descendants of Canaan as black people from Africa, and they used the curse on Canaan to justify slavery. But black people did not come from Canaan. Canaan was the father of the near-eastern peoples, many of whom were conquered by Joshua when Israel took the Promised Land.

4. (28-29) The end of Noah's days.

And Noah lived after the flood three hundred and fifty years. So all the days of Noah were nine hundred and fifty years; and he died.

a. **Noah lived after the flood three hundred and fifty years**: Noah was a remarkable man who served God in his own generation. Yet his last years do not seem to match the glory of his first years.

b. **All the days of Noah were nine hundred and fifty years**: Noah was man of great triumph and of weakness. His godliness is remembered in the New Testament, marking him as a man of faith (Hebrews 11:7) and a preacher of righteousness (2 Peter 2:5).

Genesis 10 – The Table of Nations

"The tenth chapter of Genesis... stands absolutely alone in ancient literature, without a remote parallel, even among the Greeks, where we find the closest approach to a distribution of peoples in genealogical framework... The Table of Nations remains an astonishing accurate document." (William F. Albright, cited in Boice)

A. The descendants of Japheth.

1. (1) The three sons of Noah: Shem, Ham, and Japheth.

Now this is the genealogy of the sons of Noah: Shem, Ham, and Japheth. And sons were born to them after the flood.

> a. **This is the genealogy of the sons of Noah**: This may mark another transition in the records that Moses collected to compile the book of Genesis.
>
> b. **And sons were born to them after the flood**: God told humanity to multiply after the flood, and this indicates that they did. Humanity and life went on.

2. (2) The sons of Japheth.

The sons of Japheth *were* Gomer, Magog, Madai, Javan, Tubal, Meshech, and Tiras.

> a. **The sons of Japheth**: He was the father of the Indo-European peoples, those stretching from India to the shores of Western Europe. They are each linked by linguistic similarities that often seem invisible to the layman but are much more obvious to the linguist.
>
> b. **Gomer**: From this son of Japheth came the Germanic peoples, from whom came most of the original peoples of Western Europe. These include the original French, Spanish, and Celtic settlers.
>
> c. **Magog... Tubal, Meshech**: These settled in the far north of Europe and became the Russian peoples.

d. **Madai**: From this son of Japheth came the ancient Medes and they populated what are now Iran and Iraq. The peoples of India also came from this branch of Japheth's family.

e. **Javan**: From this son of Japheth came the ancient Greeks, whose seafaring ways are described in Genesis 10:5.

3. (3) The sons of Gomer.

The sons of Gomer *were* Ashkenaz, Riphath, and Togarmah.

a. **Ashkenaz**: From this son of Gomer came the peoples who settled north of Judea into what we call the Fertile Crescent.

b. **Togarmah**: From this son of Gomer came the Armenians.

4. (4-5) The sons of Javan (the ancient Greeks).

The sons of Javan *were* Elishah, Tarshish, Kittim, and Dodanim. From these the coastland *peoples* of the Gentiles were separated into their lands, everyone according to his language, according to their families, into their nations.

a. **The sons of Javan were**: Geographic names that spring from these names in this chapter abound. Linguists have no trouble seeing the connection between **Kittim** and Cyprus, **Rodanim** and Rhodes, **Gomer** and Germany, **Meschech** and Moscow, **Tubal** and Tobolsk.

b. **Everyone according to his language, according to their families, into their nations**: These divisions of mankind developed into **language**, genetic (**families**) and ethnic (**nations**) divisions.

B. **The descendants of Ham.**

1. (6) The sons of Ham.

The sons of Ham *were* Cush, Mizraim, Put, and Canaan.

a. **Ham**: The descendants of Ham are the peoples who populated Africa and the Far East.

b. **Cush**: Apparently, this family divided into two branches early. Some founded Babylon (notably, **Nimrod**) and others founded Ethiopia.

c. **Mizraim**: This is another way the Bible refers to Egypt. **Put** refers to Libya, the region of North Africa west of Egypt. **Canaan** refers to the peoples who originally settled the land we today think of as Israel and its surrounding regions.

2. (7-12) The sons of Cush.

The sons of Cush *were* Seba, Havilah, Sabtah, Raamah, and Sabtechah; and the sons of Raamah *were* Sheba and Dedan. Cush begot Nimrod; he

began to be a mighty one on the earth. He was a mighty hunter before the LORD; therefore it is said, "Like Nimrod the mighty hunter before the LORD." And the beginning of his kingdom was Babel, Erech, Accad, and Calneh, in the land of Shinar. From that land he went to Assyria and built Nineveh, Rehoboth Ir, Calah, and Resen between Nineveh and Calah (that *is* the principal city).

a. **Cush begot Nimrod**: One son of Cush worthy of note is **Nimrod**. He was a **mighty one on the earth**, but not in a good way. He ruled over **Babel**, which was the first organized rebellion of humans against God. The name **Nimrod** itself means, "let us rebel."

b. **Like Nimrod the mighty hunter before the LORD**: The context shows that this is not a compliment of Nimrod. The idea is that Nimrod was an *offense* before the face of God.

i. "This is not talking about Nimrod's ability to hunt wild game. He was not a hunter of animals. He was a hunter of men – a warrior. It was through his ability to fight and kill and rule ruthlessly that his kingdom of the Euphrates valley city states was consolidated." (Boice)

ii. A Jerusalem Targum says: "He was powerful in hunting and in wickedness before the Lord, for he was a hunter of the sons of men, and he said to them, 'Depart from the judgment of the Lord, and adhere to the judgment of Nimrod!' Therefore it is said: 'As Nimrod the strong one, strong in hunting, and in wickedness before the Lord'" (cited in Morris).

iii. Ginzberg quotes from a Jewish legend: "The great success that attended all of Nimrod's undertakings produced a sinister effect. Men no longer trusted in God, but rather in their own prowess and ability, an attitude to which Nimrod tried to convert the whole world."

iv. "Hence it is likely that Nimrod, having acquired power, used it in tyranny and oppression; and by rapine and violence founded the domination which was the first distinguished by the name of a *kingdom* on the face of the earth. How many kingdoms have been founded in the same way, in various ages and nations from that time to the present! From the Nimrods of the earth, God deliver the world!" (Clarke)

3. (13-14) The sons of Mizraim.

Mizraim begot Ludim, Anamim, Lehabim, Naphtuhim, Pathrusim, and Casluhim (from whom came the Philistines and Caphtorim).

4. (15-19) The sons of Canaan.

Canaan begot Sidon his firstborn, and Heth; the Jebusite, the Amorite, and the Girgashite; the Hivite, the Arkite, and the Sinite; the Arvadite, the Zemarite, and the Hamathite. Afterward the families of the Canaanites were dispersed. And the border of the Canaanites was from Sidon as you go toward Gerar, as far as Gaza; then as you go toward Sodom, Gomorrah, Admah, and Zeboiim, as far as Lasha.

    a. **Canaan begot Sidon**: The family of **Sidon**, the son of Canaan, went north and is related to the Hittites and Lebanese.

    b. **And the Sinite**: Many people believe the Oriental peoples descended from the **Sinites**.

5. (20) The spread of the descendants of Ham.

These *were* **the sons of Ham, according to their families, according to their languages, in their lands** *and* **in their nations.**

C. The descendants of Shem.

1. (21-22) The sons of Shem.

And *children* **were born also to Shem, the father of all the children of Eber, the brother of Japheth the elder. The sons of Shem** *were* **Elam, Asshur, Arphaxad, Lud, and Aram.**

    a. **Children were born also to Shem**: From Shem comes **Elam**, who was an ancestor of the Persian peoples; **Asshur**, who was the father of the Assyrians; **Lud** was father to the Lydians who lived for a time in Asia Minor; and **Aram** was father to the Arameans, who we also know as the Syrians. **Arphaxad** was the ancestor of Abram and the Hebrews.

2. (23) The sons of Aram.

The sons of Aram *were* **Uz, Hul, Gether, and Mash.**

    a. **Uz**: Later, a region in Arabia was named after this son of Aram. Job came from the land of Uz (Job 1:1).

3. (24-30) The sons and descendants of Arphaxad.

Arphaxad begot Salah, and Salah begot Eber. To Eber were born two sons: the name of one *was* **Peleg, for in his days the earth was divided; and his brother's name** *was* **Joktan. Joktan begot Almodad, Sheleph, Hazarmaveth, Jerah, Hadoram, Uzal, Diklah, Obal, Abimael, Sheba, Ophir, Havilah, and Jobab. All these** *were* **the sons of Joktan. And their dwelling place was from Mesha as you go toward Sephar, the mountain of the east.**

a. **All these were the sons of Joktan**: The names after the son of **Joktan** (son of Eber, son of Salah, son of Arphaxad) are all associated with various Arabic peoples.

b. **And Jobab**: The one named **Jobab** may be the one we know as *Job* in the Old Testament.

4. (31) The spread of the descendants of Shem.

These *were* the sons of Shem, according to their families, according to their languages, in their lands, according to their nations.

5. (32) Summary statement: the nations after the flood.

These *were* the families of the sons of Noah, according to their generations, in their nations; and from these the nations were divided on the earth after the flood.

a. "Hence one must consider this chapter of Genesis a mirror in which to discern that we human beings are, namely, creatures so marred by sin that we have no knowledge of our own origin, not even of God Himself, our Creator, unless the Word of God reveals these sparks of divine light to us from afar... This knowledge the Holy Scriptures reveal to us. Those who are without them live in error, uncertainty, and boundless ungodliness; for they have no knowledge about who they are and whence they came." (Luther, cited in Boice)

Genesis 11 – Mankind after the Flood; the Tower of Babel

A. The tower of Babel.

1. (1-4) A tower in the land of **Shinar**.

Now the whole earth had one language and one speech. And it came to pass, as they journeyed from the east, that they found a plain in the land of Shinar, and they dwelt there. Then they said to one another, "Come, let us make bricks and bake *them* thoroughly." They had brick for stone, and they had asphalt for mortar. And they said, "Come, let us build ourselves a city, and a tower whose top is in the heavens; let us make a name for ourselves, lest we be scattered abroad over the face of the whole earth."

> a. **Now the whole earth had one language and one speech**: If we accept the Biblical teaching that mankind has a common origin in Adam, then this simply makes sense: that there was a time when humanity spoke one language instead of the hundreds on the earth today.
>
> b. **The land of Shinar**: **Shinar** was a term used also of Babylon (Genesis 10:10). The multiplied descendants from the ark came together to build a great city and tower, in rebellion against God's command to spread out over the earth (Genesis 9:1).
>
> c. **"Let us make bricks and bake them thoroughly" …they had asphalt for mortar**: Using baked bricks and asphalt for mortar, men built a tower that was both strong and waterproof, even as Noah used the same material in waterproofing the ark (Genesis 6:14). Later Moses' mother used the same material in waterproofing Moses' basket (Exodus 2:3).
>
> > i. "Archaeology has revealed that this type of kiln-fired brick and asphalt construction was common in ancient Babylon." (Morris)

d. **Come, let us build ourselves a city**: The *heart* and the *materials* relevant to the tower of Babel show that it was not only disobedient to God's command to *fill the earth* (Genesis 9:1), but it also shows man did not believe God's promise to never again flood the earth. A waterproof tower was made to protect man against a future deluge.

i. This was a strong statement of *self* against *God*. When they said **let us build ourselves a city, and a tower whose top is in the heavens**, they meant it.

e. **A tower whose top is in the heavens**: The top of the tower was intended to be **in the heavens**. It is doubtful they thought they could build a tower *to* heaven. It is more likely they built the tower as an observation point of the heavens; it was built "unto the heavens." Most astrological and occult practices have a history back to Babel.

i. If they really wanted to build a tower to reach heaven, it is unlikely they would start on the plain of Shinar, which is about Sea Level. Common sense says they would start on one of the nearby mountains.

ii. This **tower** was real. The ancient Greek historian Herodotus said the tower of Babel still stood in his day and he had seen it.

2. (5-9) God scatters them over the whole earth.

But the LORD came down to see the city and the tower which the sons of men had built. And the LORD said, "Indeed the people *are* one and they all have one language, and this is what they begin to do; now nothing that they propose to do will be withheld from them. "Come, let Us go down and there confuse their language, that they may not understand one another's speech." So the LORD scattered them abroad from there over the face of all the earth, and they ceased building the city. Therefore its name is called Babel, because there the LORD confused the language of all the earth; and from there the LORD scattered them abroad over the face of all the earth.

a. **The LORD came down to see the city and the tower**: The personal character of the language indicates this perhaps was a time when God came down in the form of a man, in the Person of Jesus Christ.

b. **Let Us go down**: This plural reference to **Us** is another subtle reference to the Trinity.

c. **Nothing that they propose to do will be withheld from them**: The potential of fallen man is terrible and powerful. When we think of the horrific accomplishments of evil from men in the 20th century, the great ability of men and nations is a painful consideration.

d. **So the LORD scattered them abroad**: The forced separation of men from Babel was more God's mercy than His judgment. God, in dividing man both linguistically and geographically, put a check on the power of his fallen nature.

e. **The LORD confused the language of all the earth**: The division of the languages is a fascinating subject. Modern linguists know man did not invent language, any more than man invented his own circulatory or nervous system. Most modern linguists believe language is so unique that the only way they can explain it apart from God is to say that it was part of a *unique* evolutionary process.

> i. Language cannot be the product of man putting together sounds all by himself. For example, there are many universal human sounds (like the "raspberry" sound) that are not part of any human language. If man invented language on his own, it would make sense for some language to use that sound.
>
> ii. Language is so complex because languages exist as whole systems, not as small parts put together. Most modern linguists believe all languages come from one original language.

f. **From there the LORD scattered them abroad over the face of all the earth**: Think what it was like for a family to leave the area of Babel and go out on their own. They must look for a suitable place to live, and once they found it, they must exist by hunting and gathering, living in crude dwellings or caves until they could support themselves by agriculture and taking advantage of the natural resources. Families would multiply rapidly, develop their own culture, and their own distinctive biological and physical characteristics influenced by their environment. In the small population, genetic characteristics change very quickly, and as the population of the group grew bigger, the changes stabilized and became more or less permanent.

> i. The whole account of what happened at Babel with its anti-God dictator, its organized rebellion against God, and its direct distrust of God's promise shows man hasn't gotten any better since the flood. Time, progress, government, and organization have made man *better off*, but not *better*.
>
> ii. Now God will begin to make man *better*, and He will start as He always starts: with a man who will do His will, even if he does not do His will perfectly.

B. The line of Adam through Shem to Abram.

1. (10-25) From Shem to Terah, the father of Abram.

This is the genealogy of Shem: Shem was one hundred years old, and begot Arphaxad two years after the flood. After he begot Arphaxad, Shem lived five hundred years, and begot sons and daughters. Arphaxad lived thirty-five years, and begot Salah. After he begot Salah, Arphaxad lived four hundred and three years, and begot sons and daughters. Salah lived thirty years, and begot Eber. After he begot Eber, Salah lived four hundred and three years, and begot sons and daughters. Eber lived thirty-four years, and begot Peleg. After he begot Peleg, Eber lived four hundred and thirty years, and begot sons and daughters. Peleg lived thirty years, and begot Reu. After he begot Reu, Peleg lived two hundred and nine years, and begot sons and daughters. Reu lived thirty-two years, and begot Serug. After he begot Serug, Reu lived two hundred and seven years, and begot sons and daughters. Serug lived thirty years, and begot Nahor. After he begot Nahor, Serug lived two hundred years, and begot sons and daughters. Nahor lived twenty-nine years, and begot Terah. After he begot Terah, Nahor lived one hundred and nineteen years, and begot sons and daughters.

a. **This is the genealogy of Shem**: This genealogy is of special note because it will eventually be part of the Messianic line. It is followed in genealogical record of Luke 3.

b. **Nahor lived twenty-nine years, and begot Terah**: These were the grandfather and father of Abraham. The promise to bring forth the deliverer from the seed of the woman (Genesis 3:15) would find its fulfillment through this family.

2. (26-28) The family of Terah in Ur of the Chaldeans.

Now Terah lived seventy years, and begot Abram, Nahor, and Haran. This is the genealogy of Terah: Terah begot Abram, Nahor, and Haran. Haran begot Lot. And Haran died before his father Terah in his native land, in Ur of the Chaldeans.

a. **Now Terah lived seventy years, and begot Abram:** Genesis 11:26 is the first mention of **Abram**. Abram (later changed to *Abraham*) is mentioned 312 times in 272 verses in the Bible. He is arguably the most famous man of the Old Testament, and one of the most influential men in history.

i. The Book of Genesis covers more than 2,000 years and more than 20 generations. Yet, it spends almost a third of its text on the life of one man – Abram.

b. **Terah begot Abram**: Abram is unique in the way he is called *the friend of God* (James 2:23); *Abraham, Your friend forever* (2 Chronicles 20:7); *Abraham, My friend* (Isaiah 41:8).

i. We all know the value of having friends in high places. Abram had a Friend in the highest place! Once Abraham Lincoln received a request for a pardon from a man who deserted the army. When he was told the man had no friends, Lincoln said "I will be his friend," and he pardoned him.

ii. Men and women in the Bible are famous for many different things, but Abram is great for his *faith*. Moses was the great lawgiver; Joshua a great general; David a great king, and Elijah a great prophet. Most of us know we can never be great in those things, but we can be great people of faith. We can be friends of God.

iii. If you despair in knowing you do not have Abram's faith, take comfort in knowing you have Abram's God. He can build in you the faith of Abram because He built it in Abram himself.

iv. You do have faith. You buy a ticket to a sporting event and show up, having faith the ticket is good. You fly in an airplane because you have faith in the airline's equipment, mechanics, and pilots. You plan a weekend based on the weather report. And you do this even though sometimes there are ticket scandals, sometimes planes crash, and sometimes the weatherman is wrong; but you still have faith. God can build the faith you have.

3. (29-30) The family of Abram and his brother Nahor.

Then Abram and Nahor took wives: the name of Abram's wife *was* **Sarai, and the name of Nahor's wife, Milcah, the daughter of Haran the father of Milcah and the father of Iscah. But Sarai was barren; she had no child.**

a. **Then Abram and Nahor took wives**: Abram's wife **Sarai** (her name means *contentious*) was barren, unable to bear children.

b. **Abram's wife was Sarai... she had no child**: Because the name **Abram** means *father*, it must have been an awkward embarrassment for Abram to explain that he had no children. But his present lack of children will play an important role in God's plan of redemption.

4. (31-32) The family of Terah and their travels from Ur of the Chaldeans to Haran.

And Terah took his son Abram and his grandson Lot, the son of Haran, and his daughter-in-law Sarai, his son Abram's wife, and they went out with them from Ur of the Chaldeans to go to the land of Canaan; and they came to Haran and dwelt there. So the days of Terah were two hundred and five years, and Terah died in Haran.

a. **They went out with them from Ur of the Chaldeans to go to the land of Canaan**: Abram's story begins in **Ur of the Chaldeans** (Babylon). Joshua 24:2 describes Abram before the LORD called him. He was from a family of idol worshippers and was probably an idol worshipper himself (notwithstanding Jewish legends).

> i. Abram came from a family of idol worshippers. Later, when Abram's grandson Jacob went back to Abram's relatives, they were still worshipping idols.

b. **And they came to Haran and dwelt there**: Acts 7:2-4 makes it clear the call of Genesis 12:1-3 came to Abram while he still lived in Ur. When he received this call from God he was only halfway obedient in at least two ways.

- First, he brought his father **Terah** (and nephew Lot) with him, when the Lord called Abram *out of your country, from your family* (Genesis 12:1).
- Second, Abram stopped and, at least for a time, **dwelt** in **Haran**, and not to where God promised, *a land that I will show you* (Genesis 12:1).

> i. "They start together for Canaan. So far so good; at least, it looks so. The travelling is wearisome, and many are the murmurings. The huge caravan has not gone very far before the proposal is made that they should be satisfied with the move which they had made, and remain at Haran. True, it was not Canaan, but it might do as well." (Spurgeon)

> ii. "Half-way obedience increases our responsibility, because it is a plain confession that we know the Lord's will, though we do it not. Abram had received the call, and knew that he had done so, else why had he come to Haran? He admitted, by going as far as Haran, that he ought to go the whole way to Canaan; and so, by his own action he left himself without excuse." (Spurgeon)

c. **Terah died in Haran**: Sometimes we can gain meaning from names in the Bible. The name **Terah** means *delay*. The name **Haran** means *parched, barren*. When Abram was in partial obedience, then delay and barrenness marked his life. When we knowingly disobey God, we often delay the outworking of His plan in our lives and we also experience barrenness.

> i. "The result of this to Abram was the absence of privilege. God spoke not to his servant in Haran: neither dream, nor vision, nor voice came to him in the place of hesitancy. The Lord loved him, but hid his face from him, and denied him the visits of his grace." (Spurgeon)

Genesis 12 – God's Call of Abram; Abram in Egypt

A. God's promise to Abram.

1. (1-3) God's previous covenant with Abram.

Now the LORD had said to Abram:

**"Get out of your country,
From your family
And from your father's house,
To a land that I will show you.
I will make you a great nation;
I will bless you
And make your name great;
And you shall be a blessing.
I will bless those who bless you,
And I will curse him who curses you;
And in you all the families of the earth shall be blessed."**

a. **Now the LORD had said to Abram**: In Acts 7:2-4, God revealed through Stephen that this promise was made to Abram *when he was in Mesopotamia, before he dwelt in Haran*. Genesis 12:1-3 *repeats* a promise that God **had said to Abram**. God repeated the promise now that his father was dead and Abram was compelled to a more complete obedience.

i. Abram's partial obedience did not take God's promise away. Instead, it meant the fulfillment of the promise was delayed until Abram was ready to do what the LORD told him to do.

ii. Abram would certainly become a giant of faith, even being the father of the believing (Galatians 3:7); yet he did not start as a hero of faith. We see Abram as an example of *growing* in faith and obedience.

iii. More important than Abram's faith was God's promise. Notice how often God says **I will** in these verses. Genesis chapter 11 is all about the plans of man. Genesis chapter 12 is all about the plans of God. Genesis 12:1-3 explains how God promised Abram a land, a nation, and a blessing.

b. **To a land I that I will show you**: After stating He wanted Abram to leave his country and his relatives, God promised Abram a **land**. Specifically, God promised the land of Canaan, what might be called "greater Israel."

c. **I will make you a great nation**: God promised to make a **nation** from Abram. He will have children and grandchildren and further descendants, enough to populate a **great nation**.

d. **And make your name great**: God promised to bless Abram and to **make his name great**. There is probably no more honored name in history than the name of Abram, who is honored by Jews, Muslims, and Christians.

e. **I will bless those who bless you, and I will curse him who curses you**: God also promised He would **bless those who bless you** and to **curse him who curses you**. This promise – inherited by the covenant descendants of Abram, the Jewish people – remains true today and is a root reason for the decline and death of many empires.

i. "When the Greeks overran Palestine and desecrated the altar in the Jewish temple, they were soon conquered by Rome. When Rome killed Paul and many others, and destroyed Jerusalem under Titus, Rome soon fell. Spain was reduced to a fifth-rate nation after the Inquisition against the Jews; Poland fell after the pogroms; Hitler's Germany went down after its orgies of anti-Semitism; Britain lost her empire when she broke her faith with Israel." (Barnhouse)

ii. This is also one reason why the United States has been so blessed. The United States was one of the first modern nations to grant full citizenship and protection to Jewish people.

iii. This promise has also affected the church. The times when the church took upon itself the persecution of the Jewish people were dark times not only for the Jews but also for the church.

f. **In you all the families of the earth shall be blessed**: Not only was Abram promised blessing, but God also promised to *make him* a blessing, even to the point where **all the families of the earth** would be blessed in Abram. This amazing promise was fulfilled in the Messiah that came from Abram's lineage. God's blessing to Abram was not for his own sake, or even the sake of the Jewish nation to come. It was for the whole world, for **all the families of the earth** through Jesus Christ.

i. *And the Scripture, foreseeing that God would justify the Gentiles by faith, preached the gospel to Abraham beforehand, saying, "In you all the nations shall be blessed." So then those who are of faith are blessed with believing Abraham* (Galatians 3:8-9).

ii. *And they sang a new song, saying: "You are worthy to take the scroll, and to open its seals; for You were slain, and have redeemed us to God by Your blood out of every tribe and tongue and people and nation* (Revelation 5:9). The work of Jesus will touch every people group on the earth.

iii. Boice quoted the observation of Martin Luther, who said the promise **in you all the families of the earth shall be blessed** should be written "in golden letters and should be extolled in the languages of all people," for "who else... has dispensed this blessing among all nations except the Son of God, our Lord Jesus Christ?"

iv. This also indicated a missionary vision that God intended Abraham's covenant descendants to have. They were to look beyond themselves to all nations, to **all the families of the earth**. "There, you see, was the missionary character of the seed of Abraham, if they had but recognized it. God did not bless them for themselves alone, but for all nations: 'In thee shall all families of the earth be blessed'" (Spurgeon).

2. (4) Abram's departure from Haran.

So Abram departed as the LORD had spoken to him, and Lot went with him. And Abram *was* seventy-five years old when he departed from Haran.

a. **And Lot went with him**: This was more partial obedience by Abram. God commanded him to go out *from your family* (Genesis 12:1) yet he brought his nephew Lot. Lot would not be a blessing to Abram. He would be nothing but trouble and inconvenience.

b. **Abram was seventy-five years old when he departed from Haran**: Abram came into the land of Canaan at this advanced age. Fathering a child through Sarai seemed a long-forgotten hope.

3. (5-6) Abram's arrival in Canaan.

Then Abram took Sarai his wife and Lot his brother's son, and all their possessions that they had gathered, and the people whom they had acquired in Haran, and they departed to go to the land of Canaan. So they came to the land of Canaan. Abram passed through the land to the place of Shechem, as far as the terebinth tree of Moreh. And the Canaanites *were* then in the land.

a. **All their possessions that they had gathered, and the people whom they had acquired in Haran**: Abram left Ur of the Chaldeans with his father and his nephew Lot, stopping in **Haran** long enough to acquire many **possessions** and **people**.

b. **So they came to the land of Canaan**: Abram came into **Canaan** as a stranger, to live in a land populated by tribes that were set in violence and sin (Genesis 34:1-5) but would become even worse (Genesis 15:16).

c. **Abram passed through the land to the place of Shechem**: This was Abram's first stopping point in Canaan. He came to a notable oak tree (**the terebinth tree of Moreh**).

i. The name **Shechem** means *shoulder*. It probably gets its meaning from the *geography* of the area. The idea may be that the two hills Gerazim and Ebal were like "shoulders" with Shechem in the midst of them. Shechem was not only in the midst of two mountains but it was also right in the middle of Canaan.

- This is where Jacob came safely when he returned with his wives and children from his sojourn with Laban (Genesis 33:18).
- This is where Jacob bought a piece of land from a Canaanite named Hamor, for 100 pieces of silver (Genesis 33:19).
- This is where Jacob built an altar to the Lord and called it *El Elohe Israel* (Genesis 33:20). This established the connection between Jacob and what became known as *Jacob's well*.
- Shechem was the place where Dinah, the daughter of Jacob, was raped – and the sons of Jacob massacred the men of the city in retaliation (Genesis 34).
- This was the plot of ground that Jacob gave his son Joseph, land Jacob had conquered from the Amorites with his sword and bow in an unrecorded battle (Genesis 48:22).
- This is where the bones of Joseph were eventually buried when they were carried up from Egypt (Joshua 24:32).
- This is where Joshua made a covenant with Israel, renewing their commitment to the God of Israel and proclaiming: *as for me and my house, we will serve the Lord* (Joshua 24).
- Shechem's New Testament name is *Sychar* – where Jesus met the Samaritan woman at the well in John 4 (John 4:5-6).

d. **And the Canaanites were then in the land**: Abram came to the land God promised, yet the Canaanites were still **in the land**. They had no intention of giving the land to Abram, and would not give it up until they were forced out some 400 years later.

4. (7-9) God appears to Abram in Canaan.

Then the LORD appeared to Abram and said, "To your descendants I will give this land." And there he built an altar to the LORD, who had appeared to him. And he moved from there to the mountain east of Bethel, and he pitched his tent *with* Bethel on the west and Ai on the east; there he built an altar to the LORD and called on the name of the LORD. So Abram journeyed, going on still toward the South.

a. **Then the LORD appeared to Abram**: Once Abram was in the land, God reminded him of His promise. The **land** Abram saw belonged to Abram and his descendants. It was actual **land** that Abram saw with his physical eyes.

b. **To your descendants I will give this land**: Abram never owned any of this land except the burial plot he bought (Genesis 23:14-20). Yet God's promise was enough evidence to assure Abram that he did indeed own the whole country.

c. **And there he built an altar to the LORD**: The altar was important to Abram because it was a place to meet with God, to offer sacrifice for sin, to show submission to God, and to worship God.

i. Christians have an altar also (Hebrews 13:10). We meet with God at our own place where we remember the sacrifice Jesus made for sin (Ephesians 5:2), where we submit to God as living sacrifices (Romans 12:1), and where we offer the sacrifice of praise (Hebrews 13:15).

d. **He pitched his tent**: Even in the land God gave him, Abram never lived in a house – he always lived in a **tent**. Tents are the home of those who are just passing through and do not put down permanent roots.

i. We too are to live like tent-dwellers, as pilgrims on this earth (1 Peter 2:11). We should live as people who have their permanent dwelling place in heaven, not on earth. Too many Christians want to build mansions on earth and think they would be happy with tents in heaven.

ii. A pilgrim is someone who leaves home and travels to a specific destination. A pilgrim isn't a drifter; a pilgrim has a goal. Abram's goal was God's heavenly city (Hebrews 11:8-10, 14-16), and this is also our goal.

B. Abram in Egypt.

1. (10) Abram's faith is tested by famine.

Now there was a famine in the land, and Abram went down to Egypt to dwell there, for the famine was severe in the land.

a. **There was a famine in the land**: A **famine** was a serious problem. Many people died from hunger, and it was right for Abram to be concerned about famine and feeding his family. But Abram was wrong in thinking God would not provide for his needs in the place where God called him to live. After all, God called Abram to Canaan and not to Egypt.

i. Abram, like most of us, found it easier to trust God in the far-off promises than in the right-now needs.

b. **Abram went down to Egypt**: When we are tested in this way, we often believe our actions are all right because no harm can come. Though God blessed and protected Abram even in Egypt, he came away with excess baggage and a rebuke from a pagan king. Harm came from his trip to **Egypt**.

i. The harm especially shows up later when a slave girl named Hagar – whom Sarai received when in Egypt – became a source of great trouble to Abram's family.

2. (11-13) Sensing potential danger in Egypt, Abram persuades Sarai to lie on his behalf.

And it came to pass, when he was close to entering Egypt, that he said to Sarai his wife, "Indeed I know that you *are* a woman of beautiful countenance. Therefore it will happen, when the Egyptians see you, that they will say, 'This is his wife'; and they will kill me, but they will let you live. Please say you *are* my sister, that it may be well with me for your sake, and that I may live because of you."

a. **I know that you are a woman of beautiful countenance**: Abram was concerned about his 60-year-old wife's attractiveness to the Egyptians. This shows Sarai was not only a woman of particular beauty but also that not every culture worships youthful appearance the way modern culture does.

i. The long lifespan of Abram and Sarai also helps to explain her beauty. Since Abram lived to be 175 and Sarai to 127, this was only middle age for her, perhaps corresponding to what we think of as her thirties.

ii. A Jewish legend says when Abram went into Egypt, he tried to hide Sarai in a box. When Egyptian customs officials asked what he had in the box, he said, "barley." "No," they said, "it contains wheat." "Very well," answered Abram. "I'll pay the custom on wheat." Then the officers said it contained pepper. Abram said he would pay the custom charges on pepper. Then the officers said it contained gold. Abram said he would pay the custom charges on gold. Then the officers said it contained precious stones. Abram said he would pay the custom charges on precious stones. By this time, the officers insisted on opening the box. When they did, all of Egypt shined with the beauty of Sarai. These same legends say that in comparison to Sarai, all other women looked like monkeys. She was even more beautiful than Eve (cited in Ginzburg).

b. **Please say you are my sister**: This was in fact a half-truth. Sarai was Abram's half-sister (Genesis 20:12). Yet this half-truth was a whole lie. Abram's intent here was clearly to deceive, and he trusted in his deception to protect him instead of trusting in the LORD.

i. If we want to do something wrong, we can find some good reasons to do it. If we can't think of the reasons our self, the devil is happy to suggest them.

ii. Ideally Abram would say, "God promised me children, and I don't have them yet; therefore, I know I am indestructible until God's promise is fulfilled, because God's promises are always true. God will protect me and my wife Sarai."

3. (14-15) Sarai is taken into Pharaoh's house.

So it was, when Abram came into Egypt, that the Egyptians saw the woman, that she was very beautiful. The princes of Pharaoh also saw her and commended her to Pharaoh. And the woman was taken to Pharaoh's house.

a. **The Egyptians saw the woman, that she was very beautiful**: Sarai attacked attention both because she was **very beautiful** and because she was the companion of an obviously wealthy and influential man (Abram).

b. **The woman was taken into Pharaoh's house**: Understanding the place Abram and Sarai have in God's redemptive plan, we realize how serious this was. God did not want Sarai's womb to be defiled by a gentile king, because the Messiah would come from her line of descendants.

4. (16-20) Abram leaves Egypt after being rebuked by Pharaoh.

He treated Abram well for her sake. He had sheep, oxen, male donkeys, male and female servants, female donkeys, and camels. But the LORD plagued Pharaoh and his house with great plagues because of Sarai, Abram's wife. And Pharaoh called Abram and said, "What *is* this you have done to me? Why did you not tell me that she *was* your wife? Why did you say, 'She *is* my sister'? I might have taken her as my wife. Now therefore, here is your wife; take *her* and go your way." So Pharaoh commanded *his* men concerning him; and they sent him away, with his wife and all that he had.

a. **He treated Abram well for her sake**: God blessed Abram even when he didn't do what he should. God continued to protect Abram, even when Abram acted like a liar. God did not call back His promise to Abram, because the promise depended on God and not on Abram.

b. **What is this you have done to me?** Sadly, a pagan king had to rebuke Abram. God's divine protection of Abram and Sarai shows that if he would have trusted in God and told the truth, everything would have been all right.

> i. But God is in the business of growing Abram into a man of great faith, and this requires circumstances where Abram must trust God. "Faith is not a mushroom that grows overnight in damp soil; it is an oak tree that grows for a thousand years under the blast of the wind and rain" (Barnhouse).

Genesis 13 – God Promises Abram the Land Again

A. Abram and Lot separate.

1. (1-4) Abram returns to the land promised to him.

Then Abram went up from Egypt, he and his wife and all that he had, and Lot with him, to the South. Abram was very rich in livestock, in silver, and in gold. And he went on his journey from the South as far as Bethel, to the place where his tent had been at the beginning, between Bethel and Ai, to the place of the altar which he had made there at first. And there Abram called on the name of the LORD.

a. **To the place where his tent had been at the beginning**: Even though Abram came back from Egypt with great riches, he returned to the same **place** as before. He was right back where he started. Essentially, Abram's time in Egypt was *wasted* time. God could have and would have provided for his needs in Canaan, even in a time of famine (Genesis 12:10).

i. Abram should not have used the blessing God brought to him in Egypt as a justification for going there. Even though God is great enough to bring good even when we disobey, there is still a cost built into disobedience.

ii. Abram's unbelief took him from his place of worship; it led him into sin, and caused him to lead others into sin. It made him more confident in his ability to lie than in the protecting power of God. It even broke apart his family for a while. Finally, even an ungodly king rightly rebuked him.

b. **To the place of the altar which he had made there at first**: Yet, at this point Abram did what he should. Instead of torturing himself about his past sin, he got busy doing what he needed to do: living with the tent as a pilgrim and the **altar** as a worshipper, calling on the name of the LORD.

i. The church has always had the challenge of what to do with believers who slip into sin and want to come back into the church. For example, in the third century, the heroes of the faith were the martyrs and the confessors, but there were also many *lapsed* believers who failed under the threat of persecution. Some churches were too lax, admitting those lapsed ones back as if nothing happened. Some were too harsh toward the lapsed, saying they could never come back to the church and be used of God. Most churches did the right thing: they allowed the lapsed back, but basically as beginners again, not pretending as if nothing happened.

ii. Here, Abram came back into the Promised Land basically as a beginner. He came back to Bethel, back with the tent and the altar, back doing what he should.

iii. God wants us to walk in our *first* love and our *first* works (Revelation 2:4-5).

2. (5-7) Contention between Abram's and Lot's hired workers.

Lot also, who went with Abram, had flocks and herds and tents. Now the land was not able to support them, that they might dwell together, for their possessions were so great that they could not dwell together. And there was strife between the herdsmen of Abram's livestock and the herdsmen of Lot's livestock. The Canaanites and the Perizzites then dwelt in the land.

a. **Lot also, who went with Abram**: God commanded Abram to leave his family behind when he came to the land of Canaan (Genesis 12:1), but Abram brought his nephew Lot along with him. Trouble like this was the result.

i. This conflict came after Abram did the right thing. When we get right with God, we can often expect attack from the devil.

b. **There was strife between the herdsmen of Abram's livestock and the herdsmen of Lot's livestock**: Something had to be done about this strife between the estates of Abram and Lot, because they could not continue a conflict like this before the unbelieving inhabitants of Canaan.

i. When the **Canaanites and the Perizzites then dwelt in the land**, and saw the men of Abram and Lot fighting, they must have thought, "Oh, they're just like us. They say they worship another God, a God they say is the true God, but I see they are really just like us."

ii. "Many people will never listen to what any believer says because of what some believers are." (Barnhouse)

c. **Their possessions were so great**: There was a great difference between the riches of Abram and the riches of Lot. They both had great wealth, but Lot's wealth *possessed him*. Abram had great **possessions**, but they did not possess him.

3. (8-9) Abram's generous offer to Lot.

So Abram said to Lot, "Please let there be no strife between you and me, and between my herdsmen and your herdsmen; for we *are* brethren. *Is* not the whole land before you? Please separate from me. If *you take* the left, then I will go to the right; or, if *you go* to the right, then I will go to the left."

a. **Is not the whole land before you?** Since Abram was the eldest, and God gave all the land to Abram (not to Lot), it was pure generosity on Abram's part that caused him to make this offer to Lot.

b. **If you take the left, then I will go to the right**: Abram was able to fight when the occasion demanded it. He did not yield to Lot out of weakness, but out of love and trust in God. A few acres of grazing land didn't seem worth fighting for to a man who lived with an eternal perspective.

i. God was glorified when Paul, out of love, waived his right to be supported by the gospel (1 Corinthians 9:14-18). God was glorified when Jesus, out of love, waived his right to an existence that knew no human suffering or trial by experience (Philippians 2:5-11).

ii. Abram fulfilled the New Testament principle of love: *Let each of you look out not only for his own interests, but also for the interests of others* (Philippians 2:4).

c. **If you go to the right, then I will go to the left**: Right or left, Abram knew he could trust God. He did it because he learned God would provide for his needs, and he did not have to worry about being too generous. Abram knew whatever Lot chose God would make sure Abram prospered.

i. In Egypt, Abram thought he had to take his fate into his own hands. He had to look out for himself. Now, he was wiser and was willing to let God look out for his interests. Right or left, it didn't matter to Abram, because God would be there.

ii. Because he trusted in God, Abram did not have to be obsessed with his own rights and neither do we. Everything we receive is the free gift of God and has nothing to do with our concept of rights.

4. (10-13) Lot chooses his portion of land.

And Lot lifted his eyes and saw all the plain of Jordan, that it *was* well watered everywhere (before the LORD destroyed Sodom and Gomorrah)

like the garden of the LORD, like the land of Egypt as you go toward Zoar. Then Lot chose for himself all the plain of Jordan, and Lot journeyed east. And they separated from each other. Abram dwelt in the land of Canaan, and Lot dwelt in the cities of the plain and pitched *his* tent even as far as Sodom. But the men of Sodom *were* exceedingly wicked and sinful against the LORD.

> a. **Like the garden of the LORD**: Lot made his choice purely based on what he could see with his **eyes**. He cared only for the material abundance of the land, and cared nothing for how it would impact him and his family spiritually.
>
>> i. As much as anything, faith means we do not walk by what we see, but by what we know to be true in God: *For we walk by faith, not by sight* (2 Corinthians 5:7). Abram walked by faith; Lot walked only by sight.
>
> b. **Pitched his tent even as far as Sodom**: It was only this far for now, but later Lot became a leader of this sinful city. Valuing only the things that can be seen increased his wealth temporarily, but Lot would eventually lose it all.
>
>> i. Of course Lot thought, "I can serve God as well there as here. They probably need a witness." But he deceived himself, as many since him have done. Jeremiah 17:9 states, *The heart is deceitful above all things, and desperately wicked; who can know it?*
>
>> ii. "In the end, he who sought this world lost it, and he who was willing to give up anything for the honour of God found it." (Maclaren)
>
>> iii. It wasn't Lot's choice that led his heart astray. His heart was already astray, and it was demonstrated by his choice.

B. God confirms His promise to Abram.

1. (14-15) God promises the land to Abram and to his descendants forever.

And the LORD said to Abram, after Lot had separated from him: "Lift your eyes now and look from the place where you are; northward, southward, eastward, and westward; for all the land which you see I give to you and your descendants forever."

> a. **After Lot had separated from him**: God wanted to talk to Abram alone after Lot left. This was a promise made to Abram, not to Abram's nephew.
>
>> i. This promise of the land had been made to Abram when he lived in Ur of the Chaldeans (Genesis 12:1-3, Acts 7:2-4). God now repeated the promise.

> b. **All the land which you see I give to you**: God also wanted to remind Abram that even though Abram had been generous enough to grant some of the land to his nephew Lot, God still said the land belonged to Abram.

2. (16) God reminds Abram of His promise to give Abram many descendants.

"And I will make your descendants as the dust of the earth; so that if a man could number the dust of the earth, *then* your descendants also could be numbered."

> a. **I will make your descendants as the dust of the earth**: This was quite a promise to make to a childless man in his seventies or eighties. Yet Abram knew to walk by faith and not by sight.
>
> b. **Your descendants**: Again, this promise of many descendants was made to Abram when he lived in Ur of the Chaldeans (Genesis 12:1-3, Acts 7:2-4). To assure Abram, God repeated the promise.

3. (17-18) Abram walks through the land God gave to him.

"Arise, walk in the land through its length and its width, for I give it to you." Then Abram moved *his* tent, and went and dwelt by the terebinth trees of Mamre, which *are* in Hebron, and built an altar there to the LORD.

> a. **Arise, walk in the land through its length and its width, for I give it to you**: As a token of Abram's reception of the land by faith, God wants Abram to *explore* the land of promise, to walk through it as if it were his, though he did not have a record of ownership to the land yet.
>
>> i. In the same way, God wants us to *explore* a land of promise, for us – His Word – where God has *given to us exceedingly great and precious promises* (2 Peter 1:4), where He has given us *all things that pertain to life and godliness* (2 Peter 1:3). He wants us to walk through this land, possessing it by faith.
>
> b. **Dwelt by the terebinth trees of Mamre, which are in Hebron**: The name **Mamre** means, *vision*. **Hebron** means *communion*. Abram once again walked in the LORD's vision for him and in communion with the LORD.
>
> c. **And built an altar there to the LORD**: Abram built another **altar**. He lived life in constant awareness of the need for a sacrificial atonement and covering.

Genesis 14 – Abram Rescues Lot and Meets Melchizedek

A. Abram rescues Lot from the confederacy of kings.

1. (1-10) The rebellion of the five kings.

And it came to pass in the days of Amraphel king of Shinar, Arioch king of Ellasar, Chedorlaomer king of Elam, and Tidal king of nations, that they made war with Bera king of Sodom, Birsha king of Gomorrah, Shinab king of Admah, Shemeber king of Zeboiim, and the king of Bela (that is, Zoar). All these joined together in the Valley of Siddim (that is, the Salt Sea). Twelve years they served Chedorlaomer, and in the thirteenth year they rebelled. In the fourteenth year Chedorlaomer and the kings that *were* with him came and attacked the Rephaim in Ashteroth Karnaim, the Zuzim in Ham, the Emim in Shaveh Kiriathaim, and the Horites in their mountain of Seir, as far as El Paran, which is by the wilderness. Then they turned back and came to En Mishpat (that *is*, Kadesh), and attacked all the country of the Amalekites, and also the Amorites who dwelt in Hazezon Tamar. And the king of Sodom, the king of Gomorrah, the king of Admah, the king of Zeboiim, and the king of Bela (that is, Zoar) went out and joined together in battle in the Valley of Siddim against Chedorlaomer king of Elam, Tidal king of nations, Amraphel king of Shinar, and Arioch king of Ellasar; four kings against five. Now the Valley of Siddim *was full of* asphalt pits; and the kings of Sodom and Gomorrah fled; *some* fell there, and the remainder fled to the mountains.

> a. **Chedorlaomer and the kings that were with him came and attacked**: The people who lived in Canaan in the days of Abram were like humanity in general. There were many among them interested in conquest and domination. This confederation of kings who **rebelled** against Chedorlaomer wanted to be free from his dominion.

i. Archaeologist Nelson Glueck documented the destruction left by these kings: "I found that every village in their path had been plundered and left in ruins, and the countryside was laid waste. The population had been wiped out or led away into captivity. For hundreds of years thereafter, the entire area was like an abandoned cemetery, hideously unkempt, with all its monuments shattered and strewn in pieces on the ground" (cited in Morris).

b. **Now the Valley of Siddim was full of asphalt pits**: There were fearful **asphalt pits** in this region, and **some fell there**. The Hebrew here is a good example of how the language uses repetition to show emphasis.

i. "The Hebrew way of saying *full of bitumen pits* is: *pits, pits of bitumen*. Repetition expresses abundance, plenitude, etc." (Leupold)

2. (11-12) The four kings take Lot and all his possessions.

Then they took all the goods of Sodom and Gomorrah, and all their provisions, and went their way. They also took Lot, Abram's brother's son who dwelt in Sodom, and his goods, and departed.

a. **They also took Lot**: Because Lot was **Abram's brother's son**, the group of four kings involved Abram. Abram was a man of honor and a guardian of his family, so he would fight for his nephew's life and safety.

b. **And his goods**: Since Lot lived among the wicked people of Sodom, we are not surprised he was also taken captive.

i. "Those believers who conform to the world must expect to suffer for it." (Spurgeon)

3. (13-14) Abram hears of Lot's captivity and marshals an army.

Then one who had escaped came and told Abram the Hebrew, for he dwelt by the terebinth trees of Mamre the Amorite, brother of Eshcol and brother of Aner; and they *were* allies with Abram. Now when Abram heard that his brother was taken captive, he armed his three hundred and eighteen trained *servants* who were born in his own house, and went in pursuit as far as Dan.

a. **Abram the Hebrew**: This is the first use of the term **Hebrew** in the Bible. It was probably a reference to the fact that Abram came from beyond the Euphrates River, and had *passed over* the river to come to Canaan.

i. "The word Hebrew comes from a root that means *passed over*. The Septuagint translates it *the passenger*." (Barnhouse)

b. **He armed his three hundred and eighteen trained servants**: This demonstrates the great wealth of Abram. Any man who could assemble 318 servants capable of fighting must be very rich.

c. **Trained servants**: Abram was a man who walked in faith, yet he was also a prudent man. Abram kept his own personal army, and he apparently kept them trained and ready to defend his interests.

d. **Went in pursuit as far as Dan**: Abram's army pursued the confederacy of four kings for a long distance to the north. The city of Dan is not far from the northern border of Israel.

  i. The gates of the city of **Dan** from Abram's time have been discovered by archaeologists and can be viewed at the Israeli national park at Dan.

4. (15-17) Abram leads his army to victory over the four kings.

He divided his forces against them by night, and he and his servants attacked them and pursued them as far as Hobah, which is north of Damascus. So he brought back all the goods, and also brought back his brother Lot and his goods, as well as the women and the people. And the king of Sodom went out to meet him at the Valley of Shaveh (that is, the King's Valley), after his return from the defeat of Chedorlaomer and the kings who *were* with him.

a. **He divided his forces against them by night**: Abram had military wisdom. Using the clever tactic of a night attack with his army split into two groups, he succeeded in rescuing Lot and recovering all the plunder (**all the goods**) seized by the partnership of the four kings.

b. **Also brought back his brother Lot and his goods**: Unfortunately, Lot moved right back to where he was before in Sodom. He refused this warning from God and would eventually lose everything when Sodom and Gomorrah were ultimately judged (Genesis 19:24-25).

  i. We may see a story in the account of Abram's rescue of Lot. We were those off in sin and shame, rescued by one who left his safety and happiness. Our kinsman redeemer went to great trouble and distance, and with His courage and daring defeated the mighty enemy that had put us in bondage, and He took all the enemy's spoil.

B. Abram and Melchizedek.

1. (18-20) Abram meets Melchizedek.

Then Melchizedek king of Salem brought out bread and wine; he *was* the priest of God Most High. And he blessed him and said:

"Blessed be Abram of God Most High,
Possessor of heaven and earth;
And blessed be God Most High,
Who has delivered your enemies into your hand."

And he gave him a tithe of all.

a. **Then Melchizedek**: We have no idea of where **Melchizedek** came from, how he came to be in Canaan, how he came to be a worshipper and priest of the true God, and how Abram came to know about him. We only know he was there.

b. **Melchizedek king of Salem**: The name **Melchizedek** means *King of Righteousness*. He was the **king of Salem**, and Salem was the original Jeru*salem*, and Melchizedek was **the priest of God Most High**. He was a worshipper and priest of the true God, ruling over Jerusalem even in those ancient times.

　i. One thing that makes Melchizedek unique was he was both a **king** and a **priest**. History shows that it is often dangerous to combine religious and civic authority. God forbade the kings of Israel to be priests and the priests to be kings. In 2 Chronicles 26:16-23, King Uzziah tried to do the work of a priest, and God struck him with leprosy. Melchizedek was an exception.

　ii. Melchizedek was the **priest of God Most High**. *El Elyon* means "Highest God," like saying "Supreme Being." Melchizedek is an example of a worshipper of the true God, even a **priest of God Most High** yet not related to Abram or other known covenant people of God.

c. **Brought out bread and wine**: Melchizedek served Abram **bread and wine**. Perhaps he even served them in a manner looking forward to our redeeming sacrifice, as the bread and wine of Passover and the Lord's Table look at our redeeming sacrifice, Jesus Christ.

d. **He was the priest of God Most High**: Melchizedek, as priest, did two things. He **blessed** Abram and he **blessed** God. Melchizedek showed that a priest must connect with both God and man and has a ministry to both God and man.

　i. Though Melchizedek seems like an obscure figure, he is in fact an important Old Testament person. Psalm 110:4 says the priesthood of the Messiah is a priesthood according to the *order of Melchizedek*, as opposed to being of the order of Aaron. Hebrews chapters 5 through 7 show this is an important idea.

　ii. Hebrews 7:3 described Melchizedek as *without father, without mother, without genealogy, having neither beginning of days nor end of life, but made like the Son of God, remains a priest continually*. Because of this passage, some have thought Melchizedek was actually a pre-Bethlehem appearance of Jesus.

iii. Others have suggested he was Seth, Noah's son, or Job, or an angel; or even some have fancifully speculated Melchizedek was an outer-space visitor, an "unfallen Adam" from another planet, sent to observe the progress of God's work of redemption for this fallen race. *These suggestions are bizarre and have no Biblical foundation.*

iv. "The question cannot be said to be settled completely… otherwise, the identity of Melchizedek would have been agreed on by Bible scholars long ago" (Morris). We can say with confidence that if Melchizedek was not an appearance of Jesus Himself, at the very least he is a remarkable type or picture of Jesus.

e. **And he gave him a tithe of all**: Abram gave unto the LORD and he did it through giving to Melchizedek a **tithe of all**. This referred to one tenth of his *assets*, not his *income*.

i. It was almost as if Abram and Melchizedek worked to see who could bless the other more. Melchizedek blessed Abram out of his resources, and Abram blessed Melchizedek out of his resources. This is a great attitude for us to have in the community of believers, an attitude of mutual blessing.

2. (21-24) Abram refuses the plunder from the battle.

Now the king of Sodom said to Abram, "Give me the persons, and take the goods for yourself." But Abram said to the king of Sodom, "I have raised my hand to the LORD, God Most High, the Possessor of heaven and earth, that I *will take* nothing, from a thread to a sandal strap, and that I will not take anything that is yours, lest you should say, 'I have made Abram rich'– except only what the young men have eaten, and the portion of the men who went with me: Aner, Eshcol, and Mamre; let them take their portion."

a. **Take the goods for yourself**: As seemed proper, the king of Sodom wanted to reward Abram for all he did in recovering what was taken by the partnership of the four kings, and he offered Abram a tremendous amount of plunder.

b. **I will take nothing**: Yet, Abram would not take any of the plunder, the spoil taken from Sodom and Gomorrah and recovered. This was because of a vow he made to **God Most High** – a phrase he used *after* hearing Melchizedek use this particular title for God (Genesis 14:19). The phrase **I have raised my hand to the LORD** indicates that Abram made the vow.

c. **Lest you should say, "I have made Abram rich"**: Abram refused any portion of the plunder because he would not allow anyone say that a man had made Abram rich. Abram determined that all of the credit for his success and wealth should go to God and God alone.

i. If success does come when we pursue human measures of success, using man-centered wisdom and methods, how can we really say that God gave the success? It is much better to follow God's wisdom so that when success comes He gets the glory, and it is evident to everyone that it was His work.

d. **Let them take their portion**: However, at the same time, Abram did not impose his principles on his Amorite allies (Genesis 14:13). They were entitled to as much of the spoil as was appropriate under the customs of the time.

Genesis 15 – God Confirms the Covenant with Abram

A. God speaks to Abram's fears and doubts with a promise.

1. (1) The word of the Lord comes to Abram in a vision.

After these things the word of the Lord came to Abram in a vision, saying, "Do not be afraid, Abram. I *am* your shield, your exceedingly great reward."

> a. **After these things the word of the Lord came to Abram**: The **word of the Lord** came to the people of the Bible in many different ways. It might come by a personal appearance of God, by an audible voice, by visions or dreams, by the ministry of angels, by the working of the Spirit of God upon the mind, by the making alive of a passage of Scripture to the heart, or by the ministry of a prophet or preacher. Here, **the word of the Lord came to Abram in a vision**.
>
> b. **Do not be afraid… I am your shield, your exceedingly great reward**: There was a good reason for God to say this. Abram had just defeated a much larger army made up of a partnership of four kings. He had reason to be afraid, expecting an attack of retribution.
>
> c. **Your shield… your reward**: Abram needed a **shield**, because he expected to be attacked. He needed **reward**, because he had denied himself great reward offered from the king of Sodom (Genesis 14:21-24).
>
>> i. God told Abram that though he had sacrificed for His sake, he would not be the loser for it. God would more than make up what Abram gave unto the Lord.
>>
>> ii. God knows how to become the answer to our need. "I do not think that any human mind can ever grasp the fullness of meaning of these four words, 'I am thy reward.' God himself the reward of his faithful people" (Spurgeon).

iii. "If God be our reward, let us take care that we do really enjoy him. Let us exult in him, and let us not be pining after any other joy." (Spurgeon)

d. **Do not be afraid**: God told Abram this because he *was* afraid, and afraid for good reasons. Yet God also gave him a *reason* to put away his fear. God doesn't tell us **do not be afraid** without giving us a reason to put away our fear.

2. (2-3) Abram honestly expresses his doubts.

But Abram said, "Lord GOD, what will You give me, seeing I go childless, and the heir of my house is Eliezer of Damascus?" Then Abram said, "Look, You have given me no offspring; indeed one born in my house is my heir!"

a. **Lord GOD, what will You give me**: Certainly, Abram appreciated the promise from God. At the same time, there was perhaps a sense in which it sounded empty to Abram. It was as if Abram said, "What good is it that You are my shield and reward? The only thing I've ever wanted with any passion in my life is a son. Where are the descendants You promised me?"

i. It is as if Abram meant, "LORD, You have prospered me materially and now promise to give me more, and to protect me. But what good is it if I don't have a descendant to give it to? I want the son You promised to give me!"

ii. **Eliezer of Damascus** was Abram's chief assistant, his main servant and associate. He was a good man, but not a son to Abram.

b. **Look, You have given me no offspring**: Abram's bold honesty before the LORD is a wonderful example of prayer. Instead of holding in his frustration, he brought it before God with an honest heart.

c. **You have given me no offspring**: To some degree, this question doubted God. Yet we can discern the difference between a doubt that *denies* God's promise and a doubt that *desires* God's promise. Abram *wanted* to believe and looked to God to strengthen his faith.

3. (4-5) God speaks to Abram's doubts with a promise.

And behold, the word of the LORD came to him, saying, "This one shall not be your heir, but one who will come from your own body shall be your heir." Then He brought him outside and said, "Look now toward heaven, and count the stars if you are able to number them." And He said to him, "So shall your descendants be."

a. **This one shall not be your heir**: Abram would not end his days with Eliezer as his only **heir**. God would indeed fulfill the promise made long before, originally recorded in Genesis 12:2 and 13:15-16. Abram needed to be reminded of the promises of God, and we also need the reminders.

b. **One who will come from your own body shall be your heir**: This promise was repeated to Abram with such clarity and certainty that it was reasonable to suppose that he expected it would be soon fulfilled. Yet in the chronology of Abram's life, the fulfillment of *this* promise was still 15 years away.

> i. No wonder the writer to the Hebrews says: *And we desire that each one of you show the same diligence to the full assurance of hope until the end, that you do not become sluggish, but imitate those who through faith and patience inherit the promises* (Hebrews 6:11-12). We need faith and patience to inherit God's promises.

c. **From your own body**: God explained exactly what He meant in His promise to Abram. He meant that it wasn't a spiritual descendant who would inherit the promise (such as Eliezer), but an actual flesh-and-blood descendant. This was necessary, because we sometimes *misunderstand* God's promises.

d. **Look now toward heaven, and count the stars if you are able to number them**: God not only *told* Abram the promise again, but He *confirmed* it with an illustration. The stars in the sky showed how vast the number of Abram's descendants would be.

> i. One of those descendants – the greatest of his descendants – would be the *Bright and Morning Star* (Revelation 22:16).

4. (6) Abram's response of faith to God's promise.

And he believed in the LORD, and He accounted it to him for righteousness.

a. **And he believed in the LORD**: When Abram put his trust in God, specifically in God's promise to him (descendants leading to the Messiah), God credited (**accounted**) this belief to Abram's account as righteousness.

> i. There are essentially two types of righteousness: righteousness we *accomplish* by our own efforts, and righteousness *accounted* to us by the work of God when we believe.

> ii. Since none of us can be good enough to accomplish perfect righteousness, we must have God's righteousness accounted to us by doing just what Abram did: **he believed in the LORD**.

> iii. God's accounting is not pretending. God does not account to us a pretended righteousness, but a real one in Christ (Romans 4:1-3).

b. **And He accounted it to him for righteousness**: This is one of the clearest expressions in the Bible of the truth of salvation by grace, through faith. This is the first time *believe* is used in the Bible and the first time *righteousness* is used in the Bible. This is the New Testament gospel in the Hebrew Scriptures, later quoted four times in the New Testament.

i. *What then shall we say that Abraham our father has found according to the flesh? For if Abraham was justified by works, he has something to boast about, but not before God. For what does the Scripture say? "Abraham believed God, and it was accounted to him for righteousness."* (Romans 4:1-3)

ii. *Does this blessedness then come upon the circumcised only, or upon the uncircumcised also? For we say that faith was accounted to Abraham for righteousness. How then was it accounted? While he was circumcised, or uncircumcised? Not while circumcised, but while uncircumcised.* (Romans 4:9-10)

iii. *And not being weak in faith, he did not consider his own body, already dead (since he was about a hundred years old), and the deadness of Sarah's womb. He did not waver at the promise of God through unbelief, but was strengthened in faith, giving glory to God, and being fully convinced that what He had promised He was also able to perform. And therefore "it was accounted to him for righteousness." Now it was not written for his sake alone that it was imputed to him, but also for us. It shall be imputed to us who believe in Him who raised up Jesus our Lord from the dead.* (Romans 4:19-24)

iv. *Therefore He who supplies the Spirit to you and works miracles among you, does He do it by the works of the law, or by the hearing of faith? – just as Abraham "believed God, and it was accounted to him for righteousness." Therefore know that only those who are of faith are sons of Abraham.* (Galatians 3:5-7)

c. **He accounted it to him for righteousness**: Romans 4:9-10 makes much of the fact this righteousness was accounted to Abram before he was circumcised (later happening in Genesis 17). No one could say Abram was made righteous *because* of his obedience or fulfillment of religious law or ritual. It was faith alone that caused God to account Abram as righteous.

i. "When the article of justification has fallen, everything has fallen... This is the chief article from which all other doctrines have flowed... It alone begets, nourishes, builds, preserves, and defends the church of God; and without it the church of God cannot exist for one hour." (Luther, cited in Boice)

d. **He believed in the LORD, and He accounted it to him for righteousness**: The faith that made Abram righteous wasn't so much believing *in* God (as we usually speak of believing in God), as it was *believing God*. Those who only believe *in* God (in the sense of believing He exists) are merely on the same level as demons (James 2:19).

B. God speaks to Abram's doubt with a covenant.

1. (7-8) Abram's doubts surface again.

Then He said to him, "I *am* the LORD, who brought you out of Ur of the Chaldeans, to give you this land to inherit it." And he said, "Lord GOD, how shall I know that I will inherit it?"

a. **Then He said to him**: We don't know if the events beginning with Genesis 15:7 followed close upon what happened in Genesis 15:1-6; the flow of the text seems to indicate they did.

b. **I am the LORD, who brought you out of Ur of the Chaldeans, to give you this land to inherit it**: This wasn't the first time this promise was given (see also Genesis 12:1-3, 12:7, and 13:15-17). Yet this was a dramatic and clear restatement of God's promise to give the land to Abram and his covenant descendants.

c. **Lord GOD, how shall I know that I will inherit it**: The power and clarity of the promise makes us somewhat surprised by Abram's response. Abram boldly asked God for *proof* of the *promise*.

i. Though God had just accounted Abram as righteous, Abram could still demonstrate some degree of doubt, as indicated by his question, **"How shall I know that I will inherit it?"** Abram experienced what many of those who are accounted righteous do. It was as if he said, "I believe when I hear God say it, but five minutes later, I'm not sure — please prove it to me."

ii. "What! Abraham, is not God's promise sufficient for thee? ... Ah, beloved! faith is often marred by a measure of unbelief; or, if not quite unbelief, yet there is a desire to have some token, some sign, beyond the bare promise of God." (Spurgeon)

iii. Abram had no title deed to the land, no certificate of ownership that another person would recognize. Abram had nothing to make anyone else believe he actually owned the land. All he had was the promise of God.

2. (9-11) Abram prepares to make a covenant with God.

So He said to him, "Bring Me a three-year-old heifer, a three-year-old female goat, a three-year-old ram, a turtledove, and a young pigeon." Then he brought all these to Him and cut them in two, down the middle, and placed each piece opposite the other; but he did not cut the birds in

two. And when the vultures came down on the carcasses, Abram drove them away.

> a. **A three-year-old heifer, a three-year-old female goat, a three-year-old ram, a turtledove, and a young pigeon**: This reads more like a shopping list for a strange pagan ceremony than something the LORD would ask for. Yet Abram understood perfectly what God asked him to prepare for.
>
> b. **Cut them in two... and placed each piece opposite the other**: Abram knew exactly what to do with these animals; he understood that according to the custom of his time, God told him to get a contract ready for signing.
>
>> i. In those days, contracts were made by the sacrificial cutting of animals, with the split carcasses of the animals lying on the ground. The covenant was made when parties to the agreement walked through the animal parts together, repeating the terms of the covenant. *The LORD made a covenant* in Genesis 15:18 is literally, "the LORD cut a covenant."
>>
>> ii. Jeremiah 34:18-20 makes reference to this same practice of a covenant made by cutting animals and repeating the oath of the covenant as one walks through the animal parts.
>>
>> iii. The symbolism was plain. First, this is a covenant so serious, it is sealed with blood. Second, if I break this covenant, let this same bloodshed be poured out on my animals and me.
>>
>> iv. When Abram had his doubts and wanted assurance from the LORD, God said to him clearly, "Let's sign a contract and settle this once for all."
>
> c. **And when the vultures came down on the carcasses, Abram drove them away**: As Abram waited for the LORD to appear and walk through the carcasses with him (to sign the covenant), God didn't come right away. He had to wait and fight off the vultures until God appeared to complete the covenant ceremony.
>
>> i. Abram had reason to expect that God would come down and walk through the animal parts with him, because God had previously appeared to him in some way (Genesis 12:7). It seems that Abram knew that God was capable of taking some physical form.

3. (12-16) Prologue to the covenant.

Now when the sun was going down, a deep sleep fell upon Abram; and behold, horror *and* great darkness fell upon him. Then He said to Abram: "Know certainly that your descendants will be strangers in a land *that is* not theirs, and will serve them, and they will afflict them

four hundred years. And also the nation whom they serve I will judge; afterward they shall come out with great possessions. Now as for you, you shall go to your fathers in peace; you shall be buried at a good old age. But in the fourth generation they shall return here, for the iniquity of the Amorites *is* not yet complete."

> a. **Now when the sun was going down**: As evening came, God had not yet appeared to walk through the animal parts with Abram and seal the covenant. Instead, God caused a **deep sleep** to fall upon Abram. Apparently, at least part of what followed came to Abram in a dream while he was under this **deep sleep**.
>
> b. **Know certainly that your descendants will be strangers in a land that is not theirs, and will serve them**: Abram wanted concrete proof from God, and God would soon sign the covenant. Yet Abram needed to know he would have land and descendants, but all would not go well with his descendants in the future. This was a dreadful aspect to an amazing promise.
>
>> i. After God told him some of the hardship that would befall his descendants, Abram might have said, "If that is what is going to happen, I don't want any children." This was a complicated blessing.
>
> c. **They will afflict them four hundred years**: Specifically, God told Abram of the slavery and hardship Israel would endure in Egypt (Exodus 1:1-14). Though the land was given to Abram and his covenant descendants, there would be this long period where they lived outside the land and in affliction. Yet after four generations they would **return here** (Canaan), and come **with great possessions**.

4. (17-21) The covenant is made.

And it came to pass, when the sun went down and it was dark, that behold, there appeared a smoking oven and a burning torch that passed between those pieces. On the same day the Lord made a covenant with Abram, saying: "To your descendants I have given this land, from the river of Egypt to the great river, the River Euphrates– the Kenites, the Kenezzites, the Kadmonites, the Hittites, the Perizzites, the Rephaim, the Amorites, the Canaanites, the Girgashites, and the Jebusites."

> a. **When the sun went down and it was dark**: As Abram was either asleep or perhaps still groggy from the deep sleep, he saw God do an amazing thing. Abram saw God pass through the animal parts all by Himself, while Abram watched on the sidelines.
>
> b. **A smoking oven and a burning torch that passed between those pieces**: In walking through the sacrificed animals in the covenant ceremony, God

represented Himself by two emblems – a **smoking oven and a burning torch**.

> i. The **smoking oven** reminds us of the many times smoke or a cloud represented the presence of God:
>
> - As the pillar of cloud with Israel in the wilderness (Exodus 13:21-22).
> - As the smoke on Mount Sinai (Exodus 19:18).
> - As the cloud of God's Shekinah glory (1 Kings 8:10-12).
>
> ii. The **burning torch** reminds us of the many times fire represented the presence of God:
>
> - As the pillar of fire with Israel in the wilderness (Exodus 13:21-22).
> - As the burning bush displaying the presence of God before Moses (Exodus 3:4).
> - As the fire from heaven that at times consumed sacrifices that pleased God (1 Kings 18:38, 1 Chronicles 21:26, 2 Chronicles 7:1).

c. **On the same day the LORD made a covenant with Abram**: God, represented by the smoking oven and the burning torch, passed through the animal parts by Himself; as Abram watched, God showed this was a *unilateral* covenant. Abram never signed the covenant, because he passively watched while God signed it for both of them in the ritual.

> i. Therefore, the certainty of the covenant God made with Abram is based on who God is, not on who Abram is or what Abram would do. This covenant could not fail, because God cannot fail.
>
> ii. In a sense, the Father walked through the broken and bloody body of Jesus to establish His covenant with us, and God signed it for both of us. We merely enter into the covenant by faith; we don't *make* the covenant with God.

d. **The LORD made a covenant with Abram**: By entering into this contract, there is a sense in which God said, "If I don't keep My word, let *Me* be put asunder." God put His Deity on the line to confirm His oath to Abram.

> i. God alone signed this covenant; Abram did not haggle with God over the terms. God established and Abram accepted. Abram could not break a contract he never signed!
>
> ii. "A Divine covenant is not a mutual agreement on equal terms between two parties, but a Divine promise assured." (Maclaren)

e. **I have given this land, from the river of Egypt to the great river, the River Euphrates**: By quoting the specific lands Abram's descendants would inherit, God made it clear this was not a *figurative* spiritual promise. It was real, and through this promise, Israel would inherit real **land**.

i. "For a very brief time, under Solomon (1 Kings 8:65) and possibly again under Jeroboam II (2 Kings 14:25), the children of Israel ruled all this territory, as a token of the final and permanent possession they will have in the future." (Morris)

Genesis 16 – Hagar and the Birth of Ishmael

A. Sarai gives her servant girl Hagar to Abram.

1. (1-2) Sarai proposes a child for Abram through Hagar.

Now Sarai, Abram's wife, had borne him no *children*. And she had an Egyptian maidservant whose name was Hagar. So Sarai said to Abram, "See now, the L<small>ORD</small> has restrained me from bearing *children*. Please, go in to my maid; perhaps I shall obtain children by her." And Abram heeded the voice of Sarai.

> a. **Now Sarai, Abram's wife, had borne him no children**: Many years before this, God promised Abram that he would have many descendants (Genesis 12:2). To this point, he had **no children** through his wife Sarai.

> b. **She had an Egyptian maidservant**: Hagar was almost certainly part of what Abram received during his time in Egypt (Genesis 12:16).

>> i. "Very likely Hagar was one of the slaves given to him by Pharaoh when he dismissed him and Sarah; and you know what trouble Hagar brought into the family. If Abraham had lived the separated life, and had not fallen into the customs of those round about him, he would not have had that sin and sorrow concerning Hagar; nor would he have had that righteous rebuke from Abimelech, the king of Gerar, when again he had acted deceitfully with regard to his wife." (Spurgeon)

> c. **See now, the L<small>ORD</small> has restrained me from bearing children**: Sarai understood that God was sovereign over the womb. He had promised descendants to Abram and Sarai, and they had not yet come after many years. *There was a lot of pain in these words.*

>> • The pain of hope deferred making the heart sick (Proverbs 13:12).

>> • The pain of prayers not yet answered.

>> • The pain of arms that had never yet held her own child.

- The pain of public shame.
- The pain of blaming God for one's problems; unbelief is a sin, but it is also a sickness, one that carries a lot of pain.

d. **Please, go in to my maid; perhaps I shall obtain children by her**: Sarai encouraged Abram to take part in what was, in that day, essentially a surrogate mother arrangement. According to custom, the child would be considered to be the child of Abram and Sarai, not Abram and Hagar.

i. Sarai could justify this as a way to fulfill God's promise. "Abram, God promised that you would be the father of many nations and He didn't specifically mention me. Maybe you're the father of many nations, but I'm not the mother."

ii. Nevertheless, this was against God's will for many reasons.

- It was a sin of unbelief in God and His promise: Sarai believed in God's sovereignty over the womb, then acted against it.
- It was a sin against God's plan for marriage: that one man and one woman come together in a one-flesh relationship.
- It was a sin against Abram and Sarai's marriage: this surrogacy wasn't done in a doctor's office, but in a bedroom.

e. **And Abram heeded the voice of Sarai**: Sarai wasn't the first woman to be tormented by the thought, *maybe my husband would be better off with someone else*. It was bad for Sarai to hold on to that thought; it was *much worse* for Abram to heed the voice of Sarai on this matter.

i. A godly Christian wife has a lot of wisdom for her husband, and many husbands learn the value of listening to the wisdom of their wives. Yet no wife is infallible, and Abram was responsible for his sin of heeding the unwise, unbelief-based advice of his wife.

ii. Abram should have said something like this: "Sarai, bless your heart – but *you're* my wife and we're in this together. Difficult as it is, let's believe God all over again for a miracle. I don't want to sin against God and our marriage with this Egyptian servant girl."

iii. Ginzberg quotes a Jewish tradition, saying that before they came to live in the Promised Land, Abram and Sarai regarded their childlessness as punishment for not living in the land. But now they were in the land for ten years, and they still had no children. Sarai probably felt it was time to do something. Perhaps she thought along the lines of an old (unbiblical) proverb, "God helps those who help themselves."

2. (3-4) Abram agrees with Sarai's suggestion.

Then Sarai, Abram's wife, took Hagar her maid, the Egyptian, and gave her to her husband Abram to be his wife, after Abram had dwelt ten years in the land of Canaan. So he went in to Hagar, and she conceived. And when she saw that she had conceived, her mistress became despised in her eyes.

a. **Sarai, Abram's wife, took Hagar her maid, the Egyptian, and gave her to her husband Abram to be his wife**: They each acted according to unbelief. Abram did not actually marry Hagar, but he acted towards her as a man should only act towards his wife.

b. **After Abram dwelt ten years in the land**: It had been more than **ten years** since the promise was made regarding Abram's descendants. By most accounts, **ten years** seems like a long time to wait for the promise of God.

i. The whole practice of surrogate parentage was somewhat common in the ancient world and may have been acceptable to God on other occasions; but it wasn't for Abram, the friend of God and the man of faith. God had a different path for him.

ii. Abram and Sarai were discouraged enough that they approached the problem of no children by leaving God out of the matter. It was as if they said, "*With God out of the equation, how do we solve this?*" This was wrong for many reasons.

- God is never out of the equation.
- Men and women of faith must walk in faith – not in unbelief.
- Men and women of faith must see seeing things in the realm of the spirit, not only in the material world.

iii. The long wait for the promise discouraged them and made them vulnerable to acting in the flesh. Yet even after this, it would still be more than 13 years until the child of promise came.

iv. When we impatiently try to fulfill God's promises in our own effort, it may prolong the time until the promise is actually fulfilled. Jacob had to live as an exile for 25 years, because he thought he had to arrange the fulfillment of God's promise to get his father's blessing. Moses had to tend sheep for 40 years in the desert after he tried to arrange the fulfillment of God's promise by murdering an Egyptian.

v. It is much better to receive God's help than to try and help Him with our own wisdom and even unbelief. "Those who are truly zealous for God frequently reach for fruit without first dying. Unfortunately much Christian work is done in this way, and while there is conception, the child that is born can never be the heir. Christian work that is done merely through the zeal of human effort without counting the body as dead, and Sarai as good as dead, may produce great revival campaigns with but a few genuinely saved, large church memberships with many tares among the wheat" (Barnhouse).

c. **So he went in to Hagar, and she conceived**: Abram certainly acted according to his own power and wisdom when he agreed to inseminate Hagar and did not trust in God's ability to provide an heir through Sarai. But this wasn't a matter of a sensual romance. According to some of the customs of the day, Hagar would actually sit on the lap of Sarai as Abram inseminated her, to show that the child would legally belong to Sarai, as Hagar was merely a substitute for Sarai.

i. We understand this from the similar occasion of using a servant as a surrogate mother in the case of Rachel's giving of Bilhah to Jacob when Rachel was barren. In that context, Genesis 30:3 reads: *So she said, "Here is my maid Bilhah; go in to her, and she will bear a child on my knees, that I also may have children by her."*

ii. The phrase "bear a child on my knees" refers to the ancient practice of surrogate-adoption. Some believe that the phrase refers only to a symbolic placement of the child on the knees of one who adopts it. Others believe that it refers to the surrogate sitting on the lap of the adoptive mother during both insemination and birth. For example, referring to Genesis 30:3, the Twentieth Century Bible Commentary says: "These words are probably intended literally, and not merely as figurative adoption."

iii. We should not regard the idea that Hagar was inseminated and gave birth "on the knees" of Sarai as a certainty – we don't know enough about the ancient practice, and even if it were an ancient custom, it doesn't mean that it was followed in every case. But it certainly is a reasonable possibility.

d. **And she conceived**: From Sarai's perspective, a terrible thing happened – Abram succeeded in making Hagar pregnant. This proved beyond all doubt the failure to provide a son to Abram was the fault of Sarai, not her husband. In a culture that so highly valued childbearing, mothering the child of a wealthy and influential man like Abram gave a servant girl like Hagar greater status, and made her appeared more blessed than Sarai.

i. This is a good reminder that *results* are not enough to justify what we do before God. It's not right to say, "Well, they got a baby out of it. It must have been God's will." The flesh profits nothing (John 6:63), but it can *produce* something. Doing things in the flesh may get results, and we may be sorry we got them.

ii. Whatever a man or woman attempts to do without God will be a miserable failure – or an even more miserable success.

e. **Her mistress became despised in her eyes**: Hagar began to think of herself as better and greater than Sarai. A bad situation became worse.

3. (5-6) Sarai's anger towards Hagar.

Then Sarai said to Abram, "My wrong *be* upon you! I gave my maid into your embrace; and when she saw that she had conceived, I became despised in her eyes. The LORD judge between you and me." So Abram said to Sarai, "Indeed your maid is in your hand; do to her as you please." And when Sarai dealt harshly with her, she fled from her presence.

a. **My wrong be upon you**: Sarai blamed the whole situation on Abram, and for good cause. He should have acted as the spiritual leader and told his wife that God was able to perform what He promised, and they didn't need to try to perform God's promise by disobeying Him and relying on man's strength and wisdom.

b. **I became despised in her eyes**: Hagar's contempt for Sarai started the problem. She couldn't resist displaying an inappropriate haughtiness, thinking her pregnancy somehow showed her to be better than Sarai.

c. **Indeed your maid is in your hand; do to her as you please**: Abram seemed to make a bad situation worse by turning the situation over to Sarai and not taking care of the child he was father to. Yet in this, he also put his relationship with Sarai first, and that was good.

i. These terribly complicated and difficult family situations often arise out of our disobedience. All things considered, it is much easier to live life trusting in and obedient unto the LORD. God wants to spare us from these complications and difficulties.

d. **When Sarai dealt harshly with her, she fled from her presence**: Sarai's cruelty collided with Hagar's pride, and all Hagar could think to do was to run. Even with nowhere to go, **she fled from her presence** – probably headed back to Egypt, her original home.

B. **Hagar flees from Abram and Sarai.**

1. (7-9) The Angel of the LORD appears to Hagar and instructs her.

Now the Angel of the LORD found her by a spring of water in the wilderness, by the spring on the way to Shur. And He said, "Hagar, Sarai's maid, where have you come from, and where are you going?" She said, "I am fleeing from the presence of my mistress Sarai." The Angel of the LORD said to her, "Return to your mistress, and submit yourself under her hand."

a. **Now the Angel of the Lord found her by a spring of water**: Hagar's escape led her to a **spring**. Perhaps she was afraid to go further and leave this supply of water. In her difficulty, **the Angel of the Lord** met her.

b. **And He said**: Seemingly, **the Angel of the Lord** was a physical presence who spoke with Hagar as one person speaks to another. We don't have the sense that this was a mere spiritual impression or a voice in the wind. There was a person physically present with Hagar, and that person was **the Angel of the Lord**.

i. Later in the text, it shows that Hagar understood that this physically-present Person was *God Himself*. When God Himself is physically present, we understand that it is a pre-incarnate appearance of Jesus Christ.

ii. We understand this because of God the Father it says: *No one has seen God at any time. The only begotten Son, who is in the bosom of the Father, He has declared Him* (John 1:18), and no man has ever seen God in the Person of the Father (1 Timothy 6:16). Therefore, if God physically appeared and spoke as one Person to another in the Old Testament, we understand this as an appearance of the eternal Son, the Second Person of the Trinity, before His incarnation in Bethlehem.

- The **Angel of the Lord** would later appear to Abraham (Genesis 22).
- The **Angel of the Lord** would later appear to Moses (Exodus 3).
- The **Angel of the Lord** would later appear to Balaam (Numbers 22).
- The **Angel of the Lord** would later appear to Israel collectively (Judges 2).
- The **Angel of the Lord** would later appear to Gideon (Judges 6).
- The **Angel of the Lord** would later appear to Samson's parents (Judges 13).
- The **Angel of the Lord** would later appear to David (2 Samuel 24).
- The **Angel of the Lord** would later appear to Elijah (1 Kings 19).

iii. *This is the first appearance of* **the Angel of the Lord** in the Bible. He didn't first appear to Noah or Enoch or Abrahm. The **Angel of the Lord** first appeared to a single mother-to-be who had a pride problem and was mistreated by the woman who put her into the whole mess.

  iv. All this makes us amazed at God's love for the unlikely, and we should never forget that He often delights in doing this.

 c. **Where have you come from, and where are you going**: The **Angel of the LORD** asked an important and insightful question. In Hagar's pride and misery, she acted without thinking, "Where have I come from?" "Where am I going?"

  i. Remembering those two questions would save us from a lot of trouble.

  ii. Hagar thought she knew: *I come from the most terrible place ever. I'm going nowhere.* The Angel of the LORD told her, I've got a plan for you – let's move forward on it.

 d. **Return to your mistress, and submit yourself under her hand**: The Angel of the Lord told her to *repent*. If she changed her direction, there was an inherent promise – *obey Me and I will protect you.* Jesus didn't exactly tell Hagar to go back to an abusive household; He made an implied promise of protection.

2. (10-12) The promise of the Angel of the LORD to Hagar.

Then the Angel of the LORD said to her, "I will multiply your descendants exceedingly, so that they shall not be counted for multitude." And the Angel of the LORD said to her:

"Behold, you *are* with child,
And you shall bear a son.
You shall call his name Ishmael,
Because the LORD has heard your affliction.
He shall be a wild man;
His hand *shall be* against every man,
And every man's hand against him.
And he shall dwell in the presence of all his brethren."

 a. **I will multiply your descendants exceedingly**: God not only implied a promise of protection, He also gave a clear promise of staggering blessing. The unborn son of Hagar would be the father of uncountable descendants.

  i. As the promise was fulfilled, Ishmael became the ancestor of the Arab people, just as his later half-brother Isaac would become the ancestor of the Jewish people.

  ii. This makes the conflict between Arab and Jew even more tragic: *they are brothers* and share a common father in Abraham.

 b. **You shall call his name Ishmael**: Ishmael was given a great promise, not only in the number of his descendants, but also in that he was the first one in the Bible given his name before he was born. *God had a plan for this boy and his descendants.* God doesn't give a name if He doesn't have a plan.

   i. Many Christians today think they know God's plan for the **descendants** of **Ishmael**, the Arabic people: God wants to wipe them out because of their hatred of Jews and their persecution of Christians. This reaction is not rooted in the Bible, especially in this passage of Genesis 16. Consider:

   - God could have allowed Hagar and her unborn child to die in the wilderness – He didn't allow it. God specifically intervened so that wouldn't happen.
   - God could have allowed Hagar to live, but to disappear from the life and household of Abraham and Sarah, but He didn't allow that.
   - One may argue that Ishmael's conception was because of sin and unbelief; but God could have erased him from the story, and *God chose not to.* This part of the story is God's doing, not man's doing.
   - God *specifically commanded Hagar to go back*, to *stay in the story.* We can know that *God's story for the Arabic people is not finished.*

   ii. We should also remember that angelic visitations, Jesus visitations, continue to this day among the descendants of Ishmael. The Angel of the LORD was not done visiting Ishmael.

c. **You shall call his name Ishmael, because the LORD has heard your affliction**: The name Ishmael means *God will hear.* We may take this as a prompting to pray for revival and spiritual awakening among the Arab peoples, because when they cry out to Jesus, *God will hear.*

d. **He shall be a wild man; his hand shall be against every man, and every man's hand against him**: The life of Hagar's son would not be easy, but God would still look over him and sustain him.

   i. Remember that the ill effect of this – **a wild man, his hand shall be against every man, every man's hand against him** – has been mostly seen in violence and murder among Arabs themselves. They kill each other even more than they kill Jews and Christians. For their own sake, even more than ours, we pray: *God, bring salvation to the Arab people.*

3. (13-16) God's blessing and protection of Hagar and Ishmael.

Then she called the name of the LORD who spoke to her, You-Are-the-God-Who-Sees; for she said, "Have I also here seen Him who sees me?" Therefore the well was called Beer Lahai Roi; observe, *it is* **between**

Kadesh and Bered. So Hagar bore Abram a son; and Abram named his son, whom Hagar bore, Ishmael. Abram was eighty-six years old when Hagar bore Ishmael to Abram.

    a. **You-Are-the-God-Who-Sees**: Hagar knew this was no mere angel who appeared to her. The Angel of the LORD was also **the-God-Who-Sees**, the same One watching over Hagar and the yet-to-be-born Ishmael.

        i. After meeting with *El Roi* (**You-Are-the-God-Who-Sees**), Hagar knew that if God could be with her in the wilderness, He would be with her in having to submit to Sarai also. It's as if Hagar said to God, "You have looked upon me, and now I can look upon You." That face-to-face relationship with God transforms.

    b. **So Hagar bore Abram a son**: Apparently, Hagar did return with a submitted heart. She told the whole story to Abram and Sarai, and Abram named the child **Ishmael**, just as instructed in the meeting with the Angel of the LORD Hagar described.

        i. Hagar might have said when she returned, "I fled from you all because I was so miserable and thought I could not continue here. But the LORD met me and told me He would see me through. He told me to come back and submit to you, so that is why I'm here."

        ii. Hagar thought her circumstances needed transformation; in fact, *she* needed transformation. "If we seek to change our circumstances, we will jump from the frying pan into the fire. We must be triumphant exactly where we are. It is not a change of climate we need, but a change of heart. The flesh wants to run away, but God wants to demonstrate His power exactly where we have known our greatest chagrin" (Barnhouse).

        iii. Christians today have an even more clear and wonderful promise of this than Hagar ever had. We have the promise of Jesus: *Behold, I am with you always, even unto the end of the age* (Matthew 28:20).

- If you have to submit in difficult circumstances, *God sees.*
- If you ache under the pain of ministry, *God sees.*
- If you just feel like running, *God sees.*
- God has met you, sent Jesus near, and gives you new hope.

Genesis 17 – God Reaffirms the Covenant

A. An appearance from God, a change of name for Abram.

1. (1-2) God appears to Abram when he is 99 years old.

When Abram was ninety-nine years old, the Lord appeared to Abram and said to him, "I *am* Almighty God; walk before Me and be blameless. And I will make My covenant between Me and you, and will multiply you exceedingly."

> a. **When Abram was ninety-nine years old**: Abram was 75 years old when he left Haran (Genesis 12:4). He was 86 years old when the son Ishmael was born of Hagar, the servant girl (Genesis 16:15-16). He had waited some 25 years for the fulfilment of God's promise to give a son through Sarai. It had been some 13 years since his last recorded word from God.
>
> b. **The Lord appeared to Abram**: This was another appearance of God in the person of Jesus, who took on a temporary human appearance before His incarnation on earth (as with Hagar in Genesis 16:7-9).
>
> c. **I am Almighty God**: God's first words to Abram made an introduction and a declaration of His being. By this name *El Shaddai* (God Almighty), God revealed His Person and character to Abram. However, there is some debate as to what exactly the name *El Shaddai* means.
>
>> i. Kidner: "A traditional analysis of the name is 'God (*el*) who (*sa*) is sufficient (*day*).'"
>>
>> ii. Clarke: "*El shaddai, I am God all-sufficient*; from *shadah*, to *shed*, to *pour out*. I am that God who *pours* out *blessings*, who gives them *richly, abundantly, continually.*"
>>
>> iii. Donald Barnhouse took the approach that the Hebrew word *shad* means "chest" or "breast." It may have in mind the strength of a man's chest (God Almighty) or the comfort and nourishment of a woman's breast (God of Tender Care).

iv. Leupold explained that *Shaddai* comes from the root *shadad*, which means "to display power."

v. The Septuagint – a translation of the Hebrew scriptures into Greek before the time of Jesus – translates **Almighty** with the Greek word *pantokrator*, the "One who has His hand on everything."

d. **Walk before Me and be blameless**: After the proclamation of His name *El Shaddai*, God then told Abram what was expected of him. It was first revelation and then expectation. This communicates the principle that we can only do what God expects of us when we know who He is, and we know it in a full, personal, and real way.

i. The word **blameless** literally means "whole." God wanted *all* of Abram, a total commitment.

e. **I will make My covenant between Me and you**: God also reminded Abram He had not forgotten the covenant. Though it had been some 25 years since the promise was first made, and though it maybe seemed to Abram God forgot, God didn't forget anything.

i. The last time we are told the Lord communicated with Abram directly was some 13 years before (Genesis 16:15-16). Seemingly, Abram had 13 years of "normal" fellowship with God, waiting for the promise all the time. It would be understandable if, at times during those 13 years, Abram felt that God forgot His promise.

ii. "All these thirteen years, so far as Scripture informs us, Abram had not a single visit from his God. We do not find any record of his either doing anything memorable or having so much as a single audience with the Most High." (Spurgeon)

iii. Abram was becoming a great man of faith, but you don't make a great man of faith overnight. It takes years of God's work in them, years of almost mundane trusting in God, perhaps interrupted with a few spectacular encounters with the Lord.

2. (3-8) God refers to specific terms of the covenant He has not forgotten.

Then Abram fell on his face, and God talked with him, saying: "As for Me, behold, My covenant is with you, and you shall be a father of many nations. No longer shall your name be called Abram, but your name shall be Abraham; for I have made you a father of many nations. I will make you exceedingly fruitful; and I will make nations of you, and kings shall come from you. And I will establish My covenant between Me and you and your descendants after you in their generations, for an everlasting covenant, to be God to you and your descendants after you. Also I give to you and your descendants after you the land in which you

are a stranger, all the land of Canaan, as an everlasting possession; and I will be their God."

a. **Abram fell on his face**: As this seems to be a direct, personal appearance of God, Abram did the proper and reverent thing; he **fell on his face**, showing submission and giving honor to God.

b. **No longer shall your name be called Abram, but your name shall be Abraham**: To encourage Abram's faith in the promise of descendants through Sarai, God changed Abram's name from **Abram** (father of many) to **Abraham** (father of many nations).

i. There was, no doubt, a sense in which **Abram**, "father of many," was a hard name to bear for a man who was the father of none, especially in a culture where inquiry about one's personal life was a courteous practice. Now, God went a step further and made his name "father of many nations." It was almost crazy for a childless man to have such a name.

ii. Think of when Abraham announced his name change to others. They must have thought he wanted to *escape* the burden of his name. Instead, he increased the burden.

iii. There are many wonderful name changes in the Bible, such as when God changed Jacob's name to *Israel* (Genesis 32:28), and when He changed Simon's name to *Peter* (Mark 3:16). God promises a wonderful new name to every overcomer in Him (Revelation 2:17).

iv. God gives us many names in faith (saint, righteous, chosen, royal priesthood, sons of God, and so forth), and He knows He will accomplish the meaning of the name in us – even it if seems somewhat crazy.

c. **Father of many nations... exceedingly fruitful... make nations of you, and kings shall come from you**: In almost every dimension, God made the long-delayed promise to Abraham *greater*. Never before had God specifically said that *multiple* **nations** would come from Abraham (a singular *nation* was promised in Genesis 12:2). Never before had God specifically said that **kings** would descend from Abraham.

i. "Oh! those glorious 'wills' and 'shalls.' Brethren, ye cannot serve the Lord with a perfect heart until first your faith gets a grip of the divine 'will' and 'shall.'" (Spurgeon)

d. **I will establish My covenant between Me and you and your descendants after you in their generations, for an everlasting covenant**: God also specifically promised that the covenant He originally made with Abram in Genesis 12:1-3 would be passed to his chosen **descendants**, those not yet born. The covenant was not only for Abram, but it was **an everlasting covenant**.

e. **I give to you and your descendants after you the land… for an everlasting possession**: The specific promise of **the land** was made *not* only to Abraham, but also to his covenant **descendants**. This **everlasting covenant** was just as valid for them as it was for Abraham himself. **The land** was and is God's covenant promise to the Jewish people.

3. (9-14) God institutes a sign of the covenant for Abraham and his descendants.

And God said to Abraham: "As for you, you shall keep My covenant, you and your descendants after you throughout their generations. This is My covenant which you shall keep, between Me and you and your descendants after you: Every male child among you shall be circumcised; and you shall be circumcised in the flesh of your foreskins, and it shall be a sign of the covenant between Me and you. He who is eight days old among you shall be circumcised, every male child in your generations, he who is born in your house or bought with money from any foreigner who is not your descendant. He who is born in your house and he who is bought with your money must be circumcised, and My covenant shall be in your flesh for an everlasting covenant. And the uncircumcised male child, who is not circumcised in the flesh of his foreskin, that person shall be cut off from his people; he has broken My covenant."

a. **This is My covenant which you shall keep**: This begins the command regarding circumcision. The cutting and removal of the foreskin of every male among Abraham's covenant descendants marked them as those who were in the covenant. Since this covenant was made with the literal, genetic **descendants** of Abraham through the promise of God, it was appropriate that this sign of the covenant be given to those born into the covenant and was associated with the reproductive part of their body.

i. "Circumcision indicated to the seed of Abraham that there was a defilement of the flesh in man which must for ever be taken away, or man would remain impure, and out of covenant with God." (Spurgeon)

b. **Every male child among you shall be circumcised**: For the first time, God gave Abraham something to *do* in regard to the covenant. He told him that his descendants must take upon themselves a **sign of the covenant**, showing they received the covenant by faith.

c. **You shall be circumcised in the flesh of your foreskins**: The sign was circumcision, the cutting away of the male foreskin. God chose this sign for many important reasons.

i. Circumcision was not unknown in the world at that time. It was a ritual practiced among various peoples.

ii. There were undoubtedly hygienic reasons, especially making sense in the ancient world. "There is some medical evidence that this practice has indeed contributed to the long-lasting vigor of the Jewish race." (Morris) McMillen, in *None of These Diseases*, noted studies in 1949 and 1954 that showed a remarkably low rate of cervical cancer for Jewish women, because they mostly have husbands who are circumcised.

iii. But more importantly, circumcision is a cutting away of the flesh and an appropriate **sign of the covenant** for those who should put no trust in the flesh.

iv. Also, because circumcision deals with the organ of procreation, it was a reminder of the special seed of Abraham, which would ultimately bring the Messiah.

d. **He who is eight days old among you shall be circumcised**: Since the covenant descendants of Abraham are born into that covenant by their natural birth, it logically followed that the **sign of the covenant** should be given to them in their infancy.

i. In Colossians 2:11-12, the Apostle Paul connected the ideas of circumcision and Christian baptism. His idea was that in Jesus we are *spiritually* circumcised, and we were also buried with Jesus in baptism. Paul did not say that baptism is the sign of the covenant Christians receive and live under, the new covenant. Even if that connection is made, it is important to note that one was genetically born into the covenant described here in Genesis 17. One is not genetically born into the new covenant; one is born into it by God's grace through faith. It is wrong and harmful to make the analogy, "babies were circumcised, so babies should be baptized."

ii. "In the type the seed of Abraham are circumcised; you draw the inference that all typified by the seed of Abraham ought to be baptised, and I do not cavil at the conclusion; but I ask you, who are the true seed of Abraham? Paul answers in Romans 9:8, 'They which are the children of the flesh, these are not the children of God: but the children of the promise are counted for the seed.'" (Spurgeon)

iii. "As many as believe in the Lord Jesus Christ, whether they be Jews or Gentiles, are Abraham's seed. Whether eight days old in grace, or more or less, every one of Abraham's seed has a right to baptism. But I deny that the unregenerate, whether children or adults, are of the spiritual seed of Abraham." (Spurgeon)

e. **He who is eight days old among you shall be circumcised**: God probably commanded the circumcision of children to take place on the eighth day because this is the day when an infant's immune system is at the optimum level for such a procedure.

i. McMillen also notes newborn children have a peculiar susceptibility to bleeding between the second and fifth days of life. It seems an important blood-clotting agent, vitamin K, is not formed in the normal amount until the fifth to seventh day of life. Another blood-clotting agent, prothrombin, is at its highest levels in infants on precisely the eighth day of life, making the eighth day the safest, earliest day to circumcise an infant.

f. **The uncircumcised male child... he has broken My covenant**: Those who rejected circumcision rejected the **sign of the covenant**. They were no friends of the covenant God made with Abraham. It wasn't that circumcision made them a part of the covenant (faith did), but rejection of circumcision was a rejection of the covenant.

i. Unfortunately, through the centuries, the Jews began to trust more in the *sign* of the covenant (circumcision) than in the *God* of the covenant, believing that circumcision by itself was sufficient and necessary to save. Paul refutes this idea extensively, especially in light of the finished work of Jesus (Galatians 5:1-15).

ii. Therefore, Christians are free to either circumcise or not. One may do so for social or hygienic reasons, but it doesn't get us any closer to God: *For in Christ Jesus neither circumcision nor uncircumcision avails anything, but faith working through love* (Galatians 5:6).

iii. Again, Paul spoke of circumcision and baptism in Colossians 2:11-12, connecting them without saying they are the same thing. In this sense, at least, they are connected: circumcision did not save a Jewish man, but refusing to be circumcised meant disobedience to the covenant, and perhaps rejection of it. In the same sense, being baptized does not save us, but no Christian should refuse baptism.

B. The promise of a son to both Abraham and Sarah.

1. (15-16) The promise is stated: a son will come through Sarai.

Then God said to Abraham, "As for Sarai your wife, you shall not call her name Sarai, but Sarah *shall be* her name. And I will bless her and also give you a son by her; then I will bless her, and she shall be a *mother of* nations; kings of peoples shall be from her."

a. **As for Sarai your wife, you shall not call her name Sarai, but Sarah shall be her name**: There is only a subtle difference between **Sarai** and

Sarah, but it is an important difference. **Sarah** indicates a higher standing and status than **Sarai**.

> i. "*Sarai* signifies *my lady*, or *my princess*, which confines her dominion to one family; but *Sarah* signifies either a *lady* or *princess*, simply and absolutely without restriction, or *the princess of a multitude*." (Poole)

b. **And I will bless her and also give you a son by her**: By emphasizing the word "**her**," God made it plain that this son will not come about by another surrogate-mother situation (as with Hagar and Ishmael). Sarah herself would give birth, even though it was past her time in life to do so (Sarah was about 90 years old at this time).

2. (17-18) Abraham's response to the promise.

Then Abraham fell on his face and laughed, and said in his heart, "Shall *a child* be born to a man who is one hundred years old? And shall Sarah, who is ninety years old, bear *a child*?" And Abraham said to God, "Oh, that Ishmael might live before You!"

a. **Then Abraham fell on his face and laughed**: Abraham's laugh didn't seem to be one of cynical doubt, but instead of rejoicing in something he knew was impossible by all outward appearance, but that God could perform.

b. **Shall a child be born to a man who is one hundred years old**: Abraham knew both he and Sarah were well past the time people normally have children. Yet Abraham believed, and in Romans 4:17-21, Paul wonderfully described Abraham's faith in this promise.

> i. *In the presence of Him whom he believed; God, who gives life to the dead and calls those things which do not exist as though they did; who, contrary to hope, in hope believed, so that he became the father of many nations, according to what was spoken, "So shall your descendants be." And not being weak in faith, he did not consider his own body, already dead (since he was about a hundred years old), and the deadness of Sarah's womb. He did not waver at the promise of God through unbelief, but was strengthened in faith, giving glory to God, and being fully convinced that what He had promised He was also able to perform.* (Romans 4:17-21)

c. **Oh, that Ishmael might live before You**: At the same time, Abraham didn't really understand God's promise completely. He perhaps thought God simply meant Ishmael would be Sarah's spiritual son. Abraham – like all of us – found it hard to trust God for more than what he could conceive of.

3. (19-22) God repeats the promise and names the child who will come forth from Abraham and Sarah.

Then God said: "No, Sarah your wife shall bear you a son, and you shall call his name Isaac; I will establish My covenant with him for an everlasting covenant, and with his descendants after him. And as for Ishmael, I have heard you. Behold, I have blessed him, and will make him fruitful, and will multiply him exceedingly. He shall beget twelve princes, and I will make him a great nation. But My covenant I will establish with Isaac, whom Sarah shall bear to you at this set time next year." Then He finished talking with him, and God went up from Abraham.

> a. **Sarah your wife shall bear you a son, and you shall call his name Isaac**: The son will be named **Isaac** (laughter) because he would be such a joy to his parents, but also to always remind Abraham he laughed at God's promise to give him a son through Sarah at this late age.
>
> b. **As for Ishmael, I have heard you. Behold, I have blessed him**: Ishmael *will* be blessed. God would answer Abraham's prayer for blessing on Ishmael, making **him fruitful** and to **multiply him exceedingly**. Nevertheless, the covenant and its promises would pass only through the son to come, the son of promise.

4. (23-27) Abraham carries out God's command of circumcision.

So Abraham took Ishmael his son, all who were born in his house and all who were bought with his money, every male among the men of Abraham's house, and circumcised the flesh of their foreskins that very same day, as God had said to him. Abraham was ninety-nine years old when he was circumcised in the flesh of his foreskin. And Ishmael his son was thirteen years old when he was circumcised in the flesh of his foreskin. That very same day Abraham was circumcised, and his son Ishmael; and all the men of his house, born in the house or bought with money from a foreigner, were circumcised with him.

> a. **And circumcised the flesh of their foreskins that very same day, as God had said to him**: Abraham's belief in the covenant was proved by his obedience to the command. What we really believe will show in our actions.
>
> b. **That very same day Abraham was circumcised**: Abraham's obedience was *complete* (**every male among the men of Abraham's house**), it was *prompt* (**that very same day**), and it was *daring* (to virtually incapacitate all his fighting men at the same time).
>
>> i. Abraham didn't need to pray about this. He didn't need to grow or transition into this. God said it, and he did it. This is a wonderful example of obedience from a great man of faith.

Genesis 18 – The Promise of Isaac Confirmed

A. Abraham welcomes important visitors.

1. (1-5) Abraham invites the LORD and two others to a meal.

Then the LORD appeared to him by the terebinth trees of Mamre, as he was sitting in the tent door in the heat of the day. So he lifted his eyes and looked, and behold, three men were standing by him; and when he saw *them*, he ran from the tent door to meet them, and bowed himself to the ground, and said, "My Lord, if I have now found favor in Your sight, do not pass on by Your servant. Please let a little water be brought, and wash your feet, and rest yourselves under the tree. And I will bring a morsel of bread, that you may refresh your hearts. After that you may pass by, inasmuch as you have come to your servant." They said, "Do as you have said."

a. **Then the LORD appeared**: Apparently, this happened a short time after the events of Genesis 17. In Genesis 17:21, God said Sarah would give birth one year later, and at this time she was not yet pregnant; so this couldn't be more than three months after the events in Genesis 17.

b. **Then the LORD appeared to him by the terebinth trees**: Here again, the LORD came to Abraham in human appearance. This is another presentation of Jesus in human form before His incarnation, here among the **three men** visiting Abraham.

i. We can assume that this was God, in the Person of Jesus Christ, appearing to Abraham before His incarnation and birth at Bethlehem. We assume this because of God the Father it says, *No one has seen God at any time. The only begotten Son, who is in the bosom of the Father, He has declared Him* (John 1:18), and no man has ever seen God in the Person of the Father (1 Timothy 6:16). Therefore, if God appeared to someone in human appearance in the Old Testament (and no one has seen God the Father) it makes sense the appearance is of the eternal Son, the Second Person of the Trinity, before His incarnation in Bethlehem.

c. **The terebinth trees of Mamre**: This was a significant place in Abraham's life. Abraham moved to **Mamre** when he came back into the promised land from Egypt and built an altar there (Genesis 13:18), and apparently stayed there some time (Genesis 14:13). Abraham purchased a field and cave at **Mamre**, using it for Sarah's burial (Genesis 23:17-19). Abraham himself was buried there (Genesis 25:9), and his son Isaac was also buried there (Genesis 49:30, 50:13).

d. **Behold, three men were standing by him**: Though we don't know if Abraham immediately understood the identity of his visitors, he did honor the leader of these three as his superior (**bowed himself to the ground**).

i. Though the LORD (in the Person of Jesus Christ) appeared to Abraham twice before (Genesis 12:7, 17:1), we don't know if Jesus looked the same each time, or if Abraham simply knew who it was by some sort of intuition or spiritual knowledge.

e. **He ran from the tent door to meet them**: According to his godliness and the customs of that culture, Abraham enthusiastically offered the hospitality of his house to these travelers.

2. (6-8) Sarah and Abraham prepare a meal for their visitors.

So Abraham hurried into the tent to Sarah and said, "Quickly, make ready three measures of fine meal; knead it and make cakes." And Abraham ran to the herd, took a tender and good calf, gave it to a young man, and he hastened to prepare it. So he took butter and milk and the calf which he had prepared, and set it before them; and he stood by them under the tree as they ate.

a. **Abraham hurried into the tent**: Abraham's urgency seems to go beyond the great sense of hospitality that was common in his time. Abraham understood there was something special about these three visitors.

b. **Abraham ran to the herd**: Though Abraham and Sarah hurried to prepare this meal for their visitors, it still took considerable time to make and serve the food. The sense is that Abraham and Sarah themselves did this work, instead of commanding servants to do it for them.

3. (9-10) God reconfirms His promise of a son.

Then they said to him, "Where is Sarah your wife?" So he said, "Here, in the tent." And He said, "I will certainly return to you according to the time of life, and behold, Sarah your wife shall have a son." (Sarah was listening in the tent door which was behind him.)

a. **Where is Sarah your wife**: They called her according to her new name, given just a few weeks before (Genesis 17:15-16).

b. **I will certainly return to you according to the time of life, and behold, Sarah your wife shall have a son**: This promise of regeneration (**return to you according to the time of life**) was specifically made to Abraham. Sarah also was miraculously regenerated, but this promise was to Abraham.

c. **Sarah your wife shall have a son**: It seems that God dramatically repeated this promise to Abraham in a relatively short time (previously in Genesis 17:17-22). Like Abraham, we *need* to hear God's promises over and over again. It is a way God uses to encourage and develop our faith: *So then faith comes by hearing, and hearing by the word of God* (Romans 10:17).

4. (11-12) Sarah's reaction to God's promise.

Now Abraham and Sarah were old, well advanced in age; *and* Sarah had passed the age of childbearing. Therefore Sarah laughed within herself, saying, "After I have grown old, shall I have pleasure, my lord being old also?"

a. **Sarah had passed the age of childbearing**: By all outward circumstance, there was good reason for Sarah to laugh at the literal fulfillment of this promise. She **had passed the age of childbearing**, which literally seems to mean, "the manner of women had ceased to be with Sarah." She had stopped menstruating and had gone through menopause.

i. Even accounting for their long lives (Abraham lived to be 175 and Sarah 127), they were both well past middle age. It would take a miracle of God for them to have literal children through normal means.

b. **Therefore Sarah laughed within herself**: Significantly, this is what Sarah (and Abraham) *most wanted all their lives* – to have a child of their own. Yet they found it hard to believe God's promise when He said He would grant it to them.

i. It is strangely characteristic of us to believe God's promise for a long, long, time, enduring through much discouragement along the way, until the promise is *almost there*, and then we find doubt. We are grateful that He is greater than our doubts.

c. **After I have grown old, shall I have pleasure**: Sarah laughed within herself at this promise. She could not believe God would literally grant this child as the result of normal sexual relations.

i. Leupold translates Genesis 18:12, "After I have become worn out, have I enjoyed sexual delight and my lord too is an old man?" Leupold then observed, "The matter is not put very delicately by Sarah."

ii. It may be, even after the dramatic promises of Genesis 17, Abraham and Sarah found some way to spiritualize God's promise, making it mean something other than what God intended. Here, God made it plain: Abraham and Sarah would have normal sexual relations and produce a baby.

5. (13-15) God answers Sarah's laugh.

And the LORD said to Abraham, "Why did Sarah laugh, saying, 'Shall I surely bear *a child*, since I am old?' Is anything too hard for the LORD? At the appointed time I will return to you, according to the time of life, and Sarah shall have a son." But Sarah denied it, saying, "I did not laugh," for she was afraid. And He said, "No, but you did laugh!"

a. **Why did Sarah laugh**: God heard Sarah's laugh even though she *laughed within herself*. The sense was, her laugh could not be heard normally, but God heard it nevertheless. There was nothing hidden before the LORD.

i. We might live very differently if we remembered that God hears and knows everything we think and say.

b. **At the appointed time I will return to you**: When Sarah laughed at God's twice-given promise, we might think God would take the promise away. Instead, God responded by dealing with her sin of unbelief, not by taking away the promise.

i. *If we are faithless, He remains faithful; He cannot deny Himself* (2 Timothy 2:13).

c. **Is there anything too hard for the LORD**: God would demonstrate through Abraham and Sarah that there is *nothing* **too hard for the LORD**, and that God can even triumph over the weak faith of His people.

i. **Hard** is the same Hebrew word for *wonderful* in Isaiah 9:6: *For unto us a Child is born, unto us a Son is given… And His name will be called Wonderful.* Jesus is our "wonderful" One, and He isn't too **hard** or wonderful for God to give unto us.

d. **The LORD said to Abraham**: Significantly, God dealt with **Abraham** about this, not Sarah herself, because Abraham was the head of his home. God promised that it would happen, and **at the appointed time**.

B. Abraham intercedes for the cities of Sodom and Gomorrah.

1. (16-19) God decides to reveal to Abraham the fate of Sodom and Gomorrah.

Then the men rose from there and looked toward Sodom, and Abraham went with them to send them on the way. And the LORD said, "Shall I hide from Abraham what I am doing, since Abraham shall surely become a great and mighty nation, and all the nations of the earth

shall be blessed in him? For I have known him, in order that he may command his children and his household after him, that they keep the way of the LORD, to do righteousness and justice, that the LORD may bring to Abraham what He has spoken to him."

> a. **Abraham went with them to send them on the way**: In that day, it was customary for a hospitable host to accompany his guests on their journey for a while as they departed.
>
> b. **And the LORD said**: God asked Himself a question. He didn't do this because He didn't know what to do or needed to process His thinking. God asked Himself this question to reveal His thinking to us, the readers of Genesis.
>
> c. **Shall I hide from Abraham what I am doing**: Because of what God would bring from Abraham (**a great and mighty nation**), and because Abraham had to be a great leader (**that he may command his children and his household after him**), God determined to reveal to Abraham what He would soon do with Sodom and Gomorrah.
>
>> i. The reasons stated in this passage are important. God's purpose in revealing this to Abraham was not just to share interesting or shocking information, and it wasn't to simply satisfy Abraham's curiosity. God wanted to do something in Abraham's life through what He would reveal to him.

2. (20-21) God tells Abraham He will see if Sodom and Gomorrah are worthy of judgment.

And the LORD said, "Because the outcry against Sodom and Gomorrah is great, and because their sin is very grave, I will go down now and see whether they have done altogether according to the outcry against it that has come to Me; and if not, I will know."

> a. **Because the outcry against Sodom and Gomorrah is great**: The offense of these cities was **great**, their sin was **very grave**, and we may suppose that this **outcry** came from many sources.
>
> - God and His holy justice cried out against Sodom and Gomorrah.
> - On-looking angelic beings cried out against Sodom and Gomorrah.
> - The multitude of victims of Sodom and Gomorrah's depravity cried out against those cities.
> - Creation itself was affected by their unnatural transgression, and cried out against them.
>
> b. **I will go down now and see**: Because the judgments of the Lord are true and righteous (Psalm 19:9, Revelation 16:7), God would only judge

Sodom and Gomorrah on direct, accurate knowledge. We are not told this because God did not know, but to demonstrate to us the thorough character of God's knowledge and integrity.

3. (22-26) Abraham asks an important question: Will God destroy the righteous with the wicked?

Then the men turned away from there and went toward Sodom, but Abraham still stood before the LORD. And Abraham came near and said, "Would You also destroy the righteous with the wicked? Suppose there were fifty righteous within the city; would You also destroy the place and not spare it for the fifty righteous that were in it? Far be it from You to do such a thing as this, to slay the righteous with the wicked, so that the righteous should be as the wicked; far be it from You! Shall not the Judge of all the earth do right?" So the LORD said, "If I find in Sodom fifty righteous within the city, then I will spare all the place for their sakes."

a. **The men turned away from there and went toward Sodom, but Abraham still stood before the LORD**: We see the two **men** were actually the angels who visited Sodom in Genesis 19. The third person in the party was actually the **LORD** Himself.

b. **And Abraham came near**: Abraham **came near** to the LORD. Effective intercession is a matter of drawing near to God so we can pray with *His* heart.

c. **Would You also destroy the righteous with the wicked**: In discussing this question, in a sense, Abraham reminded the LORD of His own nature and principles (**shall not the Judge of all the earth do right**). Abraham thought that God, as a righteous **Judge**, could not and would not punish the innocent in the same way as the guilty.

i. Effective prayer speaks knowing who God is, and how God works in a particular situation. Effective prayer doesn't see itself as a passive spectator in what God does, but effective prayer acts as if it must actually remind God in prayer.

ii. We might find it remarkable Abraham even *cared* about the people of Sodom and Gomorrah. He might have just prayed, "LORD, get my nephew Lot out of there first," but he didn't. Abraham's heart was full of sorrow and compassion, even for the wicked of Sodom and Gomorrah.

d. **If I find in Sodom fifty righteous within the city, then I will spare all the place for their sakes**: God said this because Abraham asked. When Abraham drew near to the LORD and prayed according to God's revealed nature and will, God agreed. The LORD said that He would **spare** the city if there were 50 righteous there.

4. (27-33) Abraham bargains with God for Sodom and Gomorrah.

Then Abraham answered and said, "Indeed now, I who *am but* dust and ashes have taken it upon myself to speak to the Lord: Suppose there were five less than the fifty righteous; would You destroy all of the city for *lack of five*?" So He said, "If I find there forty-five, I will not destroy *it*." And he spoke to Him yet again and said, "Suppose there should be forty found there?" So He said, "I will not do *it* for the sake of forty." Then he said, "Let not the Lord be angry, and I will speak: Suppose thirty should be found there?" So He said, "I will not do *it* if I find thirty there." And he said, "Indeed now, I have taken it upon myself to speak to the Lord: Suppose twenty should be found there?" So He said, "I will not destroy *it* for the sake of twenty." Then he said, "Let not the Lord be angry, and I will speak but once more: Suppose ten should be found there?" And He said, "I will not destroy *it* for the sake of ten." So the LORD went His way as soon as He had finished speaking with Abraham; and Abraham returned to his place.

> a. **Suppose there were five less than the fifty righteous**: In his first exchange with God, Abraham established a principle – that God would not destroy the righteous with the wicked. With that principle established, it was then just a matter of numbers. How many righteous people would God spare the city for?
>
>> i. Abraham's intercession was effective because it was *specific*. He talked about specific numbers with God, and not only in broad, general terms. Often our prayers are ineffective because we really don't ask the LORD to *do* anything. Instead, we often just toss wishes up to heaven.
>
> b. **Let not the Lord be angry, and I will speak**: Abraham continued his intercession with a bold humility. He was not proud or arrogant before the Lord, yet he still continued to ask.
>
>> i. Abraham's humility was demonstrated in that nowhere in his prayer did he ask why or did he demand that God explain Himself and His actions.
>
> c. **Suppose ten should be found there**: Abraham was a skilled negotiator and he prevailed upon God to lower the number of righteous required to spare the city. First by units of five, then by units of ten, until the number settled at ten.
>
>> i. It is impossible to miss the persistence of Abraham in intercession. Abraham did not stop asking at 40 or 50 and say simply, "Now it's

in the LORD's hands" or "The LORD will do what the LORD will do." Abraham shows us that there are times when an intercessor must feel that the eternal destiny of men and women depends on the intercessor's prayer.

ii. This is the kind of heart God wanted to draw out of Abraham; a heart that cared so much for people made in the image of God that he worked hard to intercede on behalf of a city that deserved judgment. This was the heart a great leader of a large and mighty nation needed to have.

iii. Remember, there is a sense in which all this negotiation was in vain, because Sodom and Gomorrah *were* destroyed. There were *not* ten righteous people in the city, only four; and surely God knew how many righteous people there actually were in the cities. Yet God specifically revealed the fate of these cities to Abraham to draw out of him an intercessor's heart of love, so even before the time of Jesus, Abraham could be *conformed into the image of His Son* (Romans 8:29), who is Himself an intercessor (Hebrews 7:25).

d. **Abraham returned to his place**: We wonder if Abraham should not have continued the negotiations because there were only four righteous in the city. Would God have spared the city for four if Abraham had asked? Perhaps Abraham felt Lot would surely have brought six people beyond his own family to God in his time in Sodom.

Genesis 19 – The Destruction of Sodom and Gomorrah

A. The two angels come to Sodom.

1. (1-3) Lot convinces the angelic visitors to stay with him.

Now the two angels came to Sodom in the evening, and Lot was sitting in the gate of Sodom. When Lot saw *them*, he rose to meet them, and he bowed himself with his face toward the ground. And he said, "Here now, my lords, please turn in to your servant's house and spend the night, and wash your feet; then you may rise early and go on your way." And they said, "No, but we will spend the night in the open square." But he insisted strongly; so they turned in to him and entered his house. Then he made them a feast, and baked unleavened bread, and they ate.

> a. **Now the two angels came to Sodom**: The two visitors that departed from Abraham in Genesis 18:22 as he and the Lord continued their conversation now **came to Sodom**. For the first time they are identified as angelic beings, who first accompanied the Lord as He visited Abraham at Mamre (Genesis 18:1-2).
>
> > i. We have no reason to believe that Lot *knew* that these were **angels**; to him, they probably seemed to be distinguished guests with an air of righteousness and morality about them.
>
> b. **Lot was sitting in the gate of Sodom**: There was a steady progression of compromise in Lot's life. He went from looking toward Sodom (Genesis 13:10), to pitching his tent toward Sodom (Genesis 13:12), to living in Sodom (Genesis 14:12), and losing everything when Sodom was attacked. Now, Lot sat in **the gate of Sodom**, indicating he was a civic leader.
>
> > i. The **gate** area of an ancient city was sort of a town-hall where the important men of the city judged disputes, conferred with one another, and supervised those who entered and left the city.

ii. Lot himself was a righteous man who was grieved by the sin he saw around him (2 Peter 2:7-8), but because of his deep compromise few of his family and none of his friends were saved. Compromise destroyed his testimony.

c. **He insisted strongly; so they turned in to him and entered his house**: The hospitality Lot offered to the visitors was not unusual, but the urgency with which he offered it was.

2. (4-5) The wickedness and depravity of the men of Sodom.

Now before they lay down, the men of the city, the men of Sodom, both old and young, all the people from every quarter, surrounded the house. And they called to Lot and said to him, "Where are the men who came to you tonight? Bring them out to us that we may know them *carnally*."

a. **Where are the men who came to you tonight? Bring them out to us**: These citizens of Sodom clearly came to homosexually abuse and rape these two visitors. They were willing to break all principles of hospitality and morality for their own violent and sexual gratification.

b. **The men of the city... both old and young, all the people from every quarter, surrounded the house**: This shows that *the entire city* was given over to this violence and immorality, and that this behavior wasn't unusual, but accepted among **the men of Sodom**.

i. In Ezekiel 16, God later condemned and rebuked the great sin of Judah in the latter days of the divided monarchy. He compared Jerusalem to the ancient city of Sodom, saying they were like sisters. Then, God compared the sins of Sodom to the sins of Jerusalem at that time: *Look, this was the iniquity of your sister Sodom: She and her daughter had pride, fullness of food, and abundance of idleness; neither did she strengthen the hand of the poor and needy. And they were haughty and committed abomination before Me; therefore I took them away as I saw fit* (Ezekiel 16:49-50).

ii. The point of the Ezekiel passage was not to say that the *only* sins of Sodom that made them targets of judgment were the sins of pride, idleness, injustice to the poor, and such. Instead, those were the sins of Sodom also shared by her later "sister" Jerusalem. The Genesis text makes it plain that God was also grieved by their sexual violence and immorality, which is probably included in the Ezekiel list of sins under the words *committed abomination*.

c. **That we may know them carnally**: The sin of the men of Sodom was plainly connected to their homosexuality. There is no doubt the Bible declares homosexual conduct is sin (Romans 1:26-28).

i. Both the Hebrew scriptures (Leviticus 18:22, 20:13) and the Greek scriptures (Romans 1:26-28) condemn homosexual conduct. *Jesus Himself* affirmed the Old Testament's condemnation of homosexual conduct when He said, *do not think that I came to destroy the Law or the Prophets. I did not come to destroy but to fulfill* (Matthew 5:17). Jesus also affirmed the Biblical ideal of marriage consisting of one man and one woman joined in a life-long relationship (Matthew 19:4-6).

ii. The Bible condemns homosexual conduct in the same context as it condemns incest and bestiality (as in Leviticus 18:22, 20:13). If we decide that pleasure is the ultimate goal of sex and the measure of its morality (the mentality of if it feels good, do it), then there is no standing to say that incest or bestiality are sin.

iii. Homosexual advocates have an interest in saying homosexuals are exactly like everyone else, except they love and have sex with people of their own gender. Yet when the conduct of homosexuals is observed, this is not the case. Statistics often demonstrate that on average, male homosexuals have far more partners and much more promiscuous and public sex than heterosexuals.

iv. It may well be that one of the reasons why males pursue and give in to homosexual desires is because they want to immerse themselves in a lifestyle of dangerous sex with no inhibitions or obstacles, and sense that sex with other men is an easier path to this. No wonder Paul connects "burning lust" and *a debased mind* with male homosexuality in Romans 1:27-28.

v. Homosexual activists have an interest in saying that 10% or more of the population is homosexual, but the most reliable statistics show only 2.3% of men in their 20's and 30's report ever having had a homosexual experience. Only 1.1% reported being exclusively homosexual. These low figures agree with several other surveys and those conducted in Britain and France.

vi. Homosexual activists have an interest in saying they were born into their deviation, often with the sense that God deliberately created their homosexual desires and He intends they should fulfill those desires. All attempts thus far to prove this have been based more on wishful thinking than solid biological research, but if it were found to be the case, it wouldn't make a difference in a Biblical understanding of homosexual desire and conduct. The Bible teaches we are all born with a predisposition to sin. It shouldn't surprise us that some 2% of the population finds this predisposition expressed in homosexual desire.

vii. Homosexual activists have an interest in defining themselves as "gay," a word that used to mean "happy" or "carefree." But "gay" is a poor description of a lifestyle that has such a high rate of death, disease, and suicide.

3. (6-9) Lot bargains for the life and safety of his guests.

So Lot went out to them through the doorway, shut the door behind him, and said, "Please, my brethren, do not do so wickedly! See now, I have two daughters who have not known a man; please, let me bring them out to you, and you may do to them as you wish; only do nothing to these men, since this is the reason they have come under the shadow of my roof." And they said, "Stand back!" Then they said, "This one came in to stay *here*, and he keeps acting as a judge; now we will deal worse with you than with them." So they pressed hard against the man Lot, and came near to break down the door.

a. **Please, my brethren, do not do so wickedly**: This was a difficult argument for Lot to make. He and the men of Sodom had a completely different standard for deciding what was wicked and what was not. The men of Sodom thought they were pursuing pleasure, and did not care that Lot thought it was wicked.

i. The difference in their standards points to an important question: If we abandon the Bible's guide for sexual morality, what guide for sexual morality will we follow? To simply do as one pleases is not enough.

b. **I have two daughters who have not known a man; please, let me bring them out to you, and you may do to them as you wish**: Lot's offer to the mob was horrible and cannot be justified. The men of Sodom showed a shocking demonstration of depravity, but we are just as shocked at the willingness of Lot to give up his daughters to the mob as we are at the sinful desire of the mob itself.

i. We understand this terrible description a *little* more when we consider the low place of women in the pre-Christian world and the very high place of any guest in one's home. Under the sacred obligations of hospitality, it was often understood that a guest was to be protected more than one's own family.

c. **This one came in to stay here, and he keeps acting like a judge**: The men of Sodom mocked Lot, and they rejected his feeble efforts to provide moral and spiritual leadership.

i. Perhaps Lot thought that through compromise he might reach these men, but just the opposite happened. They had no respect for him whatsoever, even though his friendly-first approach led him to call such wicked men **my brethren**.

4. (10-11) Angelic protection at the door.

But the men reached out their hands and pulled Lot into the house with them, and shut the door. And they struck the men who *were* at the doorway of the house with blindness, both small and great, so that they became weary *trying* to find the door.

> a. **The men reached out their hands and pulled Lot into the house with them, and shut the door**: It must have taken great, perhaps supernatural, strength to do what the angels did at the door. Perhaps for the first time, Lot began to understand that his guests were more than men.
>
> b. **They struck the men who were at the doorway of the house with blindness**: Obviously, the work of striking the men blind was supernatural. Now, the mob had a physical blindness that matched their moral blindness.

B. The angels' deliverance of Lot.

1. (12-14) The angels warn Lot; Lot warns his family.

Then the men said to Lot, "Have you anyone else here? Son-in-law, your sons, your daughters, and whomever you have in the city– take *them* out of this place! For we will destroy this place, because the outcry against them has grown great before the face of the LORD, and the LORD has sent us to destroy it." So Lot went out and spoke to his sons-in-law, who had married his daughters, and said, "Get up, get out of this place; for the LORD will destroy this city!" But to his sons-in-law he seemed to be joking.

> a. **Have you anyone else here**: The angels were not *omniscient*, knowing everything. Knowing the number and location of the members of Lot's family was something that spiritual beings could easily observe, but at this point even these angels did not know it apart from Lot's answer.
>
>> i. Spurgeon saw something instructive in the angels' question, "**have you anyone else here?**" The question shows the concern we should have for the salvation of not only ourselves, but our whole house.
>
> b. **To his sons-in-law**: Lot's daughters were unmarried and had not known a man (Genesis 19:8). These men were **sons-in-law** by the ancient practice of binding betrothal, not yet by marriage.
>
> c. **We will destroy this place… the LORD has sent us to destroy it**: For the first time, Lot heard of the work of these supernatural guests – **to destroy** Sodom and Gomorrah. Sodom was destined for judgment, but God wanted to spare Lot and his family.

d. **He seemed to be joking**: This was the clear effect of Lot's life of compromise. When he spoke with utmost seriousness to his sons-in-law about the judgment of God, they did not believe him. Not even *they* would be saved from the judgment to come.

> i. The life of Lot shows us that it is possible to have a saved soul and a wasted life. Lot would be rescued, but his life would accomplish nothing, as in 1 Corinthians 3:15: *If anyone's work is burned, he will suffer loss; but he himself will be saved, yet so as through fire.*

2. (15-16) The angels try to hurry Lot and his family.

When the morning dawned, the angels urged Lot to hurry, saying, "Arise, take your wife and your two daughters who are here, lest you be consumed in the punishment of the city." And while he lingered, the men took hold of his hand, his wife's hand, and the hands of his two daughters, the LORD being merciful to him, and they brought him out and set him outside the city.

a. **Arise, take your wife and your two daughters**: There was now no mention of the two sons-in-law. They would be left behind as **the angels urged Lot** to escape the coming destruction and judgment on Sodom.

> i. In their urging of Lot, we see that these angels may serve as a pattern of evangelism.
>
> - They went after Lot, going to him and his house.
> - They warned him of what was going to happen, and in plain words.
> - They **urged Lot**, urging him to flee destruction.

b. **While he lingered**: Too much of Lot's heart was in Sodom, so he did not have an urgency to leave the city. A lack of *urgency* to obey God (even when it is necessary and good) is a common sign of compromise and a backslidden condition.

> i. **The men took hold of his hand**: "I thought, as I read my text, that it gave us a striking example of doing all we can. Lot and his wife, and the two daughters—well, that was four—the angels had only four hands, so they did all that they could—there was a hand for each. You notice the text expressly says, they took hold of the hand of Lot, and the hand of his wife, and the hand of his two daughters. There were no more persons, and no more helping hands, so that there was just enough instrumentality, but there was not a hand to spare" (Spurgeon).

c. **They brought him out and set him outside the city**: In Genesis 18, Abraham asked God to spare the cities of Sodom and Gomorrah if there were ten righteous found there. Because there were not ten righteous people, God did not spare the city, but He still answered the *heart* of Abraham's prayer by bringing Lot and his family out of Sodom, even if it was almost against Lot's will.

> i. Lot was in the worst of all possible places. He had too much of the world to be happy in the LORD, and too much of the LORD to be happy in the world.

3. (17-22) The escape from Sodom.

So it came to pass, when they had brought them outside, that he said, "Escape for your life! Do not look behind you nor stay anywhere in the plain. Escape to the mountains, lest you be destroyed." Then Lot said to them, "Please, no, my lords! Indeed now, your servant has found favor in your sight, and you have increased your mercy which you have shown me by saving my life; but I cannot escape to the mountains, lest some evil overtake me and I die. See now, this city is near *enough* to flee to, and it is a little one; please let me escape there (*is* it not a little one?) and my soul shall live." And he said to him, "See, I have favored you concerning this thing also, in that I will not overthrow this city for which you have spoken. Hurry, escape there. For I cannot do anything until you arrive there." Therefore the name of the city was called Zoar.

> a. **Escape for your life! Do not look behind you**: The angels seemed far more urgent to rescue Lot and his family than they were to be rescued. This is strange, but common in spiritual things.
>
> b. **Please, no, my lords**: Lot seemed pathetic and whimpering in his prayer, especially in contrast to the bold intercession of Abraham in Genesis 18.
>
> c. **I cannot do anything until you arrive there**: This answers Abraham's question, *Shall not the Judge of all the earth do right?* (Genesis 18:25). God, bound by His own righteousness and honor, *could not* bring this judgment on Sodom until the few righteous people were rescued.
>
> d. **Therefore the name of the city was called Zoar**: The name **Zoar** means *small* or *insignificant*. It was the **little** city Lot bargained with the angel about.

C. God's judgment of Sodom and Gomorrah.

1. (23-26) The cities destroyed, and Lot's wife is turned to a pillar of salt.

The sun had risen upon the earth when Lot entered Zoar. Then the LORD rained brimstone and fire on Sodom and Gomorrah, from the LORD out of the heavens. So He overthrew those cities, all the plain, all

the inhabitants of the cities, and what grew on the ground. But his wife looked back behind him, and she became a pillar of salt.

a. **When Lot entered Zoar. Then the LORD**: As the angel said in Genesis 19:22, judgment could not come upon Sodom and Gomorrah until Lot and his family were safe in Zoar; otherwise, it would violate God's promise to Abraham, at least in principle.

b. **Then the LORD rained brimstone and fire on Sodom and Gomorrah**: These cities were judged completely and severely, but only after God confirmed their great wickedness and gave them a righteous witness in Lot.

i. Today, some think these cities are buried under the Dead Sea, and their complete destruction is a testament to God's judgment and grace in delivering His righteous people.

ii. Before this destruction, the area of Sodom was unbelievably beautiful and productive, *like the garden of the LORD* (Genesis 13:10). Yet this great privilege and blessing did not turn their hearts toward God.

iii. As well, the people of Sodom and Gomorrah saw more of the power, grace, and mercy of God than any of the other people of the region. They had been delivered from ruin by God's work through Abraham. They heard the testimony from Melchizedek and saw the example of Melchizedek and Abraham. They had great blessing and great evidence of God's care for them, yet they rejected it all.

c. **But his wife looked back behind him, and she became a pillar of salt**: Lot's wife was turned to a pillar of salt because she **looked back behind**, after the angels had specifically warned, *do not look behind you* (Genesis 19:17). Some think she lingered behind and was caught up in the cataclysm somehow, but it was probably a unique judgment of God on her for the state of her heart. Her looking back likely showed a love for Sodom and regret for its destruction.

i. "The word *looked back* has the connotation of *looking intently*. It might possibly be rendered *lagged back*, or maybe even *returned back*." (Morris)

ii. In referring to the end times, Jesus said something interesting in Luke 17:32: *Remember Lot's wife*. In other words, as we see the end of the age, no Christian should have a heart like Lot's wife. We should not have a heart that longs for a corrupt and passing world. We should not have a heart that will in some sense regret the judgment God will bring on it.

iii. We need to look *forward* to our deliverance, not *back* at a world passing away and ripe for judgment.

2. (27-29) Abraham learns of Sodom and Gomorrah's destruction.

And Abraham went early in the morning to the place where he had stood before the LORD. Then he looked toward Sodom and Gomorrah, and toward all the land of the plain; and he saw, and behold, the smoke of the land which went up like the smoke of a furnace. And it came to pass, when God destroyed the cities of the plain, that God remembered Abraham, and sent Lot out of the midst of the overthrow, when He overthrew the cities in which Lot had dwelt.

a. **Abraham went early in the morning to the place where he had stood before the LORD**: We sense that Abraham, with deeply moved memory of the previous day, wanted to remember his meeting with God.

b. **He saw, and behold, the smoke of the land which went up like the smoke of a furnace**: When Abraham saw the smoke of the cities and their destruction, he knew that his request was answered. God delivered Lot before the destruction came.

i. **He saw**: Spurgeon used these verses to think about what emotions are appropriate for the believer as they look upon God's judgment on the wicked.

- They should have a humble submission to God's will.
- They should have a deep sense of gratitude for their rescue.
- They should have an increased watchfulness over their own life.
- They should remember the great evil of sin.

3. (30-32) Lot and his daughters live in a wilderness cave.

Then Lot went up out of Zoar and dwelt in the mountains, and his two daughters were with him; for he was afraid to dwell in Zoar. And he and his two daughters dwelt in a cave. Now the firstborn said to the younger, "Our father is old, and there is no man on the earth to come in to us as is the custom of all the earth. Come, let us make our father drink wine, and we will lie with him, that we may preserve the lineage of our father."

a. **Then Lot went up out of Zoar and dwelt in the mountains**: We don't know why Lot and his daughters became dissatisfied with Zoar, or why the people of Zoar became dissatisfied with them. Yet for some reason, they left the small city of Zoar and went to the **mountains** and **dwelt in a cave**.

b. **Let us make our father drink wine**: Lot and his family lost everything in the destruction of Sodom and Gomorrah. Even so, they quickly had a stock of **wine**. They either brought this with them or they obtained it in Zoar.

c. **We will lie with him, that we may preserve the lineage of our father**: This is a remarkable – and seemingly desperate sin from Lot's daughters. Some suggest that they believed that the whole world had perished with Sodom and Gomorrah, and it was now their responsibility to repopulate the earth through their father. However, their brief time in Zoar was enough to show there were other people.

> i. Living in the low moral environment of Sodom had a great and harmful effect on Lot's family. His compromise affected far more than himself.

4. (33-38) Moab and Ammon are born from this incestuous relationship.

So they made their father drink wine that night. And the firstborn went in and lay with her father, and he did not know when she lay down or when she arose. It happened on the next day that the firstborn said to the younger, "Indeed I lay with my father last night; let us make him drink wine tonight also, and you go in *and* lie with him, that we may preserve the lineage of our father." Then they made their father drink wine that night also. And the younger arose and lay with him, and he did not know when she lay down or when she arose. Thus both the daughters of Lot were with child by their father. The firstborn bore a son and called his name Moab; he is the father of the Moabites to this day. And the younger, she also bore a son and called his name Ben-Ammi; he is the father of the people of Ammon to this day.

a. **The firstborn went in and lay with her father**: We may be uncomfortable with the idea that the Bible includes the record of such disgraceful sins.

> i. Yet Donald Barnhouse observed: "It is far better for children to learn the facts of life from the Word of God where sin is condemned than from dirty words on alley walls, or from lewd stories. No one can escape knowledge of sin… these things are never mentioned without being accompanied by the stern warnings that God hates sin and punishes it."

> ii. "Ironically, in his own drunkenness Lot carried out the shameful act that he himself had suggested to the men of Sodom: he lay with his own daughters." (Sailhamer)

b. **Moab; he is the father of the Moabites… Ben-Ammi; he is the father of the people of Ammon**: Their descendants would become enemies and obstacles for Israel, just like the descendants of Ishmael. Lot's life ended in ruin in regard to the past, the present, and the future – and all because of his love for the world and the compromise that came from that love.

Genesis 20 – Abraham Lies About Sarah Again

A. Abraham's lie, God's protection.

1. (1-2) Abraham lies again, in a similar manner as before.

And Abraham journeyed from there to the South, and dwelt between Kadesh and Shur, and stayed in Gerar. Now Abraham said of Sarah his wife, "She *is* my sister." And Abimelech king of Gerar sent and took Sarah.

> a. **Abraham journeyed from there to the South**: After the destruction of Sodom and Gomorrah, Abraham moved. Perhaps he did not want to live in the hills overlooking the destroyed region any longer, and be reminded of those people and the judgment that came upon them.
>
> b. **Abraham said of Sarah his wife, "She is my sister"**: Abraham's concern was probably not because Sarah looked like a young beauty at 90 years of age. We can surmise that she was reasonably attractive at that age, but more importantly she was connected to one of the richest and most influential men of the region. In that day, a harem was sometimes more of a political statement than a romantic statement.
>
>> i. At the same time, we should not ignore the idea of Sarah's continued attractiveness even in old age. "She had in some measure been physically rejuvenated, in order to conceive, bear, and nurse Isaac, and possibly this manifested itself in renewed beauty as well" (Morris).
>
> c. **She is my sister**: This is the same lie Abraham told back in Genesis 12:10-13. He showed that it was easy to slip back into sinful habits. Abraham stumbled in a place that he had stumbled before. Instead of trusting God to keep his family together, he devised his own plan to do it. His plan would fail completely.
>
>> i. Age does not automatically sanctify us. Unless yielded to the Spirit of God, we will repeat in our old age the sinful patterns of our youth.

2. (3-7) God threatens judgment upon Abimelech for taking Sarah.

But God came to Abimelech in a dream by night, and said to him, "Indeed you *are* a dead man because of the woman whom you have taken, for she *is* a man's wife." But Abimelech had not come near her; and he said, "Lord, will You slay a righteous nation also? Did he not say to me, 'She *is* my sister'? And she, even she herself said, 'He *is* my brother.' In the integrity of my heart and innocence of my hands I have done this." And God said to him in a dream, "Yes, I know that you did this in the integrity of your heart. For I also withheld you from sinning against Me; therefore I did not let you touch her. Now therefore, restore the man's wife; for he *is* a prophet, and he will pray for you and you shall live. But if you do not restore *her*, know that you shall surely die, you and all who *are* yours."

> a. **Indeed you are a dead man**: This was a scary thing to hear from God, even in a dream. But the point had to be made to Abimelech, even though he could truly say he acted **in the integrity of my heart and innocence of my hands**.
>
>> i. This may seem drastic, but something important was concerned. "Suppose Abimelech had taken Sarah and God had not intervened? Two seeds would have been at the door to Sarah's womb, and to this day an element of doubt would cling to the ancestry of our Lord" (Barnhouse).
>
> b. **I know that you did this in the integrity of your heart**: Because Abimelech's **heart** was right in this regard, God kept him from worse sin. God's protecting power can guide even a pagan king (Proverbs 21:1).
>
>> i. Despite Abraham's failure to really trust God in the situation, God did not abandon him. He would not *let* Abimelech touch Sarah. Her womb was going to bring forth the son of promise, who would eventually bring forth God's Messiah. God would not leave this matter up to man.
>
> c. **For he is a prophet, and he will pray for you**: Even though Abraham was in sin, he was still **a prophet** and man of powerful prayer. God's mercy did not leave Abraham, even though Abraham didn't trust God the way he should.

B. Abraham is rebuked again.

1. (8-10) Abraham once again suffers rebuke from a heathen king.

So Abimelech rose early in the morning, called all his servants, and told all these things in their hearing; and the men were very much afraid. And Abimelech called Abraham and said to him, "What have you done

to us? How have I offended you, that you have brought on me and on my kingdom a great sin? You have done deeds to me that ought not to be done." Then Abimelech said to Abraham, "What did you have in view, that you have done this thing?"

> a. **You have done deeds to me that ought not to be done**: It is sad to see that Abimelech – the pagan king – was in the right, and Abraham – the man of God – was in the wrong, and Abimelech told Abraham so.
>
> b. **What did you have in view, that you have done this thing**: This was a logical question for Ahimelech to ask Abraham. Abraham certainly did not have the LORD **in view** when he lied and failed to trust God.

2. (11-13) Abraham's excuse.

And Abraham said, "Because I thought, surely the fear of God *is* not in this place; and they will kill me on account of my wife. But indeed *she* is truly my sister. She is the daughter of my father, but not the daughter of my mother; and she became my wife. And it came to pass, when God caused me to wander from my father's house, that I said to her, 'This is your kindness that you should do for me: in every place, wherever we go, say of me, "He is my brother."'"

> a. **Surely the fear of God is not in this place**: This was Abraham's excuse for his sinful deception, but the real problem was that the **fear of God** wasn't in Abraham. If he really respected the LORD, His commandments, His promises, and His protection, then Abraham would have never trusted in his *own* efforts to keep his family safe and together.
>
> b. **Indeed she is truly my sister**: This was another attempt to justify his lie, by saying it was really the truth. But a half-truth, said with intent to deceive, is always a whole lie.
>
> c. **When God called me to wander from my father's house**: This was an indirect way of blaming God for the problem. Abraham claimed that God sent him out on this dangerous journey upon which Abraham had to protect himself.
>
> > i. "There is a terrible meaning in this verb *wander* which Abraham uses. The Hebrew word occurs exactly fifty times in Scripture and never in a good sense. It is used of animals going astray, of a drunken man reeling, or staggering, of sinful seduction, of a prophet's lies causing the people to err, of the path of a lying heart. Six other words are translated *wander*, any one of which Abraham might have used, but he used the worst word available." (Barnhouse)
> >
> > ii. "Abraham should have said: 'Forgive me, Abimelech, for dishonoring both you and my God. My selfish cowardice overwhelmed me, and

I denied my God by fearing that He who called me could not take care of me. He is not as your gods of wood and stone. He is the God of glory. He is the living God, the Creator, the most High God, possessor of heaven and earth. He told me He would be my shield and my exceeding great reward, and supplier of all my needs… In sinning against Him, I sinned against you. Forgive me, Abimelech.'" (Barnhouse)

3. (14-18) Abimelech's gift recompenses Sarah, and Abraham prays for him.

Then Abimelech took sheep, oxen, and male and female servants, and gave *them* **to Abraham; and he restored Sarah his wife to him. And Abimelech said, "See, my land is before you; dwell where it pleases you." Then to Sarah he said, "Behold, I have given your brother a thousand** *pieces* **of silver; indeed this vindicates you before all who** *are* **with you and before everybody." Thus she was reproved. So Abraham prayed to God; and God healed Abimelech, his wife, and his female servants. Then they bore** *children***; for the LORD had closed up all the wombs of the house of Abimelech because of Sarah, Abraham's wife.**

a. **Abimelech took sheep, oxen, and male and female servants, and gave them to Abraham**: In showing such generosity to Abraham, Abimelech was essentially heaping coals of fire on Abraham's head (as in Romans 12:20). This was somewhat backwards; Abraham should have given gifts to Abimelech because Abraham was in the wrong.

i. Also, it is interesting to see that Abraham *accepted* these gifts when he had refused gifts from a pagan king previously (Genesis 14:21-24), because he wanted no one to think a man had made him rich. Here, because of Abraham's compromise, he found it hard to reclaim the same high moral ground.

b. **I have given your brother a thousand pieces of silver**: We can imagine the irony in Abimelech's voice when he referred to Abraham as Sarah's **brother**.

c. **Thus she was reproved**: The ancient Hebrew word for **reproved** is *yakach*. It has the idea of "set right," so it is debatable if Sarah was *set right* by Abimelech's rebuke, or if she was *found to be right* because of her humble submission in this occasion. In a sense, both were true.

Genesis 21 – The Birth of Isaac

A. The birth of Isaac.

1. (1) God fulfills His promise to Abraham and Sarah.

And the LORD visited Sarah as He had said, and the LORD did for Sarah as He had spoken.

> a. **The LORD visited Sarah as He had said**: It took a long time (25 years) for this promise to come to pass, but God was faithful to His promise. God's promises never fail.
>
> b. **As He had spoken**: The promise of a son was not fulfilled because Abraham was perfect in his obedience, but because God was faithful to His Word.
>
>> i. Some promises of God are conditional and depend on something we must do. Other promises of God are unconditional, and God will fulfill them not because of what we do, but because of who He is.

2. (2-7) The child is named Isaac.

For Sarah conceived and bore Abraham a son in his old age, at the set time of which God had spoken to him. And Abraham called the name of his son who was born to him– whom Sarah bore to him– Isaac. Then Abraham circumcised his son Isaac when he was eight days old, as God had commanded him. Now Abraham was one hundred years old when his son Isaac was born to him. And Sarah said, "God has made me laugh, and all who hear will laugh with me." She also said, "Who would have said to Abraham that Sarah would nurse children? For I have borne him a son in his old age."

> a. **Abraham called the name of his son who was born to him; whom Sarah bore to him; Isaac**: Originally, the name **Isaac** was something of a rebuke of the laughter of Abraham and Sarah (Genesis 17:17-19 and 18:12-15), but God turned a gentle rebuke into an occasion for joy.

b. **Isaac:** Isaac became a wonderful type or picture of the Messiah to come, Jesus Christ.

- Both were specially promised sons.
- Both conceptions were miraculous.
- Both were born after a period of delay.
- Both mothers were given assurance by truth of God's omnipotence (Genesis 18:13-14; Luke 1:34, 37).
- Both were given names rich with meaning before they were born.
- Both births occurred at God's appointed time (Genesis 21:2; Galatians 4:4).
- Both births were accompanied by great joy (Genesis 21:6; Luke 1:46-47; 2:10-11).

B. The conflict between Ishmael and Isaac.

1. (8-11) Sarah wants Abraham to cast out both Hagar and Ishmael.

So the child grew and was weaned. And Abraham made a great feast on the same day that Isaac was weaned. And Sarah saw the son of Hagar the Egyptian, whom she had borne to Abraham, scoffing. Therefore she said to Abraham, "Cast out this bondwoman and her son; for the son of this bondwoman shall not be heir with my son, *namely* with Isaac." And the matter was very displeasing in Abraham's sight because of his son.

a. **The child grew and was weaned:** Some ancients say children were not weaned until 12 years of age and some say five years, but the most reliable research indicates an age of three. Isaac was young.

b. **And Sarah saw the son of Hagar... scoffing:** This conflict between the two sons was almost inevitable, even though they were approximately 13 years apart in age. Abraham found it hard to agree with Sarah's complaint, when he did not want to reject his son through Hagar, Ishmael.

i. Notice the conflict came *from* Ishmael unto Isaac. Ishmael was the one **scoffing** at Isaac. In Galatians 4:22-29, the Apostle Paul used this conflict as an illustration of the conflict between those born of the promise and those born of the flesh.

ii. In Galatians 4, the Jewish legalists who troubled the Galatians protested *they* were children of Abraham and thus blessed. Paul admitted they were children of Abraham, but they were like Ishmael, not Isaac! The legalists claimed Abraham as their father. Paul asked who was their *mother*, Hagar or Sarah? Ishmael was born of a slave, and born according to the flesh. Isaac was born of a freewoman, and born according to promise. Even so, the legalists promoted a relationship with God based in bondage and according to the flesh. The true gospel of grace offers liberty in Jesus Christ and is a promise received by faith.

iii. Even as Ishmael and his descendants have persecuted Isaac and his descendants, we should not be surprised that the modern-day people who follow God, yet in reliance upon human strength and wisdom (the flesh), do in fact persecute those who follow God in faith through the promise.

2. (12-14) Under God's instruction, Abraham puts out Hagar and Ishmael.

But God said to Abraham, "Do not let it be displeasing in your sight because of the lad or because of your bondwoman. Whatever Sarah has said to you, listen to her voice; for in Isaac your seed shall be called. Yet I will also make a nation of the son of the bondwoman, because he *is* your seed." So Abraham rose early in the morning, and took bread and a skin of water; and putting *it* on her shoulder, he gave *it* and the boy to Hagar, and sent her away. Then she departed and wandered in the Wilderness of Beersheba.

a. **Whatever Sarah has said to you, listen to her voice**: Perhaps Abraham did not want to give up Ishmael because he considered the son of Hagar something of a backup plan. If something should happen to Isaac, there would always be Ishmael. God did not want Abraham to trust in a backup son or in a backup plan. God wanted Abraham to trust in Him.

i. Abraham might have been tempted to reject Sarah's counsel just because it was Sarah who offered it. Instead he sought the Lord in the matter, did what Sarah suggested, and did so apparently without feeling he merely gave in to Sarah's demands.

b. **Sent her away**: God's solution was clear – get rid of the son of the flesh. There was to be no reconciliation with the flesh, no peaceful coexistence. The son of the flesh must simply be put away forever.

i. The solution is the same in our own battle between trusting in the flesh and trusting in the Holy Spirit: *cast out this bondwoman and her son*. Law and grace cannot live together as principles for our Christian life, and there is no question we belong to the free, not the bondwoman.

c. **Then she departed and wandered in the Wilderness of Beersheba**: It may have seemed ruthless of Abraham to do this, but it was exactly what God wanted, and exactly what needed to happen.

i. Flesh and blood do not make the strongest bond God wants us to honor. There are circumstances where we can do nothing other than put away family for the glory of God.

ii. God wants us to be ruthless with the flesh in the same manner: *And those who are Christ's have crucified the flesh with its passions and desires* (Galatians 5:24).

d. **Took bread and a skin of water**: Abraham was a wealthy man and could certainly afford to give them more supplies, even giving them a donkey or several pack animals. Yet Abraham realized that without God's help, no matter what he gave them, it would not be enough. But *with* God, things would turn out all right.

3. (15-18) God preserves Ishmael and Hagar in the desert.

And the water in the skin was used up, and she placed the boy under one of the shrubs. Then she went and sat down across from *him* at a distance of about a bowshot; for she said to herself, "Let me not see the death of the boy." So she sat opposite *him*, and lifted her voice and wept. And God heard the voice of the lad. Then the angel of God called to Hagar out of heaven, and said to her, "What ails you, Hagar? Fear not, for God has heard the voice of the lad where he is. Arise, lift up the lad and hold him with your hand, for I will make him a great nation."

a. **The water in the skin was used up**: As Hagar and Ishmael traveled away from Abraham, their supplies eventually ran out. Their water **was used up** and Hagar left Ishmael under the shade of **one of the shrubs**, expecting their soon death in the wilderness.

i. "Behold the compassion of a mother for her child expiring with thirst, and remember that such a compassion ought all Christians to feel towards souls that are perishing for lack of Christ, perishing eternally, perishing without hope of salvation." (Spurgeon)

b. **God heard the voice of the lad**: As Hagar **lifted her voice and wept**, God answered. Curiously, God answered in response to **the voice of the lad** instead of specifically to Hagar's weeping. In some way, Ishmael cried out for mercy and help.

c. **Fear not, for God has heard the voice of the lad where he is**: Despite the desperate problem in the wilderness, God's promise gave Hagar and Ishmael reason to **fear not**. God showed special favor to Ishmael because he was a descendant of Abraham.

d. **I will make him a great nation**: Though Ishmael was not the son to receive the covenant promise, God was not *against* him. The descendants of Ishmael became **a great nation**, the Arabic people.

4. (19-21) God's provision for Hagar and Ishmael.

Then God opened her eyes, and she saw a well of water. And she went and filled the skin with water, and gave the lad a drink. So God was with the lad; and he grew and dwelt in the wilderness, and became an archer. He dwelt in the Wilderness of Paran; and his mother took a wife for him from the land of Egypt.

a. **Then God opened her eyes, and she saw a well of water**: Whether the miracle was in the creation of a water source or the revealing of an existing water source, God provided for Hagar and Ishmael.

i. Spurgeon explained the likeness between Hagar and the one who needs God. "As in Hagar's case, *the supply of their necessities is close at hand*: the well is near. Secondly, it often happens that that supply *is as much there as if it had been provided for them and for them only*, as this well seemed to have been. And, thirdly, *no great exertion is needed to procure from the supply already made by God all that we want*. She filled her bottle with water — a joyful task to her; and she gave the lad drink."

b. **So God was with the lad**: The idea is emphasized that God was not against Ishmael and his descendants. God **was with** Ishmael, and had a promise for his future.

C. Abraham makes a covenant with a Philistine king.

1. (22-24) Abraham makes a no-hostility treaty with Abimelech.

And it came to pass at that time that Abimelech and Phichol, the commander of his army, spoke to Abraham, saying, "God is with you in all that you do. Now therefore, swear to me by God that you will not deal falsely with me, with my offspring, or with my posterity; but that according to the kindness that I have done to you, you will do to me and to the land in which you have dwelt." And Abraham said, "I will swear."

a. **Abimelech... spoke to Abraham**: This was probably not the same Abimelech of Genesis 20. **Abimelech** was the *title* of a ruler among the Canaanites, not a specific name. This ruler and **Phichol, the commander of his army**, met with Abraham.

b. **God is with you in all that you do**: Abimelech noticed this because of Abraham's integrity and because of the blessing evident in his life. Abraham had the greatest of all blessings: the presence of God in his life.

i. "I think that the greatest blessing God ever gives to a man is his own presence. If I had my choice of all the blessings of this life, I certainly should not ask for wealth, for that can bring no ease; and I certainly should not ask for popularity, for there is no rest to the man upon whose words men constantly wait, and it is a hard task one has to perform in such a case as that; but I should choose, as my highest honor, to have God always with me." (Spurgeon)

c. **Swear to me by God that you will not deal falsely with me**: Because God had so blessed Abraham, he was a man of great wealth, influence, and power. Abimelech knew that it was important to have Abraham in favor towards him and his descendants. Abraham agreed, saying "**I will swear.**"

2. (25-31) In return for the treaty, Abraham clears up a dispute about an important well.

Then Abraham rebuked Abimelech because of a well of water which Abimelech's servants had seized. And Abimelech said, "I do not know who has done this thing; you did not tell me, nor had I heard *of it* **until today." So Abraham took sheep and oxen and gave them to Abimelech, and the two of them made a covenant. And Abraham set seven ewe lambs of the flock by themselves. Then Abimelech asked Abraham, "What** *is the meaning of these* **seven ewe lambs which you have set by themselves?" And he said, "You will take** *these* **seven ewe lambs from my hand, that they may be my witness that I have dug this well." Therefore he called that place Beersheba, because the two of them swore an oath there.**

a. **Then Abraham rebuked Abimelech because of a well**: Because Canaan had no significant rivers and a great reliance upon rain, **a well** was an important and strategic property. Apparently, Abraham was in possession of **a well of water** that **Abimelech's servants had seized**. The man of faith did not simply accept this wrong; he **rebuked Abimelech because of a well**.

b. **Abraham took sheep and oxen and gave them to Abimelech, and the two of them made a covenant**: The **sheep and oxen** were probably used as sacrifices to make or cut the covenant, as in Genesis 15:7-21.

c. **You will take these seven ewe lambs from my hand**: The **seven ewe lambs** were special gifts from Abraham to Abimelech to show favor and offer some compensation for his loss of access to the well. Abraham understood his own property rights, but was not greedy or miserly. The acceptance of the seven lambs was Abimelech's recognition that Abraham had **dug this well** and it belonged to him.

d. **Therefore he called that place Beersheba**: This was a descriptive name. **Beersheba** means *watering place, well of underground water*. Some understand the Biblical name **Beersheba** as *well of seven* or *well of the oath*. **Beersheba** would become a notable place in Israel's continuing history, and continues today as an important city in modern Israel (Beer-Sheva).

- Abraham's son Isaac dug this well again, and he built an altar in Beersheba (Genesis 26:23–33).
- Abraham's grandson Jacob stopped in Beersheba as he left the promised land (Genesis 28:10–15, 46:1–7).
- When Israel took possession of the promised land, Beersheba became the territory of the tribe of Simeon and Judah (Joshua 15:28, 19:2).
- Samuel's sons were judges in Beersheba (I Samuel 8:2).
- King Saul fortified Beersheba in his battles against the Amalekites (I Samuel 14:48, 15:2–9).
- The prophet Elijah found refuge at Beersheba when Jezebel ordered him killed (I Kings 19:3).
- The prophet Amos mentioned Beersheba in regard to idolatry (Amos 5:5 and 8:14).

i. The phrase *from Dan to Beersheba* would later become a proverbial phrase describing the entire land of Israel, from north (Dan) to south (Beersheba). This is seen in passages such as Judges 20:1, 1 Samuel 3:20, 2 Samuel 3:10, 1 Kings 4:25, and many others.

3. (32-34) Abraham calls on the name of the LORD.

Thus they made a covenant at Beersheba. So Abimelech rose with Phichol, the commander of his army, and they returned to the land of the Philistines. Then *Abraham* planted a tamarisk tree in Beersheba, and there called on the name of the LORD, the Everlasting God. And Abraham stayed in the land of the Philistines many days.

a. **Abraham planted a tamarisk tree in Beersheba**: After the successful treaty, Abraham did something that looked forward to coming decades and generations. A **tamarisk tree** takes a long time to grow, but Abraham knew God had promised the land to him and his descendants forever.

b. **Called on the name of the LORD, the Everlasting God**: Even through this time of conflict in his family and among his neighbors, Abraham kept a real, live walk with God. Conflict did not drive him away from God, but he allowed it to push him closer to the LORD.

Genesis 22 – Abraham Is Willing to Offer Isaac

A. God's command to Abraham and his response.

1. (1-2) God tests the faith of Abraham.

Now it came to pass after these things that God tested Abraham, and said to him, "Abraham!" And he said, "Here I am." Then He said, "Take now your son, your only *son* Isaac, whom you love, and go to the land of Moriah, and offer him there as a burnt offering on one of the mountains of which I shall tell you."

> a. **God tested Abraham**: This was not so much a test to *produce* faith, as it was a test to *reveal* faith. God built Abraham slowly, piece by piece, year by year, into a man of faith. This test would reveal some of the faith God had built into Abraham.
>
>> i. "I cannot imagine a greater test than that which the Lord applied to Abraham. The Jews usually say that Abraham was tried ten times. Surely on this occasion he was tried ten times in one." (Spurgeon)
>
> b. **Here I am**: Abraham's quick answer to the call is a wonderful example of how the man or woman of faith should respond to God. When Abraham said, "**Here I am,**" it meant that he was ready to be taught, ready to obey, ready to surrender, and he was ready to be examined by God.
>
> c. **Take now your son, your only son Isaac**: Significantly, God called Isaac **your only son Isaac**, when in fact Abraham had another son, Ishmael. Since Ishmael was put away from Abraham's family (Genesis 21:8-14), as far as God's covenant was concerned, Abraham had only one son.
>
> d. **Your only son Isaac, whom you love**: Counting from Genesis 1:1, this is the first mention of **love** in the Bible. This first mention comes in the context of the love between father and son, connected with the idea of the sacrificial offering of the son.
>
>> i. Every phrase of God's command to Abraham was like a knife.

- Take now your son.
- Your only son Isaac.
- Whom you love.
- Offer him there.
- As a burnt offering.

e. **Offer him there as a burnt offering**: God told Abraham to offer him as a **burnt offering**. This was not an offering that was burned alive, but one with the life first taken by sacrifice and then the body completely burnt before the LORD.

i. Abraham lived as a sojourner, a pilgrim, in the land of Canaan. The priests of many of the Canaanite gods said their gods demanded human sacrifice. The people of Canaan found nothing especially strange about human sacrifice, but Abraham had believed Yahweh was different.

ii. With this command, Abraham might have wondered if Yahweh, the God of the covenant and creator of heaven and earth, was like the pagan gods the Canaanites and others worshipped. By the end of this story, Abraham knew that God was *not* like the pagan gods that demanded human sacrifice. In truth, He was just the opposite.

iii. How would we react if God told us to do such a thing? Many years ago, Jack Smith, a columnist for the L.A. Times, wrote about this Biblical incident. He said he would have told God to mind his own business. That's what the world always says to God.

iv. It can't be denied that either out of madness or demonic deception, some have done terrible things and justified it along these lines. In 1993, a man named Andrew Cate was sentenced to 60 years in prison after being convicted of fatally shooting his 2-year-old daughter, then walking naked through his neighborhood carrying her body. Cate claimed he was acting out the biblical story of Abraham and Isaac, and God would do a miracle to win his brother to Christianity. Cate believed God would miraculously stop him at the last moment before killing his daughter. The man was obviously deranged. What Abraham did was something completely unique in God's redemptive history, given for a specific purpose once-for-all fulfilled. There is no way God would ever direct someone to do this same thing today. As will be shortly demonstrated, a significant point of this story is the demonstration that God *did not*, in fact, want this kind of sacrifice.

f. **Offer him there as a burnt offering**: This test was difficult in yet another aspect, because it seemed to contradict the previous promise of God. God had already promised *in Isaac your seed shall be called* (Genesis 21:12). It seemed strange and contradictory to kill the son who was promised to carry on the covenant when it had not yet been fulfilled in him. It seemed as if God commanded Abraham to kill the very promise God made to him.

> i. Abraham had to learn the difference between trusting the promise and trusting the Promiser. We can put God's promise before God Himself and feel it is our responsibility to bring the promise to pass, even if we have to disobey God to do it. Trust the Promiser no matter what, and the promise will be taken care of.

> ii. "Brethren, there are times with us when we are called to a course of action which looks as though it would jeopardise our highest hopes… It is neither your business nor mine to fulfill God's promise, nor to do the least wrong to produce the greatest good. To do evil that good may come is false morality, and wicked policy. For us is duty, for God is the fulfillment of his own promise, and the preservation of our usefulness." (Spurgeon)

e. **To the land of Moriah… on one of the mountains of which I shall tell you**: There was a specific *place* God commanded Abraham to go, a particular spot where this would happen. God carefully directed each detail of this drama.

2. (3) Abraham's immediate response of faith.

So Abraham rose early in the morning and saddled his donkey, and took two of his young men with him, and Isaac his son; and he split the wood for the burnt offering, and arose and went to the place of which God had told him.

a. **So Abraham rose early**: There is no sign of hesitation on Abraham's part. Abraham **rose early in the morning** to do this. It must have been a sleepless night for Abraham.

> i. Abraham's obedience showed that he trusted God, even *when he did not understand*. Sometimes we say, "I'm not going to obey or believe until I understand it all," but that is to put myself on an equal standing with God.

> ii. Abraham's obedience showed that he didn't *debate or seek counsel from others*. He knew what to do and refused to use stalling tactics.

> iii. Abraham's obedience showed that he trusted God, *even when he did not feel like it*. There is not a line in this text about how Abraham felt, not because he didn't feel, but because he walked by faith, not feelings.

iv. "But there is not a word of argument; not one solitary question that even looks like hesitation. 'God is God,' he seems to say, and it is not for me to ask him why, or seek a reason for his bidding. He has said it: 'I will do it.'" (Spurgeon)

v. God trained Abraham over many decades, bringing him to this place of great trust. In just the last chapter, God asked Abraham to give up Ishmael in a less severe way. God used that, and everything else, to train up Abraham and build great faith in him.

b. **Saddled his donkey**: The phrasing suggests that Abraham did this work personally; he **saddled his donkey** and **he split the wood**. Though he had plenty of servants to do this for him, Abraham did it himself, even in his old age. Perhaps this was because he was filled with nervous energy.

i. "He was a sheik and a mighty man in his camp, but he became a wood-splitter, thinking no work menial if done for God, and reckoning the work too sacred for other hands. With splitting heart he cleaves the wood. Wood for the burning of his heir! Wood for the sacrifice of his own dear child!" (Spurgeon)

c. **Went to the place of which God had told him**: In wonderful, trusting obedience, Abraham went right to the spot **which God had told him**. He did this even though it would have been easier in Abraham's eyes if God had asked Abraham to lay his own life down instead of the life of his son.

B. Abraham's offering of Isaac.

1. (4-8) Abraham journeys to the place of sacrifice with Isaac.

Then on the third day Abraham lifted his eyes and saw the place afar off. And Abraham said to his young men, "Stay here with the donkey; the lad and I will go yonder and worship, and we will come back to you." So Abraham took the wood of the burnt offering and laid it on Isaac his son; and he took the fire in his hand, and a knife, and the two of them went together. But Isaac spoke to Abraham his father and said, "My father!" And he said, "Here I am, my son." Then he said, "Look, the fire and the wood, but where is the lamb for a burnt offering?" And Abraham said, "My son, God will provide for Himself the lamb for a burnt offering." So the two of them went together.

a. **On the third day**: Abraham came to the place on **the third day**. The region of Moriah is associated with Mount Moriah, which is modern-day Jerusalem (2 Chronicles 3:1).

i. Abraham had three long days to think over what God commanded him to do. This made the test even more severe. "To be burnt quick to death upon the blazing fagot is comparatively an easy martyrdom, but to hang in chains roasting at a slow fire, to have the heart hour by hour pressed as in a vice, this it is that trieth faith; and this it was that Abraham endured through three long days" (Spurgeon).

b. **I will go yonder and worship**: This is the first use of the word **worship** in reference to God in the Bible. The Hebrew word *shachah* simply means, *to bow down*. While Abraham and Isaac did not go to the mount to have a time of joyful praise, they did go to bow down to the LORD.

c. **And we will come back to you**: Abraham was full of faith when he spoke to the young men who were with him. He believed that both he and Issac would return; that **we will come back**, and he told them so.

i. This does not mean that Abraham somehow knew this was only a test and God would not really require this of him. Instead, Abraham's faith was in understanding that should he kill Isaac, God would raise him from the dead, because God had promised Isaac would carry on the line of blessing and the covenant.

ii. He knew *in Isaac your seed shall be called* (Genesis 21:12), and Isaac had yet to have any children. God had to let him live *at least* long enough to have children. "If Isaac shall die, there is no other descendant left, and no probabilities of any other to succeed him; the light of Abraham will be quenched, and his name forgotten" (Spurgeon).

iii. Hebrews 11:17-19 clearly explains this principle: *By faith Abraham, when he was tested, offered up Isaac, and he who had received the promises offered up his only begotten son, of whom it was said, "In Isaac your seed shall be called," concluding that God was able to raise him up, even from the dead, from which he also received him in a figurative sense.*

iv. Abraham knew anything was possible, but it was *impossible* that God would break His promise. He knew God was not a liar. To this point in Biblical history, we have no record of anyone being raised from the dead, so Abraham had no precedent for this faith, apart from God's promise. Yet Abraham knew God was able. God could do it.

d. **Abraham took the wood of the burnt offering and laid it on Isaac his son**: Isaac received the wood for his own sacrifice from his father, and he carried it to the hill of sacrifice.

e. **He took the fire in his hand, and a knife**: Abraham took the knife up the hill. He didn't leave it behind or pretend to forget it. This was a further demonstration of his obedience, and of his trust that if necessary, God would raise Isaac from the dead.

i. "That knife was cutting into his own heart all the while, yet he took it. Unbelief would have left the knife at home, but genuine faith takes it." (Spurgeon)

f. **The two of them went together**: This literally means *the two of them went in agreement*. Isaac did this knowingly and willingly. The phrase is repeated twice for emphasis.

g. **My son, God will provide for Himself the lamb for a burnt offering**: Abraham knew God would provide a sacrifice, but where? Where was the lamb? That question had been asked by all the faithful, from Isaac to Moses to David to Isaiah, all the way to the time of John the Baptist when he declares: *Behold! The Lamb of God who takes away the sin of the world!* (John 1:29)

i. At this time, Abraham didn't know *how* God would provide. He still trusted in the ability of God to raise Isaac from the dead, but he wouldn't stop trusting just because he didn't know *how* God would fulfill His promise.

ii. We have a remarkable picture of the work of Jesus at the cross, thousands of years before it happened. The son of promise willingly went to be sacrificed in obedience to his father, carrying the wood of his sacrifice up the hill, all with full confidence in the promise of resurrection.

2. (9) Isaac willingly lies down on the altar.

Then they came to the place of which God had told him. And Abraham built an altar there and placed the wood in order; and he bound Isaac his son and laid him on the altar, upon the wood.

a. **Then they came to the place**: Apparently, even on Mount Moriah there was a specific place God told Abraham to stop, because this was the **place** to do this.

b. **Abraham built an altar there and placed the wood in order; and he bound Isaac**: At this time, Abraham was more than 100 years old and Isaac would have been able to escape his coming death had he chosen to. Yet he submitted to his father perfectly. In remembering Abraham's faith, we should never forget *Isaac's* faith.

i. Some Jewish commentators think Isaac was in his thirties at the time of this event. "The younger man, perhaps five-and-twenty — so Josephus thinks — possibly thirty-three years of age, and, if so, very manifestly the type of Christ, who was about that age when he came to die" (Spurgeon).

c. **Upon the wood**: As an obedient son, Isaac laid down on the wood, ready to be sacrificed.

3. (10-14) God's merciful reprieve.

And Abraham stretched out his hand and took the knife to slay his son. But the Angel of the LORD called to him from heaven and said, "Abraham, Abraham!" So he said, "Here I am." And He said, "Do not lay your hand on the lad, or do anything to him; for now I know that you fear God, since you have not withheld your son, your only *son*, from Me." Then Abraham lifted his eyes and looked, and there behind *him* was a ram caught in a thicket by its horns. So Abraham went and took the ram, and offered it up for a burnt offering instead of his son. And Abraham called the name of the place, The-LORD-Will-Provide; as it is said to this day, "In the Mount of The LORD it shall be provided."

a. **Abraham stretched out his hand and took the knife to slay his son**: We must believe Abraham was completely willing to plunge the knife into Isaac, because his faith was in God's ability to raise Isaac from the dead, not in God's desire to stop the sacrifice. Abraham didn't think this was a drama or a mere ceremony.

i. "Notice the obedience of this friend of God – it was no playing at giving up his son: it was really doing it. It was no talking about what he could do, and would do, perhaps, but his faith was practical and heroic." (Spurgeon)

ii. One may say, "It's not fair or right. God told Abraham to do something and then told him not to do it. If God really wanted to test Abraham, He should have made him plunge the knife into his son's chest."

iii. Yet God often takes the *will* for the *deed* with his people. When He finds them truly *willing* to make the sacrifice He demands, He often does not require it. This is how we can be martyrs without ever dying for Jesus. We live the *life* of a martyr right now.

iv. But, "Often there are believers who wonder how they may know the will of God. We believe that ninety per cent of the knowing of the will of God consists in willingness to do it before it is known" (Barnhouse).

b. **Do not lay your hand on the lad, or do anything to him**: With this, God emphatically showed Abraham that He was *not* like the pagan gods worshipped by the Canaanites and others, gods that demanded human sacrifice and were pleased by it. God strongly and clearly demonstrated that He did *not* want human sacrifice.

c. **You have not withheld your son, your only son, from Me**: Abraham displayed his heart towards God in that he was willing to give up his only son. God displays His heart towards us in the same way, by giving His *only begotten Son* (John 3:16).

> i. When God asked Abraham for the ultimate demonstration of love and commitment, He asked for Abraham's son. When God the Father wanted to show us the ultimate demonstration of His love and commitment to us, He gave us His Son. We can say to the LORD, "Now I know that You love me, seeing You have not withheld Your Son, Your only Son from me."

d. **Abraham went and took the ram, and offered it up for a burnt offering instead of his son**: All the while, God still required a sacrifice. God didn't call off the sacrifice. Instead, He required that there be a substitute provided by God Himself.

e. **Abraham called the name of the place**: The naming of the place was significant. Abraham called it **The LORD Will Provide** (*Jehovah Jireh*); **In this mount, it shall be provided**.

> i. Abraham didn't name the place in reference to what *he* experienced. He didn't name it *Mount Trial* or *Mount Agony* or *Mount Obedience*. Instead, he named the hill in reference to what *God* did; he named it *Mount Provision*. He named it knowing God would provide the ultimate sacrifice for salvation on that hill someday.

> ii. Earlier, Isaac asked his father where the sacrifice was, and Abraham answered, *God will provide for Himself the lamb* (Genesis 22:8). In naming the place *Jehovah Jireh*, "Abraham says nothing about himself at all, but the praise is unto God, who sees and is seen; the record is, 'Jehovah will provide.' I like that self-ignoring; I pray that we, also, may have so much strength of faith that self may go to the wall" (Spurgeon).

> iii. **As it is said to this day**: Apparently, Moses meant even in his own day, men looked at that hill and said, **"In the Mount of the LORD it shall be provided."** Abraham, and later Moses, recognized that God *did* **provide**, and it pointed to the ultimate sacrifice when God would provide Himself. "God provided a ram instead of Isaac. This was sufficient for the occasion as a type; but that which was typified by the ram is infinitely more glorious. In order to save us God provided *God*. I cannot put it more simply. He did not provide an angel, nor a mere man, but God himself" (Spurgeon).

iv. This is also a prophecy of Jesus' rising from the dead on the *third day*, as 1 Corinthians 15:4 says *He rose again the third day according to the Scriptures*. This is one place where the Old Testament indicates the Messiah would rise again the third day. It says so through the picture of Isaac. Isaac was "reckoned dead" by Abraham as soon as God gave the command, and Isaac was "made alive" (risen) three days later.

v. Isaac's life as a picture of Jesus becomes even clearer:

- Both were loved by their father.
- Both offered themselves willingly.
- Both carried wood up the hill of their sacrifice.
- Both were sacrificed on the same hill.
- Both were delivered from death on the third day.

4. (15-19) God reconfirms His promise to Abraham in light of his faith.

Then the Angel of the Lord called to Abraham a second time out of heaven, and said: "By Myself I have sworn, says the Lord, because you have done this thing, and have not withheld your son, your only son–blessing I will bless you, and multiplying I will multiply your descendants as the stars of the heaven and as the sand which is on the seashore; and your descendants shall possess the gate of their enemies. In your seed all the nations of the earth shall be blessed, because you have obeyed My voice." So Abraham returned to his young men, and they rose and went together to Beersheba; and Abraham dwelt at Beersheba.

a. **The Angel of the Lord called to Abraham**: This would seem to be the voice of God the Son Himself, the unique *messenger* or **Angel of the Lord**. The message following seems to be in the first person (**By Myself I have sworn**). Jesus the Messiah, God the Son, was uniquely present at this remarkable event.

b. **You have done this thing, and have not withheld your son, your only son**: For the third time, God refers to Isaac as Abraham's **only son** (previously in Genesis 22:2 and 22:12).

c. **Blessing I will bless you**: Abraham knew the **blessing** that comes to those who trust God's promise, and trust it so completely that they will take action on that belief. Trusting in God's power to raise his only son from the dead, Abraham received this great **blessing**.

d. **I will multiply your descendants**: Abraham's obedience was based on trust in God's promise to bring descendants through Isaac (Genesis 21:12). Therefore, God repeated and emphasized that promise after Abraham's remarkable obedience.

e. **As the stars of the heaven and as the sand which is on the seashore**: According to Morris, by rough calculations, the number of stars in the sky and grains of sand on the seashore are the same: 10 to the 25th power.

f. **In your seed all the nations of the earth shall be blessed, because you have obeyed My voice**: The promise to bring forth the Messiah from Abraham's lineage was also repeated (earlier in Genesis 12:3). The Messiah – **the only son** of God the Father – would fulfill this promise of blessing to **all the nations of the earth**.

5. (20-24) The listing of Nahor's family.

Now it came to pass after these things that it was told Abraham, saying, "Indeed Milcah also has borne children to your brother Nahor: Huz his firstborn, Buz his brother, Kemuel the father of Aram, Chesed, Hazo, Pildash, Jidlaph, and Bethuel." And Bethuel begot Rebekah. These eight Milcah bore to Nahor, Abraham's brother. His concubine, whose name was Reumah, also bore Tebah, Gaham, Thahash, and Maachah.

a. **Milcah also has borne children to your brother Nahor**: When Abraham left Ur of the Chaldeans, he also left his brother **Milcah** (Genesis 11:27-29). Here we learn of the children born to Abraham's brother, back in Ur.

b. **Bethuel begot Rebekah**: One son of Milcah named **Bethuel** had a daughter named **Rebekah**. She is mentioned because she will later become the wife of Abraham's son Isaac.

c. **His concubine**: This is the first mention of a **concubine** in the Bible. In addition to his wife **Milcah**, Nahor also took a concubine named **Reumah**.

i. Matthew Poole gave a good explanation of a **concubine**: "A *concubine* was an inferior kind of wife, taken according to the common practice of those times, subject to the authority of the principal wife, and whose children had no right of inheritance, but were endowed with gifts."

ii. This taking of an additional wife or concubine was recognized as legal and was culturally accepted in the ancient world, including the world Abraham and the patriarchs lived in. However, it was never in God's plan. We know this because of the pattern given in Genesis 2:24, that *a man should leave his father and mother and be joined to his wife, and they shall become one flesh*. In speaking upon the Genesis 2:24 principle, Jesus clearly told us that this was God's intention *at the beginning* (Matthew 19:4-6). God never gave a specific command against polygamy until the New Testament, but God showed in principle that it was never His heart. In addition, whenever we see the family life of a polygamous household in the Bible, those families are marked by chaos and conflict.

Genesis 23 – Sarah Dies and Is Buried

A. The death of Sarah.

1. (1) The death of Sarah.

Sarah lived one hundred and twenty-seven years; *these were* the years of the life of Sarah.

> a. **Sarah lived one hundred and twenty-seven years**: Sarah is the only woman in the Bible whose age at death is recorded. This gives us some measure of how highly she is regarded in the Bible.
>
> b. **The life of Sarah**: Nowhere in the Bible are we told to look to Mary the mother of Jesus as an example of a godly woman. Twice we are told to look to Sarah as such an example (Isaiah 51:1-2 and 1 Peter 3:3-6).

2. (2) Abraham's mourning.

So Sarah died in Kirjath Arba (that is, Hebron) in the land of Canaan, and Abraham came to mourn for Sarah and to weep for her.

> a. **Abraham came to mourn for Sarah**: Abraham felt his loss of Sarah deeply and wasn't afraid to mourn, though he did not sorrow as those without hope (1 Thessalonians 4:13).
>
>> i. "That is, he set himself deliberately to all the functions of a mourner." (Boice)
>
> b. **And to weep for her**: Abraham's mourning was demonstrated in an appropriate way. The man of great faith, the friend of God, wept for the loss of Sarah's companionship. There was nothing weak or unbelieving about the tears of this man of faith.
>
>> i. "To weep for a loved one is to show that we have been close, that the loss is keenly felt, that death is an enemy, and that sin has brought this sad punishment upon the human race." (Boice)

B. Abraham buys land for Sarah's burial.

1. (3-9) Abraham speaks with the sons of Heth.

Then Abraham stood up from before his dead, and spoke to the sons of Heth, saying, "I *am* a foreigner and a visitor among you. Give me property for a burial place among you, that I may bury my dead out of my sight." And the sons of Heth answered Abraham, saying to him, "Hear us, my lord: You *are* a mighty prince among us; bury your dead in the choicest of our burial places. None of us will withhold from you his burial place, that you may bury your dead." Then Abraham stood up and bowed himself to the people of the land, the sons of Heth. And he spoke with them, saying, "If it is your wish that I bury my dead out of my sight, hear me, and meet with Ephron the son of Zohar for me, that he may give me the cave of Machpelah which he has, which *is* at the end of his field. Let him give it to me at the full price, as property for a burial place among you."

a. **I am a foreigner and a sojourner among you**: Abraham did not feel this way because he came from Ur of the Chaldeans. It was because he recognized his real home was heaven. Moses knew the same, and commanded Israel to know it (Leviticus 25:23). David also knew this truth (1 Chronicles 29:14 and Psalm 39:12).

b. **Give me property for a burial place among you**: Abraham had a particular **property** in mind – **the cave of Machpelah**. It was in the land of **Ephron the son of Zohar**. In his travels around Canaan, Abraham had earlier lived in this area and here built an altar to God (Genesis 13:18). He knew this **cave** and was willing to pay **the full price** for it.

2. (10-16) Abraham negotiates with Ephron the Hittite for the land of Sarah's tomb.

Now Ephron dwelt among the sons of Heth; and Ephron the Hittite answered Abraham in the presence of the sons of Heth, all who entered at the gate of his city, saying, "No, my lord, hear me: I give you the field and the cave that is in it; I give it to you in the presence of the sons of my people. I give it to you. Bury your dead!" Then Abraham bowed himself down before the people of the land; and he spoke to Ephron in the hearing of the people of the land, saying, "If you *will give it*, please hear me. I will give you money for the field; take it from me and I will bury my dead there." And Ephron answered Abraham, saying to him, "My lord, listen to me; the land is *worth* four hundred shekels of silver. What is that between you and me? So bury your dead." And Abraham listened to Ephron; and Abraham weighed out the silver for Ephron which he had named in the hearing of the sons of Heth, four hundred shekels of silver, currency of the merchants.

a. **I give you the field and the cave**: This way of negotiating the price was typical of ancient and modern practices in that culture. As a gesture of kindness, the selling party may offer to give the property in question to the buyer, until the buyer insists on paying a price.

i. Ephron the Hittite followed the cultural customs of bargaining. First, the seller offered to *give* the item – confident that the buyer would refuse the ceremonial offer. When the buyer refused to receive it as a gift, the seller suggested a price, which he claimed was modest but was really very high. This was understood to be the starting point, and from there the bargaining began.

b. **Abraham bowed himself down to the people of the land**: Abraham showed how a follower of God should conduct business with the world: *courteously, fairly, prudently*. In not giving a counter-offer to the suggested price of **four hundred shekels of silver**, Abraham was remarkably generous in his dealings with Ephron.

i. "They who, under the sanction of religion, trample under foot the decent forms of civil respect, supposing that because they are religious, they have a right to be rude, totally mistake the spirit of Christianity." (Clarke)

3. (17-20) Abraham buys the field and buries Sarah.

So the field of Ephron which was in Machpelah, which was before Mamre, the field and the cave which was in it, and all the trees that *were* in the field, which *were* within all the surrounding borders, were deeded to Abraham as a possession in the presence of the sons of Heth, before all who went in at the gate of his city. And after this, Abraham buried Sarah his wife in the cave of the field of Machpelah, before Mamre (that is, Hebron) in the land of Canaan. So the field and the cave that is in it were deeded to Abraham by the sons of Heth as property for a burial place.

a. **Were deeded to Abraham as a possession**: The text emphasizes this property was Abraham's land by deed, not only by the promise of God. If this was the only piece of land Abraham ever owned in the land promised to him, it showed that he was a real man of faith.

b. **Abraham buried Sarah his wife in the cave of the field of Machpelah**: This is where Isaac and Ishmael buried Abraham (Genesis 25:9). Isaac and Rebekah were both buried here (Genesis 49:31). Jacob buried Leah here (Genesis 49:31), and Joseph buried Jacob here (Genesis 50:13). The cave of **Machpelah** (near **Hebron**) was the great tomb of the Patriarchs.

Genesis 24 – A Bride for Isaac

A. Abraham's commission to his servant.

1. (1-4) Abraham sends out a servant to seek out a bride for his son.

Now Abraham was old, well advanced in age; and the LORD had blessed Abraham in all things. So Abraham said to the oldest servant of his house, who ruled over all that he had, "Please, put your hand under my thigh, and I will make you swear by the LORD, the God of heaven and the God of the earth, that you will not take a wife for my son from the daughters of the Canaanites, among whom I dwell; but you shall go to my country and to my family, and take a wife for my son Isaac."

a. **The oldest servant of his house, who ruled over all that he had**: The servant named *Eliezer* held this position before (Genesis 15:2). Since he is described as **the oldest servant of his house**, this was likely Eliezer. He held a position of great honor and responsibility, managing **all that** Abraham **had**.

i. **The LORD had blessed Abraham in all things**: "That is the short history of his long life; God told him that he would bless him, and he did so. 'The Lord had blessed Abraham in all things.' What! when he commanded him to slay his son? Yes; he 'had blessed him in all things.' What! when he took away his wife Sarah? Yes, for 'the Lord had blessed Abraham in all things.' Perhaps, if his life had been without troubles, that sentence would not have been true" (Spurgeon).

b. **Put your hand under my thigh**: According to ancient custom, this described a solemn and serious oath. Abraham was extremely concerned that Isaac not be married to a Canaanite bride, making his servant **swear by the LORD, the God of heaven and the God of the earth**.

i. "The person binding himself put his hand under the thigh of the person to whom he was to be bound; *i.e.*, he put his hand on the *part* that bore the mark of *circumcision*, the sign of God's covenant… Our ideas of delicacy may revolt from the *rite* used on this occasion; but, when the nature of the covenant is considered, of which *circumcision* was the *sign*, we shall at once perceive that this rite could not be used without producing sentiments of reverence and godly fear, as the contracting party must know that the God of this covenant was a consuming fire." (Clarke)

c. **Take a wife for my son Isaac**: Abraham was clear that he did not want Isaac to have a Canaanite wife, and that the wife should be found among Abraham's ancestors in Ur of the Chaldees (**go to my country and to my family**).

2. (5-9) The mission clearly defined.

And the servant said to him, "Perhaps the woman will not be willing to follow me to this land. Must I take your son back to the land from which you came?" But Abraham said to him, "Beware that you do not take my son back there. The LORD God of heaven, who took me from my father's house and from the land of my family, and who spoke to me and swore to me, saying, 'To your descendants I give this land,' He will send His angel before you, and you shall take a wife for my son from there. And if the woman is not willing to follow you, then you will be released from this oath; only do not take my son back there." So the servant put his hand under the thigh of Abraham his master, and swore to him concerning this matter.

a. **Abraham said to him**: Apparently, Abraham anticipated that he might die while his servant was gone, so the instructions were made perfectly clear.

b. **Beware that you do not take my son back there**: Isaac, the son of promise, never once left the Promised Land. His wife was to come to *him*, as Isaac stayed in the land of Canaan. This principle was so important that if the woman would not come with the servant, it was better for Isaac to not have a wife (**only do not take my son back there**).

c. **To your descendants I give this land**: Abraham insisted on this, because God made a covenant promise to Abraham and his **descendants** that the land of Canaan was theirs. Abraham understood that the covenant promise was passed on to Isaac, not Ishmael.

B. **The servant's mission fulfilled.**

1. (10-14) Eliezer's prayer to God.

Then the servant took ten of his master's camels and departed, for all his master's goods *were in* his hand. And he arose and went to Mesopotamia,

to the city of Nahor. And he made his camels kneel down outside the city by a well of water at evening time, the time when women go out to draw *water*. Then he said, "O LORD God of my master Abraham, please give me success this day, and show kindness to my master Abraham. Behold, *here* I stand by the well of water, and the daughters of the men of the city are coming out to draw water. Now let it be that the young woman to whom I say, 'Please let down your pitcher that I may drink,' and she says, 'Drink, and I will also give your camels a drink'– *let* her *be the one* You have appointed for Your servant Isaac. And by this I will know that You have shown kindness to my master."

    a. **The servant took ten of his master's camels and departed**: Abraham's **servant** (likely Eliezer) led a large and impressive caravan. They carried such substantial riches that it could be said with poetic exaggeration, **all his master's goods were in his hand**. The journey was long. The straight-line distance from Canaan to Ur of the Chaldeans was some 500 miles (800 kilometers), but the most common route was about 900 miles (1,450 kilometers).

    b. **To the city of Nahor**: This probably refers to the place known as Ur of the Chaldees. Two men named **Nahor** were associated with this place: the grandfather of Abraham (Genesis 11:24-26) and the brother of Abraham (Genesis 11:26-29). It was **the city of Nahor** in this sense.

    c. **O LORD God of my master Abraham, please give me success this day**: As Abraham's servant arrived at his master's ancestral city, he first had a practical concern, to water **his camels**. He then had a spiritual concern, asking for God's guidance through providential circumstances.

        i. This is sometimes a bad way to discern God's will. Generally speaking, circumstances alone can be a dangerous way to discern God's will. We have a way of ignoring circumstances that speak against our desired outcome (or we attribute those circumstances to the devil), while focusing on the circumstances that speak for our desired outcome.

        ii. But in this case, Eliezer established what he would look for *before* anything happened. He wasn't making up the standard as the process unfolded.

    d. **Drink, and I will also give your camels a drink**: Abraham's servant asked God to show him the woman chosen to be Isaac's wife through an offer to provide water for his ten camels. Eliezer was wise enough to ask for a sign that was remarkable, but (in human terms) possible. He didn't tempt God by asking for fire to fall from heaven or for protection as he leapt from an unsafe height.

e. **Let her be the one**: In praying this prayer, there was a sense in which Eliezer set the odds against finding someone. It would take a remarkable woman to volunteer for this tedious task.

> i. Considering that a camel may drink up to 20 gallons, watering ten camels meant at least an hour of hard work.

f. **By this I will know**: Abraham's servant cared nothing about the woman's appearance. He wanted a woman of character, a woman whom God had chosen.

2. (15) God answers the servant's prayer before it was finished.

And it happened, before he had finished speaking, that behold, Rebekah, who was born to Bethuel, son of Milcah, the wife of Nahor, Abraham's brother, came out with her pitcher on her shoulder.

a. **Before he had finished speaking**: Isaiah 65:24 speaks of this kind of gracious answer to prayer: *It shall come to pass that before they call, I will answer; and while they are still speaking, I will hear.*

b. **Rebekah... came out with her pitcher on her shoulder**: The servant did not yet *know* the prayer was answered; only time would prove it. The woman **Rebekah** was the granddaughter of Abraham's brother **Nahor**.

3. (16-21) The servant, though surprised, waits for complete confirmation of his prayer.

Now the young woman was very beautiful to behold, a virgin; no man had known her. And she went down to the well, filled her pitcher, and came up. And the servant ran to meet her and said, "Please let me drink a little water from your pitcher." So she said, "Drink, my lord." Then she quickly let her pitcher down to her hand, and gave him a drink. And when she had finished giving him a drink, she said, "I will draw *water* for your camels also, until they have finished drinking." Then she quickly emptied her pitcher into the trough, ran back to the well to draw *water*, and drew for all his camels. And the man, wondering at her, remained silent so as to know whether the LORD had made his journey prosperous or not.

a. **The young woman was very beautiful to behold**: We generally regard the Bible as being given to understatement. When we read Rebekah was **very beautiful to behold**, we should understand Rebekah was indeed *very* **beautiful**.

> i. Rebekah is one of the women whom the Bible specifically says was **beautiful**. The others are Sarah (Genesis 12:11-14), Rachel (Genesis 29:17), Abigail (1 Samuel 25:3), Bathsheba (2 Samuel 11:2), Tamar

(2 Samuel 14:27), Queen Vashti of the Persians (Esther 1:11), Esther (Esther 2:7), and the daughters of Job (Job 42:15).

b. **The servant ran to meet her**: The servant did not think it was unspiritual to introduce himself to Rebekah; yet, he certainly did not do anything to suggest that she should provide water for the camels. Prayer is no substitute for action.

c. **And drew for all his camels**: As Rebekah began the hard work of watering all the camels, the servant did not stop her. He wanted a woman who would not only *say* that she would water the camels, but who would actually *do* the hard work. He was amazed as he watched her do this (**wondering at her**).

i. Perhaps Eliezer knew that for some, it is much easier to talk like a servant than to actually serve. He wanted to see if she had a servant's *heart*, not only a servant's *talk*.

4. (22-28) The servant, when the bride has been chosen, gives her rich gifts even before the marriage to the father's son.

So it was, when the camels had finished drinking, that the man took a golden nose ring weighing half a shekel, and two bracelets for her wrists weighing ten *shekels* of gold, and said, "Whose daughter *are* you? Tell me, please, is there room in your father's house for us to lodge?" So she said to him, "I am the daughter of Bethuel, Milcah's son, whom she bore to Nahor." Moreover she said to him, "We have both straw and feed enough, and room to lodge." Then the man bowed down his head and worshiped the Lord. And he said, "Blessed *be* the Lord God of my master Abraham, who has not forsaken His mercy and His truth toward my master. As for me, being on the way, the Lord led me to the house of my master's brethren." So the young woman ran and told her mother's household these things.

a. **When the camels had finished drinking**: Abraham's servant let Rebekah complete the difficult job of providing water to his ten camels.

b. **A golden nose ring… two bracelets for her wrists weighing ten shekels of gold**: After Rebekah fulfilled the sign Abraham's servant prayed for, he immediately revealed precious gifts for her. This was a sign of his generosity and the wealth of the master he represented.

c. **Whose daughter are you**: Having already revealed the gifts indicating that Rebekah was the answer to the servant's prayer, he then asked about her family. He praised God when he found out that she was related to Abraham's family.

d. **Being on the way, the LORD led me**: This showed the mentality of the servant. He felt it was his duty to be **on the way**, and to trust that God would guide him along the way.

> i. It is hard to steer a parked car. If we want to be guided by the LORD, we should be on our way.

e. **The young woman ran and told her mother's household these things**: It is easy to picture Rebekah's excitement. A day that likely started as any other turned out to be a remarkable, life-changing day.

5. (29-33) Laban entertains the servant.

Now Rebekah had a brother whose name was Laban, and Laban ran out to the man by the well. So it came to pass, when he saw the nose ring, and the bracelets on his sister's wrists, and when he heard the words of his sister Rebekah, saying, "Thus the man spoke to me," that he went to the man. And there he stood by the camels at the well. And he said, "Come in, O blessed of the LORD! Why do you stand outside? For I have prepared the house, and a place for the camels." Then the man came to the house. And he unloaded the camels, and provided straw and feed for the camels, and water to wash his feet and the feet of the men who *were* with him. Food was set before him to eat, but he said, "I will not eat until I have told about my errand." And he said, "Speak on."

> a. **Rebekah had a brother whose name was Laban**: The father of Rebekah was *Bethuel*, who was still alive (Genesis 24:50). Yet it seems that Laban took the lead in representing the family. Perhaps Laban was already known for his ability to make a deal to his advantage.
>
> b. **When he saw the nose ring, and the bracelets on his sister's wrists**: Laban's eyes were on the riches the servant brought. He was motivated to show appropriate hospitality to this mysterious visitor and to warmly greet him: "**Come in, O blessed of the LORD!**"
>
> c. **I will not eat until I have told about my errand**: Abraham's servant was focused on his mission and would not be distracted from its fulfillment.
>
>> i. "Like every true servant of Christ, he put his master's business before his own ease or comfort; even before the question of necessary food. When a man begins to think more of his eating than of doing the will of God, he ceases to be a true-hearted minister." (Spurgeon)

6. (34-49) The servant tells his story and the purpose of his visit.

So he said, "I *am* Abraham's servant. The LORD has blessed my master greatly, and he has become great; and He has given him flocks and herds, silver and gold, male and female servants, and camels and

donkeys. And Sarah my master's wife bore a son to my master when she was old; and to him he has given all that he has. Now my master made me swear, saying, 'You shall not take a wife for my son from the daughters of the Canaanites, in whose land I dwell; but you shall go to my father's house and to my family, and take a wife for my son.' And I said to my master, 'Perhaps the woman will not follow me.' But he said to me, 'The LORD, before whom I walk, will send His angel with you and prosper your way; and you shall take a wife for my son from my family and from my father's house. You will be clear from this oath when you arrive among my family; for if they will not give *her* to you, then you will be released from my oath.' And this day I came to the well and said, 'O LORD God of my master Abraham, if You will now prosper the way in which I go, behold, I stand by the well of water; and it shall come to pass that when the virgin comes out to draw water, and I say to her, "Please give me a little water from your pitcher to drink," and she says to me, "Drink, and I will draw for your camels also,"– *let* her be the woman whom the LORD has appointed for my master's son.' But before I had finished speaking in my heart, there was Rebekah, coming out with her pitcher on her shoulder; and she went down to the well and drew *water*. And I said to her, 'Please let me drink.' And she made haste and let her pitcher down from her *shoulder*, and said, 'Drink, and I will give your camels a drink also.' So I drank, and she gave the camels a drink also. Then I asked her, and said, 'Whose daughter are you?' And she said, 'The daughter of Bethuel, Nahor's son, whom Milcah bore to him.' So I put the nose ring on her nose and the bracelets on her wrists. And I bowed my head and worshiped the LORD, and blessed the LORD God of my master Abraham, who had led me in the way of truth to take the daughter of my master's brother for his son. Now if you will deal kindly and truly with my master, tell me. And if not, tell me, that I may turn to the right hand or to the left."

> a. **I am Abraham's servant**: Abraham had left Ur of the Chaldees several decades before, and his family may have wondered how he fared. Here, **Abraham's servant** explained that **the LORD has blessed my master greatly**. He went on to describe the blessing mainly in material terms.
>
>> i. "The phrase, 'my master', is the refrain of this chapter; the word 'master' occurs twenty- two times. Eliezer did not aspire to any independence of Abraham, or of Abraham's son. His thoughts were of his master; his words were in praise of his master; his deeds on behalf of his master. He was not his own, but the bond-servant of another. This is also our position." (Spurgeon)

b. **To him he has given all that he has**: Abraham's servant explained that his master had only one heir, and that this son would inherit all his master's wealth.

c. **The Lord, before whom I walk, will send His angel with you and prosper your way**: Eliezer explained his master Abraham's great faith in God. Abraham never doubted that God would lead the servant to the right woman for Isaac.

d. **If you will deal kindly and truly with my master, tell me**: Abraham's servant understood that they would say yes or no to his **master**, not to him. He truly represented his master, not himself.

i. Eliezer is a wonderful example of the master's faithful messenger:

- He told them that his master was great.
- He told them his master's son was the heir.
- He wanted one who would leave her old home and live with the master's son.
- He pressed for a reply.

ii. "'Well,' says one, 'I am glad you have spoken to us; I will think it over.' No, friend, I do not mean that. I do not want you to think it over. You have had enough of thinking; I pray that God's Spirit may lead you to an immediate decision." (Spurgeon)

C. Rebekah is brought to Isaac.

1. (50-53) The family agrees to give Rebekah to Isaac and Abraham's servant gives more gifts.

Then Laban and Bethuel answered and said, "The thing comes from the Lord; we cannot speak to you either bad or good. Here is Rebekah before you; take *her* and go, and let her be your master's son's wife, as the Lord has spoken." And it came to pass, when Abraham's servant heard their words, that he worshiped the Lord, *bowing himself* to the earth. Then the servant brought out jewelry of silver, jewelry of gold, and clothing, and gave *them* to Rebekah. He also gave precious things to her brother and to her mother.

a. **Laban and Bethuel answered**: In light of the evident hand of God's providence, and the wealth of the servant's master, the answer seemed obvious to Rebekah's brother and father. They quickly decided that **the thing comes from the Lord** and that **the Lord has spoken**.

b. **The servant brought out jewelry of silver, jewelry of gold, and clothing**: The gifts given to Rebekah at the well were only the beginning.

With an agreement from Rebekah and her family for marriage to Isaac, she received even greater gifts as a sign she would become one with the one who would inherit all Abraham's wealth.

c. He also gave precious things to her brother and to her mother: When an agreement of marriage had been made, it was customary for the bridegroom (or his representative) to give the family of the bride gifts as a dowry to demonstrate his financial ability to provide for the bride.

2. (54-60) The servant intends to depart quickly; Rebekah agrees.

And he and the men who were with him ate and drank and stayed all night. Then they arose in the morning, and he said, "Send me away to my master." But her brother and her mother said, "Let the young woman stay with us a *few* days, at least ten; after that she may go." And he said to them, "Do not hinder me, since the LORD has prospered my way; send me away so that I may go to my master." So they said, "We will call the young woman and ask her personally." Then they called Rebekah and said to her, "Will you go with this man?" And she said, "I will go." So they sent away Rebekah their sister and her nurse, and Abraham's servant and his men. And they blessed Rebekah and said to her:

"Our sister, *may* you *become*
The *mother* of thousands of ten thousands;
And may your descendants possess
The gates of those who hate them."

a. **Send me away to my master**: Abraham's servant was focused and urgent regarding his mission. After a 900-mile (1,450 kilometer) journey, he stayed one night at his destination and then wanted to return that great distance.

b. **Let the young woman stay with us a few days**: Rebekah's family first wanted their departure delayed some **ten** days. Eliezer remained focused on his mission and replied, **Do not hinder me, since the LORD has prospered my way**.

i. "He thought, perhaps, that there were more golden bracelets to be had, that he was parting with his sister rather too cheaply, that he must not let the priceless gem go out of his hands too soon." (Spurgeon)

c. **I will go**: Rebekah showed a remarkable willingness to leave everything she knew in order to be with a bridegroom she had never seen. Her words **"I will go"** were worthy words of faith.

d. **Do not hinder me… I will go**: The servant was determined to leave promptly, and Rebekah was determined to make her home with her new husband. She understood that her loyalty should be with her new family.

> i. "If the world does not succeed in persuading the believer to abide in the world, it will seek to delay his exit… When you decide to go with the Lord, the world will applaud your devotion but will say, 'Don't rush. Abide a few days, at least ten, and then go.'" (Barnhouse)

3. (61-67) Rebekah is brought unto Isaac and they marry.

Then Rebekah and her maids arose, and they rode on the camels and followed the man. So the servant took Rebekah and departed. Now Isaac came from the way of Beer Lahai Roi, for he dwelt in the South. And Isaac went out to meditate in the field in the evening; and he lifted his eyes and looked, and there, the camels were coming. Then Rebekah lifted her eyes, and when she saw Isaac she dismounted from her camel; for she had said to the servant, "Who is this man walking in the field to meet us?" The servant said, "It is my master." So she took a veil and covered herself. And the servant told Isaac all the things that he had done. Then Isaac brought her into his mother Sarah's tent; and he took Rebekah and she became his wife, and he loved her. So Isaac was comforted after his mother's *death.*

a. **So the servant took Rebekah and departed**: We can well imagine the conversations Rebekah and Eliezer had on the journey. She wanted to know all she could about Isaac, whom she loved without ever seeing, and he would be delighted to tell her.

b. **She took a veil and covered herself**: The covering with a veil signified chastity, modesty, and submission. This was how Rebekah wanted to meet the man she would marry.

c. **Isaac went out to meditate in the field in the evening**: This was the first mention of Isaac since he was left on top of Mount Moriah (Genesis 22:19). We see nothing of Isaac from the time of his rescue from death (which might be thought of as a symbolic resurrection) to the time he was united with his bride.

> i. In all this, we see the coming together of Isaac and Rebekah as a remarkable picture of the coming together of Jesus and His people.
>
> - A father desired a bride for his son.
> - A son was accounted as dead and raised from the dead.
> - A nameless servant was sent forth to get a bride for the son.
> - The servant's name was actually *Eliezer*, meaning "God of help" or "helper."

- The lovely bride was divinely met, chosen, and called, and then lavished with gifts.
- She was entrusted to the care of the servant until she met her bridegroom.

ii. The way Isaac and Rebekah came to each other is also instructive. They served and sought God (Isaac did **meditate in the field**), and God brought them together. They were more concerned with the will of God than with the idea that love is purely a matter of *feeling*.

iii. "May I say of this chapter. It records what actually was said and done; but at the same time, it bears within it allegorical instruction with regard to heavenly things. The true minister of Christ is like this Eleazar of Damascus; he is sent to find a wife for his Master's son. His great desire is, that many shall be presented unto Christ in the day of his appearing, as the bride, the Lamb's wife." (Spurgeon)

d. **She became his wife, and he loved her**: Isaac loved his bride, and Jesus loves His Church. We may summarize the pictures of Isaac, Rebekah, Jesus, and the Church.

i. *Both Rebekah and the Church:*
- Were chosen for marriage before they knew it (Ephesians 1:3-4).
- Were necessary for the accomplishment of God's eternal purpose (Ephesians 3:10-11).
- Were destined to share in the glory of the son (John 17:22-23).
- Learned of the son through his representative.
- Must leave all with joy to be with the son.
- Were loved and cared for by the son.

ii. *Both Isaac and Jesus:*
- Were promised before their coming.
- Finally appeared at the appointed time.
- Were conceived and born miraculously.
- Were given a special name before birth.
- Were offered up in sacrifice by the father.
- Were brought back from the dead.
- Were head of a great company to bless all people.
- Prepared a place for their bride.
- Had a ministry of prayer until united with the bride.

Genesis 25 – Abraham's Death; Jacob and Esau Born to Isaac

A. Abraham's latter life and death.

1. (1-4) Abraham marries again and has many children by Keturah.

Abraham again took a wife, and her name was Keturah. And she bore him Zimran, Jokshan, Medan, Midian, Ishbak, and Shuah. Jokshan begot Sheba and Dedan. And the sons of Dedan were Asshurim, Letushim, and Leummim. And the sons of Midian *were* Ephah, Epher, Hanoch, Abidah, and Eldaah. All these *were* the children of Keturah.

> a. **Abraham again took a wife**: This was after the death of Sarah, recorded in Genesis 23:1-2 and 23:19. There was nothing wrong with Abraham taking another **wife** after Sarah's death.
>
> b. **Here name was Keturah**: It is easy to forget that Abraham had a second wife, and he fathered six more sons through her. In total, Abraham had eight sons: Isaac through Sarah, Ishmael through Hagar, and these six through **Keturah**.
>
> c. **She bore him Zimran, Jokshan, Medan, Midian, Ishbak, and Shuah**: These sons would themselves become the fathers of distinct peoples. For example, the Midianites came from **Midian**. These sons through Keturah were also a further demonstration that in Abraham's marriage to Sarah, whatever fertility problems that existed were on the part of Sarah, not Abraham.

2. (5-6) Abraham is careful to set Isaac apart as the child of promise.

And Abraham gave all that he had to Isaac. But Abraham gave gifts to the sons of the concubines which Abraham had; and while he was still living he sent them eastward, away from Isaac his son, to the country of the east.

a. **Abraham gave all that he had to Isaac**: Abraham gave his wealth to Isaac, and he gave the promise of the land God had promised to him to Isaac (**he sent them eastward, away from Isaac his son**).

b. **Abraham gave gifts to the sons of the concubines**: The only such relationship we know of in Abraham's life was with Hagar (Genesis 16:1-4). Perhaps this is also a reference to Keturah, letting us know that though she was Abraham's wife (Genesis 25:1), in regard to God's covenant promise to Abraham and his descendants, she was not on the same level as Sarah.

3. (7-11) Abraham's death and burial.

This is the sum of the years of Abraham's life which he lived: one hundred and seventy-five years. Then Abraham breathed his last and died in a good old age, an old man and full *of years*, and was gathered to his people. And his sons Isaac and Ishmael buried him in the cave of Machpelah, which is before Mamre, in the field of Ephron the son of Zohar the Hittite, the field which Abraham purchased from the sons of Heth. There Abraham was buried, and Sarah his wife. And it came to pass, after the death of Abraham, that God blessed his son Isaac. And Isaac dwelt at Beer Lahai Roi.

a. **Then Abraham breathed his last and died**: Abraham passed from the scene, being one of the most important men of the Bible. He is mentioned 70 times in the New Testament alone. Only Moses is mentioned more times in the New Testament (80 times).

b. **Died in a good old age, an old man and full of years**: Abraham lived a remarkably long life of **one hundred and seventy-five years**. By many measures his life was not perfect, but he was a man of faith, who had a real relationship with God, of remarkable obedience, and a true friend of God (2 Chronicles 20:7 and James 2:23).

i. Adam Clarke wrote a good eulogy of Abraham: "Above all as a *man of God*, he stands unrivaled; so that under the most exalted and perfect of all dispensations, the Gospel of Jesus Christ, he is proposed and recommended as the *model* and *pattern* according to which the faith, obedience, and perseverance of the followers of the Messiah are to be formed. Reader, while you admire the *man*, do not forget the *God* that made him so great, so good, and so useful. Even Abraham had nothing but what he had received; from the free unmerited mercy of God proceeded all *his* excellences; but he was a *worker together with God*, and therefore *did not receive the grace of God in vain*. Go thou, believe, love, obey, and persevere in like manner."

c. **After the death of Abraham, that God blessed his son Isaac**: Abraham was a great man, but he was only a man. God's work passed on from one generation to the next. Now, God would carry on the work of the covenant first promised to Abraham through Isaac.

4. (12-18) The life and descendants of Ishmael.

Now this is the genealogy of Ishmael, Abraham's son, whom Hagar the Egyptian, Sarah's maidservant, bore to Abraham. And these *were* the names of the sons of Ishmael, by their names, according to their generations: The firstborn of Ishmael, Nebajoth; then Kedar, Adbeel, Mibsam, Mishma, Dumah, Massa, Hadar, Tema, Jetur, Naphish, and Kedemah. These *were* the sons of Ishmael and these *were* their names, by their towns and their settlements, twelve princes according to their nations. These *were* the years of the life of Ishmael: one hundred and thirty-seven years; and he breathed his last and died, and was gathered to his people. (They dwelt from Havilah as far as Shur, which is east of Egypt as you go toward Assyria.) He died in the presence of all his brethren.

a. **Now this is the genealogy of Ishmael**: Here the twelve sons of **Ishmael** are named. With so many sons to carry on his family name, Ishmael was a blessed man. However, he was not blessed with the inheritance of the covenant God made to Abraham.

b. **Twelve princes… one hundred and thirty-seven years… was gathered to his people… he died in the presence of all his brethren**: All of these descriptions show what a *blessed* man **Ishmael** was. Though he did not receive the Abrahamic covenant, God's blessing and hand was upon him.

B. **The children of Isaac: Jacob and Esau.**

1. (19-23) The conception of Jacob and Esau.

This is the genealogy of Isaac, Abraham's son. Abraham begot Isaac. Isaac was forty years old when he took Rebekah as wife, the daughter of Bethuel the Syrian of Padan Aram, the sister of Laban the Syrian. Now Isaac pleaded with the Lord for his wife, because she was barren; and the Lord granted his plea, and Rebekah his wife conceived. But the children struggled together within her; and she said, "If *all is* well, why *am I like* this?" So she went to inquire of the Lord. And the Lord said to her:

**"Two nations are in your womb,
Two peoples shall be separated from your body;
One people shall be stronger than the other,
And the older shall serve the younger."**

a. **Now Isaac pleaded with the Lord for his wife, because she was barren**: Even the son of promise did not come into the promise easily. It only came through waiting and prayer. We can trust that the prayers of a husband for his wife have a special effectiveness.

b. **The Lord granted his plea, and Rebekah his wife conceived**: This prayer was answered, but some 20 years after Isaac and Rebekah first married (Genesis 25:20, 26). Their faith and persistence in prayer was tested and invited to grow through many years. As well, these were the only children born to Isaac and Rebekah.

c. **So she went to inquire of the Lord**: The struggle that seemed to take place in Rebekah's womb made her seek God. As she sought Him, the Lord spoke to her regarding number of children in her womb, their gender, and the destiny of those sons in her womb.

i. It is good to desire that the Lord would speak to us, but we must realize we do not hear perfectly from God. We can become far too confident in our ability to hear from the Lord, and forget that it is easy for us to stop listening when God wants to keep speaking. We may add to what the Lord is saying, or hear it clearly but misunderstand the timing or application of what the Lord says to us.

ii. In connection with God's eternal word (as was the case with Rebekah here), God gave a unique gift to *perfectly* listen, a gift given only in connection with the revelation of His written, eternal word.

d. **Two nations are in your womb**: What God said is simple; Rebekah would give birth to twins. The twins would each father nations. One shall be greater than the other, and the younger will be greater than the older.

i. Jewish legends say Jacob and Esau tried to kill each other in the womb. Also, every time Rebekah went near an idol's altar, Esau would get excited in the womb, and when she would go near a place where the Lord was worshipped, Jacob would get excited. Of course, these should be regarded as nothing more than legends.

e. **And the older shall serve the younger**: In this case, God chose to go against the accepted pattern of the younger serving the older. In Romans 9:10-13, the Apostle Paul used this choice of Jacob over Esau before their birth as an illustration of God's sovereign choice.

i. God's choice of Isaac instead of Ishmael seems more logical to us. Yet His choice between Jacob and Esau, regarding which one would be the heir of God's covenant of salvation, was just as valid, though in some ways it seemed to make less sense.

ii. Paul wrote that God's choice was not based on the performance of Jacob or Esau. The choice was made when they were *not yet being born, nor having done any good or evil* (Romans 9:11).

iii. God announced these intentions to Rebekah before the children were born (**the older shall serve the younger**), and repeated His verdict long after Jacob and Esau had both passed from the earth (*Jacob I have loved, but Esau I have hated*, Malachi 1:2-3).

iv. Some object, questioning the fairness of God making such a choice before Jacob or Esau were born. Yet we should regard the *love* and the *hate* God spoke of in Malachi 1:2-3 and Romans 9:10-13 as having to do with His purpose in choosing one of these two to become the heir of the covenant of Abraham. In that regard, God's preference could rightly be regarded as a display of *love* towards Jacob and *hate* towards Esau. The real thought in Malachi 1 and Romans 9 is much more like "accepted" and "rejected" more than it is like our understanding of the terms "loved" and "hated."

v. God did *not* hate Esau in the sense of cursing him to a doomed life in either this world or the next. All told, Esau was indeed a blessed man, and in some ways more well-adjusted than Jacob (Genesis 33:4-9). Yet in regard to the inheritance of the covenant, it could be rightly said that God hated Esau and loved Jacob.

vi. "A woman once said to Mr. Spurgeon, 'I cannot understand why God should say that He hated Esau.' 'That,' Spurgeon replied, 'is not my difficulty, madam. My trouble is to understand how God could love Jacob.'" (Newell in *Romans, Verse by Verse*)

vii. Our greatest error in considering the choices of God is to think God chooses for arbitrary reasons, as if His choices were random and senseless. God chooses according to His divine wisdom, love, and goodness. We may not be able to understand God's reasons for choosing, and they are reasons He alone knows and answers to, but God's choices are not random or capricious.

2. (24-26) The birth of Jacob and Esau.

So when her days were fulfilled *for her* to give birth, indeed *there were* twins in her womb. And the first came out red. *He was* like a hairy garment all over; so they called his name Esau. Afterward his brother came out, and his hand took hold of Esau's heel; so his name was called Jacob. Isaac was sixty years old when she bore them.

a. **Indeed there were twins in her womb**: The truth of the unseen promise was fulfilled by something that could be seen. When the time came for them to be born, there were in fact twins in Rebekah's womb and God's word was proved true.

b. **And the first came out red**: The circumstances surrounding the birth of each child were responsible for their names. **Esau** referred to the hairiness and hair color of the first-born child. **Jacob** referred to the way the second-born was holding on to the heel of his brother.

i. Additionally, the idea of a "heel-catcher" *meant* something in that day. It had the idea of "trickster," "con-man," "scoundrel," or "rascal." It wasn't a compliment.

3. (27-28) The different characters of Jacob and Esau.

So the boys grew. And Esau was a skillful hunter, a man of the field; but Jacob was a mild man, dwelling in tents. And Isaac loved Esau because he ate *of his* game, but Rebekah loved Jacob.

a. **Esau was a skillful hunter, a man of the field; but Jacob was a mild man**: Like so many siblings in a family, Jacob and Esau were very different from each other in their personality and tastes; and as is sometimes the case, each parent had a favorite child.

b. **Jacob was a mild man**: The Hebrew word for **mild** has the idea of "wholeness," instead of someone who is weak or effeminate. The Hebrew word *tam* (**mild**) is used of Job in Job 1:8: *Then the LORD said to Satan, "Have you considered My servant Job, that there is none like him on the earth, a <u>blameless</u> and upright man, one who fears God and shuns evil?"*

4. (29-34) Esau sells his birthright to Jacob.

Now Jacob cooked a stew; and Esau came in from the field, and he was weary. And Esau said to Jacob, "Please feed me with that same red stew, for I am weary." Therefore his name was called Edom. But Jacob said, "Sell me your birthright as of this day." And Esau said, "Look, I *am* about to die; so what is this birthright to me?" Then Jacob said, "Swear to me as of this day." So he swore to him, and sold his birthright to Jacob. And Jacob gave Esau bread and stew of lentils; then he ate and drank, arose, and went his way. Thus Esau despised *his* birthright.

a. **Jacob cooked a stew; and Esau came in from the field**: Here, each son acted consistently with his own natural inclination. Esau hunted and Jacob cooked.

b. **Sell me your birthright as of this day**: Jacob knew that the **birthright** was valuable and he wanted it. Passages like Deuteronomy 21:17 and 1 Chronicles 5:1-2 tell us the *birthright* involved both a material and a spiritual dynamic. The son of the birthright received a double portion of the inheritance, and he also became the head of the family and the spiritual leader upon the passing of the father.

i. In the case of *this* family, the birthright determined who would inherit the covenant God made with Abraham; the covenant of a land, a nation, and the Messiah.

c. **I am about to die**: Esau's thought wasn't that he was so hungry that he would die without food. Instead the idea was, "I will die one day anyway, so what good is this birthright to me?"

d. **Swear to me as of this day**: Jacob acted in the character of his name, acting like a heel-catcher. He was acting like a scoundrel or a rascal in taking advantage of his brother.

i. Jacob was guilty of scheming in the flesh to gain something God said was already his. Yet we should remember the far greater blame was placed on Esau, who **despised his birthright**.

ii. According to Leupold, Martin Luther drew attention to an important fact: this was not a valid transaction, because Jacob tried to purchase what was already his, and Esau tried to sell something that didn't belong to him.

e. **And sold his birthright to Jacob**: Esau thought little of the spiritual heritage connected to the birthright. He valued only material things, so a spiritual birthright meant little to him when his stomach was hungry. Many, if not most people, also place little value on spiritual things.

i. "History shows that men prefer illusions to realities, choose time rather than eternity, and the pleasures of sin for a season rather than the joys of God forever. Men will read trash rather than the Word of God, and adhere to a system of priorities that leaves God out of their lives. Multitudes of men spend more time shaving than on their souls; and multitudes of women give more minutes to their makeup than to the life of the eternal spirit. Men still sell their birthright for a mess of pottage." (Barnhouse)

ii. Spiritually speaking, many today despise their birthright. Ephesians 1:3-14 shows us a treasury of riches that are ours by birthright in Jesus:

- Every spiritual blessing.
- The blessing of being chosen in Jesus.
- Adoption into God's family.
- Complete acceptance by God in Jesus.
- Redemption from our slavery to sin.

- True and total forgiveness.
- The riches of God's grace.
- The revelation and knowledge of the mystery of God's will.
- An eternal inheritance.
- The guarantee of the indwelling Holy Spirit.

Far too many neglect or trade away this birthright for cheap entertainment, momentary popularity, or passing pleasures.

f. **Thus Esau despised his birthright**: Esau's character as a *fornicator* and *profane person* (according to Hebrews 12:16) shows God was entirely correct in choosing Jacob over Esau to carry on the birthright, even though Jacob was younger.

i. Though Esau's character was not the *basis* for God's choosing (He chose Jacob over Esau before they were born), Esau's character ultimately showed the wisdom of God's choice.

Genesis 26 – Isaac Sins Like Abraham

A. Isaac repeats Abraham's mistakes.

1. (1) Isaac responds to famine by going towards Egypt.

There was a famine in the land, besides the first famine that was in the days of Abraham. And Isaac went to Abimelech king of the Philistines, in Gerar.

> a. **There was a famine in the land**: Though Isaac lived in the land God promised to his father Abraham and his descendants, it did not mean that life in the land would be without trouble or challenge. As there was a famine in the days of Abram (Genesis 12:10), so there was a famine in Isaac's day.
>
> b. **Isaac went to Abimelech king of the Philistines, in Gerar**: Isaac began to go south towards Egypt, as Abram did in famine (Genesis 12:10). It seems that Isaac thought to travel along the famous road between Egypt and Canaan that went along the Mediterranean Sea.
>
>> i. **Gerar** was the same place where Isaac's father Abraham met another Abimelech, and almost compromised his wife (Genesis 20:1-18). A similar story, similar both in the way man acted and the way God acted would play out with Abraham's son.
>>
>> ii. The ruler of Gerar was called **Abimelech** as a title, not as a personal name. This is why both Abraham and Isaac dealt with Abimelech (Genesis 20, Genesis 26).

2. (2-5) God proclaims the covenant to Isaac.

Then the LORD appeared to him and said: "Do not go down to Egypt; live in the land of which I shall tell you. Dwell in this land, and I will be with you and bless you; for to you and your descendants I give all these lands, and I will perform the oath which I swore to Abraham your father. And I will make your descendants multiply as the stars of

heaven; I will give to your descendants all these lands; and in your seed all the nations of the earth shall be blessed; because Abraham obeyed My voice and kept My charge, My commandments, My statutes, and My laws."

a. **Do not go down to Egypt**: As Isaac journeyed south, God warned him not to go any further. Isaac was to always **live in the land** that God told him to live in. The Son of Promise was always to live in the land of promise; if Isaac did, God promised to **be with** him and to **bless** him.

b. **I will perform the oath which I swore to Abraham your father**: In theory, it was possible for the covenant to end with the passing of Abraham, but God was true to His word. The covenant God made with Abraham was not only unto Abraham, but unto his chosen descendants also (Genesis 17:7-8). This fulfilled a specific promise made in Genesis 17:19.

i. This formal repetition of the covenant included the three essential aspects first communicated in Genesis 12:2-3 and repeated afterwards, including the promise of:

- A land (**all these lands**).
- A nation (**your descendants multiply as the stars of heaven**).
- A blessing (**in your seed all the nations of the earth shall be blessed**).

c. **Because Abraham obeyed My voice and kept My charge**: God said that He kept the covenant with Isaac because of Abraham's obedience. A close look at Abraham's life shows that his obedience wasn't complete or constant; yet God recognized it.

i. God could say this of Abraham because Abraham was declared righteous by faith (Genesis 15:6), and as far as God was concerned, all He saw in Abraham was the righteousness of Jesus.

3. (6-8) Abimelech takes Rebekah because Isaac says she is his sister.

So Isaac dwelt in Gerar. And the men of the place asked about his wife. And he said, "She *is* my sister"; for he was afraid to say, "*She is* my wife," *because he thought,* **"lest the men of the place kill me for Rebekah, because she *is* beautiful to behold." Now it came to pass, when he had been there a long time, that Abimelech king of the Philistines looked through a window, and saw, and there was Isaac, showing endearment to Rebekah his wife.**

a. **So Isaac dwelt in Gerar**: Isaac obeyed God's warning and stayed in the land; yet he lived among the people in Canaan, closer than he had before, and this would bring trouble.

b. **And he said, "She is my sister"; for he was afraid to say, "She is my wife"**: Isaac went from such a high spiritual experience (Genesis 26:1-5) to such blatant sin because of the weakness of his own flesh, and also because of his father's bad example.

> i. Peter, with his confession and wrong counsel to Jesus, was a perfect example of how sin can follow upon an outpouring of God's blessing. For good reason, 1 Corinthians 10:12 says: *Therefore let him who thinks he stands take heed lest he fall.*

c. **Lest the men of the place kill me for Rebekah, because she is beautiful to behold**: The Bible doesn't teach we are bound by what are known as generational curses, but it is often the case that the sins of the fathers are found in the children. This may be because those sins of the flesh have been nurtured in the same environment and patterned by a previous generation.

d. **There was Isaac, showing endearment to Rebekah his wife**: When Abimelech saw this, he made the logical conclusion, understanding the true nature of their relationship.

> i. The King James Version has an interesting translation here, saying Isaac was *sporting with* Rebekah.

4. (9-11) Isaac is rebuked by a pagan king, even as his father was.

Then Abimelech called Isaac and said, "Quite obviously she *is* your wife; so how could you say, 'She *is* my sister'?" And Isaac said to him, "Because I said, 'Lest I die on account of her.'" And Abimelech said, "What is this you have done to us? One of the people might soon have lain with your wife, and you would have brought guilt on us." So Abimelech charged all *his* people, saying, "He who touches this man or his wife shall surely be put to death."

a. **Quite obviously she is your wife**: What Isaac thought could be hidden was obvious to others. This is often the case with sin among God's people.

b. **What is this you have done to us**: In a similar manner to the rebuke of Pharaoh to Abraham (Genesis 12:18-19) and of Abimelech's predecessor to Abraham (Genesis 20:10), this ruler of Gerar rebuked Isaac for his deception.

c. **He who touches this man or his wife shall surely be put to death**: Even as God protected his father Abraham and mother Sarah (even in the midst of sinful conduct), Isaac and Rebekah were also protected.

B. Isaac digs the wells.

1. (12-14) Isaac becomes wealthy, as Abraham was before him.

Then Isaac sowed in that land, and reaped in the same year a hundredfold; and the LORD blessed him. The man began to prosper, and continued prospering until he became very prosperous; for he had possessions of flocks and possessions of herds and a great number of servants. So the Philistines envied him.

    a. **Then Isaac sowed in that land**: Prosperity came to Isaac as the blessing upon his hard work. He probably received enough of an inheritance from his father that he did not have to work, but worked hard nonetheless, and God blessed it and **he became very prosperous**.

    b. **So the Philistines envied him**: Isaac's prosperity prompted the envy of his neighbors. This was another problem that came from living in close company to the Philistines of Gerar.

2. (15-17) Isaac leaves Gerar.

Now the Philistines had stopped up all the wells which his father's servants had dug in the days of Abraham his father, and they had filled them with earth. And Abimelech said to Isaac, "Go away from us, for you are much mightier than we." Then Isaac departed from there and pitched his tent in the Valley of Gerar, and dwelt there.

    a. **Now the Philistines had stopped up all the wells**: Wells were precious, and they were difficult and expensive to dig. It was a significant attack to destroy someone's wells. This shows how severe the envy of the Philistines was towards Isaac.

        i. These particular wells were dug in the days of Abraham (Genesis 21:30) and had served Abraham and his son for many years.

    b. **Isaac departed from there and pitched his tent in the Valley of Gerar**: Isaac didn't want to continue the battle, and was confident that God would take care of him if he **departed**. He did, but did not go far.

3. (18-19) Isaac digs the wells of Abraham.

And Isaac dug again the wells of water which they had dug in the days of Abraham his father, for the Philistines had stopped them up after the death of Abraham. He called them by the names which his father had called them. Also Isaac's servants dug in the valley, and found a well of running water there.

    a. **Isaac dug again the wells of water which they had dug in the days of Abraham**: Isaac went back to the same resources that had sustained his father and all he possessed (Genesis 21:25-31). It took faith, work, and commitment to dig the wells again, but the provision was there when Isaac sought it diligently.

i. For nomadic herdsmen, even great ones like Abraham and Isaac, *water was life*. In some seasons of the year, human or animal life could not be sustained without water from wells. These wells were not a luxury, but a necessity.

  ii. There is a powerful illustration here of the spiritual life. The spiritual resources that sustained previous generations are available for us today, *if we will seek them with faith, work, and commitment*.

 b. **He called them by the names which his father had called them**: Isaac honored the provision that his father received by calling the wells by the same name.

  i. Using this as a spiritual illustration, we might say that the wells of *peace*, of *power*, of *grace*, of *wisdom*, of *transformation* are all available for the believer today as they were for previous generations. The question is whether a present generation will have the faith, the work, and the commitment to dig the wells again.

 c. **Found a well of running water**: It seems that Isaac even found something that Abraham didn't. Isaac found the best kind of well – one **of running water**. This was the best kind of provision, and came to Isaac as he received the provision once enjoyed by his father Abraham.

4. (20-23) Three wells and their names.

But the herdsmen of Gerar quarreled with Isaac's herdsmen, saying, "The water *is* ours." So he called the name of the well Esek, because they quarreled with him. Then they dug another well, and they quarreled over that *one* also. So he called its name Sitnah. And he moved from there and dug another well, and they did not quarrel over it. So he called its name Rehoboth, because he said, "For now the LORD has made room for us, and we shall be fruitful in the land." Then he went up from there to Beersheba.

 a. **He called the name of the well Esek**: The first well was named *contention*, because it made others jealous. It seems that though Isaac called these wells by the names Abraham had previously given (Genesis 26:18), he also named them in light of his present circumstances.

 b. **He called its name Sitnah**: The second well was named *opposition* for the same reason.

 c. **He called its name Rehoboth**: The third well was named *roominess*, because it was far enough to not be a problem. Isaac saw this as a testimony to God's faithfulness and blessing (**now the LORD has made room for us, and we shall be fruitful in the land**).

i. Isaac saw these wells as they rightly were: the blessing of God. He saw them more as God's gracious blessing than the result of his hard work.

d. **Then he went up from there to Beersheba**: God used the conflicts to lead Isaac back to **Beersheba**, where Abraham had been before. Because God repeatedly demonstrated His faithfulness to Isaac, he knew that he could be blessed and fruitful wherever God led him (**we shall be fruitful in the land**).

i. Of course, none of this lessens the responsibility of those who unjustly opposed Isaac. God used their sinful contention against Isaac, but it was still sin.

C. God's blessing upon Isaac.

1. (24-25) God again confirms His promise to Isaac for Abraham's sake.

And the LORD appeared to him the same night and said, "I *am* the God of your father Abraham; do not fear, for I *am* with you. I will bless you and multiply your descendants for My servant Abraham's sake." So he built an altar there and called on the name of the LORD, and he pitched his tent there; and there Isaac's servants dug a well.

a. **The LORD appeared to him the same night**: Isaac's father Abraham had many personal appearances of the LORD. This seems to be the first such experience for Isaac.

b. **Do not fear, for I am with you**: In the atmosphere of greater contention between Isaac's herdsmen and the Philistine herdsmen, Isaac had reason to be afraid. Here, God told Isaac to put any such fears away.

c. **For My servant Abraham's sake**: God kept His covenant with Isaac for **Abraham's sake**. After the same pattern, God keeps His covenant with us for Jesus' sake.

d. **So he built an altar there... he pitched his tent there... dug a well**: Isaac walked in the same paths of his father Abraham. Altars and tents marked Abraham's life, demonstrating a life of worship and trust. Isaac lived that, calling **on the name of the LORD**, and enjoyed the additional blessing of another **well**.

2. (26-31) The natives make peace with Isaac because the LORD is with him, just as happened with Abraham.

Then Abimelech came to him from Gerar with Ahuzzath, one of his friends, and Phichol the commander of his army. And Isaac said to them, "Why have you come to me, since you hate me and have sent me away from you?" But they said, "We have certainly seen that the LORD

is with you. So we said, 'Let there now be an oath between us, between you and us; and let us make a covenant with you, that you will do us no harm, since we have not touched you, and since we have done nothing to you but good and have sent you away in peace. You are now the blessed of the LORD.'" So he made them a feast, and they ate and drank. Then they arose early in the morning and swore an oath with one another; and Isaac sent them away, and they departed from him in peace.

> a. **Why have you come to me, since you hate me and have sent me away from you**: Isaac's question was logical. He was pushed out of Gerar by the contention of the herdsmen of Gerar. He had every reason to believe he was not welcome – and he went towards Beersheba.
>
> b. **We have certainly seen that the LORD is with you**: Abimelech gave a surprising response. He and others could *see* that the covenant God, Yahweh, was with Isaac and had blessed him. He came to ask for peace and a blessing from Isaac, this wonderfully blessed man, because he knew that God was **with** him, and that **you are now the blessed of the LORD**.
>
>> i. We see the tremendous practical wisdom of Isaac's actions. He didn't respond to evil with more evil, and he sought God's provision along the pattern of ancient ways.
>
> c. **They departed from him in peace**: After a **feast** marking their covenant of peace, Abimelech departed from Isaac.

3. (32-33) God's blessing for Isaac in the form of a well.

It came to pass the same day that Isaac's servants came and told him about the well which they had dug, and said to him, "We have found water." So he called it Shebah. Therefore the name of the city is Beersheba to this day.

> a. **It came to pass the same day**: God brought many blessings to Isaac at once. He enjoyed a rich season of blessing.
>
> b. **We have found water**: Abraham was a man of altars, and Jacob would be a man of tents. Isaac was a man of wells, and he knew God's constant provision. He knew by experience God could provide in many different ways, not just one.
>
>> i. **So he called it Sheba**: "Like Isaac, after you have drunk of the waters of 'contention' and 'hatred', you will be brought to Rehoboth, where you shall have 'room', yea, even to Beer-sheba, 'the well of the oath', or 'the seventh well', 'the well of satiety', where your enemies shall seek your favor, and glorify your Lord." (Spurgeon)

4. (34-35) Esau marries, becoming a grief to his parents.

When Esau was forty years old, he took as wives Judith the daughter of Beeri the Hittite, and Basemath the daughter of Elon the Hittite. And they were a grief of mind to Isaac and Rebekah.

a. **He took as wives Judith the daughter of Beeri the Hittite, and Basemath the daughter of Elon the Hittite**: Esau, the son of Isaac and twin brother of Jacob, went against the pattern established by Abraham, that his descendants should not marry the women of Canaan (Genesis 24:3-4).

b. **They were a grief of mind to Isaac and Rebekah**: This shows Esau's character as a *fornicator* and *profane person* (Hebrews 12:16).

Genesis 27 – Jacob Deceptively Gains the Blessing of Isaac

A. Rebekah and Jacob plot to deceive Isaac.

1. (1-4) Isaac's deathbed request to Esau.

Now it came to pass, when Isaac was old and his eyes were so dim that he could not see, that he called Esau his older son and said to him, "My son." And he answered him, "Here I am." Then he said, "Behold now, I am old. I do not know the day of my death. Now therefore, please take your weapons, your quiver and your bow, and go out to the field and hunt game for me. And make me savory food, such as I love, and bring *it* to me that I may eat, that my soul may bless you before I die."

> a. **Now it came to pass, when Isaac was old**: Isaac believed his time had come to die, and this was his way of settling his affairs, sort of a last will and testament. His old age was evident in his weakened eyesight (**his eyes were so dim that he could not see**).
>
>> i. **Isaac was old**, but perhaps not near death. Martin Luther calculated Isaac's age to be 137 at this point; he lived to be 180. Isaac lived 43 more years.
>
> b. **Make me savory food, such as I love**: Isaac asked for food, but he seemed to mostly glory in Esau's power as a manly hunter. We later find that he actually could not taste the difference between what Esau hunted in the field and what his wife Rebekah could prepare from the flock. It wasn't the taste of the food that attracted him, but how he prized the thought of Esau as a mighty hunter.
>
> c. **That my soul may bless you before I die**: Strangely, Isaac insisted on giving the blessing to Esau, the one whom God did not choose (Genesis 25:23), who despised his birthright, and who married pagan wives. It seems

Isaac rejected godly thinking and spiritual wisdom, and instead thought only of food and common, man-centered ideas of might.

> i. In the willfulness of his old age, he was determined to pass on the blessing to Esau, despite what the LORD had said and what the boys had shown in their lives. The fact Isaac tried to dispense the blessing *secretly* showed he knew what he wanted to do was wrong. Sadly, in this house, no one trusted anyone else.

2. (5-10) Rebekah advises Jacob to deceive his father Isaac.

Now Rebekah was listening when Isaac spoke to Esau his son. And Esau went to the field to hunt game and to bring *it*. So Rebekah spoke to Jacob her son, saying, "Indeed I heard your father speak to Esau your brother, saying, Bring me game and make savory food for me, that I may eat it and bless you in the presence of the LORD before my death.' Now therefore, my son, obey my voice according to what I command you. Go now to the flock and bring me from there two choice kids of the goats, and I will make savory food from them for your father, such as he loves. Then you shall take *it* to your father, that he may eat *it*, and that he may bless you before his death."

> a. **Rebekah was listening when Isaac spoke to Esau**: The account here does not specifically tell us that Rebekah spied upon Isaac and Esau in some inappropriate sense. The *feeling* that this was scheming and spying is here, but it is possible that she casually overheard this important conversation. When **Esau went to the field to hunt**, Rebekah was ready with her plan.

> b. **Now therefore, my son, obey my voice according to what I command you**: Instead of trusting God to fulfill what He had promised in Genesis 25:23, Rebekah used manipulative scheming to accomplish what she thought was God's plan – and, likely, also her preference.

>> i. "Good men have gone very wrong when they have thought of aiding in the fulfillment of promises and prophecies. See how Rebecca erred in trying to get the promised blessing for Jacob. We had better leave the Lord's decrees in the Lord's hands." (Spurgeon)

> c. **I will make savory food from them for your father, such as he loves**: Rebekah knew her husband well enough to know that he couldn't tell the difference between what she prepared and what Esau might bring home from hunting.

3. (11-17) Preparations are made for Jacob's deceptive attempt to steal the blessing.

And Jacob said to Rebekah his mother, "Look, Esau my brother is a hairy man, and I *am* a smooth-*skinned* man. Perhaps my father will

feel me, and I shall seem to be a deceiver to him; and I shall bring a curse on myself and not a blessing." But his mother said to him, *"Let* your curse *be* on me, my son; only obey my voice, and go, get *them* for me." And he went and got *them* and brought them to his mother, and his mother made savory food, such as his father loved. Then Rebekah took the choice clothes of her elder son Esau, which *were* with her in the house, and put them on Jacob her younger son. And she put the skins of the kids of the goats on his hands and on the smooth part of his neck. Then she gave the savory food and the bread, which she had prepared, into the hand of her son Jacob.

a. **Perhaps my father will feel me, and I shall seem to be a deceiver to him**: Jacob, true to his name (trickster or scoundrel), was happy to go along with this plan. His only concern was if it would *succeed*.

i. When we are willing to abandon the question of right and wrong, and when our only concern is what *works*, we agree with the modern idea of *pragmatism*, as many in the church do today.

b. **He went and got them and brought them to his mother**: Once Jacob overcame his fear of getting caught in his deception, he was ready to carry it out. Rebekah manipulated both Isaac and Jacob, but Jacob was willing to be manipulated.

c. **His father… Rebekah… Esau… Jacob**: Significantly, at this point, each person in this drama acted in man-centered wisdom and energy, not according to divine or spiritual wisdom and energy. Even Esau, in agreeing to Isaac's plan to give him the birthright, disregarded his previous promise to allow Jacob to have the birthright.

i. All four of them – Isaac, Rebekah, Jacob, and Esau – did not trust each other. Worse yet, they did not trust the Lord. Each one of them schemed and plotted against each other and against God. "The whole story reflects no credit upon any of the persons concerned" (Spurgeon).

ii. The worst aspect of this all is they seem to regard the blessing as *magical*, as something detached from God's wisdom and will. But in giving the blessing, the most Isaac could do was to recognize *God's* call and blessing on Jacob. Only God could truly bestow the blessing. Esau could receive the blessing from Isaac a hundred times, but it only mattered if God in heaven honored it.

B. Jacob receives the blessing that Isaac intended for Esau.

1. (18-27a) Jacob lies to his father, pretending to be Esau.

So he went to his father and said, "My father.' And he said, "Here I am. Who *are* you, my son?" Jacob said to his father, "I *am* Esau your

firstborn; I have done just as you told me; please arise, sit and eat of my game, that your soul may bless me." But Isaac said to his son, "How *is it* that you have found it so quickly, my son?" And he said, "Because the LORD your God brought *it* to me." Then Isaac said to Jacob, "Please come near, that I may feel you, my son, whether you *are* really my son Esau or not." So Jacob went near to Isaac his father, and he felt him and said, "The voice is Jacob's voice, but the hands *are* the hands of Esau." And he did not recognize him, because his hands were hairy like his brother Esau's hands; so he blessed him. Then he said, "*Are* you really my son Esau?" He said, "I *am*." He said, "Bring *it* near to me, and I will eat of my son's game, so that my soul may bless you." So he brought *it* near to him, and he ate; and he brought him wine, and he drank. Then his father Isaac said to him, "Come near now and kiss me, my son." And he came near and kissed him; and he smelled the smell of his clothing,

> a. **I am Esau your firstborn**: Sometimes it is difficult to discern a lie, and whether a statement is sin or not comes back to the question of intent; but other times it is not difficult at all, and here Jacob clearly lied to his father.
>
> b. **Because the LORD your God brought it to me**: Jacob, the scoundrel, did not hesitate to give credit to God as part of his deception.
>
> > i. Jacob could do this, because his only concern was for *what worked*. Since he (rightly) knew that God wanted him to have the birthright, he justified any lie or other sin he committed in the pursuit of the birthright. He likely did so telling himself that it was all for a righteous cause.
> >
> > ii. Jacob probably used the promise and calling of God as an excuse for sin; he justified it to himself by saying his sinful conduct acted towards the fulfillment of the promise of God.
>
> c. **Are you really my son Esau**: Even under repeated questioning, Jacob stayed confirmed in his lie. Partially, Jacob took advantage of his father's good nature. Isaac probably would not believe that his Jacob would lie to him so repeatedly.

2. (27b-29) The blessing is given to Jacob.

And blessed him and said:

"Surely, the smell of my son
***Is* like the smell of a field**
Which the LORD has blessed.
Therefore may God give you
Of the dew of heaven,
Of the fatness of the earth,

And plenty of grain and wine.
Let peoples serve you,
And nations bow down to you.
Be master over your brethren,
And let your mother's sons bow down to you.
Cursed *be* everyone who curses you,
And blessed *be* those who bless you!"

 a. **And blessed him**: Isaac blessed Jacob as the spiritual head of the family. *Isaac* had the right (not Ishmael) to pass on this blessing related to the covenant of Abraham. The son (Jacob or Esau) who received this blessing was able to pass it on to his descendants.

 b. **May God give you of the dew of heaven, of the fatness of the earth**: The words of the blessing were filled with pictures of the Lord's rich bounty, and they echoed some of the words of the covenant God made with Abraham.

 c. **Cursed be everyone who curses you, and blessed be those who bless you**: Again, it is important to see it wasn't the bestowal of these words upon Jacob that made him blessed. Instead, Jacob was blessed because God chose him long before (Genesis 25:23). What mattered was that *God* said *the older shall serve the younger* (back in Genesis 25:23), not that *Isaac* said **be master over your brethren**.

  i. "The point is that the sovereign will of God is done, in spite of our or any other person's opposition to it." (Boice)

C. Esau discovers Jacob's deception.

1. (30-32) Esau returns to his father with food from the hunt.

Now it happened, as soon as Isaac had finished blessing Jacob, and Jacob had scarcely gone out from the presence of Isaac his father, that Esau his brother came in from his hunting. He also had made savory food, and brought it to his father, and said to his father, "Let my father arise and eat of his son's game, that your soul may bless me." And his father Isaac said to him, "Who are you?" So he said, "I *am* your son, your firstborn, Esau."

 a. **As soon as Isaac had finished blessing Jacob**: The timing of each aspect of this story makes it all the more dramatic. **As soon as** Jacob received the blessing and left his father's presence, **Esau his brother came in from his hunting**.

 b. **That your soul may bless me**: We picture Esau hunting, returning, and preparing the food with pleasure. He would receive the blessing from his father and all the material benefits that went with it.

c. **Who are you**: This question may have seemed strange to Esau, but he remembered that his father was old and couldn't see well. Esau probably first thought this was a simple mistake.

2. (33) Isaac understands what Jacob did.

Then Isaac trembled exceedingly, and said, "Who? Where *is* the one who hunted game and brought *it* to me? I ate all *of it* before you came, and I have blessed him– *and* indeed he shall be blessed."

> a. **Isaac trembled exceedingly**: Isaac began to shake convulsively. This phrase is very strong. He was overcome with a deep sense that something had gone wrong in his plan to bless Esau instead of Isaac.
>
>> i. This phrase could be translated, "Isaac trembled most excessively with a great trembling" (Morris).
>
> b. **Isaac trembled exceedingly**: Isaac was troubled, because he knew he had tried to work against the plan God revealed in Genesis 25:23 – and God had beaten him. At this moment, Isaac realized he would always lose when he tried to resist God's will, even when he didn't like God's will. And he came to learn that despite his arrogance against God's will, God's will was glorious.
>
>> i. Later, in Hebrews 11:20, it says *By faith Isaac blessed Jacob and Esau concerning things to come.* Isaac's faith was demonstrated after his attempt to redirect the will of God was destroyed and he said of Jacob, **"and indeed he shall be blessed."**
>>
>> ii. "As soon as Isaac perceives that he has been wrong in wishing to bless Esau he does not persist in it. He will give Esau such a blessing as he may, but he does not think for a moment of retracting what he has done — he feels that the hand of God was in it. What is more, he tells his son, 'He is blessed, yea, and shall be blessed.'" (Spurgeon)

3. (34-38) Esau's reaction to the blessing given to Jacob.

When Esau heard the words of his father, he cried with an exceedingly great and bitter cry, and said to his father, "Bless me– me also, O my father!" But he said, "Your brother came with deceit and has taken away your blessing." And *Esau* said, "Is he not rightly named Jacob? For he has supplanted me these two times. He took away my birthright, and now look, he has taken away my blessing!" And he said, "Have you not reserved a blessing for me?" Then Isaac answered and said to Esau, "Indeed I have made him your master, and all his brethren I have given to him as servants; with grain and wine I have sustained him. What shall I do now for you, my son?" And Esau said to his father, "Have you

only one blessing, my father? Bless me— me also, O my father!" And Esau lifted up his voice and wept.

> a. **He cried with an exceedingly great and bitter cry**: This is about the strongest description possible to describe the depth of Esau's horror upon learning that Jacob had used deception to "take" the birthright.
>
> b. **Bless me; me also, O my father**: Esau repeated this agonized plea. Yet we understand that Esau valued his father's blessing mainly in *material* terms. He did not value the blessing's spiritual value.
>
> c. **He took away my birthright**: Both Isaac and Esau were grieved when they understood what Jacob did, and *now* Esau was concerned about the birthright. Previously (in Genesis 25:32-34), he was willing to sell his birthright for a bowl of stew, and he *despised his birthright*. Now, he wanted the material and social advantages of the birthright.
>
>> i. When he saw it as a spiritual birthright, Esau did not value the birthright; but now that he saw it in material and political terms, he wanted it.
>
> d. **For he has supplanted me these two times**: Esau failed to take responsibility for the fact that in the first of the **two times** he referred to, Esau actually *despised his birthright* (Genesis 25:34), selling it to Jacob for a bowl of stew. In the first of the two times, Esau could not truly say that Jacob ***took*** away my birthright. Esau *gave* it away, and God was Lord over the birthright anyway.
>
> e. **Esau lifted up his voice and wept**: Esau's tears were the tears of frustrated selfishness, not of regret for his own sin and despising of his birthright.
>
>> i. Hebrews 12 uses the occasion of Esau as a warning: *Looking carefully lest anyone fall short of the grace of God; lest any root of bitterness springing up cause trouble, and by this many become defiled; lest there be any fornicator or profane person like Esau, who for one morsel of food sold his birthright. For you know that afterward, when he wanted to inherit the blessing, he was rejected, for he found no place for repentance, though he sought it diligently with tears* (Hebrews 12:15-17).

4. (39-40) Isaac gives a limited blessing to Esau.

Then Isaac his father answered and said to him:

"Behold, your dwelling shall be of the fatness of the earth,
And of the dew of heaven from above.
By your sword you shall live,
And you shall serve your brother;

And it shall come to pass, when you become restless,
That you shall break his yoke from your neck."

> a. **Behold, your dwelling shall be of the fatness of the earth**: These words of Isaac sound more like a curse than a blessing. Yet, in fact, Esau ended up being a blessed man. Many years later when he met Jacob again, he could say the blessed words *I have enough, my brother* (Genesis 33:9).
>
>> i. Barnhouse (and others) indicate the blessing Isaac bestowed on Esau actually said, *"your dwelling shall be from the fatness of the earth"*; that is, Esau and his descendants would be live as nomads in mostly wilderness lands.
>
> b. **By your sword you shall live**: Whatever blessings and security Esau might enjoy, it would come as he skillfully wielded his **sword**. His life would not be easy, though it could be blessed.
>
> c. **You shall serve your brother**: Esau would be under Jacob, but not forever. The promise also was that Esau would **break his yoke from your neck** – that he would not forever serve or be under his brother Jacob.

5. (41-42) Esau's anger.

So Esau hated Jacob because of the blessing with which his father blessed him, and Esau said in his heart, "The days of mourning for my father are at hand; then I will kill my brother Jacob." And the words of Esau her older son were told to Rebekah. So she sent and called Jacob her younger son, and said to him, "Surely your brother Esau comforts himself concerning you *by intending* to kill you."

> a. **So Esau hated Jacob because of the blessing**: Esau's hatred rose against Jacob for many reasons, but mostly it was out of pride and envy. Pride, in that his brother would be preferred before him in regard to the covenant. Envy, in that his brother would enjoy greater prosperity.
>
> b. **Then I will kill my brother Jacob**: Esau's somewhat spiritual concern for the blessing of his father quickly disappeared in a bitter hatred of Jacob, a bitter hatred that also had murderous intent. Esau planned to kill Jacob as soon as Isaac died, and this was a *comfort* to Esau (**Esau comforts himself**).
>
>> i. Revenge is a comforting thought to those who feel they have been wronged like Esau, but things would not work out as Esau had hoped or planned. He vowed to kill his brother after the death of his father, thinking it was soon (**the days of mourning for my father are at hand**), yet Isaac lived much longer, perhaps another 43 years.

ii. Perhaps Esau was going to test just how blessed Jacob was. His intention may have been to kill him in an attempt to defeat God's revealed will regarding the birthright.

6. (43-46) Rebekah makes plans for Jacob to flee.

"Now therefore, my son, obey my voice: arise, flee to my brother Laban in Haran. And stay with him a few days, until your brother's fury turns away, until your brother's anger turns away from you, and he forgets what you have done to him; then I will send and bring you from there. Why should I be bereaved also of you both in one day?" And Rebekah said to Isaac, "I am weary of my life because of the daughters of Heth; if Jacob takes a wife of the daughters of Heth, like these *who are* the daughters of the land, what good will my life be to me?"

a. **Stay with him a few days**: The **few days** Jacob was to stay with Laban and Rebekah's family in Haran turned out to be more than 20 years. Yet God would fulfill His purpose in all of it.

b. **If Jacob takes a wife of the daughters of Heth, like these who are the daughters of the land, what good will my life be to me**: Rebekah successfully manipulated Isaac into telling Jacob to leave. This saved his life, but it is likely that this mother never saw her son again.

i. "Rebekah's diplomatic victory was complete; but she would never see her son again." (Kidner)

ii. In this tragic story, everyone lost. Each of the main characters – Isaac, Rebekah, Esau, and Jacob – schemed and maneuvered in human wisdom and energy, rejecting God's word and wisdom. Nevertheless, God *still* accomplished His purpose. The tragedy was that each of the participants suffered, because they insisted on working against God's word and wisdom.

Genesis 28 – Jacob Flees from Esau

A. Isaac's farewell to Jacob.

1. (1-2) Instructions to not take a Canaanite wife.

Then Isaac called Jacob and blessed him, and charged him, and said to him: "You shall not take a wife from the daughters of Canaan. Arise, go to Padan Aram, to the house of Bethuel your mother's father; and take yourself a wife from there of the daughters of Laban your mother's brother."

> a. **Isaac called Jacob and blessed him**: By now, Isaac had resigned himself to what he knew was the Lord's will all along – that the older would serve the younger, and that Jacob, not Esau, would receive the birthright (Genesis 25:23). He sent Jacob with blessing and instructions (**and charged him**).
>
> b. **You shall not take a wife from the daughters of Canaan**: It was essential Jacob *not* take a wife from the **daughters of Canaan**, as his brother Esau did. Jacob was the one to inherit the birthright and carry on the seed of the Messiah.

2. (3-5) The all-important transferal of Abraham's blessing.

**"May God Almighty bless you,
And make you fruitful and multiply you,
That you may be an assembly of peoples;
And give you the blessing of Abraham,
To you and your descendants with you,
That you may inherit the land
In which you are a stranger,
Which God gave to Abraham."
So Isaac sent Jacob away, and he went to Padan Aram, to Laban the son of Bethuel the Syrian, the brother of Rebekah, the mother of Jacob and Esau.**

a. **May God Almighty bless you**: Isaac blessed Jacob in the name of **God Almighty**, that is, *El Shaddai*. This title for God was previously used in Genesis 17:1, where God described Himself to Abraham with this phrase. Abraham passed the knowledge of *El Shaddai* on to his son Isaac, who now passed it on to Jacob. He first pronounced a general blessing of prosperity upon Jacob.

b. **And give you the blessing of Abraham**: After the general blessing, Isaac then gave the specific **blessing of Abraham**, the covenant blessing made to Abraham and his descendants (Genesis 12:7, 15:8, 17:7-8). This was the aspect of the birthright that Esau despised, but Jacob (who seemed equally unworthy) would gain. Jacob was the one to carry on God's promise to Abraham.

i. Jacob was promised a land (**that you may inherit the land**), a nation (**that you may be an assembly of peoples**), and a blessing (**give you the blessing of Abraham**), even as Abraham was promised (Genesis 12:1-3).

c. **To you and your descendants with you**: Jacob was by no means worthy of this blessing. Each of the four parties in the whole birthright mess acted in an unspiritual manner somewhere along the line. The amazing thing is that God brought *any* good out of all this. This was a triumph of God's sovereignty.

d. **So Isaac sent Jacob away**: Jacob would travel eastward to the region where his mother Rebekah was raised. He would not see his father Isaac again for more than 20 years, when Isaac was truly near death.

3. (6-9) Esau adds wives.

Esau saw that Isaac had blessed Jacob and sent him away to Padan Aram to take himself a wife from there, *and that* as he blessed him he gave him a charge, saying, "You shall not take a wife from the daughters of Canaan," and that Jacob had obeyed his father and his mother and had gone to Padan Aram. Also Esau saw that the daughters of Canaan did not please his father Isaac. So Esau went to Ishmael and took Mahalath the daughter of Ishmael, Abraham's son, the sister of Nebajoth, to be his wife in addition to the wives he had.

a. **Esau saw that Isaac had blessed Jacob**: *Now* the blessing and the birthright seemed important to Esau. They were important enough to him that he determined to impress his father by marrying non-Canaanite women when he saw **that Jacob had obeyed his father and his mother**.

b. **Esau went to Ishmael**: Esau avoided the Canaanite women and married women from the family of his uncle **Ishmael**.

B. Jacob meets God at Bethel.

1. (10-12) Jacob's dream of a ladder.

Now Jacob went out from Beersheba and went toward Haran. So he came to a certain place and stayed there all night, because the sun had set. And he took one of the stones of that place and put it at his head, and he lay down in that place to sleep. Then he dreamed, and behold, a ladder was set up on the earth, and its top reached to heaven; and there the angels of God were ascending and descending on it.

a. **Went toward Haran:** Jacob traveled eastward toward the ancestral lands of his grandfather Abraham (Genesis 11:31-32) and his mother Rebekah (Genesis 24:3-4).

b. **Then he dreamed**: In this desolate wilderness, Jacob had a significant dream as he used a stone for a pillow. One can only imagine the strange flood of feelings in Jacob at this moment: the fear, the loneliness, the isolation, the excitement, and the anticipation. This was an important time in Jacob's life.

c. **A ladder was set up on the earth, and its top reached to heaven; and there the angels of God were ascending and descending on it**: In Jacob's dream, there was now access to heaven. Jacob now knew God was closer than he ever thought before and there was real access and interaction between heaven and earth.

i. "The God of Bethel is a God who does concern himself with the things of earth, not a God who shuts himself up in heaven, but God who hath a ladder fixed between heaven and earth." (Spurgeon)

ii. Jesus made it clear in John 1:51 that *He* is the access to heaven. *He* is the means by which heaven comes down to us and by which we can go to heaven. Jesus Messiah is the **ladder**. *And He said to him, "Most assuredly, I say to you, hereafter you shall see heaven open, and the angels of God ascending and descending upon the Son of Man"* (John 1:51).

iii. Jesus *is* the way to heaven. He does not show us a way; He *is* the way. *Jesus said to him, "I am the way, the truth, and the life. No one comes to the Father except through Me"* (John 14:6).

2. (13-15) God speaks to Jacob.

And behold, the LORD stood above it and said: "I *am* the LORD God of Abraham your father and the God of Isaac; the land on which you lie I will give to you and your descendants. Also your descendants shall be as the dust of the earth; you shall spread abroad to the west and the east, to the north and the south; and in you and in your seed all the families

of the earth shall be blessed. Behold, I *am* with you and will keep you wherever you go, and will bring you back to this land; for I will not leave you until I have done what I have spoken to you."

>a. **I am the LORD God of Abraham your father and the God of Isaac**: Jacob had no doubt heard about the great God who appeared to Abraham and to Isaac, but now this same God met Jacob in a personal way. This was a life-changing experience for Jacob.

>b. **The land on which you lie I will give to you and your descendants**: These words were for comfort and hope to Jacob at this critical crossroads in his life. Essentially, God repeated to Jacob the terms of the covenant He gave to both Abraham (Genesis 12:1-3) and to Isaac (Genesis 26:2-5).

>>i. Before, Isaac told Jacob the covenant was his (Genesis 28:3-4), but now the voice of God Himself confirmed it. God promised him **land**, a nation (**your descendants shall be as the dust of the earth**), and a blessing (**in you and in your seed all the families of the earth shall be blessed**).

>c. **I am with you and will keep you wherever you go, and will bring you back to this land; for I will not leave you until I have done what I have spoken to you**: God gave to Jacob the same kind of promise found in Philippians 1:6: *being confident of this very thing, that He who has begun a good work in you will complete it until the day of Jesus Christ*. God won't let us go until His work is complete in us.

>>i. **Behold, I am with you**: "That God should give to Jacob bread to eat and raiment to put on was much, but it is nothing compared with 'I am with thee.' That God should send his angel with Jacob to protect him would have been much; but it is nothing compared with, 'I am with thee.' This includes countless blessings, but it is in itself a great deal more than all the blessings we can conceive of" (Spurgeon).

>>ii. God's blessing and faithfulness to Jacob is seen in the several ways that His presence is described in Jacob's life.

>>>- **Behold, I am with you** (Genesis 28:15) – This describes *present blessing*, and the indescribable blessing of God's presence.
>>>- *I will be with you* (Genesis 31:3) – This describes the wonderful promise of God's future presence and blessing.
>>>- *The God of my fathers has been with me* (Genesis 31:5) – This was Jacob's testimony of God's faithfulness and presence with him.
>>>- *God will be with you* (Genesis 48:21) – This was Jacob passing on the blessing of God's presence to the next generations.

3. (16-19) Jacob worships God, naming the place **Bethel** (*house of God*).

Then Jacob awoke from his sleep and said, "Surely the Lord is in this place, and I did not know it." And he was afraid and said, "How awesome is this place! This is none other than the house of God, and this is the gate of heaven!" Then Jacob rose early in the morning, and took the stone that he had put at his head, set it up as a pillar, and poured oil on top of it. And he called the name of that place Bethel; but the name of that city had been Luz previously.

    a. **Surely the Lord is in this place, and I did not know it**: Jacob was right in sensing the presence of the Lord there. If he thought that God was in some places but not in others, he was wrong.

        i. King David knew that God was everywhere: *Where can I go from Your Spirit? Or where can I flee from Your presence?* (Psalm 139:7)

    b. **How awesome is this place**: From his unspiritual and perhaps superstitious perspective, Jacob put too much emphasis on a particular **place**. He didn't realize that if the presence of the Lord was not with him in *every* place, then God could never fulfill His promise to him.

    c. **He called the name of that place Bethel**: The city of **Bethel** would play an important (though not glorious) role in Israel's history. Among the cities of Israel, it is second only to Jerusalem in the number of times mentioned in the Old Testament.

        i. Later, when speaking to Jacob, God referred to Himself as *the God of Bethel* (Genesis 31:13).

        ii. Bethel would eventually become a high place, known for a place of sacrifice to idols (1 Kings 13:32, Hosea 10:15, Amos 4:4).

4. (20-22) Jacob's vow unto God.

Then Jacob made a vow, saying, "If God will be with me, and keep me in this way that I am going, and give me bread to eat and clothing to put on, so that I come back to my father's house in peace, then the Lord shall be my God. And this stone which I have set as a pillar shall be God's house, and of all that You give me I will surely give a tenth to You."

    a. **If God will be with me**: This can also be translated "since God will be with me"; but knowing Jacob, he undoubtedly meant it in the sense of "*if* God will be with me." God gave him a promise, yet he still tried to bargain with God, even promising God money if He fulfilled His promise.

        i. The way Jacob prayed, it was evident God's mere word was not enough for him. He had to *see* God do it before he would believe. We should not be the same way, but we often are. God says, "*And my God shall supply all your need according to His riches in glory by Christ Jesus.*" (Philippians 4:19); He says, "*The LORD is good, a stronghold in the day of trouble; and He knows those who trust in Him,*" (Nahum 1:7). We should believe these things, even before we *see* them.

b. **Keep me in the way that I am going, and give me bread to eat and clothing to put on**: Here, Jacob spoke as if he could set the terms of his covenant with God. In his thinking, he made the deal for God instead of humbly receiving what God said would be the arrangement.

i. Jacob wasn't very submitted to God. In the next phase of his life, God taught him submission in adversity, through his Uncle Laban.

c. **Jacob made a vow**: Unfortunately, there was a great contrast between God's promise and Jacob's vow. One was totally God-centered; the other was terribly man-centered.

i. God's promise to Jacob (Genesis 28:13-15):

- *I am the LORD God.*
- *I will give to you.*
- *I am with you.*
- *I will not leave you until I have done what I have spoken.*

ii. Jacob's vow to God:

- **If God will be with me.**
- **And keep me.**
- **In this way that I am going.**
- **Give me bread and clothing.**
- **So that I come back to my father's house.**

iii. It would have been much better if Jacob had prayed like this: "Because You promised to be with me and to keep me and to provide for all my needs, and to bring me back to the land which you swore to give to my fathers and to me, I will be completely Yours, God."

iv. God was gracious enough not to take His covenant back when He saw such an unspiritual response from Jacob. Instead, He was willing to be called *the God of Abraham, the God of Isaac, and the God of Jacob* (Exodus 3:6).

Genesis 29 – Jacob's Marriages and Children

A. Jacob meets Rachel.

1. (1-3) Jacob comes to a covered well.

So Jacob went on his journey and came to the land of the people of the East. And he looked, and saw a well in the field; and behold, there *were* three flocks of sheep lying by it; for out of that well they watered the flocks. A large stone was on the well's mouth. Now all the flocks would be gathered there; and they would roll the stone from the well's mouth, water the sheep, and put the stone back in its place on the well's mouth.

    a. **And came to the land of the people of the East**: Because the LORD blessed his trip, Jacob returned to the land his mother Rebekah came from, being also the land of his grandfather Abraham.

    b. **He looked, and saw a well in the field**: As Jacob came near to the home of his mother's family, he noticed a well that was used to water the sheep. The well was covered and protected by **a large stone**.

2. (4-10) Jacob meets Rachel at the well.

And Jacob said to them, "My brethren, where *are* you from?" And they said, "We *are* from Haran." Then he said to them, "Do you know Laban the son of Nahor?" And they said, "We know him." So he said to them, "Is he well?" And they said, "*He is* well. And look, his daughter Rachel is coming with the sheep." Then he said, "Look, *it is* still high day; it is not time for the cattle to be gathered together. Water the sheep, and go and feed *them*." But they said, "We cannot until all the flocks are gathered together, and they have rolled the stone from the well's mouth; then we water the sheep." Now while he was still speaking with them, Rachel came with her father's sheep, for she was a shepherdess. And it came to pass, when Jacob saw Rachel the daughter of Laban his mother's brother, and the sheep of Laban his mother's brother, that Jacob went

near and rolled the stone from the well's mouth, and watered the flock of Laban his mother's brother.

> a. **My brethren, where are you from**: In an age before clearly marked roads and signs, Jacob didn't know where he was until he asked some of the locals. Jacob then discovered he was at his destination.
>
> b. **Do you know Laban the son of Nahor**: Jacob knew to make contact with his uncle **Laban**, his mother's brother. The shepherds not only knew Laban, they also told Jacob that Laban's **daughter Rachel** was approaching.
>
> c. **Water the sheep, and go and feed them**: Perhaps Jacob wanted the shepherd boys to leave, probably so he could speak more directly to Rachel.
>
> d. **Jacob went near and rolled the stone from the well's mouth**: Jacob also knew he had come to marry one of the daughters of Laban (Genesis 28:2), so he was more than willing to show kindness (and perhaps his strength) to Laban's daughter Rachel. The shepherd boys waited for someone to remove the stone, and Jacob did it in the presence of Rachel.

3. (11-14) Rachel arranges for her father Laban to meet Jacob.

Then Jacob kissed Rachel, and lifted up his voice and wept. And Jacob told Rachel that he *was* her father's relative and that he *was* Rebekah's son. So she ran and told her father. Then it came to pass, when Laban heard the report about Jacob his sister's son, that he ran to meet him, and embraced him and kissed him, and brought him to his house. So he told Laban all these things. And Laban said to him, "Surely you are my bone and my flesh." And he stayed with him for a month.

> a. **Jacob kissed Rachel, and lifted up his voice and wept**: Initially, Rachel must have been quite surprised when a man she never met before greeted her, kissed her, then cried out and wept.
>
> b. **Jacob told Rachel that he was her father's relative**: Rachel had been told about her aunt Rebekah, who married a wealthy and distant relative to the family.
>
> c. **He stayed with him for a month**: Laban showed this great hospitality, not only because of custom, and not only because Jacob was his nephew; Laban also knew that Jacob would inherit a significant fortune from his father Isaac.

B. Laban's deal with Jacob.

1. (15-20) Jacob offers to work for seven years as a dowry to receive Rachel in marriage.

Then Laban said to Jacob, "Because you *are* my relative, should you therefore serve me for nothing? Tell me, what *should* your wages *be*?"

Now Laban had two daughters: the name of the elder was Leah, and the name of the younger was Rachel. Leah's eyes were delicate, but Rachel was beautiful of form and appearance. Now Jacob loved Rachel; so he said, "I will serve you seven years for Rachel your younger daughter." And Laban said, "*It is* better that I give her to you than that I should give her to another man. Stay with me." So Jacob served seven years for Rachel, and they seemed *only* a few days to him because of the love he had for her.

a. **What should your wages be**: This might sound like a nice offer, but really Laban let Jacob know if he wanted to remain among them, he must stay as a hired servant. Jacob was the son of a man of tremendous wealth. Certainly he was not lazy, but he wasn't used to hard work. Servants did the hard work back home; now Jacob was the servant.

i. Jacob's reaction in this situation would reveal much of his character. This demonstrates the principle that you never know what kind of servant you are until others *treat* you like a servant.

b. **Now Jacob loved Rachel**: Not only was Rachel **beautiful of form and appearance**, but she was also the first friendly face Jacob met in the area. It is understandable why he had a love at first sight attachment to Rachel.

c. **Leah's eyes were delicate**: There is some dispute as to exactly what this phrase means. Some think it means her eyes were bad and she couldn't see well. Others think it means her eyes were dull, not beautiful and full of life like her sister Rachel's eyes.

i. The comparison of Rachel and Leah and their respective beauty is a small clue into what was probably a complicated, conflict-filled, and competitive family life.

d. **I will serve you seven years for Rachel your younger daughter**: The offer to work for **seven years** was essentially a dowry. Though Jacob came from a family with great wealth, he left home with no money. Before he could take a woman in marriage he had to provide a dowry to demonstrate he was fit to support a family and to compensate for the taking of the daughter.

i. **Seven years** was a very generous offer, far above a normal dowry. Jacob didn't want to risk a refusal. When Laban saw how badly Jacob wanted Rachel, he knew he could take advantage of him.

e. **They seemed only a few days to him because of the love he had for her**: We notice the great **love he had for her**. The seven years of labor without pay (except for room and board) seemed to pass as quickly as a few days.

i. In this ancient culture, Jacob was not allowed to spend as much time as he wanted with Rachel. There were strict social guidelines to separate unmarried men and women.

ii. This clearly demonstrates an important principle: true love waits. Jacob was willing to wait **seven years** for Rachel.

iii. In the 1990s, there was a successful campaign among teens titled "True Love Waits." It persuaded them to take the following pledge: *Believing that true love waits, I make a commitment to God, myself, my family, those I date, my future mate and my future children to be sexually pure until the day I enter a covenant marriage relationship.* One may debate the success of the campaign, but the principle remains. Jacob was willing to wait for Rachel **because of the love he had for her**.

2. (21-25) Laban switches Leah for Rachel on the wedding night.

Then Jacob said to Laban, "Give *me* my wife, for my days are fulfilled, that I may go in to her." And Laban gathered together all the men of the place and made a feast. Now it came to pass in the evening, that he took Leah his daughter and brought her to Jacob; and he went in to her. And Laban gave his maid Zilpah to his daughter Leah as a maid. So it came to pass in the morning, that behold, it was Leah. And he said to Laban, "What is this you have done to me? Was it not for Rachel that I served you? Why then have you deceived me?"

a. **Give me my wife, for my days are fulfilled, that I may go in to her**: These words are clear enough. Even though Jacob waited and the time went quickly because of love, when the time was done, he was done waiting. He wanted to take Rachel as his wife. Laban responded by inviting guests and making a wedding (**gathered together all the men of the place and made a feast**).

b. **He took Leah his daughter and brought her to Jacob; and he went in to her**: It was possible for Jacob to be fooled because of the wedding customs of the day. According to those customs, the wife was veiled until she was finally alone with her husband in the honeymoon suite. If it was dark by the time Jacob and his new bride were alone together (something Laban would not have difficulty arranging), it helps explain how Jacob was fooled.

c. **He took Leah his daughter and brought her to Jacob**: We assume that Leah was in agreement with this. Yet even if she was not in agreement, she was under the absolute authority of her father.

i. "She may have loved Jacob secretly. She may have considered this her one chance to get a husband. She may have thought this an unsought, and therefore justifiable, opportunity to steal a march on her sister." (Leupold)

ii. The absolute authority of the father in the home of that culture also explains why Rachel allowed this to happen.

d. **So it came to pass in the morning, that behold, it was Leah**: We can imagine how Jacob felt, and how Leah felt, and of course how poor Rachel felt. All this was because of Laban's sin; or, perhaps one should say it was because of *Jacob's* sin – now the deceiver was deceived.

e. **Why then have you deceived me**: Significantly, Laban's deception towards Jacob was similar to the deception Jacob put upon his father Isaac and his brother Esau. This is an example of Jacob reaping what he had sown. Jacob exchanged the younger for the older; Laban exchanged the older for the younger.

i. When Jacob deceived his father and cheated his brother, God did not change His plan to choose Jacob to receive the birthright. Instead, God took Jacob to the school of difficult experience to discipline him. This shows that our disobedience may not derail God's plan for our life, but it will greatly affect how we end up experiencing it. One might spend 20 years working for someone like Laban while God teaches a few things.

ii. Though we can see this was God's correction upon Jacob, it in no way justified Laban's deception. The fact that God *does* work all things together for good never excuses the evil things man does.

3. (26-30) Laban agrees to give Rachel to Jacob in return for another seven years of work.

And Laban said, "It must not be done so in our country, to give the younger before the firstborn. Fulfill her week, and we will give you this one also for the service which you will serve with me still another seven years." Then Jacob did so and fulfilled her week. So he gave him his daughter Rachel as wife also. And Laban gave his maid Bilhah to his daughter Rachel as a maid. Then *Jacob* also went in to Rachel, and he also loved Rachel more than Leah. And he served with Laban still another seven years.

a. **It must not be done so in our country**: This excuse by Laban basically said, "Well, didn't we tell you? We don't do it this way around here. I thought you knew." The only reason Jacob accepted this clever trick from Laban was because he had no other option. But Laban's supposed reason was really nothing more than an excuse.

b. **Serve with me still another seven years**: The second seven years made up Jacob's post-graduate work in the school of difficult experience. Jacob's main subject in the school of difficult experience was, "You Reap What You Sow."

c. **And he served with Laban still another seven years**: Laban was a perfect picture of a deceptive manipulator. He ended up getting exactly what he wanted (both his daughters married). Yet this would turn out badly for both himself and his daughters. Oftentimes, God will judge manipulators by giving them what they in their sinful desires and methods want, yet allowing it to be loss for them.

> i. The problems in this family can be seen immediately. Not only had Jacob married two sisters, but he also allowed everyone to know that one was favored and loved more than the other. Ultimately, all these problems came from Laban's manipulative deception, and the prior sin of Jacob that brought it upon himself.
>
> ii. What should Jacob have done? Some say Jacob should have gone to Laban and told him to correct the whole mess, and simply be married to Rachel and let Leah be Laban's problem. Others believe that according to the standards of the culture, he could not have put Leah aside, because she was unable to marry another after having been given to Jacob. Perhaps he should have done the best he could have in the situation, which would have been to love his two wives equally. What a mess!

d. **He gave him his daughter Rachel as wife also**: Polygamy is not widely practiced in western culture, but we do practice *serial marriage*. When it comes to terminology, we can think of polygamy as *mass marriage* in the sense we speak about *mass murder*: someone who marries more than one at the same time. There is also *serial murder*: where a murderer kills many, but one at a time. In our modern culture, we also multiply wives to ourselves; we just do it one at a time.

> i. We can't do anything about our marriages that have broken up in the past, but each of us can do all that we can before God to make sure that from now on, it is one partner for all time.

C. Jacob's first four sons born through Leah.

1. (31) God's gracious love for Leah.

When the LORD saw that Leah was unloved, He opened her womb; but Rachel was barren.

a. **When the LORD saw that Leah was unloved**: God's compassion on Leah is touching. She was truly the innocent party in all of this mess. God can bring comfort and blessing to a wife and meet her needs even when the husband acts in an ungodly manner.

> i. "Wretched Leah sits sadly in her tent with her maid and spends her time spinning and weeping. For the rest of the household, and especially Rachel, despises her because she has been scorned by her husband, who prefers Rachel and is desperately in love with Rachel alone. She is not beautiful, not pleasing. No, she is odious and hated… There the poor girl sits; no one pays any attention to her. Rachel gives herself airs before; she does not deign to look at her. 'I am the lady of the house,' she thinks, 'Leah is a slave.' These are truly carnal things in the saintly fathers and mothers, like the things that usually happen in our houses." (Luther, cited in Boice)

b. **When the LORD saw that Leah was unloved, He opened her womb**: God was good to Leah, even when her husband wasn't, and her sister wasn't.

> i. Isaiah 54:5 says, *For your Maker is your husband, the LORD of hosts is His name*. Husbands are responsible to care for their wives. Yet when they do not, God can meet the needs of a hurting wife, needs that may be neglected by the husband.

2. (32) The birth of Reuben.

So Leah conceived and bore a son, and she called his name Reuben; for she said, "The LORD has surely looked on my affliction. Now therefore, my husband will love me."

a. **She called his name Rueben**: The first child born to Jacob, through Leah, was named **Reuben** by Leah, meaning *Behold, a son*. This was her statement to Jacob and all others that the LORD had **looked upon my affliction**.

> i. Reuben was the firstborn son of Jacob; he was the logical one to inherit the promise God had made to Abraham and passed on to Isaac and then to Jacob.

b. **Now therefore, my husband will love me**: Jacob, even though he did not love Leah, still was willing to have sex with her. This demonstrates a principle that is still true, that a man will often be willing to have sex completely apart from love, and only a foolish woman regards the willingness to have sex as proof of love. Leah was not the first, nor the last, to live under this problem of male nature.

3. (33) The birth of Simeon.

Then she conceived again and bore a son, and said, "Because the LORD has heard that I am unloved, He has therefore given me this *son* also." And she called his name Simeon.

> a. **She called his name Simeon**: The second child born to Jacob, through Leah, was named (by Leah) *Simeon*, meaning *Hearing*. Leah hoped all would notice that the LORD had heard her.
>
> b. **Because the LORD has heard that I am unloved**: Apparently, the birth of Reuben did not turn the heart of Jacob towards Leah. She was still aware he did not love her, though he still was willing to have sex with her.
>
>> i. Of course, Jacob and Leah were married, so there was nothing *sinful* in sexual relationship. But this plainly shows that Jacob, like most any man in the flesh, was able and willing to have sex with someone he did not love.
>>
>> ii. A 1995 survey asked the following question: "Have you ever had sex with a woman you have actively disliked?" 58% of men answered "yes."

4. (34) The birth of Levi.

She conceived again and bore a son, and said, "Now this time my husband will become attached to me, because I have borne him three sons." Therefore his name was called Levi.

> a. **Therefore his name was called Levi**: The third child born to Jacob, again through Leah, was named **Levi**, meaning *Attachment*. Leah still lived in the hope her husband Jacob would love her and become attached to her through the birth of these sons.
>
> b. **Now this time my husband will become attached to me**: The pain in the heart of Leah was just as evident as the hardness of Jacob's heart, and as evident as his attitude towards his wife Leah.

5. (35) The birth of Judah.

And she conceived again and bore a son, and said, "Now I will praise the LORD." Therefore she called his name Judah. Then she stopped bearing.

> a. **She called his name Judah**: The fourth son born to Jacob, again through Leah, was named **Judah**, meaning *Praise*. Apparently, Leah stopped naming her children to reflect the pain and longing in her heart. At this point, she focused on God and could praise Him.
>
> b. **Now I will praise the LORD**: To some extent, and for some period of time, Leah allowed the LORD to meet her need, and she could now praise God. Leah knew the LORD better, driven to Him by the neglect of her husband.

i. Leah, though she was neglected by Jacob and despised by Rachel, had a great purpose in God's plan. The two greatest tribes came from Leah, not Rachel: Levi (the priestly tribe) and Judah (the royal tribe). And most importantly, the Messiah came from Leah, the less-attractive sister who was neglected and despised but learned to look to the Lord and praise Him.

Genesis 30 – The Children Born to Jacob

A. Two sons born to Bilhah.

1. (1-4) Rachel, out of frustration, gives her maid Bilhah to Jacob to bear children through her.

Now when Rachel saw that she bore Jacob no children, Rachel envied her sister, and said to Jacob, "Give me children, or else I die!" And Jacob's anger was aroused against Rachel, and he said, "*Am* I in the place of God, who has withheld from you the fruit of the womb?" So she said, "Here is my maid Bilhah; go in to her, and she will bear *a child on my knees*, that I also may have children by her." Then she gave him Bilhah her maid as wife, and Jacob went in to her.

> a. **Give me children, or else I die**: Despite Rachel's great beauty, she also was near despair. No doubt Leah often said, "If I only had my sister's beauty and the love of my husband, I would be happy." No doubt Rachel often said, "If I only had sons like my sister, I would be happy." Beautiful or plain, we all have our problems.
>
>> i. This principle shows us the need to stop looking to how God deals with others and set our eyes on Him. Jesus taught the same principle to Peter (John 21:19-22).
>
> b. **Rachel envied her sister... Give me children, or else I die... Jacob's anger was aroused against Rachel**: The tension in this family was apparent. Yet in it all, Jacob saw the hand of God in the matter, even though he stated it to Rachel so directly as to be cruel (**Am I in the place of God, who has withheld from you the fruit of the womb**).
>
>> i. It is likely that Rachel was vain and conceited. She knew that Jacob worked *14 years* with no pay out of love for her, and also knew Jacob would not have worked one day for Leah.

c. **Here is my maid Bilhah; go in to her, and she will bear a child on my knees, that I also may have children by her**: Much like Sarah gave Hagar to Abraham in a surrogate-mother type arrangement (Genesis 16), Rachel gave her maid Bilhah to Jacob.

> i. The phrase **bear a child on my knees** refers to the ancient practice of surrogate-adoption. Some believe that the phrase refers only to a symbolic placement of the child on the knees of one who adopts it. Others believe that it refers to the surrogate sitting on the lap of the adoptive mother during both insemination and birth. Referring to Genesis 30:3, the Twentieth Century Bible Commentary says: "These words are probably intended literally, and not merely as figurative adoption."
>
> ii. We should not regard the idea that Bilhah was inseminated and gave birth "on the knees" of Rachel as a certainty. We don't know enough about the ancient practice, and even if it were an ancient custom, it doesn't mean that it was followed in every case, but it certainly is a reasonable possibility.

d. **She gave him Bilhah her maid as wife**: This did not mean that Jacob actually married Bilhah. It means Jacob did with Bilhah what a man should only do with his wife.

2. (5-6) The birth of Dan.

And Bilhah conceived and bore Jacob a son. Then Rachel said, "God has judged my case; and He has also heard my voice and given me a son." Therefore she called his name Dan.

a. **She called his name Dan**: Jacob's fifth son, born to him through Bilhah, the maid of Rachel, was named by Rachel **Dan**, meaning *Judgment*. Because of her own envy, she viewed this child born of the flesh as a victory and a vindication for her.

b. **God has judged my case; and He has also heard my voice and given me a son**: Rachel felt that the birth of **Dan** was proof that God **heard** her complaint. She felt strengthened in the competition against her sister Leah.

> i. "Can a woman get so low that she will hit her sister over the head with a baby? Rachel did." (Barnhouse)

3. (7-8) The birth of Naphtali.

And Rachel's maid Bilhah conceived again and bore Jacob a second son. Then Rachel said, "With great wrestlings I have wrestled with my sister, *and* indeed I have prevailed." So she called his name Naphtali.

a. **She called his name Naphtali**: Jacob's sixth son, born to him through Bilhah, the maid of Rachel, was named **Naphtali**. Rachel gave this name (meaning *wrestle*), because relationships in their home had broken down to the point where Rachel openly acknowledged the baby competition.

b. **With great wrestlings I have wrestled with my sister, and indeed I have prevailed**: This seems strange, because at this point Leah had four sons, and Rachel (through Bilhah) had two sons. Yet Rachel said that she had **prevailed**. Perhaps she meant it in the sense that now Leah seemed to have stopped having children.

B. Two sons born to Zilpah.

1. (9-11) The birth of Gad.

When Leah saw that she had stopped bearing, she took Zilpah her maid and gave her to Jacob as wife. And Leah's maid Zilpah bore Jacob a son. Then Leah said, "A troop comes!" So she called his name Gad.

a. **She took Zilpah her maid and gave her to Jacob as wife**: Leah, who has stopped bearing children, figured she could use the same surrogate-mother method to increase the number of children accounted to her, so she gave her maid Zilpah to Jacob, as Rachel had given her maid Bilhah to Jacob.

b. **She called his name Gad**: Jacob's seventh son, born to him through Zilpah, the maid of Leah, was named **Gad**, meaning *Troop* or *Good Fortune*. The wives of Jacob continued to use their children as pawns in a power struggle within the home.

i. Leah had apparently lost the peace she had when her fourth son was born; she no longer had the peace praise (*Judah*) brought.

2. (12-13) The birth of Asher.

And Leah's maid Zilpah bore Jacob a second son. Then Leah said, "I am happy, for the daughters will call me blessed." So she called his name Asher.

a. **So she called his name Asher**: Jacob's eighth son, born to him through Zilpah, the maid of Leah, was named **Asher**, meaning *Happy*. Leah was more concerned about the status the child would bring her (**all the daughters will call me blessed**) than about the child himself.

C. Leah herself bears two more sons and a daughter.

1. (14-18) The birth of Issachar.

Now Reuben went in the days of wheat harvest and found mandrakes in the field, and brought them to his mother Leah. Then Rachel said to

Leah, "Please give me *some* of your son's mandrakes." But she said to her, "*Is it* a small matter that you have taken away my husband? Would you take away my son's mandrakes also?" And Rachel said, "Therefore he will lie with you tonight for your son's mandrakes." When Jacob came out of the field in the evening, Leah went out to meet him and said, "You must come in to me, for I have surely hired you with my son's mandrakes." And he lay with her that night. And God listened to Leah, and she conceived and bore Jacob a fifth son. Leah said, "God has given me my wages, because I have given my maid to my husband." So she called his name Issachar.

    a. **Found mandrakes in the field**: The mandrake is a root, called the *love apple* in Hebrew. They were thought to increase fertility in women (and still are among some peoples). Because Leah had the mandrakes, she knew Jacob would have relations with her, believing there was a greater likelihood she would become pregnant.

        i. We don't know if the effect of the mandrakes was something biological or if it worked more as a placebo. Under the guiding hand of God, the mandrakes seemed to work in the case of Leah and Jacob. Whatever strange agencies God may allow to be used (such as mandrakes), the real factor was His sovereign will (**God listened to Leah**).

    b. **You have taken away my husband**: The hostility between Leah and Rachel was as obvious as it was painful. It must have been terrible living in a home where one wife believed the other had stolen her husband from her.

        i. This confirms the wisdom of God's original plan, as expressed in Genesis 2:24: one man to be joined to one woman in a one-flesh relationship. Later, Leviticus 18:18 forbade the marrying of sisters, and this shows why.

        ii. "Is it any wonder that this family had a history of strife and bloodshed? Children reflect the atmosphere of the home." (Barnhouse)

    c. **So she called his name Issachar**: Jacob's ninth son, born to Leah, was named **Issachar**, meaning *Reward*. Leah saw this son as a reward from God, because she was generous enough to offer her maid to Jacob.

2. (19-20) The birth of Zebulun.

Then Leah conceived again and bore Jacob a sixth son. And Leah said, "God has endowed me with a good endowment; now my husband will dwell with me, because I have borne him six sons." So she called his name Zebulun.

    a. **So she called his name Zebulun**: Jacob's tenth son, born to Leah, was named **Zebulun**, meaning *Dwelling*. In the pain of her heart, she still waited for her husband to truly love her and live with *her*, and she hoped the sheer quantity of sons would win his heart to her.

3. (21) The birth of Dinah.

Afterward she bore a daughter, and called her name Dinah.

a. **Afterward she bore a daughter**: Finally, after ten children, Jacob became father to a daughter through Leah, who was named **Dinah**. Apparently, there was nothing symbolically significant in her name.

b. **Afterward**: The ungodly competition had, in one sense, ended. Leah and the two maids would have no more children from this point on.

i. The wives fought each other as if they were in a poker game:

"I bid one wife, loved and beautiful."

"I bid one wife and four sons."

"I'll match your one wife and raise you a concubine and the concubine's two sons."

"I'll raise you another concubine and two more sons by her; plus two more sons on my own, and I'll throw in a daughter. I'll stand with one wife, one concubine, six sons, and one daughter."

Nobody was the winner at this competition.

D. Rachel herself bears a son to Jacob.

1. (22) God's sovereignty over the womb.

Then God remembered Rachel, and God listened to her and opened her womb.

a. **And opened her womb**: The idea of God's sovereignty over the womb is a repeated theme in the Bible. The purposes of God in opening one and closing the other may be completely unknowable, but God has His purpose.

- God granted twins to Rebekah (Genesis 25:21).
- He opens the womb of Leah (Genesis 29:31).
- He closed the womb of Hannah, for a time (1 Samuel 1:5).

2. (23-24) The birth of Joseph.

And she conceived and bore a son, and said, "God has taken away my reproach." So she called his name Joseph, and said, "The LORD shall add to me another son."

a. **So she called his name Joseph**: The eleventh son born to Jacob, through Rachel, was named **Joseph**, meaning *May He Add*. Rachel felt she had been vindicated by the birth of one son, but longed for more children to continue the competition with her sister Leah.

b. **God has taken away my reproach**: At this point, one might think this eleventh son would end up being the key son used to further God's redemptive purpose through this family. Yet Isaiah 55:8-9 is true: *"For My thoughts are not your thoughts, nor are your ways My ways," says the* LORD. *"For as the heavens are higher than the earth, so are My ways higher than your ways, and My thoughts than your thoughts."*

E. Jacob's agreement with Laban.

1. (25-27) Jacob knows it is time to go back to Canaan.

And it came to pass, when Rachel had borne Joseph, that Jacob said to Laban, "Send me away, that I may go to my own place and to my country. Give *me* my wives and my children for whom I have served you, and let me go; for you know my service which I have done for you." And Laban said to him, "Please *stay*, if I have found favor in your eyes, *for* I have learned by experience that the LORD **has blessed me for your sake."**

a. **Send me away, that I may go to my own place and to my country**: Though Jacob was in Haran with Laban and his daughters for more than 14 years, he knew that he belonged in the land promised to him by God, through the covenant made with his grandfather Abraham and his father Isaac. After 14 years, Jacob still called the Promised Land **my country**.

b. **Please stay, if I have found favor in your eyes, for I have learned by experience that the** LORD **has blessed me for your sake**: Laban knew Jacob was an invaluable worker for him. Laban said this knowledge was **learned by experience**. Literally this means, *learned by divination*. It is probable that Laban practiced occult divination, and by this he knew the source of blessing.

2. (28-34) Jacob negotiates a deal with Laban to start building a flock of sheep and goats for himself.

Then he said, "Name me your wages, and I will give *it*." So *Jacob* said to him, "You know how I have served you and how your livestock has been with me. For what you had before I *came was* little, and it has increased to a great amount; the LORD **has blessed you since my coming. And now, when shall I also provide for my own house?" So he said, "What shall I give you?" And Jacob said, "You shall not give me anything. If you will do this thing for me, I will again feed and keep your flocks: Let me pass through all your flock today, removing from there all the speckled and spotted sheep, and all the brown ones among the lambs, and the spotted**

and speckled among the goats; and *these* shall be my wages. So my righteousness will answer for me in time to come, when the subject of my wages comes before you: every one that is not speckled and spotted among the goats, and brown among the lambs, will be considered stolen, if *it is* with me." And Laban said, "Oh, that it were according to your word!"

> a. **The spotted and speckled among the goats; and these shall be my wages**: Jacob would take the **speckled** and **spotted** offspring, but first he had to separate the currently speckled or spotted animals from the rest of the flock. This set the probability of more **speckled** and **spotted** offspring against him.
>
>> i. Allowing the **speckled** and **spotted** sheep and goats to remain in the flock would increase the likelihood of more speckled and spotted offspring coming from the flock at large.
>
> b. **Laban said, "Oh, that it were according to your word"**: This was an agreeable deal to both parties. First, it was a foolproof way to distinguish between the flocks of Laban and Jacob. As well, Laban liked the deal because the odds were set in his favor. Jacob may have proposed in this arrangement because he was willing to trust in God.

3. (35-36) The agreement is made, and the flocks are separated.

So he removed that day the male goats that were speckled and spotted, all the female goats that were speckled and spotted, every one that had *some* white in it, and all the brown ones among the lambs, and gave *them* into the hand of his sons. Then he put three days' journey between himself and Jacob, and Jacob fed the rest of Laban's flocks.

> a. **Jacob fed the rest of Laban's flocks**: Jacob would care for the large flock of his father-in-law Laban, made up of solid-colored animals. Jacob received any **speckled** or **spotted** offspring of this flock.
>
>> i. Obviously, if there was a way Jacob could encourage these solid-colored sheep to bring forth spotted and speckled offspring, it would increase his personal wealth.
>
> b. **He put three days' journey between himself and Jacob**: To prevent the mixing of the flocks, Laban's sons took care of all the existing speckled and spotted sheep and goats, keeping them a three-day journey from the main flock.
>
> c. **Jacob fed the rest of Laban's flocks**: To make sure that the property of his employer was well taken care of, Jacob himself looked over Laban's flock.

4. (37-43) God blesses Jacob's method of breeding, and he greatly increases in wealth.

Now Jacob took for himself rods of green poplar and of the almond and chestnut trees, peeled white strips in them, and exposed the white which was in the rods. And the rods which he had peeled, he set before the flocks in the gutters, in the watering troughs where the flocks came to drink, so that they should conceive when they came to drink. So the flocks conceived before the rods, and the flocks brought forth streaked, speckled, and spotted. Then Jacob separated the lambs, and made the flocks face toward the streaked and all the brown in the flock of Laban; but he put his own flocks by themselves and did not put them with Laban's flock. And it came to pass, whenever the stronger livestock conceived, that Jacob placed the rods before the eyes of the livestock in the gutters, that they might conceive among the rods. But when the flocks were feeble, he did not put *them* in; so the feebler were Laban's and the stronger Jacob's. Thus the man became exceedingly prosperous, and had large flocks, female and male servants, and camels and donkeys.

a. **Jacob took for himself rods of green poplar and of the almond and chestnut trees**: When Jacob put these branches in the **watering troughs** of the flocks, it apparently increased the number of speckled and spotted offspring from the solid-colored flock that Jacob managed on Laban's behalf.

b. **So the feebler were Laban's and the stronger Jacob's**: Jacob also used selective breeding to increase the strength and vitality of his flock. We don't know exactly how this method worked. It is possible Jacob knew more about animal husbandry than we do today; but it is more likely Jacob did the best he knew, and God blessed it.

i. Genesis 31:10-13 tells us that Jacob saw in a dream the blessed reproduction of speckled and spotted sheep and goats. That dream was also connected with a promise of God's care for Jacob and a command to return to Canaan, the land of his family.

c. **Thus the man became exceedingly prosperous**: The ancient Hebrew says, "The man burst out exceedingly exceedingly." God blessed Jacob, but it was not because Jacob was especially good. It was because of the promises God made to Jacob (Genesis 28:13-15) and the covenant made to Abraham.

i. In the same way, blessing comes from the LORD to us not because we are great or good, but because of the covenant God has made with us through Jesus, and promises He has given us in His word.

ii. We may note Jacob's principles for prosperity:
- Don't make wealth your goal (Genesis 30:25-26).
- Don't be afraid to work for others and try to increase their wealth before or as you work to increase your own wealth (Genesis 30:27).
- Work hard, dedicating yourself to your employer's success (Genesis 30:26, 31:38-42).
- Trust God (Genesis 30:31-33).

Genesis 31 – Jacob Flees from Laban to Canaan

A. Jacob's disputes with Laban and his sons.

1. (1-2) Contention with Laban's sons causes Laban to look differently at Jacob.

Now *Jacob* heard the words of Laban's sons, saying, "Jacob has taken away all that was our father's, and from what was our father's he has acquired all this wealth." And Jacob saw the countenance of Laban, and indeed it was not *favorable* toward him as before.

> a. **Jacob has taken away all that was our father's**: It wasn't that Jacob had taken anything that belonged to Laban. Rather, it was that his wealth was increasing in proportion to Laban's wealth. The problem wasn't that Jacob stole; it was that **Laban's sons** were filled with *envy*.
>
>> i. Envy will distort the truth. Jacob had not taken anything of Laban's, but envy will lie. Therefore Jacob's sons said, **Jacob has taken away all that was our father's**.
>
> b. **The countenance of Laban… was not favorable toward him**: The envy of Laban's sons poisoned Laban's heart against Jacob. Before, Laban was entirely pleased with the agreement.
>
>> i. Envy is bad not only on its own, but also for the company it keeps: *For you are still carnal. For where there are envy, strife, and divisions among you, are you not carnal and behaving like mere men?* (1 Corinthians 3:3). *For where envy and self-seeking exist, confusion and every evil thing are there* (James 3:16).
>>
>> ii. Instead, *Love suffers long and is kind; love does not envy* (1 Cor 13:4).
>>
>> iii. God wants to deliver us from envy: *For we ourselves were also once foolish, disobedient, deceived, serving various lusts and pleasures, living in malice and envy, hateful and hating one another* (Titus 3:3).
>>
>> iv. Envy is no small sin. It put Jesus on the cross: *For he knew that they had handed Him over because of envy* (Matthew 27:18).

2. (3) God tells Jacob to return to the Promised Land.

Then the LORD said to Jacob, "Return to the land of your fathers and to your family, and I will be with you."

> a. **Return to the land of your fathers**: Even if Jacob never knew it, God prepared him for this time. First, God gave him the *desire* to go back home (Genesis 30:25). Then, his *present circumstances became unbearable*. Finally, the LORD gave *personal direction* to Jacob. Today, God may lead people after the same pattern.
>
> b. **And I will be with you**: This was the most important aspect. If God were **with** Jacob, he could be at peace and confident in any difficulty – or at least had the opportunity for peace and confidence. The promise of God's presence meant everything.

3. (4-9) Jacob explains the situation and his plan to his wives.

So Jacob sent and called Rachel and Leah to the field, to his flock, and said to them, "I see your father's countenance, that it is not *favorable* toward me as before; but the God of my father has been with me. And you know that with all my might I have served your father. Yet your father has deceived me and changed my wages ten times, but God did not allow him to hurt me. If he said thus: 'The speckled shall be your wages,' then all the flocks bore speckled. And if he said thus: 'The streaked shall be your wages,' then all the flocks bore streaked. So God has taken away the livestock of your father and given *them* to me.

> a. **But the God of my father has been with me**: Even though Laban tried to cheat Jacob, God protected him all the time. God showed Jacob that He was greater and able to overcome what any man might do to Jacob. God's presence was with Jacob, just as God had promised (Genesis 28:15).
>
>> i. This attitude was later expressed in a Psalm: *The LORD is on my side; I will not fear. What can man do to me?* (Psalm 118:6).
>
> b. **You know that with all my might I have served your father**: Jacob not only believed that he had acted properly toward Laban, but he also believed that his wives knew of his righteous conduct and Laban's unfair treatment of him.

4. (10-13) Jacob's dream of the flocks.

And it happened, at the time when the flocks conceived, that I lifted my eyes and saw in a dream, and behold, the rams which leaped upon the flocks were streaked, speckled, and gray-spotted. Then the Angel of God spoke to me in a dream, saying, 'Jacob.' And I said, 'Here I am.' And He said, 'Lift your eyes now and see, all the rams which leap on the

flocks are streaked, speckled, and gray-spotted; for I have seen all that Laban is doing to you. I *am* the God of Bethel, where you anointed the pillar *and* where you made a vow to Me. Now arise, get out of this land, and return to the land of your family.'"

    a. **The Angel of God spoke to me in a dream**: Here, we learn that the blessing of blessed production of sheep and goats described in Genesis 30:37-43 was in some way revealed to Jacob in a dream. Jacob did not only use clever agricultural methods; more importantly, he had the blessing of God.

    b. **I am the God of Bethel**: God told Jacob to go back to Bethel, back to the place where he first encountered the LORD in a personal way. This was Jacob's way of returning to his first love and first works (as would be later described in Revelation 2:4-5).

        i. **I am the God of Bethel**: It is good to remember times and places where the LORD did great works for us and has met us in wonderful ways. As we remember them, God reminds us He is still the same God who met our needs then and wants to meet our needs now.

        ii. "You remember, some of you, perhaps, the first time when pardoning love was revealed to you — when you were brought to see the love of God in the great atoning sacrifice of Jesus Christ. Well, to-night, the Lord says to you, 'I am the same God as you have ever found me. I have not changed. I change not; therefore ye sons of Jacob are not consumed, even as your father Jacob was not consumed; for I was even to him the selfsame God.'" (Spurgeon)

    c. **Arise, get out of this land, and return to the land of your family**: In this previous dream, God told Jacob to return. The land was **the land of your family**, the land promised to Abraham, Isaac, and Jacob by covenant.

5. (14-16) Leah and Rachel support Jacob in his desire to move back to Canaan.

Then Rachel and Leah answered and said to him, "Is there still any portion or inheritance for us in our father's house? Are we not considered strangers by him? For he has sold us, and also completely consumed our money. For all these riches which God has taken from our father are *really* **ours and our children's; now then, whatever God has said to you, do it."**

    a. **Is there still any portion or inheritance for us in our father's house**: Rachel and Leah noted that their father Laban had already used any potential inheritance they may have once received (**also completely consumed our money**). This meant they were happy to leave their homeland with Jacob and return to Bethel and the land promised to Jacob.

b. **Whatever God has said to you, do it**: Their support of Jacob in a costly and perhaps dangerous move was significant. It was a huge undertaking to move such a large family so far. If not for the support of his wives, Jacob perhaps would not have done what the LORD had told him to do.

i. This may be the first time in quite a while when the sisters Leah and Rachel agreed on anything. They could agree in uniting against a common enemy – their father Laban.

B. Jacob's departure from Laban.

1. (17-21) Jacob leaves without saying goodbye.

Then Jacob rose and set his sons and his wives on camels. And he carried away all his livestock and all his possessions which he had gained, his acquired livestock which he had gained in Padan Aram, to go to his father Isaac in the land of Canaan. Now Laban had gone to shear his sheep, and Rachel had stolen the household idols that were her father's. And Jacob stole away, unknown to Laban the Syrian, in that he did not tell him that he intended to flee. So he fled with all that he had. He arose and crossed the river, and headed toward the mountains of Gilead.

a. **Jacob rose and set his sons and wives on camels**: Jacob intended a quick departure, traveling as fast as possible. Jacob was wealthy enough so that his entire family could travel **on camels**.

b. **Jacob stole away, unknown to Laban the Syrian**: God already told Jacob to go and had promised him safe passage. Jacob's fear and deceptive departure showed that he lacked confidence in God and His promise, and he relied more on his own wisdom and ability.

i. "He could have announced his departure and gone in the glory of an army with banners. But fear made it impossible to reap the full measure of blessing. He sneaked away into the will of God instead of departing in triumph." (Barnhouse)

c. **Rachel had stolen the household idols that were her father's**: Rachel stole her father's **household idols** (*teraphim*). There are many potential reasons why Rachel did this.

- Perhaps she worshipped these idols and did not want to be without them.
- Perhaps she did not want her father to inquire of them, to use them as tools of divination to catch them (as he may have previously done, as in Genesis 30:27).

- Perhaps it was because such idols were often used as deeds to property and she thought that by taking the idols she took whatever inheritance might be left to Laban's children.
- Perhaps Rachel stole the *teraphim* simply to get back at her father, whom she felt had mistreated her, her husband, and her whole family.
- According to some Jewish traditions, Rachel took the *teraphim* because she wanted to keep her father Laban from idolatry.

d. **Headed toward the mountains of Gilead**: It was nearly 300 miles (482 kilometers) from Haran to the mountains of Gilead, but the journey was longer and more difficult psychologically than it was physically for Jacob. He left the place of safety, where he lived in a comfortable servitude, to go to a place where God called him, but there were many dangerous enemies (such as his brother Esau, who had sworn to kill him).

2. (22-24) Laban pursues and catches Jacob.

And Laban was told on the third day that Jacob had fled. Then he took his brethren with him and pursued him for seven days' journey, and he overtook him in the mountains of Gilead. But God had come to Laban the Syrian in a dream by night, and said to him, "Be careful that you speak to Jacob neither good nor bad."

a. **Laban was told on the third day that Jacob had fled**: This shows that Jacob and his family lived some distance from Laban. He didn't notice their departure for three days.

b. **God had come to Laban the Syrian in a dream by night**: Apparently, Laban *did* have an evil intention against Jacob. Yet God protected Jacob through this **dream by night**, telling Laban to be careful in his dealings with Jacob.

3. (25-30) Laban meets and confronts Jacob.

So Laban overtook Jacob. Now Jacob had pitched his tent in the mountains, and Laban with his brethren pitched in the mountains of Gilead. And Laban said to Jacob: "What have you done, that you have stolen away unknown to me, and carried away my daughters like captives *taken* with the sword? Why did you flee away secretly, and steal away from me, and not tell me; for I might have sent you away with joy and songs, with timbrel and harp? And you did not allow me to kiss my sons and my daughters. Now you have done foolishly in so doing. It is in my power to do you harm, but the God of your father spoke to me last night, saying, 'Be careful that you speak to Jacob neither good nor

bad.' And now you have surely gone because you greatly long for your father's house, *but* why did you steal my gods?"

> a. **In the mountains of Gilead**: At this point, Jacob was not far from the Jordan River and the Promised Land. This shows that he traveled quickly and that Laban was determined to pursue him this far.
>
> b. **Why did you flee away secretly**: Laban first tried to shame Jacob with kindness, suggesting that they would have had a celebration at his departure. Apparently, that idea was met with an unsympathetic response, so Laban threatened Jacob (**it is in my power to do you harm**).
>
>> i. **My sons and my daughters** in this context means Laban's grandsons and granddaughters.
>
> c. **Why did you steal my gods**: Laban ended his words to Jacob with an accusing question. He knew that his *teraphim* were missing and he had reason to believe that Jacob had stolen them. Laban's question shows the foolishness of idolatry. It is sad and strange to have a god that can be stolen.

4. (31-32) Jacob proclaims his innocence.

Then Jacob answered and said to Laban, "Because I was afraid, for I said, 'Perhaps you would take your daughters from me by force.' With whomever you find your gods, do not let him live. In the presence of our brethren, identify what I have of yours and take it with you." For Jacob did not know that Rachel had stolen them.

> a. **Jacob answered and said to Laban**: Jacob replied with an explanation for their secret departure (**Because I was afraid**), and with a firm belief he and his family had not taken Laban's household idols.
>
> b. **With whomever you find your gods, do not let him live**: Jacob, not knowing his beloved wife Rachel stole the household idols, proclaimed his innocence and pronounced a harsh curse on the thief, not knowing that he actually invited judgment on his own wife.

5. (33-35) Laban searches for his household idols.

And Laban went into Jacob's tent, into Leah's tent, and into the two maids' tents, but he did not find *them*. Then he went out of Leah's tent and entered Rachel's tent. Now Rachel had taken the household idols, put them in the camel's saddle, and sat on them. And Laban searched all about the tent but did not find *them*. And she said to her father, "Let it not displease my lord that I cannot rise before you, for the manner of women is with me." And he searched but did not find the household idols.

a. **Laban went into Jacob's tent**: Laban was confident that his idols had been stolen. He made a thorough search of Jacob's tents.

b. **Rachel had taken the household idols, put them in the camel's saddle, and sat on them**: Rachel learned the ways of deception well from her father – and perhaps also from her husband. She succeeded in deceiving her father about the idols.

> i. "Amid much that is sad and even sordid in this story… amid craft, deceit, and lying on almost every side, we cannot fail to see the hand of God overruling and making even the wrath of man to praise Him." (Griffith Thomas, cited in Barnhouse)

6. (36-42) Jacob rebukes his father-in-law Laban.

Then Jacob was angry and rebuked Laban, and Jacob answered and said to Laban: "What *is* my trespass? What *is* my sin, that you have so hotly pursued me? Although you have searched all my things, what part of your household things have you found? Set *it* here before my brethren and your brethren, that they may judge between us both! These twenty years I *have been* with you; your ewes and your female goats have not miscarried their young, and I have not eaten the rams of your flock. That which was torn *by beasts* I did not bring to you; I bore the loss of it. You required it from my hand, *whether* stolen by day or stolen by night. *There* I was! In the day the drought consumed me, and the frost by night, and my sleep departed from my eyes. Thus I have been in your house twenty years; I served you fourteen years for your two daughters, and six years for your flock, and you have changed my wages ten times. Unless the God of my father, the God of Abraham and the Fear of Isaac, had been with me, surely now you would have sent me away empty-handed. God has seen my affliction and the labor of my hands, and rebuked *you* last night."

a. **Then Jacob was angry and rebuked Laban**: It is likely that this anger built up in Jacob for a long time – perhaps 20 years. Perhaps in his mind, he practiced this speech over and over again.

b. **What is my trespass**: Jacob rebuked Laban and made the case for his own innocence with several examples.

- **What part of your household things have you found**: After searching, Laban found no evidence of the stolen gods he accused Jacob of taking.

- **These twenty years I have been with you**: Jacob's twenty years of faithful service proved his integrity.

- **Your ewes and your female goats have not miscarried**: This demonstrated the care Jacob showed for the success of Laban's herds.

- **I have not eaten the rams of your flock**: Jacob didn't feed or enrich himself at the expense of what belonged to Laban.

- **That which was torn by beasts I did not bring to you**: It was an ancient custom that a shepherd could bring the torn carcass of a sheep to his owner, as evidence that he was brave enough to not let the wolf devour it or take it away, and thus the shepherd would be excused. Jacob explained he didn't follow this custom, and every animal that was attacked or stolen, he replaced out of his own herd.

- **Drought consumed me, and the frost by night, and my sleep departed**: Jacob worked hard and sacrificed for the success of Laban's enterprise.

- **You have changed my wages ten times**: Jacob endured repeated unfairness from Laban as his employer.

c. **Unless the God of my father, the God of Abraham and the Fear of Isaac, had been with me, surely now you would have sent me away empty handed**: Jacob claimed that it was God's protection that sent him away in a way that prevented Laban from taking what belonged to Jacob.

i. It was good that Jacob saw God's presence and protection in all this. Unfortunately, nowhere did Jacob claim God as *his* own; he referred to God as the **Fear** of his father **Isaac** and the **God** of his grandfather **Abraham**.

C. Laban and Jacob make a covenant.

1. (43-50) Jacob and Laban make a covenant.

And Laban answered and said to Jacob, "*These* daughters are my daughters, and *these* children are my children, and *this* flock is my flock; all that you see is mine. But what can I do this day to these my daughters or to their children whom they have borne? Now therefore, come, let us make a covenant, you and I, and let it be a witness between you and me." So Jacob took a stone and set it up as a pillar. Then Jacob said to his brethren, "Gather stones." And they took stones and made a heap, and they ate there on the heap. Laban called it Jegar Sahadutha, but Jacob called it Galeed. And Laban said, "This heap *is* a witness between you and me this day." Therefore its name was called Galeed, also Mizpah, because he said, "May the LORD watch between you and me when we are absent one from another. If you afflict my daughters, or if you take other wives besides my daughters, *although* no man is with us– see, God *is* witness between you and me!"

a. **All that you see is mine**: Laban boldly said that everything Jacob had actually belonged to *him*. Yet in a supposed act of generosity, he said to Jacob, "It **is** mine but, out of the kindness of my heart, I'll let you have it."

b. **May the LORD watch between you and me when we are absent one from another**: In this covenant, Laban expressed how suspicious he was of Jacob. The idea of **Mizpah** (*watch*) is, "If you do wrong, God will see it and may He punish."

> i. "In effect, the pillar of Mizpah meant, 'If you come over on my side of this line, the pact is void and I will kill you.' The covenant breaker would need God to take care of him, because the other would shoot to kill" (Barnhouse). **Mizpah** was never meant to be a nice sentiment – despite what a Mizpah coin shared between two people might say.

2. (51-55) A pillar of separation and a parting of their ways.

Then Laban said to Jacob, "Here is this heap and here is *this* pillar, which I have placed between you and me. This heap *is* a witness, and *this* pillar *is* a witness, that I will not pass beyond this heap to you, and you will not pass beyond this heap and this pillar to me, for harm. The God of Abraham, the God of Nahor, and the God of their father judge between us." And Jacob swore by the Fear of his father Isaac. Then Jacob offered a sacrifice on the mountain, and called his brethren to eat bread. And they ate bread and stayed all night on the mountain. And early in the morning Laban arose, and kissed his sons and daughters and blessed them. Then Laban departed and returned to his place.

a. **I will not pass beyond this heap to you**: The best solution for Jacob's in-law problems was for him to separate from Laban. Therefore they set up a pillar to be a barrier between them.

> i. There is wisdom in having some separation from in-laws. The Bible says, *therefore a man shall leave his father and mother and be joined to his wife* (Genesis 2:24). Laban and Jacob seemed to have more problems than most families, so their separation was extreme.

b. **Then Laban departed and returned to his place**: After a proper goodbye, Laban saw his daughters and grandchildren for the last time. Jacob took his family to Canaan and never returned to where Laban lived.

> i. "This is the last we hear of Laban in the Bible, and it is good that this is the end of him. Laban is of the world, and Jacob needed to be freed from this world in order to live wholeheartedly for the God of his fathers." (Boice)

> ii. Morris on Laban: "Rather than seeking to follow the truth of God's plan as witnessed by Jacob, he merely resented and coveted the blessing

of God on Jacob. He finally ended up with neither. His life constitutes a sober warning to a great host of semireligious but fundamentally self-worshipping and self-seeking men and women today."

ii. Rachel and Leah were wrong to look to their father Laban for their *portion or inheritance* (Genesis 31:14) once they were married to Jacob. He now was their portion and inheritance. "Since you are saved and joined to Christ, appraise the world and ask, 'Is there yet any portion for me?' If you think there is, you are mistaken" (Barnhouse).

Genesis 32 – Jacob Prepares to Meet Esau

A. Jacob hears of Esau's approach.

1. (1-2) Jacob meets the angels of God at Mahanaim.

So Jacob went on his way, and the angels of God met him. When Jacob saw them, he said, "This is God's camp." And he called the name of that place Mahanaim.

> a. **The angels of God met him**: We don't exactly know what this means. In some way, angelic beings that are normally unseen were now made visible to Jacob, and they **met him**. Perhaps God wanted Jacob to know how great His care was for him and his family.
>
>> i. This wonderful revelation of God's presence and care came *after* Jacob finally separated from Laban, the worldly man. Separation from the world brings greater insight to the believer.
>>
>> ii. "Our Mahanaims occur at much the same time as that in which Jacob beheld this great sight. Jacob was entering upon a more separated life. He was leaving Laban and the school of all those tricks of bargaining and bartering which belong to the ungodly world." (Spurgeon)
>
> b. **This is God's camp**: Literally, Jacob observed he was in a *double camp*. He was not alone; God had a camp of **angels** to be with him at **Mahanaim**.
>
>> i. It was not as if God's angels just joined Jacob. They were with him the entire time. Now, Jacob could *see* God's angels with him and it provided great encouragement.
>>
>> ii. Angels, though "higher" beings than us, are ordained by God to be our servants (Hebrews 1:14) and they serve God's people even as they served Jesus (Matthew 4:11). In 2 Kings 6:15-17, Elisha's servant had his eyes opened to see the tremendous angelic host surrounding them.
>>
>> iii. John Paton, a missionary to the New Hebrides Islands, told of how one night hostile natives surrounded his mission's headquarters,

intent on driving the Patons out of their home and killing them. He and his wife prayed through the entire night, and when daylight finally came, their attackers were gone. A year later, the chief of the tribe became a Christian, and Paton asked the man about that night. The chief replied, "Who were all those men you had with you there?" The missionary explained only he and his wife were there. The chief insisted he had seen hundreds of big men with shining garments and swords circling the mission headquarters, so the natives were afraid to attack (Billy Graham in *Angels, God's Secret Agents*, page 3). That night in the New Hebrides Islands, there certainly was a "double camp," a group of angels to help and serve the missionary family.

iv. Spurgeon thought about the great multitude of angels that God has available for His people's help: "It may be that every star is a world, thronged with the servants of God, who are willing and ready to dart like flames of fire upon Jehovah's errands of love. If the Lord's chosen could not be sufficiently protected by the forces available in one world, he has but to speak or will, and myriads of spirits from the far-off regions of space would come thronging forward to guard the children of their king."

v. "I do not ask that you may see angels: still, if it can be, so be it. But what is it, after all, to see an angel? Is not the fact of God's presence better than the sight of the best of his creatures? Perhaps the Lord favored Jacob with the sight of angels because he was such a poor, weak creature as to his faith." (Spurgeon)

2. (3-6) Jacob's message to Esau.

Then Jacob sent messengers before him to Esau his brother in the land of Seir, the country of Edom. And he commanded them, saying, "Speak thus to my lord Esau, 'Thus your servant Jacob says: "I have dwelt with Laban and stayed there until now. I have oxen, donkeys, flocks, and male and female servants; and I have sent to tell my lord, that I may find favor in your sight.""" Then the messengers returned to Jacob, saying, "We came to your brother Esau, and he also is coming to meet you, and four hundred men are with him."

a. **Jacob sent messengers before him to Esau his brother**: Jacob, seeking to reconcile with his brother (who 20 years before swore to kill him), first began by humbling himself and beginning his message with "**your servant Jacob.**"

b. **I have oxen, donkeys, flocks, and male and female servants**: Jacob wasn't boasting. He wanted Esau to know that he was a man of wealth and that he did not come to take anything from Esau. Jacob tried to anticipate his brother's thinking and to answer Esau's concerns.

c. **He also is coming to meet you, and four hundred men are with him**: When the messengers returned, Jacob heard news that gave him great concern – Esau was **coming to meet** him with 400 men. Because Jacob could not bring himself to think the best of Esau (for understandable reasons), he was convinced the 400 men were an army intending to destroy him and his family.

3. (7-8) Jacob's fear and panicked preparation.

So Jacob was greatly afraid and distressed; and he divided the people that were with him, and the flocks and herds and camels, into two companies. And he said, "If Esau comes to the one company and attacks it, then the other company which is left will escape."

a. **Jacob was greatly afraid and distressed**: When Laban confronted Jacob with a hostile militia, Jacob boldly stood up to him and spoke his mind (Genesis 31:36-42); yet Jacob was afraid to meet Esau. This was because Jacob knew he was in the right with Laban, but he knew he was in the wrong with Esau.

i. "Jacob had just been delivered from Laban, but he was oppressed by another load: the dread of Esau was upon him. He had wronged his brother; and you cannot do a wrong without being haunted by it afterwards." (Spurgeon)

ii. Shakespeare was right when he wrote, "Conscience does make cowards of us all," (*Hamlet*, Act 3 Scene 1). As Jacob had no strength before Esau because of guilt, many Christians today are also hindered by memory of their past sins and failings.

b. **Jacob was greatly afraid and distressed**: Before Jacob left home, after his brother swore to kill him, Rebekah told Jacob *until your brother's anger turns away from you, and he forgets what you have done to him; then I will send and bring you from there* (Genesis 27:45). Rebekah never sent for Jacob; therefore, he had every reason to believe that Esau was still angry with him 20 years later.

i. But Jacob also had every reason to believe God would protect him. He seems to have forgotten God had a special camp of angels there to protect him (Genesis 32:1-2). His great fear and distress was not appropriate for someone under God's protection.

- Jacob's fear was wrong, because it followed after a great deliverance.

- Jacob's fear was wrong, because he had just had a remarkable divine visitation.
- Jacob's fear was wrong, because it probably arose out of a remembrance of his old sins.

ii. Jacob could have said, "I don't know if Esau is coming to me in peace or in war. I hope for peace, but if it is war, I trust God will protect me."

c. **He divided the people that were with him, and the flocks and herds and camels, into two companies**: In splitting his company, Jacob used human wisdom and schemes to prepare for Esau's coming. He should have trusted that God could protect all he had. Jacob forgot about God's two camps (Genesis 32:2) and tried to make his *own* **two companies**.

i. "Jacob is the type of a believer who has too much planning and scheming about him; he is a wise man according to the judgment of the world… Abraham never descended to any of the tricks by which Jacob sought to increase his flocks; he lived, like a princely man, in simple, childlike confidence in God, willing to be injured rather than to seek his own interests." (Spurgeon)

4. (9-12) Jacob's prayer.

Then Jacob said, "O God of my father Abraham and God of my father Isaac, the LORD who said to me, 'Return to your country and to your family, and I will deal well with you': I am not worthy of the least of all the mercies and of all the truth which You have shown Your servant; for I crossed over this Jordan with my staff, and now I have become two companies. Deliver me, I pray, from the hand of my brother, from the hand of Esau; for I fear him, lest he come and attack me *and* the mother with the children. For You said, 'I will surely treat you well, and make your descendants as the sand of the sea, which cannot be numbered for multitude.'"

a. **Then Jacob said**: After first reacting in fear and unbelief, Jacob did the right thing. He went to the LORD and prayed a good prayer, humble, full of faith, full of thanksgiving and God's Word.

i. "Depend upon it, it will go hard with any man who fights against a man of prayer." (Spurgeon)

- Jacob's fear was good, because it led him to prayer.
- Jacob's fear was good, because it led him to take a review of his life.

- Jacob's fear was good, because it led him to seek out a suitable promise from God.

b. **The LORD who said to me, "Return to your country and to your kindred, and I will deal well with you"**: Jacob's prayer had *God's word* (what God said in Genesis 31:3). He also quoted God's promises, **"I will surely treat you well"** (remembering God words in Genesis 28:13-15).

i. Many of our prayers fall short, because there is none of God's Word within them. Often there is none of God's Word in them, because there is little of God's Word in us. Jacob *remembered* what the LORD had said to him. He said to God, **for You said**.

ii. "Beloved, I say to you, one and all, study much the promises of God's word! Have them at your fingers' ends. Remember what things God has said to men, and when he has said them, and to what kind of men he has said them, and discover by this means how far he has said them to you." (Spurgeon)

iii. "When God gave his promise, he did, as it were, put himself in the power of those who know how to plead the promise. Every promise is so much strength given to the man who has faith in the promise, for he may with it overcome even the omnipotent God himself." (Spurgeon)

c. **I am not worthy of the least of all the mercies**: His prayer had *humility* and *thanksgiving*. Jacob understood he was not worthy of what God did for him or what he asked God to do, but he relied on what God promised and not upon his own worthiness.

i. "Notice that while Jacob thus pleads his own unworthiness he is not slow to plead God's goodness." (Spurgeon)

d. **Deliver me, I pray**: His prayer had *faith*. Jacob boldly asked God to do something, humbly giving reasons why the LORD should fulfill His word.

i. George Mueller, a great man of faith and prayer, was once asked what was the most important part of prayer. He answered: "The 15 minutes after I have said, 'Amen.'" No matter how great Jacob's prayer was, his faith would be seen in what he did *after* his prayer.

5. (13-21) Jacob sends many gifts to Esau.

So he lodged there that same night, and took what came to his hand as a present for Esau his brother: two hundred female goats and twenty male goats, two hundred ewes and twenty rams, thirty milk camels with their colts, forty cows and ten bulls, twenty female donkeys and ten foals. Then he delivered *them* to the hand of his servants, every drove by itself, and said to his servants, "Pass over before me, and put some

distance between successive droves." And he commanded the first one, saying, "When Esau my brother meets you and asks you, saying, 'To whom do you belong, and where are you going? Whose *are* these in front of you?' then you shall say, 'They are your servant Jacob's. It is a present sent to my lord Esau; and behold, he also *is* behind us.'" So he commanded the second, the third, and all who followed the droves, saying, "In this manner you shall speak to Esau when you find him; and also say, 'Behold, your servant Jacob *is* behind us.'" For he said, "I will appease him with the present that goes before me, and afterward I will see his face; perhaps he will accept me." So the present went on over before him, but he himself lodged that night in the camp.

    a. **Took what came to his hand as a present for Esau his brother**: Jacob sent such an impressive gift, because he wanted to make it completely clear to Esau that he did not need or want anything from him. It also was probably an attempt to *buy* his brother's good favor.

    b. **I will appease him with the present that goes before me, and afterward I will see his face; perhaps he will accept me**: Jacob seems to be a good example of the principle, "When all else fails, pray." As soon as he finished praying, he took up us own strategies again.

        i. After all, if Jacob really trusted God, he would be at the *head* of the procession to meet Esau, not at the *back*.

        ii. Jacob hoped, "**perhaps he will accept me**," but in Jacob's mind, perhaps not. Jacob also thought, "Perhaps he will kill me just like he said he would."

    c. **So the present went on over before him**: This gift is a good example of the way we trust in our ability to do things and make things happen apart from trusting God. A popular traditional Christian song says:

> *All to Jesus, I surrender, all to Him I freely give;*
> *I will ever love and trust Him, in His presence daily live.*
> *I surrender all, I surrender all,*
> *All to Thee, my blessed Savior, I surrender all.*

        i. But we, so often like Jacob mean, "I surrender all the goats. If that isn't enough, I will surrender all the sheep. If that isn't enough, I will surrender all the camels..." To this point, what Jacob refused to do was to surrender *himself*, truly trusting in God's promise of protection.

        ii. "What care he takes about the whole affair! We cannot blame him, under the circumstances, yet how much grander is the quiet, noble demeanour of Abraham, who trusts in God, and leaves matters more in his hands!" (Spurgeon)

B. Jacob wrestles with God.

1. (22-23) Jacob sends all his possessions over the river.

And he arose that night and took his two wives, his two female servants, and his eleven sons, and crossed over the ford of Jabbok. He took them, sent them over the brook, and sent over what he had.

a. **He took them, sent them over the brook**: This was a demonstration of his faith, because Jacob left himself no retreat. If Esau wanted to attack his group, they would quickly be backed up against the river.

b. **Sent over what he had**: Jacob spent the night alone. This was his last night on the east side of the Jordan River, and he probably spent the night in prayer.

i. God had to get Jacob alone before He dealt with him. While all the activity of the huge entourage surrounded Jacob, he could busy himself with a thousand different tasks. Once he was alone, God commanded his attention.

ii. Think of all Jacob had to pray about: thanking God, remembering all that the LORD did for him, wondering how God would fulfill His work in him. This was a significant turning point in Jacob's life and he knew it.

2. (24-25) A **Man** wrestles with Jacob.

Then Jacob was left alone; and a Man wrestled with him until the breaking of day. Now when He saw that He did not prevail against him, He touched the socket of his hip; and the socket of Jacob's hip was out of joint as He wrestled with him.

a. **A Man wrestled with him until the breaking of day**: Jacob didn't wrestle with the **Man**. Instead, **a Man wrestled with him**. Jacob didn't start out wanting anything from God; God wanted something from him. God wanted all of Jacob's proud self-reliance and fleshly scheming, and God came to take it, by force if necessary.

i. "It does not say that he wrestled with the man, but 'there wrestled a man with him.' We call him 'wrestling Jacob,' and so he was; but we must not forget the wrestling man, — or, rather, the wrestling Christ, — the wrestling Angel of the covenant, who had come to wrestle out of him much of his own strength and wisdom." (Spurgeon)

b. **A Man wrestled with him**: As the following verses show, this was no mere man. This is another special appearance of Jesus in the Old Testament before His incarnation in Bethlehem. This was God in human form.

i. "I suppose our Lord Jesus Christ did here, as on many other occasions preparatory to his full incarnation, assume a human form, and came thus to wrestle with the patriarch." (Spurgeon)

c. **Until the breaking of the day**: We can only imagine what this scene looked like. Perhaps sometimes it looked like a barroom fight, and perhaps at other times it looked like an intense wrestling match.

i. "How did Jacob ever manage to keep up his struggle throughout the entire night? I do not know. But I do know that his determination to hang in there was no greater than our frequent determination to have our own way and eventually win out over God." (Boice)

ii. "It was brave of Jacob thus to wrestle, but there was too much of self about it all. It was his own sufficiency that was wrestling with the God-man, Christ Jesus." (Spurgeon)

d. **He saw that He did not prevail against him**: As the fight progressed, it seemed Jacob was somewhat evenly matched against the **Man**, but the match was only evenly matched in appearance. The **Man** could have won easily at any time, using supernatural power.

i. Sometimes we feel man really *can* contend with God. A man or woman in rebellion against God might seem to do pretty well. The match seems even in appearance only. God can turn the tide at any moment, and He allows the match to go on for His own purposes.

ii. It isn't hard to imagine Jacob working so hard and feeling he is getting the best of his opponent, until finally the **Man** changed the nature of the struggle in a moment. Jacob must have felt very defeated.

3. (26) Jacob's plea to the **Man**.

And He said, "Let Me go, for the day breaks." But he said, "I will not let You go unless You bless me!"

a. **Let Me go, for the day breaks**: The Man let Jacob know this would not last much longer. Even though Jacob clung to him desperately, Jacob had lost. A better, greater Man defeated Jacob.

i. This is an invaluable place for everyone to come to: where God conquers us. There is something to be said for every man doing his wrestling with God, and then acknowledging God's greatness after having been defeated. We must know we serve a God who is greater than us, and we cannot conquer much of anything until He conquers us.

b. **I will not let You go unless You bless me**: This wasn't Jacob dictating terms to God as he did on previous occasions. God overcame Jacob here, and we know from Hosea 12:3-5 that Jacob sought this blessing with weeping. He knew he was defeated, yet desperately wanted a blessing from this Greater One.

> i. *He took his brother by the heel in the womb, and in his strength he struggled with God. Yes, he struggled with the Angel and prevailed; he wept, and sought favor from Him. He found Him in Bethel, and there He spoke to us; that is, the* LORD *God of hosts. The* LORD *is His memorable name.* (Hosea 12:3-5)

c. **Unless You bless me**: Through his past, Jacob was always clever and sneaky enough so he never felt the need to trust in God alone. Now he could *only* rely on the blessing of God.

> i. Jacob was reduced to the place where all he could do was to hold on to the LORD with everything he had. Jacob could not fight anymore, but he could hold on. That is not a bad place to be.

> ii. Here, God has answered Jacob's prayer in Genesis 32:9-12. Yet before Jacob could be delivered from the hand of his brother, he had to be delivered from his own self-will and self-reliance. "It is evident that, as soon as he felt that he must fall, he grasped the other 'Man' with a kind of death-grip, and would not let him go. Now, in his weakness, he will prevail. While he was so strong, he won not the blessing; but when he became utter weakness, then did he conquer" (Spurgeon).

> iii. Jacob thought the real enemy was outside of him, being Esau. The real enemy was his own carnal, fleshly nature, which had not been conquered by God.

4. (27-29) Jacob's name is changed, and he is a blessed man.

So He said to him, "What is your name?" He said, "Jacob." And He said, "Your name shall no longer be called Jacob, but Israel; for you have struggled with God and with men, and have prevailed." Then Jacob asked, saying, "Tell *me* Your name, I pray." And He said, "Why is it *that* you ask about My name?" And He blessed him there.

a. **What is your name**: Jacob must have felt a sense of shame, admitting his name was **Jacob**, with all its associations of deception and cheating. Yet this was *who he was*, and Jacob had to admit to it.

> i. We all want to name ourselves favorably. We say, "I am firm; you are stubborn; they are obstinate fools." God wouldn't allow Jacob to cover up his name, because in his case it reflected his true nature.

b. **Your name shall no longer be called Jacob, but Israel**: The name **Israel** is a compound of two words: *sarah* (meaning, *fight*, *struggle*, or *rule*) and *el* (meaning, *God*). Some take the name Israel to mean, *He who struggles with God* or *He who rules with God*. But in Hebrew names, sometimes God is not the object of the verb but the subject. *Daniel* means *God judges*, not *he judges God*. This principle shows us **Israel** likely means, *God rules*.

> i. From this point on, this son of Isaac will be called **Jacob** twice as often as he is called **Israel**. Apparently, there was still plenty of the old man left in Jacob.

> ii. "Dear friends, I am afraid that the lives of many of the Lord's chosen people alternate between 'Israel' and 'Jacob.' Sometimes we are 'strong in the Lord, and in the power of his might,' and at another time we cry, 'Who is sufficient for these things?' Like princes we prevail with God, and are true Israels; but perhaps ere the sun has gone down we limp with Jacob, and though the spirit be willing, the flesh is weak. We are Jacob before we are Israel; and we are Jacob when we are Israel; but blessed be God, we are Israels with God when we cease to be Jacobs among men." (Spurgeon)

c. **For you have struggled with God and with men, and have prevailed**: Jacob **prevailed** in the sense that he endured through his struggle until God thoroughly conquered him. When you battle with God, you only win by losing and by not giving up until you know you have lost. This is how Jacob **prevailed**.

d. **Why is it that you ask about My name**: The Man probably refused to tell Jacob His name because He figured Jacob should already know it, and it turned out that Jacob *did* know exactly who this was.

e. **And He blessed him there**: Surely, this was the blessing of being defeated by God. It was the blessing of the passing of the old (**Jacob**) life, and the coming of a new (**Israel**) life. It may also have had to do with the great idea of the blessing of Abraham, and meeting Jacob's immediate needs for security in the midst of fear. Whatever Jacob needed, God's blessing provided at the moment.

> i. We note that **He blessed him *there*** – at that particular place.
> - The place of special trial and testing.
> - The place of intense pleading to God.
> - The place of seeing the face of God.
> - The place of conscious weakness.

5. (30-32) Two memorials of this event.

And Jacob called the name of the place Peniel: "For I have seen God face to face, and my life is preserved." Just as he crossed over Penuel

the sun rose on him, and he limped on his hip. Therefore to this day the children of Israel do not eat the muscle that shrank, which *is* on the hip socket, because He touched the socket of Jacob's hip in the muscle that shrank.

> a. **Jacob called the name of the place Peniel**: The first memorial was a name. Jacob named the place **Peniel** (*Face of God*), because he *did* know the name of the *Man* who wrestled with him. He was the same One who wrestled with Jacob all his life.
>
>> i. Jacob also understood it was only by God's grace and mercy he escaped from this episode with his life. No man should be allowed to wrestle with God and live, but God was gracious.
>
> b. **He limped on his hip**: The second memorial was a perpetual limp. Jacob would remember his being conquered by God with every step he took for the rest of his life. This was a small price to pay for such a great gift.
>
>> i. "The memorial of his weakness was to be with him as long as he lived… How pleased would you and I be to go halting all our days with such weakness as Jacob had, if we might also have the blessing that he thus won!" (Spurgeon)

Genesis 33 – The Meeting of Jacob and Esau

A. Esau's warm welcome.

1. (1-2) Jacob's careful preparations.

Now Jacob lifted his eyes and looked, and there, Esau was coming, and with him were four hundred men. So he divided the children among Leah, Rachel, and the two maidservants. And he put the maidservants and their children in front, Leah and her children behind, and Rachel and Joseph last.

> a. **He divided the children among Leah, Rachel, and the two maidservants**: These preparations were not necessarily examples of unbelief or of human wisdom and strength. Yet the order of the groups shows that Jacob openly favored Rachel and her son Joseph, with **Rachel and Joseph last**.
>
> b. **He put the maidservants and their children in front**: Leah and her children were more protected than the two **maidservants**, Bilhah and Zilpah, and their respective children.

2. (3) Jacob demonstrates his submission to Esau.

Then he crossed over before them and bowed himself to the ground seven times, until he came near to his brother.

> a. **He crossed over before them**: After being conquered by God, Jacob now *led* the procession to meet Esau. This displays some change of character.
>
> b. **Bowed himself to the ground**: Jacob already sent over gifts and showed he didn't want to take anything materially from Esau. Then, by bowing down, he showed he was submitted to his brother and wanted no social power over him.
>
>> i. If Jacob had not superstitiously tried to steal the blessing 20 years before, all this would have been unnecessary. Isaac's promise to Jacob,

Let peoples serve you, and nations bow down to you. Be master over your brethren (Genesis 27:29) would have been more immediately fulfilled.

ii. It is still common to suffer some problems because we try to accomplish what we think to be God's will, or in unbelief to protect ourselves with merely human energy and wisdom. God never needs us to sin to help Him fulfill His plan in our lives.

3. (4-7) Esau warmly greets Jacob and his family.

But Esau ran to meet him, and embraced him, and fell on his neck and kissed him, and they wept. And he lifted his eyes and saw the women and children, and said, "Who *are* these with you?" So he said, "The children whom God has graciously given your servant." Then the maidservants came near, they and their children, and bowed down. And Leah also came near with her children, and they bowed down. Afterward Joseph and Rachel came near, and they bowed down.

a. **Esau ran to meet him**: This probably terrified Jacob. Surely, he thought his life would soon end. Instead, God had worked in Esau, and he only wanted to bless Jacob.

b. **Fell on his neck and kissed him, and they wept**: Esau and Jacob did not feel a need to discuss and resolve the past. God worked in both their hearts, and there was no need to discuss or argue over it all again. What was past was past.

c. **Who are these with you**: In a moving scene, Jacob introduced his large family to his brother Esau.

4. (8-11) Esau receives Jacob's gifts.

Then Esau said, "What *do* you *mean by* all this company which I met?" And he said, "*These are* to find favor in the sight of my lord." But Esau said, "I have enough, my brother; keep what you have for yourself." And Jacob said, "No, please, if I have now found favor in your sight, then receive my present from my hand, inasmuch as I have seen your face as though I had seen the face of God, and you were pleased with me. Please, take my blessing that is brought to you, because God has dealt graciously with me, and because I have enough." So he urged him, and he took it.

a. **What do you mean by all this company which I met**: Jacob's generous gifts confused Esau. He did not expect this, showing that he had no sense of superiority over Jacob or did not have a strong sense that Jacob owed him.

b. **I have enough… I have enough**: Both Esau and Jacob have a blessed testimony; they could both say, **I have enough**. *Godliness with contentment is great gain* (1 Timothy 6:6). Esau's peace and contentment showed him to be a remarkably blessed man, though he did not receive the promise of the Abrahamic covenant as he had hoped.

> i. "Although Esau did not receive the great blessing — the covenant blessing, — that having gone to Jacob who secured it by deception, yet Esau did receive a great blessing of a temporal kind, which Isaac pronounced upon him with all the fervor of a father who loved his son most ardently. Esau thus received what he most wanted, for he cared very little for the spiritual blessing, — not being a spiritual man, — and when he obtained the temporal blessing, that satisfied his heart, and he said, 'It is enough.'" (Spurgeon)

c. **So he urged him, and he took it**: Esau's receiving of the gifts was as important to the reconciliation as Jacob's giving of the gifts. When Jacob gave such generous gifts, it was his way of saying to Esau that he was sorry, and when Esau accepted the gifts, it was his way of accepting Jacob and saying he was forgiven.

> i. In that culture, one never accepted a gift from an enemy, only from a friend. To accept the gift was to accept the friendship.

B. Jacob's travels in the Promised Land.

1. (12-17) Jacob and Esau part their ways; Jacob goes to Succoth.

Then Esau said, "Let us take our journey; let us go, and I will go before you." But Jacob said to him, "My lord knows that the children *are* weak, and the flocks and herds which are nursing *are* with me. And if the men should drive them hard one day, all the flock will die. Please let my lord go on ahead before his servant. I will lead on slowly at a pace which the livestock that go before me, and the children, are able to endure, until I come to my lord in Seir." And Esau said, "Now let me leave with you *some* of the people who *are* with me." But he said, "What need is there? Let me find favor in the sight of my lord." So Esau returned that day on his way to Seir. And Jacob journeyed to Succoth, built himself a house, and made booths for his livestock. Therefore the name of the place is called Succoth.

> a. **Please let my lord go on ahead before his servant**: Jacob was glad to be reconciled with his brother, but didn't want to be too close to him. He was still afraid of Esau.

> b. **Jacob journeyed to Succoth**: Unfortunately, Jacob still acted like old Jacob instead of like new Israel, because he said he would go far to the

south with Esau to the area of Mount Seir. Instead, he allowed Esau to go a few days beyond him and then headed north towards Succoth.

> i. It's hard to try to be Jacob and Israel at the same time. We could have called him *Jak-iel* or *Israe-ob*.

c. **Built himself a house, and made booths for his lifestock**: God had appointed Abraham, Isaac, and Jacob to live in the land, but in tents as sojourners. Here was a disobedient and unwise settling down.

> i. "Yet at Succoth we read that he built booths — scarcely houses, I suppose, but more than tents. It was a compromise, and a compromise is often worse than a direct and overt disobedience of command. He dares not erect a house, but he builds a booth and thus shows his desire for a settled life." (Spurgeon)

2. (18-20) Jacob comes to Shechem.

Then Jacob came safely to the city of Shechem, which is in the land of Canaan, when he came from Padan Aram; and he pitched his tent before the city. And he bought the parcel of land, where he had pitched his tent, from the children of Hamor, Shechem's father, for one hundred pieces of money. Then he erected an altar there and called it El Elohe Israel.

a. **And he pitched his tent before the city**: It is good Jacob came to the Promised Land, and he settled there. But he came short of full obedience, because it seems God directed him to return to Bethel (Genesis 31:13).

b. **Then he erected an altar there and called it El Elohe Israel**: The altar was good, but complete obedience was better. God wants obedience first, then sacrifice. Jacob and his family will suffer in this wasted, disobedient period of time.

Genesis 34 – Simeon and Levi Massacre the Men of Shechem

A. The rape of Dinah.

1. (1-4) A local prince violates Dinah and then wants to marry her.

Now Dinah the daughter of Leah, whom she had borne to Jacob, went out to see the daughters of the land. And when Shechem the son of Hamor the Hivite, prince of the country, saw her, he took her and lay with her, and violated her. His soul was strongly attracted to Dinah the daughter of Jacob, and he loved the young woman and spoke kindly to the young woman. So Shechem spoke to his father Hamor, saying, "Get me this young woman as a wife."

> a. **Now Dinah the daughter of Leah**: This chapter contains one of the most shameful incidents in Israel's history. A terrible crime was committed against **Dinah the daughter of Leah**, but the response by her brothers was worse than the crime. When the Bible shows its leaders and heroes in such terrible, plain truth, we can know for sure that it is a book from God. Men don't normally write about themselves and their ancestors like this.
>
>> i. Leupold's preaching suggestions on the chapter give us an idea of this: "We may well wonder if any man who had proper discernment ever drew a text from this chapter… It is rightly evaluated by the more mature mind and could be treated to advantage before a men's Bible class. But we cannot venture to offer homiletical suggestions for its treatment."
>
> b. **Went out to see the daughters of the land**: We remember that Jacob brought his family to a region in the Promised Land that God didn't really want them to be in. It seems God directed him to return to Bethel (Genesis 31:13), and his time spent in the city of Shechem did much harm to his family.

i. Jacob chose a place to live for all the wrong reasons. He wanted to be close to the city (Genesis 33:18), though the city had a strong and ungodly influence. God called him to Bethel, and Jacob's poor choice of a place to live left his family open to ungodly influence.

c. **Went out to see the daughters of the land**: Dinah's desire to do this was understandable but unwise. Jacob did not make sure she was properly supervised. To allow unsupervised socialization in a pagan town was a failure of responsibility on the part of Jacob and Leah.

i. "Unattached young women were considered fair game in cities of the time, in which promiscuity was not only common but, in fact, a part of the very religious system itself." (Morris)

ii. "This occurrence serves to illustrate the low standard of morals prevalent among the Canaanites. Any unattended female could be raped, and in the transactions that ensue neither father nor son feel the need of apologizing for or excusing what had been committed." (Leupold)

iii. But try telling this to a teenager like Dinah! Teenagers often want it all, and they want it now. It is almost impossible for them to see the benefits of waiting for certain things until they are more mature.

iv. One of the ways this difficulty has been measured has been called the marshmallow test. A researcher gives this choice to a four-year-old: "I am leaving for a few minutes to run an errand, and you can have this marshmallow while I am gone, but if you wait until I return, you can have two marshmallows." Researchers at Stanford did this test in the 1960's, and a dozen years later they found the kids who grabbed the single marshmallow tended to be more troubled as adolescents. The one-marshmallow kids also scored an average of 210 points less on university entrance exams. Learning to delay gratification is important.

d. **Shechem the son of Hamor the Hivite, prince of the country, saw her, he took her and lay with her**: Jacob's lack of attention and protection was partially at fault in this tragedy. His own compromise made him less able to stand up to his own children and guide them as he should.

i. Jacob's children knew he told his brother Esau he would go south with him, but Jacob went north instead. They picked up on this and other areas of compromise and used them to justify their own compromise.

e. **He took her and lay with her, and violated her**: As for the young man named Shechem, **his soul was strongly attracted** to Dinah and he even

spoke kindly to her. Yet we cannot say he loved her, because **he violated her**.

> i. It was a soulish love Shechem had for Dinah, not a spiritual, godly, or good kind of love. He loved her for what she could be for him and give to him, not for what he could be and give to her. His heart was shown in the words **"get me this young woman as a wife."** It was a soulish "get me" kind of love.

> ii. It is possible for a man to be attracted to a woman and to show kindness to her for reasons having nothing or little to do with real love. In a desire to connect romantically with a man, a woman may willingly overlook this and hope for the best.

2. (5-7) Jacob's lack of outrage; the anger of Simeon and Levi.

And Jacob heard that he had defiled Dinah his daughter. Now his sons were with his livestock in the field; so Jacob held his peace until they came. Then Hamor the father of Shechem went out to Jacob to speak with him. And the sons of Jacob came in from the field when they heard it; and the men were grieved and very angry, because he had done a disgraceful thing in Israel by lying with Jacob's daughter, a thing which ought not to be done.

> a. **Jacob held his peace until they came**: This section gives the impression that Jacob's sons were far more offended and outraged than their father Jacob was. Upon hearing that Shechem **had defiled Dinah his daughter**, he **held his peace** until his sons returned from the fields.

> > i. Jacob's refusal to do what is right in regard to his family will encourage two of his sons to do *something*, something *terrible* in response. When God-appointed heads do not take appropriate leadership, it creates a void, which is often filled sinfully.

> b. **The sons of Jacob... and the men were grieved and very angry**: Ancient Middle Eastern cultures had a strong sense of family honor, strong enough to use violence to defend this sense of honor. In this culture, the brothers had a greater responsibility to protect their sister than the father. Yet **the sons of Jacob** would go on to defend the family's honor in unwise and sinful ways.

3. (8-12) Hamor and Shechem seek to arrange the marriage of Dinah.

But Hamor spoke with them, saying, "The soul of my son Shechem longs for your daughter. Please give her to him as a wife. And make marriages with us; give your daughters to us, and take our daughters to yourselves. So you shall dwell with us, and the land shall be before you. Dwell and trade in it, and acquire possessions for yourselves in it."

Then Shechem said to her father and her brothers, "Let me find favor in your eyes, and whatever you say to me I will give. Ask me ever so much dowry and gift, and I will give according to what you say to me; but give me the young woman as a wife."

a. **Make marriages with us; give your daughters to us, and take our daughters to yourselves**: The Canaanite's proposal to marry the daughter of Jacob was a dangerous challenge to the covenant family. Irresponsible intermarriage with the Canaanites could prove especially harmful for this family with such an important destiny in God's redemptive plan.

b. **Make marriages with us; give your daughters to us, and take our daughters to yourselves**: This was far more than a matter between a young Canaanite man and Dinah, the daughter of Jacob. If they married, it would set the pattern for future marriages between Jacob's family and the people of Canaan. The result would be the eventual and complete assimilation of Jacob's family into Canaanite culture (**so you shall dwell with us... dwell and trade in it**). The future of this covenant family as a distinct people was at risk.

c. **Whatever you say to me I will give**: Hamor and Shechem probably thought themselves generous. But their manner of negotiating the arrangement of the marriage insulted Dinah and her family even more with a "just-name-your-price" attitude. They acted as if money and marriage could make her disgrace go away.

4. (13-17) The counteroffer of Simeon and Levi: all the men of the city of Shechem should be circumcised.

But the sons of Jacob answered Shechem and Hamor his father, and spoke deceitfully, because he had defiled Dinah their sister. And they said to them, "We cannot do this thing, to give our sister to one who is uncircumcised, for that *would be* a reproach to us. But on this *condition* we will consent to you: If you will become as we *are*, if every male of you is circumcised, then we will give our daughters to you, and we will take your daughters to us; and we will dwell with you, and we will become one people. But if you will not heed us and be circumcised, then we will take our daughter and be gone."

a. **The sons of Jacob answered... and spoke deceitfully**: Their response to **Shechem and Hamor** was a planned, calculated deception.

b. **If every male of you is circumcised, then we will give our daughters to you**: Hamor and Shechem agreed to such an extreme demand because circumcision was not *only* practiced among the Israelites, but some other ancient peoples also circumcised their males. **Shechem and Hamor** knew of the practice from the rituals of other nations.

c. **For that would be a reproach to us**: From the beginning, Simeon and Levi planned evil against **Shechem and Hamor** and their people. Yet they covered their evil plan with spiritual words, and they used Dinah as a cover for their intended evil.

i. They felt justified because the men of Shechem treated Dinah their sister as a prostitute (Genesis 34:31), but they prostituted the sign of God's covenant for their own violent purpose.

5. (18-24) Hamor and Shechem convince the men of the city to go along with the plan.

And their words pleased Hamor and Shechem, Hamor's son. So the young man did not delay to do the thing, because he delighted in Jacob's daughter. He was more honorable than all the household of his father. And Hamor and Shechem his son came to the gate of their city, and spoke with the men of their city, saying: "These men *are* at peace with us. Therefore let them dwell in the land and trade in it. For indeed the land is large enough for them. Let us take their daughters to us as wives, and let us give them our daughters. Only on this *condition* will the men consent to dwell with us, to be one people: if every male among us is circumcised as they are circumcised. Will not their livestock, their property, and every animal of theirs be ours? Only let us consent to them, and they will dwell with us." And all who went out of the gate of his city heeded Hamor and Shechem his son; every male was circumcised, all who went out of the gate of his city.

a. **Their words pleased Hamor and Shechem**: Despite the obvious sacrifice involved, Hamor and Shechem were **pleased** with this plan. Beyond the obviously deep attraction Shechem had for Dinah, they were also pleased to begin to marry into a family so large, wealthy, and influential.

b. **He was more honorable than all the household of his father**: Among the Canaanites of his time and place, Shechem was **more honorable** than others. He sincerely **delighted in Jacob's daughter**.

c. **Will not their livestock, their property, and every animal of theirs be ours**: The father and son (**Hamor and Shechem**) had to convince the men of their community to receive the painful and possibly dangerous procedure of circumcision. They convinced them it was worth it because they could then **take their daughters to us as wives** and take **their livestock, property, and every animal of theirs**. The potential gain of wealth made it worth it.

d. **Every male was circumcised**: The men of Shechem agreed and all received the painful and potentially dangerous operation of circumcision.

B. Simeon and Levi destroy the city of Shechem.

1. (25) The massacre of the men of the city of Shechem.

Now it came to pass on the third day, when they were in pain, that two of the sons of Jacob, Simeon and Levi, Dinah's brothers, each took his sword and came boldly upon the city and killed all the males.

    a. **When they were in pain… each took his sword and came boldly upon the city and killed all the males**: This was not only a brutal, deceptive act, but it also disgraced God's covenant of circumcision. Surely, with this clever act of violent deception, Simeon and Levi showed themselves to be the children of *Jacob* from a bitter, competitive home environment.

        i. **In pain**: "Crudely performed, circumcision could be quite incapacitating, particularly after two or three days" (Kidner).

    b. **Came boldly**: It was a bold plan to massacre an entire community of men under the cover of their acceptance of the demand to be circumcised. It was bold in the cause of evil.

        i. "The boldness with which they executed their foul plan shows the hardness of their hearts." (Barnhouse)

2. (26-29) They rescue Dinah and plunder the city.

And they killed Hamor and Shechem his son with the edge of the sword, and took Dinah from Shechem's house, and went out. The sons of Jacob came upon the slain, and plundered the city, because their sister had been defiled. They took their sheep, their oxen, and their donkeys, what was in the city and what was in the field, and all their wealth. All their little ones and their wives they took captive; and they plundered even all that was in the houses.

    a. **They killed Hamor and Shechem his son with the edge of the sword**: There was no sparing of the sword. Even relatively good men like **Shechem** (Genesis 34:19) were **killed**. The **sons of Jacob** justified this murder and theft by saying their sister and family had been dishonored, but the punishment was clearly excessive.

    b. **Plundered the city… They took their sheep, their oxen, and their donkeys, what was in the city and what was in the field, and all their wealth**: The sons of Jacob *completely* **plundered** the city of Shechem, including taking the surviving women and children as slaves.

        i. "By way of making some amends for their sister's defilement, with dastardly treachery they slay the whole of the Shechemites, and so

3. (30-31) Jacob's reaction.

Then Jacob said to Simeon and Levi, "You have troubled me by making me obnoxious among the inhabitants of the land, among the Canaanites and the Perizzites; and since I *am* few in number, they will gather themselves together against me and kill me. I shall be destroyed, my household and I." But they said, "Should he treat our sister like a harlot?"

a. **You have troubled me by making me obnoxious**: In response to the *terrible* massacre and plundering of Shechem, Jacob seemed to only be concerned with himself and the danger of retribution against his small family (**I am few in number**). There was no concern for right and wrong, for God's righteousness, or for the death and plunder of innocents. This was *Jacob*, not *Israel* in action.

> i. "All was out of order, and threatened to become much worse. Even the heathen outside began to smell the ill savor of Jacob's disorganized family, and the one alternative was—mend or end." (Spurgeon)

> ii. "Jacob! You brought that trouble on yourself. You passed your own deceitful nature into your boys. You set them a constant example of guile. They heard you lie to Esau at Peniel and start northwest after he went southeast. They saw your interest in the fat pastures when you pitched your tent in Shechem. You said nothing when Dinah was violated… Talk to God about your own sin before talking to these boys about theirs." (Barnhouse)

b. **Should he treat our sister like a harlot**: This was Simeon and Levi's only reply. They were correct that their **sister** Dinah had been abused and treated terribly. Yet none of that justified their outrageous evils of mass murder, enslaving women and children, and theft through plunder.

> i. When Jacob was about to die, he prophesied over each of his 12 sons. This is what he said about Simeon and Levi: *Simeon and Levi are brothers; instruments of cruelty are in their dwelling place. Let not my soul enter their council; let not my honor be united to their assembly; for in their anger they slew a man, and in their self-will they hamstrung an ox. Cursed be their anger, for it is fierce; and their wrath, for it is cruel! I will divide them in Jacob and scatter them in Israel* (Genesis 49:5-7). He saw Simeon and Levi for who they were, but he rebuked them far too late.

> ii. The prophetic word of God through Jacob proved true. God did in fact both divide the tribes of Simeon and Levi, and scatter them

among Israel. But, significantly, the way it happened for each tribe was different.

- The tribe of Simeon, because of their lack of faithfulness, was effectively dissolved as a tribe, and the tribe of Simeon was absorbed into the tribal area of Judah.
- The tribe of Levi was also scattered, but because of the faithfulness of this tribe during the rebellion of the golden calf (Exodus 32:26-28), the tribe was scattered as a blessing throughout the whole nation of Israel.

iii. Both were scattered, but one as a blessing and the other as a curse.

Genesis 35 – Revival in Jacob's Life

A. Jacob returns to Bethel.

1. (1) God speaks to Jacob, calling him back to Bethel.

Then God said to Jacob, "Arise, go up to Bethel and dwell there; and make an altar there to God, who appeared to you when you fled from the face of Esau your brother."

a. **Arise, go up to Bethel and dwell there**: The whole Shechem incident happened because Jacob went to Shechem instead of Bethel, where he was supposed to be. Now at last he went where God told him to go (Genesis 31:13).

i. "The only cure for worldliness is to separate from it" (Barnhouse). Jacob had to leave Shechem and go to Bethel. There had to be a departure from one and a new direction and destination set. There was a new place for Jacob and his family to **dwell**.

ii. Genesis 34 does not mention God once, and is one of the most sordid chapters in Israel's history. Genesis 35 mentions God over and over again, more than 10 times, plus 11 more times in names such as **Bethel** and **Israel**.

b. **Make an altar there to God**: Jacob was told to go back to Bethel and resume a life of worship there. This return to the LORD would have an especially good effect on the children of Jacob. This reminds us the best thing parents can do for their children is to choose God's path themselves.

i. As Jacob looked back on his walk with God, the first meeting with God at Bethel must have seemed like a high point (Genesis 28:10-22). But to his credit, Jacob refused to think the best years of his life with God were behind him. He returned to his first love—he returned to Bethel, and God blessed it.

ii. "A revival of old memories is often most useful to us, especially to revive the memory of our conversion. The memory of the love of our espousals, when we went after the Lord into the wilderness, and were quite satisfied to be denied and disowned of all, so long as we might but dwell near to him—that memory is right good for us." (Spurgeon)

2. (2-4) The cleansing of Jacob's family.

And Jacob said to his household and to all who were with him, "Put away the foreign gods that are among you, purify yourselves, and change your garments. Then let us arise and go up to Bethel; and I will make an altar there to God, who answered me in the day of my distress and has been with me in the way which I have gone." So they gave Jacob all the foreign gods which were in their hands, and the earrings which were in their ears; and Jacob hid them under the terebinth tree which was by Shechem.

a. **Put away the foreign gods that are among you, purify yourselves**: Jacob's family only got right with God after Jacob himself did. This again shows us the tremendous leadership role men have within the family. A man resisting God will see the same effect in his children. A man who gets right with God will also see the effect in his family.

i. Jacob's children kept **foreign gods** because their mother did. Rachel kept the household idols of her father (Genesis 31:19). No matter how hard we try to teach our children godly conduct, they will continue to do what we *do*.

ii. "In families it is often well, when you see that things are wrong, just to call the household together and say, 'We must draw near unto God with peculiar earnestness, for we are going astray. We have not given up family prayer, but we must now make it special, and with double zeal draw nigh unto God.' I am afraid that some of you neglect family prayer. If you do I am sure it will work evil in your households." (Spurgeon)

b. **And change your garments**: This was an important step, both literally and as a symbol of something spiritual. Jacob wanted them to be cleaned up and in their best frame of mind to come before the God they had neglected.

i. "Throughout the Bible, garments symbolize character. The inward life of the unregenerate is compared to a polluted garment." (Barnhouse)

ii. Jude 23 gives the idea: *but others save with fear, pulling them out of the fire, hating even the garment defiled by the flesh*. Ephesians 4:22-24 gives a similar exhortation: *that you put off, concerning your former conduct, the old man which grows corrupt according to the deceitful lusts, and be renewed in the spirit of your mind, and that you put on the new man which was created according to God, in true righteousness and holiness.*

c. **And the earrings which were in their ears**: Apparently, these **earrings** also had a pagan connection. Though one could find some justification for keeping the **earrings**, they got rid of them nonetheless.

i. It is important for everyone to take stock of what they may have in their home that is ungodly or connected to the occult, and promptly get rid of those things.

ii. "He had not said anything about their earrings. Was there any hurt in their earrings? For a woman to wear an earring is not such a dreadful thing, is it? Perhaps not, but I suppose that these earrings were charms, and that they were used in certain incantations, and heathenish customs. It must have been a very sad discovery to Jacob, who himself could not have endured it, to find that wicked superstitions had come into his tents." (Spurgeon)

3. (5-7) God's protection of Jacob; he comes to Bethel.

And they journeyed, and the terror of God was upon the cities that were all around them, and they did not pursue the sons of Jacob. So Jacob came to Luz (that is, Bethel), which is in the land of Canaan, he and all the people who were with him. And he built an altar there and called the place El Bethel, because there God appeared to him when he fled from the face of his brother.

a. **The terror of God was upon the cities that were all around them, and they did not pursue the sons of Jacob**: This was God's protection on Jacob and his family. It would have been *fair* of God to leave Jacob to the consequences of his sinful lack of leadership in the family. Yet God's grace covered Jacob even when his sin had made them vulnerable.

i. Jacob and his family needed this protection, because the massacre at Shechem made them hated among the Canaanites, as Jacob feared in Genesis 34:30.

b. **He built an altar there and called the place El Bethel**: Though Jacob had sinned, he *now* did what was right before God. He did this despite the danger, and trusting God's protection. He might have justified a lack of obedience because of fear, but he trusted God instead.

i. "They came to Bethel, and I can almost picture the grateful delight of Jacob as he looked upon those great stones among which he had lain him down to sleep, a lonely man. Perhaps he hunted out the stone that had been his pillow; probably it still stood erect as part of the pillar which he had reared in memory of the goodness of God, and the vision he had seen. There were many regrets, many confessions, many thanksgivings at Bethel." (Spurgeon)

ii. It was dangerous for Jacob to set out to Bethel, but it was more dangerous for him to disobey God. The only thing that could save him was a radical obedience to the LORD. No matter what the circumstances look like, the safest thing to do is the will of God.

4. (8) The death of Deborah, Rebekah's beloved nurse.

Now Deborah, Rebekah's nurse, died, and she was buried below Bethel under the terebinth tree. So the name of it was called Allon Bachuth.

a. **Now Deborah, Rebekah's nurse, died**: We know nothing of this woman before this account. Seemingly, she came with Rebekah as a companion when she came from Haran to marry Isaac. Obviously, she was a beloved member of the family, because they named the place where she was buried **Allon Bachuth**, which means "Oak of Weeping."

b. **Rebekah's nurse**: Some commentators assume for some reason that she came to be in Jacob's household, coming from his mother's household, but we do not know for certain if this is the case.

5. (9-15) God speaks to Jacob again at Bethel.

Then God appeared to Jacob again, when he came from Padan Aram, and blessed him. And God said to him, "Your name *is* Jacob; your name shall not be called Jacob anymore, but Israel shall be your name." So He called his name Israel. Also God said to him: "I *am* God Almighty. Be fruitful and multiply; a nation and a company of nations shall proceed from you, and kings shall come from your body. The land which I gave Abraham and Isaac I give to you; and to your descendants after you I give this land." Then God went up from him in the place where He talked with him. So Jacob set up a pillar in the place where He talked with him, a pillar of stone; and he poured a drink offering on it, and he poured oil on it. And Jacob called the name of the place where God spoke with him, Bethel.

a. **Then God appeared to Jacob again… and blessed him**: When Jacob finally arrived at the place God told him to go, he immediately found great blessing. God appeared to him, God blessed him, and God called him by his new name (**Israel**).

i. The reminder of the new name was important, because Jacob had acted like the old Jacob instead of Israel. Yet God wanted to set his mind on the new man God made him to be. God does the same with us, reminding us who we are in Him. God wants us to remember and live in the great names He gives us.

ii. **Israel shall be your name**: "The next thing that came of it was a confirmation to Jacob of his title of prince, which conferred a dignity on the whole family. For a father to be a prince ennobles all the clan. God now puts upon them another dignity and nobility which they had not known before, for a holy people are a noble people" (Spurgeon).

b. **God appeared to Jacob again**: Relationship was restored. This was an excellent example of what it means to return to your first love, as in Revelation 2:4-5: Jacob *remembered* to go back to Bethel. He *repented* by getting rid of all the idols, and he *did the first works* by building an altar and worshipping God as before.

c. **The land which I gave Abraham and Isaac I give to you; and to your descendants after you I give this land**: God granted Jacob a precious reminder of his place in God's great covenant, begun with his grandfather Abraham. In this, Jacob did not need to hear anything new from God. He just needed to be reminded of what was true, and be encouraged to cling to it all.

d. **Then God went up from him in the place where He talked with him**: Seemingly, God appeared to Jacob here in bodily form. God blessed Jacob remarkably after his return to his first love. Much blessing waits for us until we *do* what God tells us to do.

e. **He poured a drink offering on it, and he poured oil on it**: Appropriately, Jacob performed sacrificial acts of worship to the God who had blessed him so much.

i. The idea of a **drink offering** is found in several places in the Bible. Exodus 29:40-41, Leviticus 23:13, and Numbers 15:5-7 show the drink offering was made with wine poured out in sacrifice before the LORD at His altar. Paul considered the pouring out of his life before God to be like the pouring out of a drink offering at God's altar (Philippians 2:17 and 2 Timothy 4:6).

ii. Jacob's heart of worship showed *gratitude* towards God. When we look back on life, we should never have the attitude that says, "I was robbed." Instead our heart should say, "God has blessed." This will probably determine if we will be perfectly miserable or perfectly delightful as we get older.

B. The birth of Benjamin and the death of Rachel.

1. (16-17) The birth of another son.

Then they journeyed from Bethel. And when there was but a little distance to go to Ephrath, Rachel labored *in childbirth*, and she had hard labor. Now it came to pass, when she was in hard labor, that the midwife said to her, "Do not fear; you will have this son also."

a. **Rachel labored in childbirth**: There seems to be none of the contentiousness and competitiveness surrounding the birth of this last son, possibly because they were all older at this time. More so, it was because they were now in the Promised Land and it just wasn't as important as before.

b. **In childbirth**: We don't know how long Jacob stayed at Bethel, but it is possible this last child was conceived at this place where Jacob came back to his first love for the Lord.

2. (18) The naming of the last son.

And so it was, as her soul was departing (for she died), that she called his name Ben-Oni; but his father called him Benjamin.

a. **She called his name Ben-Oni**: Rachel named this last child – who before would have been seen as a cause for rejoicing and victory in the competition with her sister – **Ben-Oni**, meaning "son of my sorrow."

i. Ultimately, this shows the futility of Rachel's competition with her sister Leah. Now at the time of her final "victory," all she found was *sorrow*.

b. **But his father called him Benjamin**: Jacob wisely named the child **Benjamin**, which means "son of my right hand." Perhaps he rightly sensed the special place God had for this child, or perhaps he simply prized Benjamin so greatly because he was the final link between him and the woman he most loved.

c. **Benjamin**: The right side was associated with greater strength and honor, because most people are right-handed. **Benjamin** (*son of my right hand*), therefore, has the idea of "son of my strength" or "son of my honor."

i. The idea is expressed in passages like Exodus 15:6: *Your right hand, O Lord, has become glorious in power; Your right hand, O Lord, has dashed the enemy in pieces.*

ii. The Lord is our strength and honor, as in Psalm 16:8: *I have set the Lord always before me; because He is at my right hand I shall not be moved.*

iii. God's strength and honor are for us: *My soul follows close behind You; Your right hand upholds me* (Psalm 63:8). *Though I walk in the midst of trouble, You will revive me; You will stretch out Your hand against the wrath of my enemies, and Your right hand will save me* (Psalm 138:7).

iv. Jesus sits at the *right hand* of the Father, the position of strength and honor, and we sit there with Him! *If then you were raised with Christ, seek those things which are above, where Christ is, sitting at the right hand of God* (Colossians 3:1).

3. (19-20) The death and burial of Rachel.

So Rachel died and was buried on the way to Ephrath (that is, Bethlehem). And Jacob set a pillar on her grave, which is the pillar of Rachel's grave to this day.

a. **Rachel died and was buried**: Rachel's death was a tragic fulfillment of the curse Jacob himself pronounced on the one who stole the idols of Laban (Genesis 31:32).

i. In Genesis 30:1, Rachel pleaded with Jacob, *Give me children, or else I die!* As it happened, both became true. She had children and she died as a result.

b. **Jacob set a pillar on her grave**: This also shows that even when we get right with God and return to our first love, it doesn't mean life becomes easy and comfortable. There are constant challenges for us to trust God.

i. We cannot prize comfort more than getting right with God. For some, comfort is their idol – a false god they worship with constant pursuit and attention. Some only want a *comfortable* life, not a godly life. The symbol for some Christians seems to be an easy chair, not a cross.

4. (21-22a) Reuben's sin with his father's concubine.

Then Israel journeyed and pitched his tent beyond the tower of Eder. And it happened, when Israel dwelt in that land, that Reuben went and lay with Bilhah his father's concubine; and Israel heard *about it***.**

a. **Reuben went and lay with Bilhah his father's concubine**: Reuben was the firstborn. We might expect the best conduct from him, and might expect him to most seriously receive the covenant of his fathers. Yet here, he sinned in a most offensive way against his father and entire family.

i. However, we don't have to wonder about where this sinful conduct came from. In a home so filled with strife, contention, competition, and the pursuit of the flesh, it was almost to be expected.

b. **Israel heard about it**: Through their sin Reuben, Simeon, and Levi seemed to disqualify themselves from the high calling of Abraham's blessing. It will be up to the fourth son, Judah, to bring forth the Messiah.

5. (22b-26) Jacob's 12 sons.

Now the sons of Jacob were twelve: the sons of Leah *were* **Reuben, Jacob's firstborn, and Simeon, Levi, Judah, Issachar, and Zebulun; the sons of Rachel** *were* **Joseph and Benjamin; the sons of Bilhah, Rachel's maidservant,** *were* **Dan and Naphtali; and the sons of Zilpah, Leah's maidservant,** *were* **Gad and Asher. These** *were* **the sons of Jacob who were born to him in Padan Aram.**

a. **The sons of Jacob were twelve**: From what we have seen in the last few chapters, this was not a collection of amazingly spiritual men.

i. "We are greatly amazed in reflecting upon the event as a whole that descendants of the worthy patriarch Abraham should almost immediately after his time already have sunk to the level upon which Jacob's sons stand in this chapter." (Leupold)

b. **These were the sons of Jacob**: This was actually a severely dysfunctional family. God will use this family, but not because they were such great or spiritual men, but because He chose them by His grace alone.

C. The death of Isaac.

1. (27) Jacob visits his father Isaac one last time.

Then Jacob came to his father Isaac at Mamre, or Kirjath Arba (that is, Hebron), where Abraham and Isaac had dwelt.

a. **Jacob came to his father Isaac**: More than 20 years ago, Jacob left his home thinking his father would soon die. Jacob probably never expected to see his father again before he died.

i. We should remember our times are in God's hands. We may expect a long or short life for others or ourselves and be quite wrong. Only God knows.

b. **His father Isaac**: There seemed to be nothing dramatic between Isaac and Jacob at this meeting. There are recorded no further words or blessings. It was possible Isaac was hindered by his old age.

2. (28-29) Jacob and Esau bury their father together.

Now the days of Isaac were one hundred and eighty years. So Isaac breathed his last and died, and was gathered to his people, *being* **old and full of days. And his sons Esau and Jacob buried him.**

a. **His sons Esau and Jacob buried him**: The sons had already been brought together by God's hand. Now they worked together again, united by the death of their father.

Genesis 36 – The Family of Esau

A. Esau's separation from Jacob.

1. (1-5) The wives, sons, and daughters of Esau.

Now this is the genealogy of Esau, who is Edom. Esau took his wives from the daughters of Canaan: Adah the daughter of Elon the Hittite; Aholibamah the daughter of Anah, the daughter of Zibeon the Hivite; and Basemath, Ishmael's daughter, sister of Nebajoth. Now Adah bore Eliphaz to Esau, and Basemath bore Reuel. And Aholibamah bore Jeush, Jaalam, and Korah. These were the sons of Esau who *were* born to him in the land of Canaan.

> a. **This is the genealogy of Esau, who is Edom**: The Edomite people descended from **Esau**, the son of Isaac and the twin brother of Jacob.

> b. **Esau took his wives from the daughters of Canaan**: Abraham was determined that Isaac not take a wife from among the **daughters of Canaan** (Genesis 24:37). Esau's marriage to Canaanite women caused much grief to Isaac and Rebekah (Genesis 26:34-35).

2. (6-8) The separation of Jacob and Esau.

Then Esau took his wives, his sons, his daughters, and all the persons of his household, his cattle and all his animals, and all his goods which he had gained in the land of Canaan, and went to a country away from the presence of his brother Jacob. For their possessions were too great for them to dwell together, and the land where they were strangers could not support them because of their livestock. So Esau dwelt in Mount Seir. Esau *is* Edom.

> a. **Their possessions were too great for them to dwell together**: Esau's painful cry to Isaac *Have you only one blessing, my father?* (Genesis 27:38) proved unfounded. God blessed Esau because he was a descendant of Abraham, and blessed him regarding what he really cared about – wealth.

b. **So Esau dwelt in Mount Seir**: This was land to the south and east of the Dead Sea, and became known as the land of **Edom**.

B. The descendants of Esau.

1. (9) The Edomites descend from Esau.

And this is the genealogy of Esau the father of the Edomites in Mount Seir.

a. **Esau the father of the Edomites**: Edom and the Edomites are mentioned some 130 times in the Bible. They were an important group of neighbors to Israel.

- When the Israelites came through the wilderness to the Promised Land in the time of Moses, the Edomites refused them passage through their land (Numbers 20:21). This was a source of great discouragement for the nation (Numbers 21:4).
- Even so, God commanded special regard for the Edomites among Israel: *You shall not abhor an Edomite, for he is your brother* (Deuteronomy 23:7).
- In the days of Saul, Edom was made subject to Israel (1 Samuel 14:47), and David established garrisons there (2 Samuel 8:14). But later, in the days of Joram, the son of Ahab, the Edomites became independent of Israel (2 Kings 8:16-22).
- Several of the prophets spoke about and against Edom, including Jeremiah (Jeremiah 49:17-18) and Ezekiel (Ezekiel 25:12-14).
- From the time Islam conquered the Middle East, the region has been mostly unoccupied, except for a few Bedouins and military outposts. It has been brought to nothing, as Obadiah had prophesied (the entire book of Obadiah records an extended prophecy against Edom).

b. **The Edomites in Mount Seir**: The Edomites also held the rock city of Petra, or at least its early version. This city can only be reached through a narrow, winding gorge. Petra was so defensible that it was said that a dozen men could protect Petra against a whole army.

2. (10-43) The descendants of Edom and the chiefs of the Edomites.

These *were* the names of Esau's sons: Eliphaz the son of Adah the wife of Esau, and Reuel the son of Basemath the wife of Esau. And the sons of Eliphaz were Teman, Omar, Zepho, Gatam, and Kenaz. Now Timna was the concubine of Eliphaz, Esau's son, and she bore Amalek to Eliphaz. These *were* the sons of Adah, Esau's wife. These *were* the sons of Reuel: Nahath, Zerah, Shammah, and Mizzah. These were the sons

of Basemath, Esau's wife. These were the sons of Aholibamah, Esau's wife, the daughter of Anah, the daughter of Zibeon. And she bore to Esau: Jeush, Jaalam, and Korah. These *were* the chiefs of the sons of Esau. The sons of Eliphaz, the firstborn *son* of Esau, were Chief Teman, Chief Omar, Chief Zepho, Chief Kenaz, Chief Korah, Chief Gatam, *and* Chief Amalek. These were the chiefs of Eliphaz in the land of Edom. They *were* the sons of Adah. These *were* the sons of Reuel, Esau's son: Chief Nahath, Chief Zerah, Chief Shammah, and Chief Mizzah. These *were* the chiefs of Reuel in the land of Edom. These *were* the sons of Basemath, Esau's wife. And these *were* the sons of Aholibamah, Esau's wife: Chief Jeush, Chief Jaalam, and Chief Korah. These *were* the chiefs who *descended* from Aholibamah, Esau's wife, the daughter of Anah. These *were* the sons of Esau, who is Edom, and these *were* their chiefs. These *were* the sons of Seir the Horite who inhabited the land: Lotan, Shobal, Zibeon, Anah, Dishon, Ezer, and Dishan. These *were* the chiefs of the Horites, the sons of Seir, in the land of Edom. And the sons of Lotan were Hori and Hemam. Lotan's sister was Timna. These *were* the sons of Shobal: Alvan, Manahath, Ebal, Shepho, and Onam. These *were* the sons of Zibeon: both Ajah and Anah. This *was the* Anah who found the water in the wilderness as he pastured the donkeys of his father Zibeon. These *were* the children of Anah: Dishon and Aholibamah the daughter of Anah. These *were* the sons of Dishon: Hemdan, Eshban, Ithran, and Cheran. These *were* the sons of Ezer: Bilhan, Zaavan, and Akan. These *were* the sons of Dishan: Uz and Aran. These *were* the chiefs of the Horites: Chief Lotan, Chief Shobal, Chief Zibeon, Chief Anah, Chief Dishon, Chief Ezer, and Chief Dishan. These *were* the chiefs of the Horites, according to their chiefs in the land of Seir. Now these were the kings who reigned in the land of Edom before any king reigned over the children of Israel: Bela the son of Beor reigned in Edom, and the name of his city was Dinhabah. And when Bela died, Jobab the son of Zerah of Bozrah reigned in his place. When Jobab died, Husham of the land of the Temanites reigned in his place. And when Husham died, Hadad the son of Bedad, who attacked Midian in the field of Moab, reigned in his place. And the name of his city was Avith. When Hadad died, Samlah of Masrekah reigned in his place. And when Samlah died, Saul of Rehoboth-by-the-River reigned in his place. When Saul died, Baal-Hanan the son of Achbor reigned in his place. And when Baal-Hanan the son of Achbor died, Hadar reigned in his place; and the name of his city *was* Pau. His wife's name *was* Mehetabel, the daughter of Matred, the daughter of Mezahab. And these were the names of the chiefs of Esau, according to their families and their places, by their names: Chief

Timnah, Chief Alvah, Chief Jetheth, Chief Aholibamah, Chief Elah, Chief Pinon, Chief Kenaz, Chief Teman, Chief Mibzar, Chief Magdiel, and Chief Iram. These *were* the chiefs of Edom, according to their dwelling places in the land of their possession. Esau *was* the father of the Edomites.

a. **These were the chiefs of the sons of Esau**: When we see the kings and chiefs among the descendants of Esau, we see more clearly what God meant when He said, *Jacob I have loved, but Esau I have hated* (Malachi 1:2-3 and Romans 9:13). Esau was obviously a blessed man, but he was hated and rejected in regard to being chosen to inherit the covenant God made to Abraham.

i. "If God blesses so abundantly those who are not chosen, what is the magnitude of His blessings for those who *are* chosen? If nonspiritual people experience such outpourings of merely common grace, how great must the special grace of the regenerate be!" (Boice)

b. **She bore Amalek to Eliphaz**: Notable among this list is **Amalek**. From him came the Amalekites, notable enemies of Israel (Exodus 17:8-16; Deuteronomy 25:17-19; 1 Samuel 15:1-8).

i. In addition, the names of the descendants of Esau don't reflect a godly heart.

- **Dishon** (Genesis 36:21) means *gazelle*.
- **Alvan** (Genesis 36:23) means *wicked*.
- **Ithran** (Genesis 36:26) means *advantage*.
- **Aran** (Genesis 36:28) means *mountain goat*.
- **Baal-Hanan** (Genesis 36:38) – his name embraced the false god Baal.

ii. **Jobab the son of Zerah**: "Many have supposed that *Jobab* is the same as *Job*, so remarkable for his afflictions and patience; and that *Eliphaz*... was the same who in the book of Job is called one of his friends: but there is no proper proof of this, and there are many reasons against it" (Clarke).

Genesis 37 – Joseph Is Sold into Slavery

A. Joseph's dreams.

1. (1-4) Jacob favors Joseph.

Now Jacob dwelt in the land where his father was a stranger, in the land of Canaan. This is the history of Jacob. Joseph, *being* seventeen years old, was feeding the flock with his brothers. And the lad was with the sons of Bilhah and the sons of Zilpah, his father's wives; and Joseph brought a bad report of them to his father. Now Israel loved Joseph more than all his children, because he was the son of his old age. Also he made him a tunic of *many* colors. But when his brothers saw that their father loved him more than all his brothers, they hated him and could not speak peaceably to him.

   a. **Joseph, being seventeen years old**: This begins one the remarkable life stories of the Bible and all literature.

- Enoch shows the *walk* of faith.
- Noah shows the *perseverance* of faith.
- Abraham shows the *obedience* of faith.
- Isaac shows the *power* of faith.
- Jacob shows the *discipline* of faith.
- Along these lines we could say that Joseph shows the *triumph* of faith. Joseph never complained and he never compromised.

    i. "He was loved and hated, favored and abused, tempted and trusted, exalted and abased. Yet at no point in the one-hundred-and-ten-year life of Joseph did he ever seem to get his eyes off God or cease to trust him. Adversity did not harden his character. Prosperity did not ruin him. He was the same in private as in public. He was a truly great man." (Boice)

ii. Best of all, Joseph is also a remarkably powerful picture of Jesus Christ.

b. **Now Israel loved Joseph more than all his children**: Jacob (**Israel**) was father over a troubled family. With sons from four different mothers, all living and working together, there was much rivalry and competition. Yet Jacob had a clear **favorite** – Joseph, who was **the son of his old age**.

i. We all have ideas and dreams about what a perfect family should be. By anyone's measure, Joseph's family had a lot of problems.

- As a young man, his father Jacob tried to trick his grandfather Isaac into giving him the family fortune instead of his older twin brother.
- It all fell apart and Joseph's father Jacob had to run for his life when his twin brother vowed to murder him.
- Jacob went away, more than 200 miles on foot. He did not see his father Isaac for more than twenty years, when Isaac was almost dead. There is no record that he ever saw his mother again.
- Jacob found a place with his mother's relatives, but his uncle cheated him and treated him like a slave.
- Jacob married two of his cousins, and took two more concubines (legal mistresses).
- Between them all, they had twelve sons and one daughter.
- There was constant competition and conflict among all the children and all the mothers.
- It was one great big messed-up family; still, it brought forth Joseph, and furthered God's great plan of the ages.

ii. It can be helpful to remember that Jesus Himself came from difficult family circumstances.

- Unexpectedly and under strange circumstances, His mom became pregnant well before the wedding.
- His mom and dad were quickly married, far ahead of their announced wedding date.
- Things didn't seem right with His dad's side of the family down in Bethlehem.
- When Jesus was just a young child, they had to escape as refugees, fleeing for their lives.

- They made a home back in Nazareth, where everyone knew about the strange pregnancy and the shotgun wedding.
- Jesus never got married – unusual and maybe even scandalous for a 30-year-old rabbi.
- We don't know what happened to Joseph, and His mom seemed a little pushy.
- His own brothers didn't believe in Him and called Him crazy.
- Jesus said that being in God's family was more important to Him than His biological family.
- Jesus put His mom into the care of one of His disciples, not one of His brothers.

iii. God's word to everyone is this: Your messed-up family – past, present, or future – does not mean God has forsaken you or that some cloud has come over you that will never pass. God works in and through difficult and messed-up families.

c. **Joseph brought a bad report of them to his father**: Joseph reported the bad behavior of his brothers to his father. This naturally made him even more unpopular and disliked among his brothers.

d. **Also he made him a tunic of many colors:** Jacob's favoritism of Joseph was plain to everyone, including Joseph himself. As an outward display of his favor, he gave Joseph a **tunic of many colors**. This signified a position of favor, princely standing, and birthright. It was a dramatic way of saying he was the son to receive the birthright.

i. According to Boice, the real idea behind the ancient Hebrew phrase for **tunic of many colors** is that it was a tunic extending all the way down to the wrists and ankles, as opposed to a shorter one. This was not what a workingman wore. It was a garment of privilege and status. The man who wore **a tunic of many colors** watched others as they did hard physical labor.

e. **They hated him and could not speak peaceably to him**: Jacob's favoritism of Joseph was an obvious source of conflict in the family. The brothers naturally **hated him**, because the father favored him and Joseph also reported their bad behavior.

2. (5-8) Joseph's first dream.

Now Joseph had a dream, and he told it to his brothers; and they hated him even more. So he said to them, "Please hear this dream which I have dreamed: There we were, binding sheaves in the field. Then behold, my sheaf arose and also stood upright; and indeed your sheaves stood all

around and bowed down to my sheaf." And his brothers said to him, "Shall you indeed reign over us? Or shall you indeed have dominion over us?" So they hated him even more for his dreams and for his words.

    a. **Joseph had a dream, and he told it to his brothers; and they hated him even more**: At best, Joseph showed a great lack of tact. Surely he knew how much his brothers hated to hear this dream, which set him above his brothers.

        i. The Bible tells us that God may speak through dreams, but it doesn't give us a guidebook for dream interpretation. Most of all, *know the Bible* to know the voice of God. We should expect that God speaks to us in the Bible, and if He were to speak in a dream, it would be unexpected.

    b. **Please hear this dream**: Joseph dreamed of the brothers in a grain field at harvest, each with a bunch of wheat stalks (**sheaves**). The sheaves belonged to the brothers all bowed down to the sheaf belonging to Joseph.

    c. **Shall you indeed reign over us**: The brothers understood perfectly the meaning of the dream – one day Joseph would **reign over** them and **have dominion over** them.

        i. Also relevant to this dream was the fact that it involved **sheaves** of wheat. Joseph's ultimate position of status over his brethren would be connected with grain and food.

3. (9-11) Joseph's second dream.

Then he dreamed still another dream and told it to his brothers, and said, "Look, I have dreamed another dream. And this time, the sun, the moon, and the eleven stars bowed down to me." So he told it to his father and his brothers; and his father rebuked him and said to him, "What is this dream that you have dreamed? Shall your mother and I and your brothers indeed come to bow down to the earth before you?" And his brothers envied him, but his father kept the matter *in mind*.

    a. **Then he dreamed still another dream and told it to his brothers**: If Joseph was unwise to tell the first dream (knowing how irritating it was to his brothers), then it was worse to share this second dream. The second dream was likely to cause even more resentment, because it set him not only above his brothers, but also set him above his father and mother.

        i. Joseph had the sort of pride common in the favored and blessed. He was so focused on how great his dreams were for *him*, he didn't begin to consider how the dreams would sound in the ears of *others*.

ii. At this point, Joseph was a *contrast* to Jesus. Jesus wants us to be as He was on this earth – an *others-centered* person. Joseph seems to have fallen short in this area.

iii. Though Joseph was wrong to tell these dreams, they certainly did come true. One may receive a wonderful message from God that He does not intend them to publish to others. Joseph showed a lack of wisdom here, perhaps rooted in pride.

b. **Shall your mother and I and your brothers indeed come to bow down to the earth before you**: At this point, even Jacob was a bit offended. He couldn't understand how Joseph could be exalted higher than his own father and mother.

i. This portion of Genesis possibly isn't in strict chronological order. Back in Genesis 35:16-20, Joseph's mother Rachel died. This portion of Genesis seems to backtrack somewhat.

ii. Probably, the transition point is in Genesis 37:2: *This is the genealogy of Jacob*. This likely ends the record preserved by Jacob himself (who recounted the death of Rachel), and the next line begins the record preserved by Joseph himself. These same kinds of transitions are found in Genesis 5:1, 6:9 and 25:19.

c. **The sun, the moon, and the eleven stars bowed down to me**: The idea of the stars, moon, and sun representing the family of Israel is repeated in Revelation 12:1. That passage speaks of Jesus coming from the nation of Israel.

B. Joseph's brothers sell him into slavery.

1. (12-17) Jacob sends Joseph to find his brothers keeping the sheep.

Then his brothers went to feed their father's flock in Shechem. And Israel said to Joseph, "Are not your brothers feeding *the flock* in Shechem? Come, I will send you to them." So he said to him, "Here I am." Then he said to him, "Please go and see if it is well with your brothers and well with the flocks, and bring back word to me." So he sent him out of the Valley of Hebron, and he went to Shechem. Now a certain man found him, and there he was, wandering in the field. And the man asked him, saying, "What are you seeking?" So he said, "I am seeking my brothers. Please tell me where they are feeding *their flocks*." And the man said, "They have departed from here, for I heard them say, 'Let us go to Dothan.'" So Joseph went after his brothers and found them in Dothan.

a. **His brothers went to feed their father's flock in Shechem**: Joseph's brothers had to do the hard and uncomfortable work of tending the roaming flocks of their father's sheep. Joseph stayed home and slept in his own bed, except when Jacob sent him to check on his brothers.

i. There seems nothing strange about this errand, except Joseph's brothers were in **Shechem**, a place where this family was influenced and harmed by worldly influences (Genesis 34).

b. **Please, go and see if it is well with your brothers and well with the flocks**: Here is Joseph with the coat of many colors, with long sleeves and doing no hard work. Joseph was the supervisor and his brothers were the workers.

i. In the New King James Version, when Jacob sent him, he even said **please**!

c. **Found them in Dothan**: It took some persistence, but Joseph found his brothers in Dothan. It was perhaps a 10- to 15-mile walk (16 to 24 kilometers), mostly west of Shechem.

i. Much later in Israel's history, Dothan was where Elisha saw angelic armies surrounding him, protecting him even when the Syrians came to arrest him (2 Kings 6:13-17).

2. (18) The conspiracy to kill Joseph.

Now when they saw him afar off, even before he came near them, they conspired against him to kill him.

a. **When they saw him afar off**: We can picture the brothers dreading Joseph's arrival. He came to inspect their work, and he would not hesitate to report to their father whatever they did wrong.

b. **They conspired against him to kill him**: This is shocking, and we shouldn't lose our sense of shock about it. They didn't conspire to mock or tease or bully Joseph a little bit; they **conspired against him to kill him**.

i. The sin was in their heart before it was ever acted out. Our sin problem begins in our heart and must be dealt with on a heart level. Our goal is not *only* changing our behavior, but especially to let God change our heart. Christian transformation works *from the inside out*.

3. (19-20) The plan to kill the **dreamer**.

Then they said to one another, "Look, this dreamer is coming! Come therefore, let us now kill him and cast him into some pit; and we shall say, 'Some wild beast has devoured him.' We shall see what will become of his dreams!"

a. **Look, this dreamer is coming**: Joseph's brothers mocked him as the **dreamer**. In a sense, Joseph brought this upon himself by the foolish way he spoke of his God-given dreams before his brothers.

b. **Some wild beast has devoured him**: Their plan to kill Joseph developed. They were so serious about it that they plotted the excuse they would make to their father, *knowing well how it would devastate Jacob*.

c. **We shall see what will become of his dreams**: They didn't oppose Joseph's plans, hopes, and dreams for the future. They opposed the **dreams** that came as a revelation from God. They wanted to see if they could defeat God's Word, God's announced purpose.

i. Joseph's life doesn't really tell us anything about fulfilling life dreams.

- Joseph never dreamed of being a slave.
- Joseph never dreamed of being falsely accused of rape.
- Joseph never dreamed of being forgotten in prison.
- Joseph never dreamed of being the second most powerful man in Egypt.
- Joseph never dreamed of saving the world from famine.
- God's dream for Joseph was better and greater than any dream Joseph could come up with.

ii. A focus on our life dreams can be dangerous, because we make the fulfillment of our dream the most important thing – we make it an idol. We think of Jesus as a way to accomplish *our* dream; we make Him an actor in our life story. Instead, we want play our part in God's unfolding story.

ii. Joseph's life tells us *a lot* about how God fulfills His word. The brothers were *determined* to defeat God's revealed word. *God's Word never fails.*

- What God said about Joseph *is true and would come to pass.*
- What God says about Jesus *is true and will come to pass.*

4. (21-22) Reuben's plan to rescue Joseph.

But Reuben heard it, and he delivered him out of their hands, and said, "Let us not kill him." And Reuben said to them, "Shed no blood, *but* cast him into this pit which is in the wilderness, and do not lay a hand on him"; that he might deliver him out of their hands, and bring him back to his father.

a. **But Reuben heard it, and he delivered him out of their hands**: We think of all ten brothers (leaving little Benjamin out), and wonder how they could all be so evil. There was one good among the ten. They wanted to kill Joseph first and then throw him into the pit; Reuben suggested they throw him in the pit first instead, and he got the brothers to agree to it.

i. There is something wonderful in seeing this from **Reuben**, because earlier (Genesis 35) he did a terrible thing – he had sex with one of this father's wives/concubines (Bilhah). **Reuben** wouldn't be defined only by the worst thing that he did.

b. **That he might deliver him out of their hands, and bring him back to his father**: The other brothers had their plan and Reuben had his plan. Reuben didn't try to *stop* his brothers; he tried to out-smart them.

i. Reuben could have simply rose up and said, "This is wrong! We can't do this!" Reuben wanted to be merciful to Joseph, but he also wanted to please the other brothers who hated Joseph. This failure to do the right thing meant that the good Reuben wanted to do (**bring him back to his father**) would not happen.

5. (23-25a) Joseph is cast into a pit.

So it came to pass, when Joseph had come to his brothers, that they stripped Joseph *of* his tunic, the tunic of *many* colors that *was* on him. Then they took him and cast him into a pit. And the pit was empty; *there was* no water in it. And they sat down to eat a meal.

a. **They stripped Joseph of his tunic, the tunic of many colors that was on him**: With cruel pleasure, they bullied Joseph and ripped from him the sign of his father's favor, the coat **of many colors**.

i. We picture this scene and think of how Jesus was stripped of everything before He was crucified. Jesus went up on a cross and Joseph went down in a pit, but each was stripped, declared cursed, and put into a place they could seemingly never rescue themselves from.

ii. We think first of Jesus, but we also think of the righteousness of God that clothes every believer, and how the enemy of our soul wishes us to feel naked, cursed, and helpless. None of that was true for Joseph, Jesus, or for the believer today.

b. **And they sat down to eat a meal**: The heartless character of the brothers was evident—they could eat a meal with Joseph nearby in the pit. They could sit down and enjoy their food before completing the murder of Joseph.

i. Later, Genesis 42:21 described the conviction of sin they ignored at that moment. In that passage the brothers said: *We are truly guilty concerning our brother, for we saw the anguish of his soul when he pleaded with us, and we would not hear.* When Joseph was cast into the pit, he pled with his brothers, and they ignored his cries as they ate their meal.

ii. "A physicist could compute the exact time required for his cries to go twenty-five yards to the eardrums of the brothers. But it took twenty-two years for that cry to go from the eardrums to their hearts." (Barnhouse)

6. (25b-27) The plan to sell Joseph.

Then they lifted their eyes and looked, and there was a company of Ishmaelites, coming from Gilead with their camels, bearing spices, balm, and myrrh, on their way to carry *them* **down to Egypt. So Judah said to his brothers, "What profit** *is there* **if we kill our brother and conceal his blood? Come and let us sell him to the Ishmaelites, and let not our hand be upon him, for he** *is* **our brother** *and* **our flesh." And his brothers listened.**

a. **There was a company of Ishmaelites**: We would call these Arab traders, the family that came from their great-uncle Ishmael, the other son of Abraham.

b. **What profit is there if we kill our brother and conceal his blood**: The only way to describe the brothers is *cruel* and *cold*. They were heartless to Joseph, to their father, and set themselves against God's plan. They decided that if they were going to ruin so many lives, they might as well make some money off of it.

i. This came from **Judah**, who of all the brothers became the ancestor of the Messiah. As the story of Joseph develops, **Judah** will be the brother most changed in heart and character.

c. **For he is our brother and our flesh**: "He's our **brother**, so let's *only* sell him into a life of slavery and tell dad that he's dead." What brothers!

7. (28) Joseph is sold into slavery.

Then Midianite traders passed by; so *the brothers* **pulled Joseph up and lifted him out of the pit, and sold him to the Ishmaelites for twenty** *shekels* **of silver. And they took Joseph to Egypt.**

a. **The brothers pulled Joseph up and lifted him out of the pit**: As they brought him out of the pit, perhaps Joseph felt that this was a big and cruel practical joke. Perhaps he told his brothers how sorry he was, and that he had learned his lesson and wouldn't act so superior and privileged around them anymore.

i. We don't know if we should think more highly of Joseph's brothers because they decided to spare his life or less highly of them because they figured they could get rid of him and make a little money at the same time. Apparently, they considered that their brother was only worth **twenty shekels of silver**.

b. **Sold him to the Ishmaelites for twenty shekels of silver**: If Joseph was hopeful as he was pulled out of the pit, all hope vanished when he saw the **Ishmaelites** and the exchange of money.

i. The brothers probably laughed as the **Ishmaelites** went their way to Egypt, feeling good that they didn't kill Joseph and that they made a little money in the process. Best of all, they thought they had defeated the dream, the revelation from God.

- God's word about Joseph was proved true – *no matter what his brothers did to Him*.

- God's word about Jesus was proved true – *no matter what others did to Him*.

- God's word about you will be proved true – *no matter what others do or have done*.

8. (29-32) The brothers cover their sin and lie to Jacob concerning Joseph's fate.

Then Reuben returned to the pit, and indeed Joseph was not in the pit; and he tore his clothes. And he returned to his brothers and said, "The lad *is* no *more*; and I, where shall I go?" So they took Joseph's tunic, killed a kid of the goats, and dipped the tunic in the blood. Then they sent the tunic of *many* colors, and they brought it to their father and said, "We have found this. Do you know whether it is your son's tunic or not?"

a. **Then Reuben returned to the pit, and indeed Joseph was not in the pit; and he tore his clothes**: Reuben tore his clothes as an expression of utter horror and mourning, because his weak stand for righteousness accomplished nothing. Joseph might as well be dead, because his father who loved him so would never see him again.

b. **We have found this. Do you know whether it is your son's tunic or not**: This showed the cruelty of the sons of Israel was not directed only towards the favored son, but also towards the father who favored him. This was both a heartless way to bring the news and an evil lie.

9. (33-35) Jacob's grief.

And he recognized it and said, "*It is* my son's tunic. A wild beast has devoured him. Without doubt Joseph is torn to pieces." Then Jacob tore his clothes, put sackcloth on his waist, and mourned for his son many days. And all his sons and all his daughters arose to comfort him; but he refused to be comforted, and he said, "For I shall go down into the grave to my son in mourning." Thus his father wept for him.

> a. **It is my son's tunic**: We can only imagine the pain of the father losing his beloved son, and the strange pleasure the brothers had in concealing the crime. Joseph's brothers decided to live the rest of their lives with this terrible secret.
>
> b. **Jacob tore his clothes**: This was an expression of utter horror and mourning because his beloved son was gone. His grief was understandable, but his failure to see the truth of eternal life was not.
>
> > i. This is also a powerful illustration of the principle that if we *believe* something to be so, it may as well be. Joseph was not dead, but as long as Jacob believed he was, as far as Jacob was concerned, Joseph *was* dead. In the same way, the Christian has in truth been set free from sin, but if Satan can persuade us we are under the tyranny of sin, we may as well be.
>
> c. **All his sons and all his daughters arose to comfort him**: Pretended comfort from those who both did the crime and covered it up was of no help to Jacob.

10. (36) Joseph ends up in the court of a high Egyptian official.

Now the Midianites had sold him in Egypt to Potiphar, an officer of Pharaoh and captain of the guard.

> a. **Now the Midianites had sold him in Egypt**: Egypt was a large and thriving kingdom for at least a thousand years before Joseph came. The Egyptians were wealthy and had massive natural resources. They were educated and had no real enemies at the time. When Joseph came to Egypt, some of the pyramids already looked old and the Sphinx was already carved.
>
> > i. Yet in God's eyes, the most impressive thing about Egypt was that Joseph was now there. "Though stripped of his coat, he had not been stripped of his character" (Meyer).
> >
> > ii. "This delicate child of an indulgent father, who had been clothed with a princely garment of many colors, must now wear the garb, of a slave, and march in the hot sun across the burning sand; but never was captive more submissive under cruel treatment, he endured as seeing

him who is invisible; his heart was sustained by a deep confidence in the God of his father Jacob, for 'Jehovah was with him.'" (Spurgeon)

b. **Sold him in Egypt to Potiphar, an officer of Pharaoh and captain of the guard**: Even in the midst of this horror, God did not depart from Joseph. In some ways the story will get worse, and when it does, God will still be with Joseph. God is working not only for Joseph himself, but also for the larger purposes of His redemptive plan.

i. We can thank God for His great plan.

- If Joseph's family wasn't messed up and weird, his brothers would never have sold him as a slave.
- If Joseph's brothers never sold him as a slave, then Joseph would never have gone to Egypt.
- If Joseph never went to Egypt, he would never have been sold to Potiphar.
- If Joseph was never sold to Potiphar, Potiphar's wife would never have falsely accused him of rape.
- If Potiphar's wife never falsely accused Joseph of rape, then Joseph would never have been put in prison.
- If Joseph was never put in prison, he would have never met the baker and butler of Pharaoh.
- If Joseph never met the baker and butler of Pharaoh, he would have never interpreted their dreams.
- If Joseph never interpreted their dreams, he would have never interpreted Pharaoh's dream.
- If Joseph never interpreted Pharaoh's dream, he never would have become prime minister, second in Egypt only to Pharaoh.
- If Joseph never became prime minister, he never would have wisely prepared for the terrible famine to come.
- If Joseph never wisely prepared for the terrible famine, then his family back in Canaan would have died in the famine.
- If Joseph's family back in Canaan died in the famine, then the Messiah could not have come from a dead family.
- If the Messiah did not come forth, then Jesus never came.
- If Jesus never came, then we are all dead in our sins and without hope in this world.
- We are grateful for God's great and wise plan.

Genesis 38 – Tamar and the Sin of Judah

A. Tamar's widowhood and Judah's unfairness.

1. (1-5) Judah and his three sons.

It came to pass at that time that Judah departed from his brothers, and visited a certain Adullamite whose name was Hirah. And Judah saw there a daughter of a certain Canaanite whose name was Shua, and he married her and went in to her. So she conceived and bore a son, and he called his name Er. She conceived again and bore a son, and she called his name Onan. And she conceived yet again and bore a son, and called his name Shelah. He was at Chezib when she bore him.

> a. **Judah departed from his brothers**: Judah, the fourth-born son of Jacob through Leah (Reuben, Simeon, and Levi were before him), had not yet distinguished himself as someone great among his brothers. He was the one who suggested they sell Joseph into slavery (Genesis 37:26).

> b. **And Judah saw there a daughter of a certain Canaanite whose name was Shua, and he married her**: Through an ungodly and unwise marriage to a Canaanite woman, Judah fathered three sons: **Er**, **Onan**, and **Shelah**.

>> i. Consistently, marriage with Canaanite women had been discouraged among the patriarchs and those connected to them (Genesis 24:3, 28:1, 28:8). The Canaanite neighbors were rapidly corrupting the family of Israel. Their future looked like a combination of corruption and assimilation. God had a plan to bring them out of Canaan.

2. (6-7) Er's marriage to Tamar and his death.

Then Judah took a wife for Er his firstborn, and her name was Tamar. But Er, Judah's firstborn, was wicked in the sight of the LORD, and the LORD killed him.

> a. **Her name was Tamar**: It is not surprising that Judah chose a Canaanite wife for his son Er, since he himself was married to a Canaanite.

b. **Er, Judah's firstborn, was wicked in the sight of the LORD, and the LORD killed him**: We are never told what Er's wickedness was, but obviously it was evil enough that God brought immediate judgment upon him. Growing up with a father from such a troubled family and with a mother who was a Canaanite did not help Er to live a godly life.

3. (8-10) Onan's refusal to raise up offspring for Tamar.

And Judah said to Onan, "Go in to your brother's wife and marry her, and raise up an heir to your brother." But Onan knew that the heir would not be his; and it came to pass, when he went in to his brother's wife, that he emitted on the ground, lest he should give an heir to his brother. And the thing which he did displeased the LORD; therefore He killed him also.

a. **Go in to your brother's wife and marry her, and raise up an heir to your brother**: This was done according to the custom of levirate marriage (later codified into law in Deuteronomy 25:5-10). If a man died before providing sons to his wife, it was the duty of his brothers to marry her and to give her sons. The child was considered the son of the brother who died, because the living brother only acted in his place (**Onan knew that the heir would not be his**).

i. This was done so the dead brother's name would be carried on, but also it was so the widow would have children to support her. Apart from this, she would likely live the rest of her life as a destitute widow.

b. **When he went in to his brother's wife, that he emitted on the ground, lest he should give an heir to his brother**: Onan refused to seriously regard the responsibility to father descendants for his dead brother. He was more than happy to use Tamar for his sexual gratification, but he did not want to give Tamar a son he would have to support but would be considered to be the son of Er.

i. Onan pursued sex as *only* a pleasurable experience. If he really didn't want to father a child by Tamar, he should never have had sex with her at all. He refused to fulfill his obligation to his dead brother and Tamar.

ii. Many Christians have used this passage as a proof-text against masturbation. Indeed, masturbation has been called *onanism*. However, this does not seem to be the case here. Whatever Onan did, he was not masturbating. This was not a sin of masturbation, but a sin of refusing to care for his brother's widow by giving her offspring, and the sin of a selfish use of sex.

4. (11) Judah's unfair dealing with Tamar.

Then Judah said to Tamar his daughter-in-law, "Remain a widow in your father's house till my son Shelah is grown." For he said, "Lest he also die like his brothers." And Tamar went and dwelt in her father's house.

> a. **Lest he also die like his brothers**: One can understand that Judah did not want to give his last son as a husband to Tamar. God already judged two of her previous husbands. Judah vowed he would not give Shelah as husband to Tamar as custom and righteousness commanded, but he would continually delay the fulfillment of his dishonest promise.
>
> b. **Tamar went and dwelt in her father's house**: This was no place for a young, childless widow to be. There were still additional brothers in her husband's family who could fulfill the obligation they owed to their late brother. None of this was the fault of Tamar. All the blame belonged to Judah and his sons.

B. Tamar bears a child by Judah.

1. (12-14) Judah's wife dies, and Tamar disguises herself as a prostitute.

Now in the process of time the daughter of Shua, Judah's wife, died; and Judah was comforted, and went up to his sheepshearers at Timnah, he and his friend Hirah the Adullamite. And it was told Tamar, saying, "Look, your father-in-law is going up to Timnah to shear his sheep." So she took off her widow's garments, covered *herself* with a veil and wrapped herself, and sat in an open place which was on the way to Timnah; for she saw that Shelah was grown, and she was not given to him as a wife.

> a. **She saw that Shelah was grown, and she was not given to him as a wife**: Tamar did not want to face what would be a difficult existence in that culture – life with no husband or children.
>
> b. **She was not given to him as a wife**: Tamar didn't have the option of just finding another man to marry. She was under the headship of her father-in-law Judah, and he had to *give* her a husband. *He* determined whom and when she could marry.
>
> c. **Covered herself with a veil and wrapped herself, and sat in an open place**: Knowing that Judah would be away from home (**to Timnah**), Tamar dressed herself as a prostitute and went to the place prostitutes met their customers. She planned to meet only one customer – Judah.

2. (15-18) Disguised as a prostitute, Tamar has sex with Judah and conceives.

When Judah saw her, he thought she was a harlot, because she had covered her face. Then he turned to her by the way, and said, "Please

let me come in to you"; for he did not know that she *was* his daughter-in-law. So she said, "What will you give me, that you may come in to me?" And he said, "I will send a young goat from the flock." So she said, "Will you give *me* a pledge till you send *it*?" Then he said, "What pledge shall I give you?" So she said, "Your signet and cord, and your staff that *is* in your hand." Then he gave *them* to her, and went in to her, and she conceived by him.

> a. **When Judah saw her, he thought she was a harlot, because she had covered her face**: In her disguise, Tamar successfully met Judah. After negotiating the price, Tamar demanded a pledge of the future payment of the agreed-upon price (**a young goat**).
>
> b. **Then he gave them to her, and went in to her, and she conceived by him**: When Tamar conceived, it certainly was not intended by Judah, but it was in Tamar's plan; more importantly, it was in God's plan.

3. (19-23) Tamar disappears.

So she arose and went away, and laid aside her veil and put on the garments of her widowhood. And Judah sent the young goat by the hand of his friend the Adullamite, to receive *his* pledge from the woman's hand, but he did not find her. Then he asked the men of that place, saying, "Where is the harlot who *was* openly by the roadside?" And they said, "There was no harlot in this *place*." So he returned to Judah and said, "I cannot find her. Also, the men of the place said there was no harlot in this *place*." Then Judah said, "Let her take *them* for herself, lest we be shamed; for I sent this young goat and you have not found her."

> a. **She arose and went away, and laid aside her veil**: After her meeting with Judah, Tamar immediately put away her disguise and resumed her normal life.
>
> b. **Judah sent the young goat by the hand of his friend the Adullamite, to receive his pledge from the woman's hand, but he did not find her**: Judah sent a friend to pay Tamar, and to retrieve the pledge he left with her. Because Tamar disappeared, he gave up the pledge, leaving it with her.

4. (24-26) Tamar is vindicated and Judah is reproved.

And it came to pass, about three months after, that Judah was told, saying, "Tamar your daughter-in-law has played the harlot; furthermore she *is* with child by harlotry." So Judah said, "Bring her out and let her be burned!" When she was brought out, she sent to her father-in-law, saying, "By the man to whom these belong, I *am* with child." And she said, "Please determine whose these *are*– the signet and cord, and staff."

So Judah acknowledged them and said, "She has been more righteous than I, because I did not give her to Shelah my son." And he never knew her again.

a. **She is with child by harlotry**: When the widowed, unmarried Tamar was found to be pregnant, it was evident that it was from some kind of sexual immorality. Perhaps Tamar even told others that she had **played the harlot**.

b. **Bring her out and let her be burned**: Judah did not care for Tamar, the widowed wife of two of his sons. He found it easy to pass judgment on someone who sinned just as he sinned, without passing the same judgment on himself.

c. **Please determine whose these are**: Tamar acted shrewdly and vindicated herself against the charge of harlotry. She made the logical appeal of noting that the man who hired her was just as guilty as she was.

d. **She has been more righteous than I**: However, even Judah could see through to the real issue. He was at fault for not providing for Tamar a son through his last son Shelah.

5. (27-30) Tamar gives birth to twins, Perez and Zerah.

Now it came to pass, at the time for giving birth, that behold, twins *were* in her womb. And so it was, when she was giving birth, that *the one* put out *his* hand; and the midwife took a scarlet *thread* and bound it on his hand, saying, "This one came out first." Then it happened, as he drew back his hand, that his brother came out unexpectedly; and she said, "How did you break through? This breach be upon you!" Therefore his name was called Perez. Afterward his brother came out who had the scarlet *thread* on his hand. And his name was called Zerah.

a. **Therefore his name was called Perez... his name was called Zerah**: Matthew 1:3 and Luke 3:33 each list **Perez** as an ancestor of Jesus the Messiah. God took the son of this ungodly situation and put him in the family line of the Messiah, despite the fact that neither Judah nor Tamar were examples of godliness.

i. This is a wonderful example of grace. God chose them, despite their works, to both be in the line of the Messiah and to have their role in God's plan of redemption.

b. **His brother came out who had the scarlet thread on his hand... his name was called Zerah**: The second-born son Zerah had the red thread on his wrist, but the first-born son Perez would be found in the Messianic line.

Genesis 39 – Joseph in Potiphar's House

A. Joseph in Potiphar's house.

1. (1) Potiphar, an Egyptian official, buys Joseph.

Now Joseph had been taken down to Egypt. And Potiphar, an officer of Pharaoh, captain of the guard, an Egyptian, bought him from the Ishmaelites who had taken him down there.

> a. **Potiphar, an officer of Pharaoh, captain of the guard, an Egyptian, bought him**: The name **Potiphar** means *devoted to the sun*. It was a name connected with the Egyptian religious system.
>
> b. **An officer of Pharaoh**: The ancient Hebrew word **officer** could be translated *eunuch* – one who was castrated, normally for the sake of their service. It was a common practice in ancient times to make those highest in the royal courts eunuchs, to ensure they would be wholly devoted to their king. Because this practice was common, the term came to be used for all who served in important positions in a king's court, whether they were actually eunuchs or not. Therefore, we really don't know if Potiphar was a eunuch.
>
> c. **Captain of the guard**: The idea behind this title means *chief of police*, or probably more precisely, Potiphar was head of Pharaoh's personal security force. He was a highly-trusted official in the government of Egypt.
>
> d. **Bought him from the Ishmaelites**: Joseph was a *slave*. He seemed to have no control over his destiny, but was bought and sold like a piece of property. He could have ended up with anyone, but Potiphar **bought him**.

2. (2-3) God is with Joseph.

The LORD was with Joseph, and he was a successful man; and he was in the house of his master the Egyptian. And his master saw that the LORD *was* with him and that the LORD made all he did to prosper in his hand.

a. **The LORD was with Joseph**: Joseph's ordeal was probably worse than any of us have gone through. Yet God did not abandon him, even in the smallest way. If God allowed Joseph to be a slave, then he would be a **successful man**, even as a slave.

i. We often complain to God that He put us in a terrible or difficult place. Yet God's will is that we trust Him to bless us and make us successful (as *He* measures success) wherever we are.

ii. "Externally it did not always appear that God was with him, for he did not always seem to be a prosperous man; but when you come to look into the inmost soul of this servant of God, you see his true likeness—he lived in communion with the Most High, and God blessed him." (Spurgeon)

iii. Some people think they we can't be blessed unless they are in authority, in charge of things. Jesus lived and taught a better way – a life as a *servant*.

- *If you want to be great in God's kingdom, learn to be the servant of all.* (Matthew 20:26)
- *For the Son of Man did not come to be served, but to serve.* (Matthew 20:28)
- There are many wonderful titles for Jesus the Messiah, but one of the most meaningful is *Servant of the LORD* (Matthew 12:18, Isaiah 42:1).
- We can and must learn the blessing of being a servant; if it isn't forced upon it, we can choose it.

b. **He was a successful man; and he was in the house of his master the Egyptian**: Even at this early point when it seemed Joseph had no control over circumstances – and indeed he had none – God overruled the evil or capricious choices of man to accomplish His eternal purpose.

c. **And his master saw that the LORD was with him**: By his trust in God, diligent work, and blessing from God, Joseph showed Potiphar that God was real. Followers of Jesus should live out the same principle today; others should see the difference Jesus makes in our lives by the way we work.

i. **The LORD was with him**: Think of the contrast between Joseph and his brothers. The brothers were not sold as slaves and slept in their own beds among their own families.

- Joseph was a slave, but free.
- The brothers were free, but slaves to secrets, shame, and guilt.

3. (4-6) God blesses Potiphar for Joseph's sake.

So Joseph found favor in his sight, and served him. Then he made him overseer of his house, and all *that* **he had he put under his authority. So it was, from the time** *that* **he had made him overseer of his house and all that he had, that the LORD blessed the Egyptian's house for Joseph's sake; and the blessing of the LORD was on all that he had in the house and in the field. Thus he left all that he had in Joseph's hand, and he did not know what he had except for the bread which he ate. Now Joseph was handsome in form and appearance.**

>a. **He made him overseer of his house, and all that he had he put under his authority**: Because of God's blessing and Joseph's faithfulness, God made sure Joseph was advanced in his position, even as a slave.
>
>>i. It would have been easy for Joseph to do what we so often do: think little of his present position because it seemed so bad (he was a slave, after all). But Joseph believed God could bless him right where he was, so he didn't wait for a better situation to be blessed by God.
>
>b. **The LORD blessed the Egyptian's house for Joseph's sake**: After the same principle, blessing can be brought upon our workplace because of our presence of godliness.
>
>c. **Thus he left all that he had in Joseph's hand**: Joseph rose to the top, but it took a while to happen.
>
>- Joseph was 17 years old when he was sold into slavery (Genesis 37:2).
>- He was 30 when Pharaoh promoted him (Genesis 41:46).
>- Joseph was in prison for two years before his promotion (Genesis 41:1).
>- Therefore, Joseph was in Potiphar's house for 11 years.
>
>>i. It took 11 years for the full measure of God's blessing to be accomplished in Joseph's life. 11 years seems like a long time. Many think if advancement is from God, it must come quickly. Sometimes this is the case, but not normally. Normally, God allows good things to develop slowly. Human children have the longest development time both in the womb and in childhood compared to animals. In the world of plants, it takes many years for an acorn to become an oak; a squash might grow almost overnight.
>
>d. **He left all that he had in Joseph's hand**: This means that Joseph was a hard worker. When he came to Egypt, he was at a great disadvantage. He knew nothing of the language, culture, customs, or ways of doing business.

He had to get up early and stay up late to both do his job and to learn Egyptian ways.

> i. It seems that Joseph grew up watching others work. Something happened to him in his crisis; he accepted God's transforming work. God gave Joseph great administrative skill, and now the heart of a hard-working servant was added to that.
>
> ii. Luther said, "Accordingly, Joseph was not only good and chaste, and not only diligently poured out prayers to God for his master, for the king, and for the whole land of Egypt, but he was also a most vigilant overseer and manager of the domestic tasks" (Cited in Boice).
>
> iii. When we leave **all that** we have in Jesus' **hand**, our home and life will be blessed – and for Jesus' sake.

e. **Now Joseph was handsome in form and appearance**: Joseph's appearance was of special note. The Bible only calls two other men beautiful: David (1 Samuel 16:12) and Absalom (2 Samuel 14:25). Moses was said to be a beautiful child (Exodus 2:2).

B. Joseph's resistance to temptation and its aftermath.

1. (7-10) The invitation of Potiphar's wife and Joseph's resistance.

And it came to pass after these things that his master's wife cast longing eyes on Joseph, and she said, "Lie with me." But he refused and said to his master's wife, "Look, my master does not know what is with me in the house, and he has committed all that he has to my hand. There is no one greater in this house than I, nor has he kept back anything from me but you, because you are his wife. How then can I do this great wickedness, and sin against God?" So it was, as she spoke to Joseph day by day, that he did not heed her, to lie with her *or* to be with her.

a. **His master's wife cast longing eyes on Joseph, and she said, "Lie with me"**: Potiphar's wife was undeniably forward towards Joseph. Literally, Potiphar is called *a eunuch of Pharaoh* (Genesis 39:1). If Potiphar was literally a castrated eunuch, this shows that his wife looked for sexual activity elsewhere.

> i. *Maybe Potiphar's wife felt deprived.* Perhaps Potiphar was a eunuch, and the marriage was purely a ceremonial arrangement. It may be that she felt free to pursue sexual pleasure outside the marriage. This attitude is common today, and our modern culture tells us that we are deprived unless we pursue every sexual desire we feel. This is a lie and makes our sexual desires gods that rule our life.

ii. Also, it seems that in the ancient Egypt there were low moral expectations on women, even married women. It was assumed that women would have sex outside marriage. Potiphar's wife wasn't looking for a relationship, just a good time. Again, our modern culture tells us that sex is great and often better apart from meaningful relationships. The truth – both Biblically and lived out in life – is that sex is far better in committed, married relationship; that sex *means* something.

iii. Joseph was an attractive man (Genesis 39:6) and perhaps this had something to do with it. That he seemed beyond the reach of Potiphar's wife was also probably a factor. If this was so, then she was not the first or last woman who tried to seduce a man out of a sense of challenge or in seeking self-worth. Potiphar's wife may have looked to Joseph with a desperate attempt to feel desirable and worth something.

b. **Lie with me**: This was bold and strong temptation to Joseph. It reminds us that when we face strong temptations, others have also faced the same.

i. Satan wants us to think our temptation is unique; that no other person could understand what we are going through in a particular temptation, but there is no temptation that has overtaken us except what is common among people (1 Corinthians 10:13).

ii. "Slavery itself was a small calamity compared with that which would have happened to young Joseph had he been enslaved by wicked passions." (Spurgeon)

c. **She spoke to Joseph day by day, that he did not heed her**: Joseph showed remarkable faithfulness towards God, Potiphar, and himself by resisting this temptation for so long – perhaps for up to 11 years. Many character qualities helped in this, and Joseph gave several reasons for his refusal.

i. Joseph **said to his master's wife**: He did not flirt or speak in a provocative manner with her. A foolish man would say, "It's just words, let's have a little fun." Flirting and provocative words lead to disaster.

ii. Joseph remembered his responsibilities: **my master does not know what is with me in the house, and he has committed all that he has to my hand**. He remembered how much he had to lose. Today, even the single person has much to lose – their innocence, their heart, and their capacity to truly give themselves to the one God has for them.

iii. Joseph remembered who she was: **you are his wife**. She simply did not belong to Joseph. She was given to another, and another was given to her.

iv. Joseph remembered what the act actually was, **great wickedness**: We often want to call sin by another name. Hostility and temper are *self-expression*. Pride is *self-esteem*. Gluttony is *the good life*. Covetousness is *trying to get ahead*. Perversion is *an alternative lifestyle*. Adultery is *a cry for help in a bad marriage*.

v. Joseph remembered that it was **sin against God**. This was probably a pretty risk-free proposition – there was little chance of getting caught. Joseph cared about more than *getting caught*, knowing that everything was before the eyes of God. Joseph had a real enough relationship with God that he cared about more than getting caught before human eyes. "When I regarded God as a tyrant, I thought sin a trifle; but when I knew him to be my father, then I mourned that I could ever have kicked against him. When I thought that God was hard, I found it easy to sin; but when I found God so kind, so good, so overflowing with compassion, I smote upon my breast to think that I could ever have rebelled against one who loved me so, and sought my good" (Spurgeon).

vi. Joseph **refused**: Sometimes it just comes down to that. One must refuse and say *no* to sin, even when they *feel* like saying *yes*. One must realize that there is more to live for than the desires of the body. We are more than our sexual urges, and should live like we are more.

d. **He did not heed her, to lie with her or to be with her**: Joseph was careful to never be alone with his temptation. Joseph wisely avoided being alone around Potiphar's wife (**or to be with her**).

i. We rightly admire Joseph as an example of a man or woman of God who resisted temptation. There are many in the Bible who did not always successfully resist temptation:

- Adam and Eve.
- Abraham and Moses.
- David and Solomon.
- John and Peter.

ii. There are a few others who seemed very good at resisting temptation, such as Joseph and Daniel. Still, none of these compare to Jesus. Jesus was tested and tempted in ways we can't even imagine, yet He remained perfect and sinless. *Filled with Jesus*, we can have the strength to resist temptation.

2. (11-12) Joseph resists her strong attempt at seduction.

But it happened about this time, when Joseph went into the house to do his work, and none of the men of the house was inside, that she caught him by his garment, saying, "Lie with me." But he left his garment in her hand, and fled and ran outside.

> a. **When Joseph went into the house to do his work, and none of the men of the house was inside, that she caught him**: Potiphar's wife knew Joseph avoided her, so she made a deliberate plan to trap him. Surely, it was she who arranged it that **none of the men of the house was inside**.
>
> b. **She caught him by his garment, saying, "Lie with me." But he left his garment in her hand, and fled and ran outside**: Joseph resisted this tremendous moment of temptation when he **ran outside**. Joseph did what we are all supposed to do when faced with this kind of situation: he **fled and ran**. 2 Timothy 2:22 makes it clear: *Flee also youthful lusts*.
>
>> i. If we are not actually running towards sin, we have a tendency to at least linger in its presence. But we are commanded to do the only safe thing: run away from these lusts of the flesh, and run as fast as we can.
>>
>> ii. The KJV says at Genesis 39:12, *He left the garment in her hand, and fled, and got him out*. Joseph *got him out*. No one else was going to get him out. God provides a *way* of escape (1 Corinthians 10:13), but you have to take the way out.
>
> c. **He left his garment**: The idea is not that he ran away naked, but that his outer garment was stripped off. Essentially, he left in his underwear. Joseph had to know this stand for purity would cost him dearly, but he considered it worth it.

3. (13-18) Potiphar's wife falsely accuses Joseph before Potiphar.

And so it was, when she saw that he had left his garment in her hand and fled outside, that she called to the men of her house and spoke to them, saying, "See, he has brought in to us a Hebrew to mock us. He came in to me to lie with me, and I cried out with a loud voice. And it happened, when he heard that I lifted my voice and cried out, that he left his garment with me, and fled and went outside." So she kept his garment with her until his master came home. Then she spoke to him with words like these, saying, "The Hebrew servant whom you brought to us came in to me to mock me; so it happened, as I lifted my voice and cried out, that he left his garment with me and fled outside."

> a. **A Hebrew… the Hebrew servant**: In an age when punishment was brutal and life was cheap – especially the life of a slave – Potiphar's wife knew her accusation would mean a death sentence for Joseph. That's why she didn't say his name; she didn't want to think of him as a real person.

b. **He came in to me to lie with me, and I cried out with a loud voice**: It must have offended and grieved Joseph to be accused under such an outrageous lie. Yet he did not seem to defend himself against this false accusation, even as Jesus was silent before His accusers (Isaiah 53:7 and Matthew 27:13-14).

> i. *This was not fair.* Sometimes there is a price to be paid for resisting temptation. We do this in faith, trusting God to work all things together for good for those who love God and are the called according to His purpose (Romans 8:28).

4. (19-20) Joseph is sent to prison.

So it was, when his master heard the words which his wife spoke to him, saying, "Your servant did to me after this manner," that his anger was aroused. Then Joseph's master took him and put him into the prison, a place where the king's prisoners were confined. And he was there in the prison.

a. **His anger was aroused**: Potiphar knew what kind of woman his wife was and he knew what kind of man Joseph was. His **anger** probably came because he knew that her accusation against Joseph was not true.

> i. Poor Potiphar! He was left *with* his wife and *without* Joseph, who made his whole household run well.

> ii. "Death was the only penalty Joseph could reasonably expect. His reprieve presumably owed much to the respect he had won; and Potiphar's mingled wrath and restraint may reflect a faint misgiving about the full accuracy of the charge." (Kidner)

> iii. "He never said a word, that I can learn, about Potiphar's wife. It seemed necessary to his own defense, but he would not accuse the woman; he let judgment go by default, and left her to her own conscience and her husband's cooler consideration. This showed great power; it is hard for a man to compress his lips, saying nothing when his character is at stake. So eloquent was Joseph in his silence that there is not a word of complaint throughout the whole record of his life." (Spurgeon)

b. **Then Joseph's master took him and put him into the prison**: Poor Joseph! Joseph went:

- From privilege in his father's house.
- To the pit his brothers threw him into.
- To being property in the slave market.
- To the privilege of managing Potiphar's house.

- To the principled stand against temptation.
- To the perjury of false accusation.
- To the prison of Pharaoh.

   i. We can see the *mercy* in this, because if Potiphar had believed his wife, he certainly would have put Joseph to death.

   ii. We can see the *injustice* in this, because Joseph suffered for someone else's sin. As Christians, we remember someone who perfectly resisted all temptation, who as He stood for righteousness was stripped of His garments, and who was then punished for the sins of others. We see that Jesus is the hope of all who fail under temptation.

   iii. We can see *God's hand* in all of this. All of this moves God's story forward, putting Joseph in the place where he can save his family and the whole world from coming famine, and prepare a place for them to live with him.

   iv. "He felt it a cruel thing, to be under such a slander, and to suffer for his innocence. A young man so pure, so chaste, must have felt it to be sharper than a whip of scorpions to be accused as he was; yet as he sat down in the gloom of his cell, the Lord was with him." (Spurgeon)

5. (21-23) Joseph prospers, even in prison.

But the Lord was with Joseph and showed him mercy, and He gave him favor in the sight of the keeper of the prison. And the keeper of the prison committed to Joseph's hand all the prisoners who were in the prison; whatever they did there, it was his doing. The keeper of the prison did not look into anything *that* was under *Joseph's* authority, because the Lord was with him; and whatever he did, the Lord made it prosper.

   a. **But the Lord was with Joseph and showed him mercy**: If God blessed Joseph in the pit, if He blessed Joseph the slave, we are not surprised to see that He blessed Joseph in prison. None of these terrible circumstances changed or defeated God's plan for Joseph's life.

   i. The dominating theme is that Joseph succeeded because of the blessing of God:

   - *The Lord was with Joseph, and he was a successful man.* (Genesis 39:2)

   - *His master saw that the Lord was with him and that the Lord made all he did to prosper in his hand.* (Genesis 39:3)

- *The LORD blessed the Egyptian's house for Joseph's sake; and the blessing of the LORD was on all that he had.* (Genesis 39:5)

ii. Even after Joseph was falsely accused and thrown into prison, God still blessed Joseph with His presence:

- **But the LORD was with Joseph**. (Genesis 39:21)
- **The LORD was with him**. (Genesis 39:23)

iii. "It is but of little consequence where the lot of a servant of God may be cast; like Joseph he is ever employed for his master, and God honours him and prospers his work." (Clarke)

b. **The keeper of the prison committed to Joseph's hand all the prisoners who were in the prison; whatever they did there, it was his doing**: As happened before in the house of Potiphar, Joseph rose to the top, becoming the chief administrator of the prison. Through his experience in both places, God sharpened the administrative skills Joseph needed to one day save his family and to save the whole world.

i. "The Lord was with Joseph none the less when he was cast into the prison. He knew God was with him in prison, and therefore he did not sit down sullenly in his sorrow, but he bestirred himself to make the best of his afflicted condition." (Spurgeon)

Genesis 40 – Joseph Interprets Dreams in Prison

A. Joseph meets the butler and the baker in prison.

1. (1-4) The Egyptian royal butler and baker are put into prison.

It came to pass after these things that the butler and the baker of the king of Egypt offended their lord, the king of Egypt. And Pharaoh was angry with his two officers, the chief butler and the chief baker. So he put them in custody in the house of the captain of the guard, in the prison, the place where Joseph *was* confined. And the captain of the guard charged Joseph with them, and he served them; so they were in custody for a while.

> a. **It came to pass after these things**: Joseph, still in prison, prospered in his circumstances. The end of Genesis 39 shows the great authority and responsibility Joseph had in the operations of the prison, even as a prisoner.

> b. **The butler and the baker of the king of Egypt**: The **butler** was in charge of Pharaoh's wine and the **baker** was in charge of Pharaoh's food. They were imprisoned because they **offended their lord, the king of Egypt**. By how the account will develop, it is probable there was a plot to murder the Pharaoh (perhaps by poisoning), and these two were suspects.

>> i. They were probably there on suspicion of murder, but they were really there because God wanted them to meet Joseph. *The LORD was with him.*

> c. **The captain of the guard charged Joseph with them, and he served them**: This favorable treatment of Joseph by the **captain of the guard** shows that Potiphar did not really believe the accusations his wife made against Joseph. We know this because Potiphar himself was **the captain of the guard** (Genesis 39:1).

d. **And he served them**: Though Joseph had a position of high authority in the prison, he did not use it to make others serve him. He used his high position to serve others.

2. (5-7) Joseph shows concern for the butler and baker.

Then the butler and the baker of the king of Egypt, who *were* confined in the prison, had a dream, both of them, each man's dream in one night *and* each man's dream with its *own* interpretation. And Joseph came in to them in the morning and looked at them, and saw that they *were* sad. So he asked Pharaoh's officers who *were* with him in the custody of his lord's house, saying, "Why do you look so sad today?"

a. **Joseph came in to them in the morning and looked at them, and saw that they were sad**: This is a window into the heart of Joseph. Men who are consumed with anger and bitterness do not often take a concern for the personal problems of others like this.

b. **Why do you look so sad today**: It would be easy – perhaps technically true – for Joseph to think that because of all the wrong done against him, everything should center on his own feelings and hurts. Instead, he cared that the butler and the baker looked **so sad** one day.

i. In this, Joseph shows us Jesus. An innocent Man came into our prison and lived our hardships and temptations, suffering worse than all, yet He never looks for our pity. He asks us, *Why do you look so sad today?* As Jesus lives His life through us, we will also care about the needs of others, even when our needs are apparent.

3. (8) Joseph invites them to tell him their disturbing dreams.

And they said to him, "We each have had a dream, and *there is* no interpreter of it." So Joseph said to them, "Do not interpretations belong to God? Tell *them* to me, please."

a. **Tell them to me, please**: This was not a case of mere discussion of dreams for the sake of curiosity or a form of fortunetelling. Joseph saw these men were clearly disturbed by their dreams, and approached the dreams from a desire to speak to their troubled souls.

b. **Do not interpretations belong to God**: Joseph had experience with dreams. His two dreams about his future greatness antagonized his family (Genesis 37:5-11), and he was mocked as *the dreamer* (Genesis 37:19-20).

i. Joseph was confident that **God** knew what the dreams were about. He was like the one boy who told another, "My father and I know everything." When the other boy asked a hard question, the boy just said, "That's one for my dad." Joseph knew he and his Father *together* knew everything.

c. **Do not interpretations belong to God**: God may certainly speak through dreams, and many passages of the Bible show this.

- God spoke to the pagan ruler Abimelech in a dream (Genesis 20:3).
- God spoke to Jacob in dreams (Genesis 28:12, 31:11).
- God spoke to Laban in a dream (Genesis 31:24).
- God spoke to the Midianite in a dream (Judges 7:13).
- God spoke to Solomon in a dream (1 Kings 3:5).
- God spoke to Nebuchadnezzar in a dream (Daniel 2:1).
- God spoke to Daniel in a dream (Daniel 7:1).
- God spoke to Joseph in dreams (Matthew 1:20, 2:13, 2:22).
- God spoke to Pilate's wife in a dream (Matthew 27:19).

i. In the Bible, God spoke to unbelievers or pagans in dreams almost twice as many times as He spoke to His people in dreams. We hear many stories today about how God speaks to people in the Muslim world with dreams about Jesus.

ii. It's always important to remember that not every dream is a revelation from God. Dreams can come just because our minds are busy: *A dream comes through much activity… For in the multitude of dreams and many words there is also vanity* (Ecclesiastes 5:3, 5:7).

iii. The Bible warns that false prophets might use dreams to give weight to their message (Deuteronomy 13:1-5, Jeremiah 23:25-28).

iv. Still, we should be open to ways that God might speak – even if it might be in a dream. Our message is the same: *Don't look for messages from God anywhere else than the Bible – it is God's voice.* Yet we recognize that from time to time God will choose an unusual way to speak to us, yet never against the Bible or never even equal to the Bible.

v. Around 200, the early church leader Tertullian wrote of a woman in their congregation who was a prophet. She heard the Lord's voice and saw visions during church services. She never interrupted the service with her prophecies, but told them to the leaders of the church after service was over. The messages were usually encouraging words, or some kind of supernatural knowledge or wisdom. She submitted the message to the church leaders for their judgment, and they carefully judged what she said. That's a way that God might speak today in an unusual way.

B. Joseph interprets their dreams.

1. (9-11) The butler explains his dream.

Then the chief butler told his dream to Joseph, and said to him, "Behold, in my dream a vine was before me, and in the vine *were* three branches; it *was* as though it budded, its blossoms shot forth, and its clusters brought forth ripe grapes. Then Pharaoh's cup *was* in my hand; and I took the grapes and pressed them into Pharaoh's cup, and placed the cup in Pharaoh's hand."

> a. **In my dream a vine was before me, and in the vine were three branches**: Though this dream was from God, God used figures and pictures that made sense to the butler (a **vine**, **grapes**, and serving the Pharaoh wine).

> b. **Pharaoh's cup was in my hand**: In his dream, the butler saw himself serve the Pharaoh again, restored to his former position.

2. (12-15) Joseph interprets the butler's dream and asks a favor.

And Joseph said to him, "This is the interpretation of it: The three branches *are* three days. Now within three days Pharaoh will lift up your head and restore you to your place, and you will put Pharaoh's cup in his hand according to the former manner, when you were his butler. But remember me when it is well with you, and please show kindness to me; make mention of me to Pharaoh, and get me out of this house. For indeed I was stolen away from the land of the Hebrews; and also I have done nothing here that they should put me into the dungeon."

> a. **The three branches are three days. Now within three days Pharaoh will lift up your head and restore you to your place**: There were aspects to this dream that could not have been guessed, such as the three branches representing three days. Joseph's interpretation of this dream came from God, not from his own wisdom.

>> i. Joseph was bold enough to give an interpretation that could be proved right or wrong **within three days**. In only three days, everyone knew if Joseph was correct or not.

> b. **Remember me when it is well with you**: Joseph asked the butler to work for his release. Though Joseph showed godly character in the Egyptian prison by not becoming angry and bitter in his heart, he wasn't stupid either. He wanted to get out, and used appropriate means to do so.

>> i. Joseph wasn't fatalistic; he used wisdom and common sense to get himself out of prison, *even though God was with him in prison*. Seeing God in your present circumstances doesn't mean that God wants you in those circumstances forever.

3. (16-19) The baker tells his dream and Joseph interprets it.

When the chief baker saw that the interpretation was good, he said to Joseph, "I also *was* in my dream, and there *were* three white baskets on my head. In the uppermost basket *were* all kinds of baked goods for Pharaoh, and the birds ate them out of the basket on my head." So Joseph answered and said, "This is the interpretation of it: The three baskets are three days. Within three days Pharaoh will lift off your head from you and hang you on a tree; and the birds will eat your flesh from you."

a. **When the chief baker saw that the interpretation was good**: The baker was encouraged that his companion had a good interpretation of his dream, and hoped for the same regarding his own dream.

b. **Within three days Pharaoh will lift off your head from you and hang you on a tree**: Joseph was just as faithful to deliver the message of judgment as he was to deliver the message of deliverance. This is the mark of a godly messenger, who does not fail to bring the whole message of God.

i. "How many there are who are willing to preach the cupbearer's sermon but are unwilling to preach the baker's sermon!" (Boice)

c. **The birds will eat your flesh from you**: This was a disgraceful way to die, but Joseph must have understood that the fate of the butler and the baker were each according to justice. Whatever crimes they were suspected of, the butler was innocent but the baker was guilty.

4. (20-23) The dreams come to pass exactly according to Joseph's interpretations.

Now it came to pass on the third day, *which was* Pharaoh's birthday, that he made a feast for all his servants; and he lifted up the head of the chief butler and of the chief baker among his servants. Then he restored the chief butler to his butlership again, and he placed the cup in Pharaoh's hand. But he hanged the chief baker, as Joseph had interpreted to them. Yet the chief butler did not remember Joseph, but forgot him.

a. **Now it came to pass on the third day**: The three days until Joseph was proved right must have been agonizing for the butler and the baker (though more so for the baker), yet Joseph was found to be a true messenger of God.

i. In trying to see ourselves in the Bible, we usually want to say, *I am Joseph – God can use me to reveal His Word or His mysteries to others.* There's a place for that, but it's not the best way to see ourselves here. More so, we are the butler and the baker. In this picture, Jesus is like Joseph to us.

- An innocent Man came into our prison and shared our condition.
- This Innocent Prisoner revealed God's message to us.
- The Innocent Prisoner was proved true in three days.
- Joseph shows us Jesus, whose message from God brings life or death. If you are looking for a message from God, *look to Jesus*.

iii. We may also see a great *difference* or *contrast* between Joseph and Jesus: *Joseph's word only rescued the innocent prisoner, not the guilty one.* The good news – the *greatest news* – is that the message and rescue of Jesus is for the *guilty*, also.

b. **Yet the chief butler did not remember Joseph, but forgot him**: Here, Joseph was wronged again. He thought that butler's kindness might mean his release from prison, but it was not to be. God had another purpose.

i. All men God uses greatly, He first prepares greatly. Few are willing to endure the greatness of God's preparation. God was in both the *steps* and *stops* of Joseph's life.

Genesis 41 – Joseph Interprets Pharaoh's Dream and Rises to Power

A. Pharaoh's dreams and his dilemma.

1. (1) Two years after the release of the butler and the execution of the baker…

Then it came to pass, at the end of two full years, that Pharaoh had a dream; and behold, he stood by the river.

> a. **At the end of two full years**: Joseph was in prison, forgotten by Pharaoh's butler, for two full years. There was difficulty and discouragement in those years for Joseph, but we assume he trusted God nonetheless. Many lessons come from this.
>
> - Sometimes the good we do seems unrewarded.
> - *Waiting* is a common theme in the Christian life.
> - God often appoints us to wait much longer than we would like.
> - God appoints our starts and our stops.
> - *God's hand was in this*: when the time was right, the butler knew *exactly* where to find Joseph. If he had been released earlier, who knows?
>
> b. **Pharaoh had a dream**: The following verses describe Pharaoh's strange dream.

2. (2-7) Pharaoh's disturbing dreams.

Suddenly there came up out of the river seven cows, fine looking and fat; and they fed in the meadow. Then behold, seven other cows came up after them out of the river, ugly and gaunt, and stood by the *other* cows on the bank of the river. And the ugly and gaunt cows ate up the seven fine looking and fat cows. So Pharaoh awoke. He slept and dreamed a second time; and suddenly seven heads of grain came up on one stalk,

plump and good. Then behold, seven thin heads, blighted by the east wind, sprang up after them. And the seven thin heads devoured the seven plump and full heads. So Pharaoh awoke, and indeed, it *was* a dream.

> a. **There came up out of the river seven cows**: In Pharaoh's dream, seven **fat** cows came out of the Nile and were consumed by seven **ugly and gaunt** cows. This strange dream woke him up, but he went back to sleep.
>
> b. **Seven heads of grain came up on one stalk**: In a second dream, **seven thin heads** of grain devoured **seven plump and full heads** of grain.
>
> c. **So Pharaoh awoke, and indeed, it was a dream**: This was a life-like, crazy dream, but it was *a message from God*.
>
>> i. *God speaks to us today*. He may use supernatural means and strange things, even crazy things. More normally, God speaks to us *through His Word*. We remember Hebrews 1:1-2: *God, who at various times and in various ways spoke in time past to the fathers by the prophets, has in these last days spoken to us by His Son.*

3. (8) Pharaoh's troubled spirit.

Now it came to pass in the morning that his spirit was troubled, and he sent and called for all the magicians of Egypt and all its wise men. And Pharaoh told them his dreams, but *there was* no one who could interpret them for Pharaoh.

> a. **In the morning his spirit was troubled**: Pharaoh didn't take this as merely a crazy dream. In his **spirit**, he knew that there was something important in this.
>
> b. **Pharaoh told them his dreams, but there was no one who could interpret them**: Joseph told the butler and the baker in prison, *Do not interpretations belong to God* (Genesis 40:8). The interpretation belonged to God, and He didn't give that knowledge to the **magicians** of Egypt.

4. (9-14) Joseph is called in to interpret Pharaoh's dreams.

Then the chief butler spoke to Pharaoh, saying: "I remember my faults this day. When Pharaoh was angry with his servants, and put me in custody in the house of the captain of the guard, *both* me and the chief baker, we each had a dream in one night, he and I. Each of us dreamed according to the interpretation of his *own* dream. Now there *was* a young Hebrew man with us there, a servant of the captain of the guard. And we told him, and he interpreted our dreams for us; to each man he interpreted according to his *own* dream. And it came to pass, just as he interpreted for us, so it happened. He restored me to my office, and he

hanged him." Then Pharaoh sent and called Joseph, and they brought him quickly out of the dungeon; and he shaved, changed his clothing, and came to Pharaoh.

> a. **I remember my faults this day**: The butler finally remembered Joseph and confessed the wrong he did against him. He recommended Joseph to Pharaoh as a man who interprets dreams.
>
> b. **Then Pharaoh sent and called Joseph, and they brought him quickly out of the dungeon**: When it was in the timing of God to get Joseph out of prison, it all happened **quickly**. Often, we feel there are long periods of time when God doesn't do anything, but when His timing is right, everything can come together in an instant.
>
>> i. During the times we think God isn't doing anything, He is doing the work most important to Him: developing our character and transforming us into the image of Jesus Christ.
>>
>> ii. We love the words of Romans 8:28: *And we know that all things work together for good to those who love God, to those who are the called according to His purpose.* But don't forget the next verse, Romans 8:29: *For whom He foreknew, He also predestined to be conformed to the image of His Son, that He might be the firstborn among many brethren.* God's work in our life is to conform us into the image of Jesus Christ, and that takes time.
>>
>> iii. Here we see another way that Joseph shows us Jesus, who was also taken from long obscurity to great prominence *quickly*.

5. (15-16) Pharaoh tells Joseph of his dream.

And Pharaoh said to Joseph, "I have had a dream, and *there is* no one who can interpret it. But I have heard it said of you *that* you can understand a dream, to interpret it." So Joseph answered Pharaoh, saying, "*It is* not in me; God will give Pharaoh an answer of peace."

> a. **I have had a dream, and there is no one who can interpret it**: Pharaoh's dream was actually a revelation from God. He received it, but could not understand it. It was like a person who reads the Bible, but needs help from a man or woman of God to understand.
>
> b. **It is not in me**: Pharaoh gave Joseph a golden opportunity to glorify himself, but Joseph refused. He did not use this as an opportunity to glorify himself before Pharaoh, but only to glorify God.
>
> c. **God will give Pharaoh an answer of peace**: Joseph seems much wiser and perhaps humbler than he was before. If it was true that in the past he

told his brothers his previous dreams in a self-glorying way, any such self-confidence was now gone. Joseph knew that God alone had the answer.

i. God's work of character building was being accomplished in Joseph, even when he perhaps thought nothing was happening.

6. (17-24) Pharaoh tells Joseph his dream.

Then Pharaoh said to Joseph: "Behold, in my dream I stood on the bank of the river. Suddenly seven cows came up out of the river, fine looking and fat; and they fed in the meadow. Then behold, seven other cows came up after them, poor and very ugly and gaunt, such ugliness as I have never seen in all the land of Egypt. And the gaunt and ugly cows ate up the first seven, the fat cows. When they had eaten them up, no one would have known that they had eaten them, for they *were* just as ugly as at the beginning. So I awoke. Also I saw in my dream, and suddenly seven heads came up on one stalk, full and good. Then behold, seven heads, withered, thin, *and* blighted by the east wind, sprang up after them. And the thin heads devoured the seven good heads. So I told this to the magicians, but *there was* no one who could explain it to me."

a. **Pharaoh said to Joseph**: The leader of Egypt explained the dream to Joseph, much the same way we read of it in Genesis 41:2-7.

b. **They were just as ugly as at the beginning**: More details of the dream come with the second telling. When the skinny cows ate the fat cows, they themselves did not become fat.

B. Joseph interprets Pharaoh's dream.

1. (25-32) Joseph interprets Pharaoh's dream.

Then Joseph said to Pharaoh, "The dreams of Pharaoh *are* one; God has shown Pharaoh what He is about to do: The seven good cows *are* seven years, and the seven good heads *are* seven years; the dreams *are* one. And the seven thin and ugly cows which came up after them *are* seven years, and the seven empty heads blighted by the east wind are seven years of famine. This is the thing which I have spoken to Pharaoh. God has shown Pharaoh what He *is* about to do. Indeed seven years of great plenty will come throughout all the land of Egypt; but after them seven years of famine will arise, and all the plenty will be forgotten in the land of Egypt; and the famine will deplete the land. So the plenty will not be known in the land because of the famine following, for it *will be* very severe. And the dream was repeated to Pharaoh twice because the thing is established by God, and God will shortly bring it to pass."

a. **The dreams of Pharaoh are one; God has shown Pharaoh what He is about to do**: There would be seven years of plenty and abundance, followed by another seven years of want and famine. The years of famine will be so bad that the good years **will be forgotten**.

b. **The dream was repeated to Pharaoh twice because the thing is established by God**: Joseph saw God's confirmation in the repetition of the dream. Joseph knew the principle later revealed in Deuteronomy 19:15: *by the mouth of two or three witnesses the matter shall be established*.

i. We can say of God's great message to us – the Bible – that **the thing is established by God**. It's unfashionable to say it today, but it remains a fact: *God's Word is true*. The Bible speaks in many different styles, but in each style it is *true*. It's true history, true commandments, true poetry, true wisdom, and true prophecy.

c. **God will shortly bring it to pass**: The confirmation of the dream also indicated the *urgency* of the message. This would all happen soon, **shortly**.

i. God spoke all this through Joseph, using Joseph as a guide to Pharaoh. Some of us wish God would give us such supernatural guidance.

ii. Many of us want guidance from God like a map, showing where to go and what to do. Instead, often Jesus comes as a *Guide*, saying "Stay close to Me, and I'll guide you along the way." Instead of looking for a map, look for a guide – Jesus the Guide, the Messenger from God.

2. (33-36) Joseph gives his advice to Pharaoh.

"Now therefore, let Pharaoh select a discerning and wise man, and set him over the land of Egypt. Let Pharaoh do *this*, and let him appoint officers over the land, to collect one-fifth *of the produce* of the land of Egypt in the seven plentiful years. And let them gather all the food of those good years that are coming, and store up grain under the authority of Pharaoh, and let them keep food in the cities. Then that food shall be as a reserve for the land for the seven years of famine which shall be in the land of Egypt, that the land may not perish during the famine."

a. **Let Pharaoh select a discerning and wise man**: To this point, Joseph gave Pharaoh *knowledge*, telling him what *would happen*, as revealed in the dreams that were a message from God. Now, Joseph began to apply *wisdom* to the knowledge.

i. Knowledge tells you what is going on; wisdom tells you what to do about it. Knowledge is the diagnosis; wisdom is directed to the cure. Knowledge is good and necessary – it just isn't enough.

ii. Our world has a lot more knowledge than wisdom. Our scientists, poets, politicians, and all the rest can often see what the problems are. True wisdom sees that *Jesus is the answer*.

b. **Let him appoint officers over the land, to collect one-fifth of the produce of the land of Egypt in the seven plentiful years**: In his God-given wisdom, Joseph saw that this great coming crisis needed proper administration.

- The problem had to be understood.
- The goal and the vision to meet the goal had to be formulated.
- The right people had to be put in place (**officers over the land**).
- They had to understand the big vision and their role in it.
- Someone had to make sure it was all operating according to plan.
- The work had to be measured.
- God would use a man to put all that into place – it wouldn't happen by what we normally think of as a miracle.

    i. **One-fifth** means a 20% tax. Some ancient sources suggest that Pharaoh normally took 10% of the grain in Egypt as a tax. If this were true, then Joseph doubled taxes over the next seven years.

c. **That the land may not perish during the famine**: The message of God through Pharaoh's dreams was of a true *crisis* to come. If they did not prepare, the land would **perish during the famine**. This was an urgent call to action.

i. God would meet the need through a man. "God always works through men performing tasks on the earth" (Barnhouse).

3. (37-38) Pharaoh perceives the presence of God's Spirit in Joseph.

So the advice was good in the eyes of Pharaoh and in the eyes of all his servants. And Pharaoh said to his servants, "Can we find *such a one* as this, a man in whom is the Spirit of God?"

a. **The advice was good in the eyes of Pharaoh**: Pharaoh understood that Joseph not only had the right interpretation of the dream, but also the right **advice** to respond to the message from heaven.

b. **A man in whom is the Spirit of God**: Pharaoh had plenty of priests, magicians, and holy men. What he did not have (until Joseph) was a man with **the Spirit of God**. This made Joseph stand out among the others ([38] **Can we find such a one as this**).

i. This is the first mention in the Bible of the Holy Spirit coming upon a man. We note that it was in regard to more *practical* things. Joseph didn't have to preach a sermon or lead a prayer for others to see the **Spirit of God** upon him. He could see it in his character, in his message, in his knowledge, in his wisdom, and in his humility.

ii. The presence and power of the Holy Spirit can be seen in very practical ways, in our character, in our humility.

4. (39-41) Joseph's promotion to second in the kingdom of Egypt.

Then Pharaoh said to Joseph, "Inasmuch as God has shown you all this, *there is* no one as discerning and wise as you. You shall be over my house, and all my people shall be ruled according to your word; only in regard to the throne will I be greater than you." And Pharaoh said to Joseph, "See, I have set you over all the land of Egypt."

a. **Inasmuch as God has shown you all this, there is no one as discerning and wise as you**: This was the first firm indication that Pharaoh wanted *Joseph* to be the one to save Egypt through wise planning and preparation. This probably surprised Joseph.

b. **You shall be over my house**: Joseph had the knowledge and the wisdom, but Pharaoh had a choice. He chose to give Joseph authority over *all*. He didn't say, "Thanks for the advice. I'll handle it myself." Pharaoh wisely *surrendered* to Joseph's knowledge, wisdom, and authority.

- Joseph would **be over** Pharaoh's **house**, his personal business.
- Joseph would rule **all** the **people** of Egypt according to his **word**.
- Joseph would be second in the kingdom behind Pharaoh.
- Joseph would have authority **over all the land of Egypt**.

i. Joseph only *seemed* to be an overnight success. In truth, his journey from the pit to the pinnacle took 13 hard years. This part of Joseph's story reminds us of some important principles regarding promotion and advancement.

- *Promotion and advancement is from the Lord* (Psalm 75:6-7). This is not to say that hard work, preparation, good habits, and other human aspects do not contribute to success – they clearly do. Yet even those things are gifts and abilities from God and should be regarded with humility and gratitude toward Him.
- *Promotion and advancement is never enough without the Lord*. You can't be so promoted or advance to where you stop needing Jesus. Often, promotion and success make us see our need for Jesus more than ever.
- *Jesus received the ultimate promotion or advancement*. Joseph's path from humble servant and prisoner to powerful ruler becomes a prophecy of Jesus Himself. Philippians 2:5-11 describes that ultimate promotion.

5. (42-44) The signs of Joseph's high status.

Then Pharaoh took his signet ring off his hand and put it on Joseph's hand; and he clothed him in garments of fine linen and put a gold chain around his neck. And he had him ride in the second chariot which he had; and they cried out before him, "Bow the knee!" So he set him over all the land of Egypt. Pharaoh also said to Joseph, "I *am* Pharaoh, and without your consent no man may lift his hand or foot in all the land of Egypt."

 a. **Pharaoh took his signet ring off his hand and put it on Joseph's hand**: The **signet ring** was the expression of Pharaoh's authority. Now Joseph had that authority. Once he wore the shackles of a prisoner; now he had the **signet ring** of Pharaoh.

 b. **He clothed him in garments of fine linen**: Once Joseph had the rags of a dungeon; now he had wonderful apparel, **garments of fine linen**.

 c. **Put a gold chain around his neck**: Joseph once had the chains of a slave; now he was adorned with a **gold chain**.

 d. **He had him ride in the second chariot**: Joseph once walked as a slave; now he traveled in style. He enjoyed great affluence.

 e. **Without your consent no man may lift his hand or foot**: This expresses again the idea of *authority*. Joseph once could only obey orders; now he could also give orders.

  i. In these ways, *Joseph illustrates the Child of God*. In Jesus we are given authority, apparel, adornment, and affluence.

  ii. Yet in an even greater way, *Joseph is a picture of Jesus Christ* in who He is, in what He has done, and in the place He should have in our life.

- Jesus is a messenger from God.
- Jesus speaks truth about the future.
- The plan of Jesus provides bread for life.
- Authority is given to Jesus by choice.

6. (45) Joseph is given a name and a wife.

And Pharaoh called Joseph's name Zaphnath-Paaneah. And he gave him as a wife Asenath, the daughter of Poti-Pherah priest of On. So Joseph went out over *all* the land of Egypt.

 a. **And Pharaoh called Joseph's name Zaphnath-Paaneah**: Jewish legends say each letter of Joseph's Egyptian name meant something. Linking them all together, these legends say the meaning of Joseph's Egyptian name was

"Seer – redeemer – prophet – supporter – interpreter of dreams – clever – discreet – wise."

> i. More likely the name means, *God Speaks and He Lives*, referring to God's word coming through Joseph, his own preservation, and the way he preserved both Egypt and the whole region.

b. **And he gave him as a wife Asenath**: Jewish legends (fabrications, really) say Asenath was really the daughter of Dinah and Shechem, who was many years earlier abandoned at the border of Egypt, and then adopted into the family of an Egyptian priest.

C. Joseph's life as Prime Minister.

1. (46-49) The seven years of plenty came to pass.

Joseph was thirty years old when he stood before Pharaoh king of Egypt. And Joseph went out from the presence of Pharaoh, and went throughout all the land of Egypt. Now in the seven plentiful years the ground brought forth abundantly. So he gathered up all the food of the seven years which were in the land of Egypt, and laid up the food in the cities; he laid up in every city the food of the fields which surrounded them. Joseph gathered very much grain, as the sand of the sea, until he stopped counting, for it *was* immeasurable.

> a. **Joseph was thirty years old when he stood before Pharaoh**: Joseph was a young man to have such authority. Yet he had been in God's school of trust-deepening and character-development for a long time. He was sold as a slave at 17 years of age (Genesis 37:2).

> b. **He gathered up all the food of the seven years which were in the land of Egypt**: Joseph did what was right. He actually stored up the grain during the seven years of plenty. This was a significant logistic and accounting challenge.

> c. **Joseph gathered very much grain**: It seems it was customary for Pharaoh to take 10% of the grain in Egypt as a tax. Essentially, Joseph doubled the taxes over the next seven years (Genesis 41:34 mentions *one-fifth*, that is, 20%).

2. (50-52) Joseph's two sons and his state of heart.

And to Joseph were born two sons before the years of famine came, whom Asenath, the daughter of Poti-Pherah priest of On, bore to him. Joseph called the name of the firstborn Manasseh: "For God has made me forget all my toil and all my father's house." And the name of the second he called Ephraim: "For God has caused me to be fruitful in the land of my affliction."

a. **Joseph called the name of the firstborn Manasseh**: From his Egyptian wife, Joseph fathered **Manasseh**, whose name means *forgetfulness*. This was because God made Joseph to forget all the previous pain and trial in his life. His second son is **Ephraim**, which means *fruitfulness*, because God made Joseph fruitful in Egypt.

> i. We can't be *doubly fruitful* until we are also *forgetting*. In his book *The Great Divorce*, C.S. Lewis described hell as a place where no one forgets anything, remembering every slight, every cruel exchange of words, every wrong ever done to them, and everybody is utterly unforgiving. But in heaven all these things are put away, because all things have become new.

b. **For God has made me forget... For God has caused me to be fruitful**: Joseph did not forget the faith of his fathers, even though he rose to great glory in Egypt and had an Egyptian wife. As a sign of this, his children were given Hebrew names, not Egyptian names.

3. (53-57) The seven years of famine begin.

Then the seven years of plenty which were in the land of Egypt ended, and the seven years of famine began to come, as Joseph had said. The famine was in all lands, but in all the land of Egypt there was bread. So when all the land of Egypt was famished, the people cried to Pharaoh for bread. Then Pharaoh said to all the Egyptians, "Go to Joseph; whatever he says to you, do." The famine was over all the face of the earth, and Joseph opened all the storehouses and sold to the Egyptians. And the famine became severe in the land of Egypt. So all countries came to Joseph in Egypt to buy *grain*, because the famine was severe in all lands.

a. **The famine was in all lands, but in all the land of Egypt there was bread**: Because of Joseph's wise preparation, Egypt became a supply source for the whole region, which suffered this severe famine.

b. **So all countries came to Joseph in Egypt to buy grain**: The people in Canaan – including Joseph's family – also suffered from this famine. But God made wise (though unexpected) provision for them by sending Joseph ahead of the family.

> i. *And we know that all things work together for good to those who love God, to those who are the called according to His purpose* (Romans 8:28). Joseph did not have Romans 8:28 on paper, but he had it in his heart. A Christian today may very well have it on paper, but not in the heart.

Genesis 42 – Joseph Meets His Brothers in Egypt

A. The sons of Jacob come to Egypt.

1. (1-4) Jacob sends his sons to Egypt to buy grain.

When Jacob saw that there was grain in Egypt, Jacob said to his sons, "Why do you look at one another?" And he said, "Indeed I have heard that there is grain in Egypt; go down to that place and buy for us there, that we may live and not die." So Joseph's ten brothers went down to buy *grain* in Egypt. But Jacob did not send Joseph's brother Benjamin with his brothers, for he said, "Lest some calamity befall him."

> a. **When Jacob saw that there was grain in Egypt**: We have reason to believe (based on Genesis 45:11) that this happened in the *first* year of the famine. It didn't take long for the big problems of the world to find their way to the home of Jacob. The famine was not only a world problem; it was a family problem for Jacob.
>
> b. **Why do you look at one another**: Jacob noticed a strange expression among the brothers when **Egypt** was mentioned, because the brothers knew it was likely Joseph was sold as a slave there. Their conscience made them feel terrible any time **Egypt** was mentioned.
>
>> i. "The father has noted the look of perplexity in his sons' faces... literally, the phrase means, 'to look questioningly one at the other.'" (Leupold)
>>
>> ii. "The word *Egypt* in their ears must have sounded like the word *rope* in the house of a man who has hanged himself." (Barnhouse)
>>
>> iii. Joseph's brothers lived with a terrible secret for 20 years. They never talked about it, but it never left them. Any mention of Joseph or Egypt brought back the guilt. They needed to be set free from the power of their terrible secret.

c. **Lest some calamity befall him**: Because he lost Joseph some 20 years before, Jacob lived in constant fear that he would also lose Benjamin – the other son of his favorite wife, Rachel. He kept a close, protective eye on Benjamin.

d. **Jacob did not send Joseph's brother Benjamin**: In keeping with this attitude, he demanded Benjamin be left behind. Though he had 11 sons, only one was a son of his beloved and deceased wife Rachel, and Jacob felt he must protect him.

i. *If Jacob only knew*. If he could only trust the hand of God, which he could not see! In fact, the only reason there was grain in Egypt to provide for their needs was because God sent Joseph ahead of them all. God knew what He was doing.

ii. Famine is not a good thing, but God used it. God can and does use material need and lack in our life to get us to do things we normally would never do. Normally, the brothers would never go to Egypt; but *need* drove them to Egypt.

2. (5-6) The sons of Jacob bow down before Joseph.

And the sons of Israel went to buy grain among those who journeyed, for the famine was in the land of Canaan. Now Joseph was governor over the land; and it was he who sold to all the people of the land. And Joseph's brothers came and bowed down before him with *their* faces to the earth.

a. **Bowed down before him with their faces to the earth**: They knew that in this time of famine, their lives literally depended on this Egyptian official; therefore, they paid him great respect by bowing.

b. **With their faces to the earth**: The following verses will tell us that Joseph remembered the dream he had some 20 years before, that his brothers would bow down to him (Genesis 37:5-8).

i. When Joseph's brothers plotted murder against him and sold him into slavery, they did it with the specific intention to defeat his dreams (Genesis 37:19-20). Instead, by sending Joseph to Egypt, they provided the way the dreams would be fulfilled.

ii. The great and glorious truth of God's providence is He can and does use the evil actions of man towards us to further His good plan. This never excuses man's evil, but it means God's wisdom and goodness are greater than man's evil. *Surely the wrath of man shall praise You* (Psalm 76:10).

3. (7-8) Joseph recognizes his brothers.

Joseph saw his brothers and recognized them, but he acted as a stranger to them and spoke roughly to them. Then he said to them, "Where do you come from?" And they said, "From the land of Canaan to buy food." So Joseph recognized his brothers, but they did not recognize him.

>a. **Joseph saw his brothers and recognized them, but he acted as a stranger**: Joseph spoke through an interpreter (he did not yet want to reveal that he spoke Hebrew), and did not reveal his identity to his brothers, but treated them **roughly** instead.
>
>>i. Joseph did this guided by the Holy Spirit. Remember what they said of Joseph in Genesis 41:38: *Can we find such a one as this, a man in whom is the Spirit of God?* This wasn't revenge or twisting the knife.
>>
>>ii. It all *could have* been very different, but God planned it *this way* not only to save them from famine but to *rightly* restore relationship with Joseph.
>
>b. **Joseph recognized his brothers, but they did not recognize him**: In this, Joseph is another picture of Jesus. Jesus sees who we are long before we see who He is. He recognizes you – and *Jesus still loves you.*

4. (9-17) Joseph interrogates his brothers and puts them into prison.

Then Joseph remembered the dreams which he had dreamed about them, and said to them, "You *are* spies! You have come to see the nakedness of the land!" And they said to him, "No, my lord, but your servants have come to buy food. "We are all one man's sons; we *are* honest *men*; your servants are not spies." But he said to them, "No, but you have come to see the nakedness of the land." And they said, "Your servants *are* twelve brothers, the sons of one man in the land of Canaan; and in fact, the youngest is with our father today, and one *is* no more." But Joseph said to them, "It is as I spoke to you, saying, 'You are spies!' In this *manner* you shall be tested: By the life of Pharaoh, you shall not leave this place unless your youngest brother comes here. Send one of you, and let him bring your brother; and you shall be kept in prison, that your words may be tested to see whether *there is* any truth in you; or else, by the life of Pharaoh, surely you *are* spies!" So he put them all together in prison three days.

>a. **Then Joseph remembered the dreams which he had dreamed about them**: Joseph did not play games with his bothers. Some commentators believe that if it were up to Joseph, he would have revealed himself to his brothers right then and there. But God recalled the dreams to his mind

and guided him to be an instrument for the correction and restoration of the brothers.

>i. God can, and must, sometimes use ways we think are harsh to call us to go to where He wants us to be. We must never resent it, because it was the hardness of our hearts that demanded it. *Before I was afflicted I went astray, but now I keep Your word* (Psalm 119:67).

b. **One is no more**: This was a lie and the brothers knew it. They had every reason to believe Joseph was not dead, but condemned to a life of slavery. Perhaps they had repeated the lie to themselves so often they came to believe it.

>i. *Saying* Joseph was dead didn't make him dead. *Saying* Jesus isn't alive doesn't make Him dead. Jesus is alive and among us.

5. (18-20) Joseph gives the terms for their release from prison.

Then Joseph said to them the third day, "Do this and live, *for* I fear God: If you *are* honest men, let one of your brothers be confined to your prison house; but you, go and carry grain for the famine of your houses. And bring your youngest brother to me; so your words will be verified, and you shall not die." And they did so.

>a. **Do this and live**: After three days in an Egyptian prison, the brothers were ready to agree to whatever Joseph wanted them to do. They had been humbled, and would listen to Joseph's demands. *He* had the words of life.

>b. **I fear God**: Joseph didn't want his brothers to *fear* him as much as he wanted his brothers to *trust* him. If the brothers were wise enough to consider what this really meant, it would be a great comfort to them.

>c. **If you are honest men**: Joseph's demand was clear. They had to prove they were not spies by proving they were honest and that they told the truth about the brother back home. The brothers agreed to this (**they did so**) but only reluctantly, because they knew their father would never want to let Benjamin leave home.

6. (21-24) The guilty conscience of Joseph's brothers at work.

Then they said to one another, "We *are* truly guilty concerning our brother, for we saw the anguish of his soul when he pleaded with us, and we would not hear; therefore this distress has come upon us." And Reuben answered them, saying, "Did I not speak to you, saying, 'Do not sin against the boy'; and you would not listen? Therefore behold, his blood is now required of us." But they did not know that Joseph understood *them*, for he spoke to them through an interpreter. And he turned himself away from them and wept. Then he returned to them

again, and talked with them. And he took Simeon from them and bound him before their eyes.

a. **We are truly guilty concerning our brother**: Their guilty conscience told them this complicated mess was because of the way they treated Joseph before. This was a good sign. The *quickness* with which they associated these events with their sin against Joseph meant they often remembered that sin.

i. There was not a completely logical connection between their current situation and their previous treatment of Joseph, but a guilty conscience sees every trouble as sin's penalty.

ii. The United States government has something called the Federal Conscience Fund, which collects money people send in because they know they cheated the government in some way. People have sent in money because they took army blankets for souvenirs, for cheating on postage, or on income tax. But our consciences are notoriously weak or corrupt. One man wrote the IRS and said, "I cheated on my taxes and can't sleep at night. Here is a check for $100. If I still can't sleep, I'll send the rest I owe."

b. **Therefore this distress has come upon us**: In these words, we hear the conscience of the brothers at work. Some describe the conscience as the *sundial of the soul*. It tells time well enough when there is light, but in darkness it is of no use. At night, you can shine a flashlight on a sundial and make it read any time you want it to. When the sunlight of God's word shines on our conscience, it is reliable and trustworthy; apart from that, it isn't always reliable.

i. Otherwise, our conscience can be like a circus-trained poodle. Whistle once, it stands up. Whistle twice, it rolls over. Whistle a third time, and it plays dead.

c. **He turned himself away from them and wept**: Joseph was overcome with emotion as he saw and understood this work of God in the conscience of his brothers. God had to do a deep work in the hearts of these brothers for the relationship to be reconciled.

i. There could be no quick and easy, "We are sorry, Joseph!" in this situation. God guided events so the brothers saw their sin clearly and repented completely before Joseph was revealed and relationship was restored.

ii. Yet even before the restoration, Joseph did not allow himself to be bound by bitterness and hatred. He still loved his brothers and wanted to be with them (**he returned to them again, and talked with them**).

He wasn't happy about their misery, but knew in some way it was necessary.

d. **He took Simeon from them and bound him before their eyes**: In a vivid and memorable scene, Joseph **bound** Simeon and kept him as a prisoner to guarantee the return of the brothers with Benjamin. Simeon was not mentioned as having a prominent role in the selling of Joseph, as both Reuben and Judah were (Genesis 37:21-28), so we don't know exactly why Simeon was chosen. Perhaps he volunteered.

B. Jacob's sons return home to Canaan.

1. (25-26) Joseph returns the money the brothers paid for the grain.

Then Joseph gave a command to fill their sacks with grain, to restore every man's money to his sack, and to give them provisions for the journey. Thus he did for them. So they loaded their donkeys with the grain and departed from there.

a. **Joseph gave a command**: The events that follow were not an accident nor a mistake, but something that Joseph commanded. Whether he was aware of it or not, God guided this spirit-filled man (Genesis 41:38) to do some strange things that would bring about true repentance and reconciliation with the brothers.

i. *God was working His plan through Joseph*. This wasn't just as if Joseph was playing practical jokes on his brothers or just trying to make life difficult. We don't know how much he sensed it, but this was all guided by God.

b. **To restore every man's money to his sack**: This was an unexpected and wonderful blessing. The grain had to be expensive, and Joseph put their money back in the sacks of grain appointed for each brother.

c. **And to give them provisions for the journey**: Joseph gave them more than their money back; he also gave them what they needed for **the journey**. He took care of them from beginning to end.

i. The money was hidden and would only be discovered later. We can assume that the **provisions** were given immediately and openly (otherwise they would not have been of much good). Joseph gave them what they needed to get by, but also much treasure beyond.

ii. Joseph did this for his brothers *before they were reconciled to him*. They had yet to repent or ask forgiveness – yet He loved them and cared for them. He gave to them and they didn't even know it!

iii. In the same way, Jesus gives us unexpected, undeserved blessings. Some are obvious and up front, and some are hidden to be discovered later – but He gives to us *even before we were reconciled to Him.*

- *There is extra in the sack.*
- Jesus gave to us and we didn't even know it.
- Jesus has gifts for us now and we don't even know it.

2. (27-28) The brothers find their money returned.

But as one *of them* opened his sack to give his donkey feed at the encampment, he saw his money; and there it was, in the mouth of his sack. So he said to his brothers, "My money has been restored, and there it is, in my sack!" Then their hearts failed *them* and they were afraid, saying to one another, "What is this *that* God has done to us?"

a. **He saw his money; and there it was, in the mouth of his sack**: This was a tremendous shock to the brothers. We aren't told which one it was, but it was one of the nine (remember, Simeon was imprisoned). The *last* thing they expected to see was their **money** returned.

i. *This was a test* – not from Joseph – but from God. What would they do with the money? What would be revealed about their *heart?*

- The deceptive heart would hide it.
- The lying heart would make up a story about it.
- The proud heart would think it deserved it.
- The superficial heart would think nothing of it.

ii. We are tested by what Jesus gives to us – and Jesus tests *the heart*. What we do is important, but God goes deeper than the action itself and wants to develop not only our behavior, but also our character.

b. **Their hearts failed them and they were afraid**: *This was strange*. It was as if they had just won the lottery, but they weren't happy at all. Instead, they were **afraid**. They were so afraid that **their hearts failed them** and they had to talk to each other about it.

- They were afraid, and they only knew *part* of it. they only discovered the money in one brother's sack. We don't know why they didn't immediately check the other sacks, but they did not.
- They were afraid, because they were already suspected as spies. Now, they could also be accused as thieves.
- They were afraid, because of their guilty consciences.

c. **What is this that God has done to us**: Their consciences were under such great bondage that they even regarded something good as punishment from God. A guilty conscience doesn't even know how to handle gifts from God.

i. Until we are reconciled with Jesus, we usually don't know what to do with God's gifts.

3. (29-34) The brothers return to their father Jacob and tell him the story.

Then they went to Jacob their father in the land of Canaan and told him all that had happened to them, saying: "The man *who is* lord of the land spoke roughly to us, and took us for spies of the country. But we said to him, 'We *are* honest *men*; we are not spies. We *are* twelve brothers, sons of our father; one *is* no *more*, and the youngest is with our father this day in the land of Canaan.' Then the man, the lord of the country, said to us, 'By this I will know that you *are* honest *men*: Leave one of your brothers *here* with me, take *food for* the famine of your households, and be gone. And bring your youngest brother to me; so I shall know that you are not spies, but *that* you *are* honest *men*. I will grant your brother to you, and you may trade in the land.'"

a. **Then they went to Jacob their father**: Think of what the rest of that journey was like. For several days as they traveled, many things weighed on their mind.

- How do we explain Simeon is not with us?
- How do we explain that we have both the grain and the money?
- How do we explain that *we have to go back to Egypt and bring Benjamin?*

b. **Told him all that had happened to them**: When the brothers finally made it home, they told their father Jacob the *truth*. The last time they came back missing one of the brothers, they told a lie, making up a story about Joseph being attacked by a wild animal. They even had his bloody coat of many colors to give false evidence to their lie.

i. The fact that they told the truth here was a small step but a good step. Good things often start small.

c. **We are honest men**: They *mostly* told the truth. They could say, **we are honest men** in regard to their dealings with the mysterious Egyptian, **the man who is the lord of the land**. But they were *not* honest men when they lied about Joseph's death 20 years before. They were still lying about it: **one is no more**.

i. Joseph knew they were not honest men. He didn't know the exact lie they told Jacob to explain Joseph's disappearance, but he knew they must have lied in some way. Joseph knew who they were, but he also knew what they could become.

ii. Jesus knows us better than we know ourselves. He knows you, but He also knows what you can become.

4. (35) The brothers discover that each man's money was returned.

Then it happened as they emptied their sacks, that surprisingly each man's bundle of money was in his sack; and when they and their father saw the bundles of money, they were afraid.

a. **Surprisingly each man's bundle of money was in his sack**: *They had no idea* this would happen. If anything, this surprised them more than when they found the bundle of money in the one sack. There was more than they ever thought.

i. Jesus has given you more than you know, and you will discover it piece by piece. *Keep going, keep growing in your life with Jesus.*

b. **Each man's bundle of money was in his sack**: Joseph gave them the bread of life, but He absolutely refused *any* payment. Their money was no good.

i. You can't buy the bread of life. Jesus refused any payment. We give out of gratitude because we *have* received; we don't give as if we could buy from Jesus.

c. **They were afraid**: What were they afraid of?

- They were afraid of receiving what they did not earn. *Grace tests us all.*

- They were afraid of their own conscience.

- They were afraid of Joseph – the great man they couldn't figure out. In a sense, they had to *fear* Joseph before they could be reconciled to him.

5. (36) Jacob's reaction: **All these things are against me**.

And Jacob their father said to them, "You have bereaved me: Joseph is no *more*, Simeon is no *more*, and you want to take Benjamin. All these things are against me."

a. **You have bereaved me**: Jacob spoke more truth than he knew. He said that his sons had **bereaved** him, that it was their fault that **Joseph** and **Simeon** were gone. He instinctively knew the truth, even when he couldn't prove it.

b. **Joseph is no more, Simeon is no more**: This tortured Jacob, yet *these statements were not true*. Not only was Joseph alive, but Jacob would see him soon and Joseph would rescue their whole family.

i. We don't blame Jacob for believing that Joseph was dead; he had been told a cunning lie. Yet this shows the power of a *lie believed*.

ii. When we believe lies – whether it is our fault or not – the lie has power over us. This is why we should learn and love and cherish God's truth.

- *God has forsaken me* – if believed, that lie has power.
- *I'm beyond hope* – if believed, that lie has power.
- *I can never confess my sin* – if believed, that lie has power.
- *I'm worthless* – if believed, that lie has power.

c. **And you want to take Benjamin**: Large in his mind was the fear he would lose more. Since he lost Joseph, Jacob lived to protect himself from further devastating loss.

d. **All these things are against me**: This summarized Jacob's outlook on life. Everything was against him. He had no happiness in the present and no hope for the future. He woke up and went to bed thinking, **all these things are against me**.

- *Jacob was God's chosen and still said,* **all these things are against me**.
- *Jacob was healthy and still said,* **all these things are against me**.
- *Jacob was a wealthy man and still said,* **all these things are against me**.

i. At the very moment Jacob felt **all these things are against me**, God was working out His plan. *There was a plan* in all this, even when Jacob couldn't see it or feel it. "If you drink of the river of affliction near its outfall, it is brackish and offensive to the taste, but if you will trace it to its source, where it rises at the foot of the throne of God, you will find its waters to be sweet and health-giving" (Spurgeon).

ii. The plan was not only good for Jacob and his family but would impact all history. God was *working all things together for good* (Romans 8:28).

- If Joseph's family wasn't messed up and weird, his brothers would never have sold him as a slave.
- If Joseph's brothers never sold him as a slave, then Joseph would never have gone to Egypt.

- If Joseph never went to Egypt, he would never have been sold to Potiphar.
- If Joseph was never sold to Potiphar, Potiphar's wife would never have falsely accused him of rape.
- If Potiphar's wife never falsely accused Joseph of rape, then Joseph would never have been put in prison.
- If Joseph was never put in prison, he would have never met the baker and butler of Pharaoh.
- If Joseph never met the baker and butler of Pharaoh, he would have never interpreted their dreams.
- If Joseph never interpreted their dreams, he would have never interpreted Pharaoh's dream.
- If Joseph never interpreted Pharaoh's dream, he never would have become prime minister, second in Egypt only to Pharaoh.
- If Joseph never became prime minister, he never would have wisely prepared for the terrible famine to come.
- If Joseph never wisely prepared for the terrible famine, then his family back in Canaan would have died in the famine.
- If Joseph's family back in Canaan died in the famine, then the Messiah could not have come from a dead family.
- If the Messiah did not come forth, then Jesus never came.
- If Jesus never came, then we are all dead in our sins and without hope in this world.
- We are grateful for God's great and wise plan.

iii. In all this, there is a sobering contrast between Jacob and Joseph. Joseph had far worse circumstances, but he never took the attitude **all these things are against me**.

iv. The motto of too many Christians is **all these things are against me**. Instead, our motto should be Romans 8:28: *And we know that all things work together for good to those who love God, to those who are the called according to His purpose.*

v. We note that Romans 8:28 says, *God works all things together for good*. Any one thing in isolation may not be good. God isn't saying that every individual thing is good, but that God can and will work everything together for good for His people.

6. (37) Reuben's dramatic offer.

Then Reuben spoke to his father, saying, "Kill my two sons if I do not bring him *back* to you; put him in my hands, and I will bring him back to you."

   a. **Then Reuben spoke to his father**: This was **Reuben**, the firstborn. He was the one who disgraced the family with incest (Genesis 35:22). He was the one who did too little too late to rescue Joseph before they sold him as a slave.

   b. **Kill my two sons if I do not bring him back to you**: In a dramatic gesture, Reuben was willing to lay down his own sons to give assurance to Jacob in his despair.

      i. What Reuben did as a dramatic gesture, *God did in fact*. God gave His own Son to deliver us and to rescue us in our despair.

7. (38) Jacob refuses to let Benjamin go back to Egypt with them.

But he said, "My son shall not go down with you, for his brother is dead, and he is left alone. If any calamity should befall him along the way in which you go, then you would bring down my gray hair with sorrow to the grave."

   a. **My son shall not go down with you**: Not only did Jacob insist that Benjamin would never leave the house, but he also spoke as if he only had one son.

      i. Apparently, Jacob didn't think too much of Simeon. It didn't matter to him that Simeon might spend the rest of his life in an Egyptian jail.

      ii. Many years before, God wrestled with Jacob and overcame him. Jacob was left with a limp as a reminder of that experience. Still, **my son shall not go down with you** shows that the wrestling was not yet over. There was still more to do, and more of Jacob to yield to God.

   b. **If any calamity should befall him**: At this point, Jacob could not bear to trust God again. He lived protecting himself against future pain. God was about to bring Jacob good news – greater than he had ever hoped:

   - The beloved son you believed was dead is really alive.
   - The living son has been exalted to the highest place.
   - The living son gives the bread of life.
   - The living son is the savior of the world.
   - The living son means you can trust God again.
   - The living son gives hope to the hopeless.

Genesis 43 – Joseph Meets His Brothers a Second Time

A. Jacob decides to let the brothers return to Egypt with Benjamin.

1. (1-2) Jacob gives the order to get more food.

Now the famine was severe in the land. And it came to pass, when they had eaten up the grain which they had brought from Egypt, that their father said to them, "Go back, buy us a little food."

> a. **Now the famine was severe in the land**: We have reason to believe the brothers went to Egypt for grain in the first year of the famine. *Joseph* knew it would last seven years, but his brothers did not. They probably thought it was one bad year, but second year of **famine** came quickly.
>
> b. **When they had eaten up the grain which they had brought from Egypt**: Perhaps Jacob originally thought they had enough to survive the famine and they would never need to go back with Benjamin, and never need to go back and get Simeon. The famine wore on, and eventually they ran out of food.
>
> c. **Go back, buy us a little food**: *Necessity* drove Jacob to do something he would normally never do. We might imagine Jacob prayed so hard for the famine to break, and asked God to send relief. We might imagine Jacob became angry and bitter against God for not answering those prayers. God had a plan and had something so much better for Jacob than he could ever imagine.

2. (3-5) Judah explains why they had to bring Benjamin with them to Egypt.

But Judah spoke to him, saying, "The man solemnly warned us, saying, 'You shall not see my face unless your brother *is* with you.' If you send our brother with us, we will go down and buy you food. But if you will not send *him*, we will not go down; for the man said to us, 'You shall not see my face unless your brother *is* with you.'"

a. **Judah spoke to him**: Judah continued to show himself something of a leader among his brothers.

b. **The man solemnly warned us**: Judah didn't know that **the man** was his brother Joseph, but he remembered what a strong and even fearsome person he was. He said, **you shall not see my face** unless Benjamin was with them.

3. (6-7) Jacob complains and the brothers defend what they told the Egyptian.

And Israel said, "Why did you deal *so* wrongfully with me as to tell the man whether you had still *another* brother?" But they said, "The man asked us pointedly about ourselves and our family, saying, 'Is your father still alive? Have you *another* brother?' And we told him according to these words. Could we possibly have known that he would say, 'Bring your brother down'?"

a. **Why did you deal so wrongfully with me as to tell the man whether you had still another brother**: Jacob was clearly desperate. They must have discussed this question a hundred times before, yet he brought it up again.

b. **Could we possibly have known**: The brothers gave a logical explanation to their father. The question of the Egyptian official was so unexpected, they could not have anticipated it.

4. (8-10) Judah convinces his father to let them go to Egypt with Benjamin.

Then Judah said to Israel his father, "Send the lad with me, and we will arise and go, that we may live and not die, both we and you *and* also our little ones. I myself will be surety for him; from my hand you shall require him. If I do not bring him *back* to you and set him before you, then let me bear the blame forever. For if we had not lingered, surely by now we would have returned this second time."

a. **Send the lad with me**: The reference to Benjamin as a **lad** makes us wonder how old he was at this time. Adam Clarke and others think **lad** here is better translated as *youth* or *young man* and that Benjamin was in his mid-twenties or early thirties with a family of his own (Genesis 46:21).

b. **I myself will be surety for him**: Judah put his own life on the line as a guarantee for Benjamin. This is the first good thing we see that Judah did. Previously, he was the one who had proposed the sale of Joseph. He was the one who wronged his daughter-in-law Tamar and had sex with her as a harlot.

i. Previously, Satan may have directed his attack against Joseph because he believed *he* was the one who would ultimately bring the Messiah.

To this point, God had not yet revealed which of the 12 sons of Jacob the Messiah would come from.

ii. Satan not only hated the children of Jacob for what they were, but also for what God would make of them. The devil directs the same kind of hatred against believers today, as Satan considers the destiny God has for His people.

5. (11-14) Jacob sends them with money and gifts for the Egyptian leader.

And their father Israel said to them, "If it *must be so*, then do this: Take some of the best fruits of the land in your vessels and carry down a present for the man– a little balm and a little honey, spices and myrrh, pistachio nuts and almonds. Take double money in your hand, and take back in your hand the money that was returned in the mouth of your sacks; perhaps it was an oversight. Take your brother also, and arise, go back to the man. And may God Almighty give you mercy before the man, that he may release your other brother and Benjamin. If I am bereaved, I am bereaved!"

a. **Take some of the best fruits of the land in your vessels and carry down a present for the man**: Once before, Jacob gave a generous gift to a potential enemy and it worked well (Esau in Genesis 33:10-11).

b. **Take double money in your hand**: They took **double money** with them to Egypt to buy grain and the Egyptian leader's favor. Since ten brothers went to Egypt and they took double money, there were 20 units of money. This answered exactly to the 20 pieces of silver they sold Joseph for (Genesis 37:28). The words for *silver* and **money** are the same.

c. **May God Almighty give you mercy before the man**: It was good for Jacob to say and believe this, but we sense too much fatalism and too little faith (**If I am bereaved, I am bereaved!**). Faith and fatalism aren't the same.

B. The sons of Jacob face Joseph again.

1. (15-18) Joseph invites the brothers to dinner.

So the men took that present and Benjamin, and they took double money in their hand, and arose and went down to Egypt; and they stood before Joseph. When Joseph saw Benjamin with them, he said to the steward of his house, "Take *these* men to my home, and slaughter an animal and make ready; for *these* men will dine with me at noon." Then the man did as Joseph ordered, and the man brought the men into Joseph's house. Now the men were afraid because they were brought into Joseph's house; and they said, "It is because of the money, which was returned in our sacks the first time, that we are brought in, so that

he may make a case against us and fall upon us, to take us as slaves with our donkeys."

> a. **Take these men to my home, and slaughter an animal and make ready; for these men will dine with me**: This was unusual interest and kindness. The brothers must have wondered *why* the powerful Egyptian official took such an interest in them, why he wanted to share a meal with them.
>
> > i. Joseph is a picture of Jesus: He wants to *eat* with us, meaning that Jesus wants close relationship with us. *Behold, I stand at the door and knock. If anyone hears My voice and opens the door, I will come in to him and dine with him, and he with Me* (Revelation 3:20).
>
> b. **Now the men were afraid because they were brought into Joseph's house**: Perhaps they feared that the kindness from the Egyptian leader was just to arrange their execution.

2. (19-23) The brothers explain the money and are treated well in Joseph's house.

When they drew near to the steward of Joseph's house, they talked with him at the door of the house, and said, "O sir, we indeed came down the first time to buy food; but it happened, when we came to the encampment, that we opened our sacks, and there, *each* man's money was in the mouth of his sack, our money in full weight; so we have brought it back in our hand. And we have brought down other money in our hands to buy food. We do not know who put our money in our sacks." But he said, "Peace be with you, do not be afraid. Your God and the God of your father has given you treasure in your sacks; I had your money." Then he brought Simeon out to them.

> a. **They talked with him at the door of the house**: The brothers thought it was wise to explain things to the **steward of Joseph's house** before they had to explain it to the Egyptian official himself.
>
> b. **Your God and the God of your father has given you treasure in your sacks; I had your money**: This was not a lie, because he really did have it, and he gave it back. It really was because of God's goodness that they had the money back.
>
> c. **He brought Simeon out to them**: Joseph fulfilled his promise.

3. (24-26) The brothers meet Joseph and bring their gift to him.

So the man brought the men into Joseph's house and gave *them* water, and they washed their feet; and he gave their donkeys feed. Then they made the present ready for Joseph's coming at noon, for they heard

that they would eat bread there. And when Joseph came home, they brought him the present which was in their hand into the house, and bowed down before him to the earth.

> a. **Gave them water, and they washed their feet**: The brothers expected to be seized as slaves and have everything taken from them (Genesis 43:18). Yet Joseph treated them with kindness. This love and goodness from Joseph would win them over and bring them to full repentance.
>
>> i. The brothers received the blessings of love and kindness from Joseph without knowing who he was. In the same way, God showers love and blessing upon man even when man doesn't know from whom the blessings come.
>
> b. **They brought him the present… and bowed down**: They once again fulfilled the dream Joseph had many years before. They honored this Egyptian official not only out of respect, not only out of gratitude, but also out of *need*. Sensing we *need* Jesus will prompt us to give to Him and worship toward Him.

4. (27-30) Joseph's emotional meeting with Benjamin.

Then he asked them about *their* well-being, and said, "*Is* your father well, the old man of whom you spoke? *Is* he still alive?" And they answered, "Your servant our father is in good health; he is still alive." And they bowed their heads down and prostrated themselves. Then he lifted his eyes and saw his brother Benjamin, his mother's son, and said, "*Is* this your younger brother of whom you spoke to me?" And he said, "God be gracious to you, my son." Now his heart yearned for his brother; so Joseph made haste and sought *somewhere* to weep. And he went into *his* chamber and wept there.

> a. **He asked them about their well-being**: The mysterious Egyptian official had an unusual personal concern for these brothers and their family. Surely, he did not treat other grain purchasers this way.
>
> b. **Now his heart yearned for his brother**: Joseph was especially affected at meeting his only full brother, Benjamin, whom he last saw as only a small child. He was so overcome with emotion that **he went into his chamber and wept**. He was sad and emotional because he never had a relationship with Benjamin.

5. (31-32) The dinner tables are segregated.

Then he washed his face and came out; and he restrained himself, and said, "Serve the bread." So they set him a place by himself, and them by themselves, and the Egyptians who ate with him by themselves;

because the Egyptians could not eat food with the Hebrews, for that is an abomination to the Egyptians.

a. **They set him a place by himself:** Joseph did not eat with his brothers, because at the time, Egypt was one of the most racially separated societies on earth. They believed that Egyptians came from the gods, and all other people came from lesser origins. There was little social mixing with foreigners in the Egypt of Joseph's day.

b. **And the Egyptians who ate with him by themselves:** The Egyptians would not eat with Joseph, much less the strangers from Canaan. Even with all his status and power, Joseph could still not eat with *real* Egyptians.

i. "It is known from Herodotus that Egyptians so abhorred things foreign, that priests, at least, ate and drank nothing that was imported, nor would they use utensils for eating that had been used by Greeks." (Leupold)

ii. Here, we see the wisdom of God. Before Genesis account ends, God brought the entire family of Jacob into Egypt, where they were isolated from the surrounding people for some 400 years. In that time, they multiplied greatly, increasing to the millions. If God had allowed them to remain in Canaan, they would have simply assimilated into the corrupt and godless peoples of Canaan.

iii. God not only had to take the family of Israel out of the corrupt environment of Canaan, but He had to put them among a racially separated people who would not often intermarry or mingle with them. God simply sent Joseph on ahead to make the arrangements.

6. (33-34) Joseph arranges them by order of birth and he favors Benjamin.

And they sat before him, the firstborn according to his birthright and the youngest according to his youth; and the men looked in astonishment at one another. Then he took servings to them from before him, but Benjamin's serving was five times as much as any of theirs. So they drank and were merry with him.

a. **The firstborn according to his birthright and the youngest according to his youth:** No wonder the brothers were filled with **astonishment**. This arrangement couldn't happen by chance. Statistically, the odds of placing 11 brothers in their precise order of birth are something like 1 in 40 million.

b. **Benjamin's serving was five times as much as any of theirs:** This was another test, seeing how they reacted when the younger brother was favored, because they resented it so much when Joseph was favored by his father.

i. Joseph wanted to see if there was a change in the heart of his brothers, or if they were the same men who threw him into a pit and were deaf to his cries for help.

ii. This might have been his whole motivation in asking for Benjamin. He wondered if they would take care of Benjamin on such a journey, as they failed to do with Joseph.

iii. We should expect if we fail in a test somewhere, God will make arrangements for us to take the test again another time. This is a serious reason to take the test well the first time.

Genesis 44 – Joseph Tests His Brothers

A. Joseph sends them on their way.

1. (1-3) Joseph again puts money in his brothers' bags of grain.

And he commanded the steward of his house, saying, "Fill the men's sacks with food, as much as they can carry, and put each man's money in the mouth of his sack. Also put my cup, the silver cup, in the mouth of the sack of the youngest, and his grain money." So he did according to the word that Joseph had spoken. As soon as the morning dawned, the men were sent away, they and their donkeys.

> a. **As soon as the morning dawned, the men were sent away**: The brothers left Egypt in high spirits. They were treated well, had their sacks full of grain, and Simeon was out of prison. Jacob's fear of something horrible happening seemed that it would not come to pass.

> b. **Also put my cup, the silver cup, in the mouth of the sack of the youngest, and his grain money**: As before, the grain sacks of the brothers were topped off by the money they paid for the grain. This time, Joseph ordered that his special silver cup be hidden in the sack of Benjamin. In the morning, **the men were sent away**, beginning the journey back to Canaan.

2. (4-5) Joseph's steward confronts the brothers on their journey back to Canaan.

When they had gone out of the city, *and* were not *yet* far off, Joseph said to his steward, "Get up, follow the men; and when you overtake them, say to them, 'Why have you repaid evil for good? Is not this *the one* from which my lord drinks, and with which he indeed practices divination? You have done evil in so doing.'"

> a. **Why have you repaid evil for good**: The brothers were caught in Joseph's trap. Some wrongly think that Joseph did this simply to use his position of power to torment his brothers in revenge for their cruelty towards him.

Yet knowing the character of Joseph, this wasn't the case. Guided by the hand of God, Joseph tested the hearts of his brothers and brought them to complete repentance.

b. **He indeed practices divination**: We know from other sources that ancients did use sacred cups as divination devices. It is possible (though not likely) that Joseph did also, because there was not yet specific revelation from God that such a practice was forbidden. Yet it was not *Joseph* who said he used the cup for divination, but his servant, who may have wrongly assumed Joseph's spiritual insight and wisdom were more due to this cup than to his relationship with the living God.

3. (6-10) The brothers claim they are innocent of theft.

So he overtook them, and he spoke to them these same words. And they said to him, "Why does my lord say these words? Far be it from us that your servants should do such a thing. Look, we brought back to you from the land of Canaan the money which we found in the mouth of our sacks. How then could we steal silver or gold from your lord's house? With whomever of your servants it is found, let him die, and we also will be my lord's slaves." And he said, "Now also *let* it *be* according to your words; he with whom it is found shall be my slave, and you shall be blameless."

a. **Far be it from us that your servants should do such a thing**: The brothers confidently stated they did not have the cup. This showed that they had a healthy trust in each other. If they did not trust each other, they would have immediately wondered which brother stole the cup.

b. **With whomever of your servants it is found, let him die, and we also will be my lord's slaves**: The brothers were so confident they did not have the cup (and trusted each other so much), they declared the thief should be killed and all the others taken as slaves.

c. **Now also let it be according to your words; he with whom it is found shall be my slave**: Joseph did not repeat their offer of a death sentence, because he wanted no bloodshed. Joseph had a plan for agreeing with the brothers' suggestion that the guilty parties be taken as slaves.

4. (11-13) The cup is found in Benjamin's sack.

Then each man speedily let down his sack to the ground, and each opened his sack. So he searched. He began with the oldest and left off with the youngest; and the cup was found in Benjamin's sack. Then they tore their clothes, and each man loaded his donkey and returned to the city.

a. **Then each man speedily let down his sack**: They did it quickly, because they were *certain* they were innocent. They were so certain that they had just promised that if the stolen cup was found among them, the guilty one would stay in Egypt as a slave.

b. **The cup was found in Benjamin's sack**: The planted evidence was found. According to their oath, they would now be rid of the *other* favored son. If they hated Benjamin as much as they hated Joseph, they would be *glad* at this.

c. **Then they tore their clothes**: This was an extreme expression of horror, as if someone had just died. They weren't happy at the idea of being rid of Benjamin; they were horrified. They *all* **tore their clothes** and they *all* **returned to the city**.

i. The reaction of the brothers showed that for them, this was the worst thing imaginable. The cup was found in the sack of their father's favorite son, the one he worried about the most. Now Benjamin was sentenced to a life of slavery in Egypt, if not death.

ii. *This was a radical change in the brothers.* Before, they didn't care about their father or his favored son. Now, the idea of hurting either father or son made them feel as bad as if someone had died.

d. **Each man loaded his donkey and returned**: When Joseph was taken as a slave, the brothers allowed him to go and thought nothing of it. Now, they were willing to stand with Benjamin as he faced slavery or death. This demonstrated a significant change in the heart and attitude of Joseph's brothers.

5. (14-15) The brothers humbly return to an angry Egyptian official (Joseph).

So Judah and his brothers came to Joseph's house, and he *was* still there; and they fell before him on the ground. And Joseph said to them, "What deed is this you have done? Did you not know that such a man as I can certainly practice divination?"

a. **They fell before him on the ground**: They came back to the Egyptian official with *humility*. They had been wronged; the evidence had been planted. Yet they didn't come demanding justice, but with a humble plea for mercy.

i. When they **fell before him on the ground**, once again – for the *third* time – they fulfilled the dreams Joseph had more than 20 years before (Genesis 37:5-11).

ii. When they **fell before him on the ground**, it also demonstrated that the brothers were desperate to gain favor with the Egyptian official to obtain the release of Benjamin. They knew it was a genuine disaster to lose Benjamin and to bereave their father.

b. **Did you not know that such a man as I can certainly practice divination**: Joseph spoke this way because it was important, for a while longer, to play the part of an Egyptian and not allow them to know he was a Hebrew who worshipped Yahweh.

6. (16-17) Judah commits himself and all the brothers to stick with Benjamin, even as slaves in Egypt.

Then Judah said, "What shall we say to my lord? What shall we speak? Or how shall we clear ourselves? God has found out the iniquity of your servants; here we are, my lord's slaves, both we and *he* also with whom the cup was found." But he said, "Far be it from me that I should do so; the man in whose hand the cup was found, he shall be my slave. And as for you, go up in peace to your father."

a. **God has found out the iniquity of your servants**: With these words, Judah revealed God's work among the brothers. In Judah's mind, the bothers were now destined to live the rest of their lives as slaves in Egypt because they sold Joseph as a slave, some 20 years before this.

i. The brothers were innocent of the sin of stealing the cup, but were guilty of far greater sins. In the same way, we might take pride because we are innocent of some sin or another, yet we are guilty of far greater. You can't hide from your sin. Time does not erase the guilt of your sin; only the blood of Jesus can.

ii. 22 years before, when the brothers thought to kill Joseph but threw him into a pit, he cried out to them, pleading with anguish (Genesis 42:21). Donald Barnhouse said, "A physicist could compute the exact time required for his cries to go twenty-five yards to the eardrums of the brothers. But it took twenty-two years for that cry to go from the eardrums to their hearts."

b. **Here we are, my lord's slaves, both we and he also with whom the cup was found**: With these words, Judah insisted that the brothers would stick by Benjamin, though he was the favored and more greatly blessed son. If they quickly abandoned Benjamin, it would show little change of heart from 20 years ago, when they abandoned Joseph.

i. This resignation to slavery in Egypt was all the more significant, considering these were middle-aged men who came from lives of relative privilege, wealth, and status.

B. Judah intercedes for Benjamin.

1. (18-23) Judah recounts the previous conversations with the Egyptian official.

Then Judah came near to him and said: "O my lord, please let your servant speak a word in my lord's hearing, and do not let your anger burn against your servant; for you *are* even like Pharaoh. My lord asked his servants, saying, 'Have you a father or a brother?' And we said to my lord, 'We have a father, an old man, and a child of *his* old age, *who is* young; his brother is dead, and he alone is left of his mother's children, and his father loves him.' Then you said to your servants, 'Bring him down to me, that I may set my eyes on him.' And we said to my lord, 'The lad cannot leave his father, for *if* he should leave his father, *his father* would die.' But you said to your servants, 'Unless your youngest brother comes down with you, you shall see my face no more.'"

> a. **Then Judah came near to him and said**: Judah didn't take this fatalistically. He made an appeal to the Egyptian official. Everything looked bad; the planted evidence against them seemed to seal their fate. Yet he made an appeal.
>
>> i. Judah's impassioned speech to Joseph is a model of a heartfelt, desperate appeal. Of Judah's speech, F.B. Meyer wrote: "In all literature, there is nothing more pathetic than this appeal." H.C. Leupold wrote, "This is one of the manliest, most straightforward speeches ever delivered by any man. For depth of feeling and sincerity of purpose it stands unexcelled." Barnhouse called it "the most moving address in all the Word of God."
>
> b. **My lord asked his servants**: Judah reminded the Egyptian official that all this began with *his* questions. All they wanted to do was to buy some grain. This point is emphasized again and again: **Then you said… but you said**.
>
> c. **A father, an old man, and a child of his old age, who is young; his brother is dead**: Judah naturally presented the matter in the most sympathetic way. Joseph must have inwardly smiled when he said, **his brother is dead**.

2. (24-29) Judah recounts the previous conversation with his father Jacob.

So it was, when we went up to your servant my father, that we told him the words of my lord. And our father said, 'Go back *and* buy us a little food.' But we said, 'We cannot go down; if our youngest brother is with us, then we will go down; for we may not see the man's face unless our youngest brother is with us.' Then your servant my father said to us, 'You know that my wife bore me two sons; and the one went out from me, and I said, "Surely he is torn to pieces"; and I have not seen him

since. But if you take this one also from me, and calamity befalls him, you shall bring down my gray hair with sorrow to the grave.'

    a. **Go back and buy us a little food**: Judah told the Egyptian official the events of Genesis 43:1-10.

    b. **Surely he is torn to pieces... I have not seen him since**: With these carefully chosen words, Judah did not say that Benjamin's brother was dead – only that Jacob said, "**Surely he is torn to pieces**" and that Judah had not **seen him since**. Judah remembered the cruel lie that the brothers let their father believe regarding the death of Joseph (Genesis 37:31-35).

3. (30-32) Judah explains why it is so important that Benjamin return to Canaan.

Now therefore, when I come to your servant my father, and the lad *is* not with us, since his life is bound up in the lad's life, it will happen, when he sees that the lad *is not with us*, that he will die. So your servants will bring down the gray hair of your servant our father with sorrow to the grave. For your servant became surety for the lad to my father, saying, 'If I do not bring him *back* to you, then I shall bear the blame before my father forever.'"

    a. **When he sees that the lad is not with us, that he will die**: 20 years before, Joseph's brothers didn't care about their father when they reported Joseph's supposed death (Genesis 37:31-35). Judah showed they were now greatly concerned for the feelings and welfare of their father. This was *more* evidence of a change of heart – to care when you didn't care before.

        i. This is especially significant when we think of how deeply Jacob, Judah's father, must have hurt him and the other brothers through the years of his constant favoring of Joseph and Benjamin. This was a deep wound; yet Judah's heart was changed to *care* even about the father who wounded him so deeply.

    b. **For your servant became surety for the lad to my father**: Judah also made his request *personal*. Judah's own life and standing before his father would be destroyed if Benjamin never returned.

4. (33-34) Judah offers his life for Benjamin and his father.

"Now therefore, please let your servant remain instead of the lad as a slave to my lord, and let the lad go up with his brothers. For how shall I go up to my father if the lad is not with me, lest perhaps I see the evil that would come upon my father?"

    a. **Please let your servant remain instead of the lad as a slave to my lord**: Judah dramatically offered to lay down his life for the sake of Benjamin.

This was a dramatic change from 22 years before when the brothers did not care about Joseph, Benjamin, or even their father Jacob.

i. Judah distinguished himself as the one willing to be a substitutionary sacrifice, out of love for his father and for his brethren. *This is love* – heroic self-sacrifice.

b. **How shall I go up to my father if the lad is not with me**: Judah was the one who suggested *selling* Joseph 20 years earlier (Genesis 37:26-27). Here, with heroic love, he offered to lay down his life for the favored brother. This display of sacrificial love was another example of transformation in the brothers.

i. Moses was willing to offer himself for the salvation of Israel (Exodus 32:31-32), and so was Paul (Romans 9:1-4). Sacrificial love is evidence of our transformation (John 13:34).

ii. Through this chapter. there is remarkable evidence of the changed hearts of Joseph's brothers.

- They did not resent it when Benjamin was given the favored portion (Genesis 43:34).
- They trusted each other, not accusing each other of wrong when accused of stealing the cup (Genesis 44:9).
- They stuck together when the silver cup was found. They did not abandon the favored son and allow him to be carried back to Egypt alone (Genesis 44:13).
- They completely humbled themselves for the sake of the favored son (Genesis 44:14).
- They knew their predicament was the result of their sin against Joseph (Genesis 44:16).
- They offered themselves as slaves to Egypt, not abandoning Benjamin, the favored son, their brother (Genesis 44:16).
- They showed due concern for how this might affect their father (Genesis 44:29-31).
- Judah was willing to be a substitutionary sacrifice for his brother out of love for his father and his brethren (Genesis 44:33).

Genesis 45 – Joseph is Reunited With His Brothers

A. Joseph reveals himself to his brothers.

1. (1-3) The emotional revelation.

Then Joseph could not restrain himself before all those who stood by him, and he cried out, "Make everyone go out from me!" So no one stood with him while Joseph made himself known to his brothers. And he wept aloud, and the Egyptians and the house of Pharaoh heard it. Then Joseph said to his brothers, "I am Joseph; does my father still live?" But his brothers could not answer him, for they were dismayed in his presence.

> a. **Joseph could not restrain himself before all those who stood by him**: Joseph ordered all the Egyptians out of the room and then was alone with his brothers. His great emotion showed that Joseph did not cruelly manipulate his brothers. He was directed by God to make these arrangements, and it hurt him to do it.

> b. **Joseph made himself known to his brothers**: This means that Joseph *told them* he was Joseph and perhaps *showed* his brothers that he was their brother. This may have been done with scars or birthmarks that were characteristic of their brother Joseph.

> c. **But his brothers could not answer him, for they were dismayed in his presence**: Because of the punishment they anticipated, the great emotion of Joseph, his manner of revelation, and the total shock of learning Joseph was not only alive, but right in front of them, the brothers were **dismayed**. The ancient Hebrew word for **dismayed** (*bahal*) actually means, *amazed* or frightened or even *terrified*.

>> i. *Come near to me* in Genesis 45:4 implies the brothers cringed back in terror. Jewish legends (which are *only* legends) say the brothers were so

shocked, that their souls left their bodies, and it was only by a miracle of God their souls came back.

ii. Their dismay was a preview, a prophecy of what will happen when the Jewish people again see Jesus and see Him for who He is: *And I will pour on the house of David and on the inhabitants of Jerusalem the Spirit of grace and supplication; then they will look on Me whom they pierced. Yes, they will mourn for Him as one mourns for his only son, and grieve for Him as one grieves for a firstborn* (Zechariah 12:10).

2. (4-8) Joseph's testimony.

And Joseph said to his brothers, "Please come near to me." So they came near. Then he said: "I *am* Joseph your brother, whom you sold into Egypt. But now, do not therefore be grieved or angry with yourselves because you sold me here; for God sent me before you to preserve life. For these two years the famine *has been* in the land, and *there are* still five years in which *there will* be neither plowing nor harvesting. And God sent me before you to preserve a posterity for you in the earth, and to save your lives by a great deliverance. So now it was not you *who* sent me here, but God; and He has made me a father to Pharaoh, and lord of all his house, and a ruler throughout all the land of Egypt.

a. **Do not therefore be grieved or angry with yourselves because you sold me here**: Joseph honestly stated their sin of many years before. Yet in compassion, Joseph did not want them to be **grieved** or **angry** with themselves. Joseph was past his grief and anger and wanted his brothers to also be past it.

b. **God sent me before you to preserve life**: Joseph did not diminish what the brothers did (**whom you sold into Egypt**). Yet he saw that God's purpose in it all was greater than the evil of the brothers.

i. When we are sinned against, we are tempted to fail in one or both of these areas. We are tempted to pretend that the offending party never did it, or we are tempted to ingore the over-arching hand of God in every circumstance.

ii. It is fair to ask, "Why *was* Joseph in Egypt? Was it because of the sin of his brothers or because of the good plan of God?" The answer is that both aspects were true.

c. **God sent me before you to preserve a posterity for you in the earth, and to save your lives by a great deliverance**: All Joseph's sorrows were for a purpose. God used them to preserve his family and provide the conditions for it to become a nation. Joseph was a victim of men, but God turned it around for His glory. None of it was for a loss.

i. If this family did not go into Egypt, then they would assimilate among the pagan tribes of Canaan and cease to become a distinctive people. God had to put them in a place where they could grow, yet remain a distinctive nation.

ii. Years ago, Rabbi Harold Kushner wrote a remarkably wide-selling book titled *When Bad Things Happen to Good People*. It sold more than a half a million copies before going to paperback and was on the *New York Times* best-seller list for a whole year. The whole point of his book was to say God is all loving but not all powerful; that God is good, but not sovereign. So when bad things happen to good people, it is because events are out of God's control. Kushner advised his readers to "learn to love [God] and forgive him despite his limitations." Whatever Kushner described, it was not the God of the Bible, the God displayed in Joseph's life.

iii. "How wonderfully those two things meet in practical harmony – the free will of man and the predestination of God! Man acts just as freely and just as guiltily as if there were no predestination whatever; and God ordains, arranges, supervises, and over-rules, just as accurately as if there were no free will in the universe." (Spurgeon)

d. **So now it was not you who sent me here, but God**: Joseph realized *God* ruled his life, not good men, not evil men, not circumstances, or fate. God was in control, and because God was in control, all things worked together for good.

B. Joseph sends his brothers home.

1. (9-15) Joseph tells his brothers to go home and to bring their father and find protection from the famine.

"Hurry and go up to my father, and say to him, 'Thus says your son Joseph: "God has made me lord of all Egypt; come down to me, do not tarry. You shall dwell in the land of Goshen, and you shall be near to me, you and your children, your children's children, your flocks and your herds, and all that you have. There I will provide for you, lest you and your household, and all that you have, come to poverty; for *there are* still five years of famine."' And behold, your eyes and the eyes of my brother Benjamin see that *it is* my mouth that speaks to you. So you shall tell my father of all my glory in Egypt, and of all that you have seen; and you shall hurry and bring my father down here." Then he fell on his brother Benjamin's neck and wept, and Benjamin wept on his neck. Moreover he kissed all his brothers and wept over them, and after that his brothers talked with him.

a. **Thus says your son Joseph**: This was the message Joseph wanted his brothers to bring to their father. When Jacob eventually heard this, it was one of the greatest days of his life. He had the joy of learning that the favored son, who would save his brethren, who was given up for dead, is now alive.

b. **He kissed all his brothers and wept over them**: Joseph was affectionate and loving to **all his brothers**. Joseph did not exclude those who had been especially cruel to him. His heart was open to his brothers, both as a group and as individuals.

c. **After that his brothers talked with him**: This was a wonderful conversation. There was a lot to catch up on.

2. (16-24) Pharaoh and Joseph send the brothers home with many gifts.

Now the report of it was heard in Pharaoh's house, saying, "Joseph's brothers have come." So it pleased Pharaoh and his servants well. And Pharaoh said to Joseph, "Say to your brothers, 'Do this: Load your animals and depart; go to the land of Canaan. Bring your father and your households and come to me; I will give you the best of the land of Egypt, and you will eat the fat of the land. Now you are commanded— do this: Take carts out of the land of Egypt for your little ones and your wives; bring your father and come. Also do not be concerned about your goods, for the best of all the land of Egypt is yours.'" Then the sons of Israel did so; and Joseph gave them carts, according to the command of Pharaoh, and he gave them provisions for the journey. He gave to all of them, to each man, changes of garments; but to Benjamin he gave three hundred *pieces* **of silver and five changes of garments. And he sent to his father these** *things*: **ten donkeys loaded with the good things of Egypt, and ten female donkeys loaded with grain, bread, and food for his father for the journey. So he sent his brothers away, and they departed; and he said to them, "See that you do not become troubled along the way."**

a. **Joseph gave them carts, according to the command of Pharaoh, and he gave them provisions for the journey**: The sons of Israel received transportation, provision, garments, and riches because of who their favored brother was. Pharaoh blessed the sons of Jacob for Joseph's sake.

i. "To return to Canaan with 'carts from Egypt' was the cultural equivalent of landing a jumbo jet among a tribe of isolated savages. It would be the stuff legends are made of." (Boice)

b. **See that you do not become troubled along the way**: The idea behind the words "**become troubled**" is literally *become angry* or *quarrel*. Joseph knew as soon as these men left his presence, they would be tempted to act in selfish, unspiritual ways. They had to anticipate and guard against this.

3. (25-28) Jacob hears the good news – that Joseph lives.

Then they went up out of Egypt, and came to the land of Canaan to Jacob their father. And they told him, saying, "Joseph is still alive, and he is governor over all the land of Egypt." And Jacob's heart stood still, because he did not believe them. But when they told him all the words which Joseph had said to them, and when he saw the carts which Joseph had sent to carry him, the spirit of Jacob their father revived. Then Israel said, "*It is* enough. Joseph my son is still alive. I will go and see him before I die."

a. **He did not believe them**: Jacob was told Joseph was dead and believed it. Then he was told Joseph was alive, and he did not believe it until his sons told him the words of Joseph and showed him the blessings that came to them through Joseph. Then he believed Joseph was alive, though he had not yet seen him.

i. By analogy, we can say that the only way people will know Jesus is alive is if we tell them His words and show them His blessings in our lives.

b. **It is enough. Joseph my son is still alive**: Knowing that the favored son was alive – back from the dead, as it were – changed Israel's testimony from *all these things are against me* (Genesis 42:36) to **it is enough**.

i. This testimony of faith came from **Israel**, not *Jacob*. When Jacob was in charge, we saw a whining, self-pitying, complaining, unbelieving type of man. In contrast Israel, the man God had conquered, had a testimony of *faith*.

ii. Jacob often struggled with doubts and fears, but here he believed in Joseph the way we should believe in Jesus.

- Jacob believed, because he had enough evidence to convince him.
- Jacob acted, because he had conviction great enough to move him.

Genesis 46 – The Family of Jacob Comes to Egypt

A. The family comes to Egypt.

1. (1-4) God speaks to Jacob on the way to Egypt.

So Israel took his journey with all that he had, and came to Beersheba, and offered sacrifices to the God of his father Isaac. Then God spoke to Israel in the visions of the night, and said, "Jacob, Jacob!" And he said, "Here I am." So He said, "I *am* God, the God of your father; do not fear to go down to Egypt, for I will make of you a great nation there. I will go down with you to Egypt, and I will also surely bring you up *again*; and Joseph will put his hand on your eyes."

> a. **Israel took his journey with all that he had, and came to Beersheba**: Jacob left nothing behind, and came to the southernmost outpost of Canaan on the way to Egypt. Israel stopped there to honor God with **sacrifices**.
>
> > i. Both Abraham (Genesis 22:19) and Isaac (Genesis 26:23) lived for a time at **Beersheba**.
> >
> > ii. Israel's grandfather Abraham planted a tamarisk tree in Beersheba many years before and had called on the name of the Lord there (Genesis 21:33). Isaac received a special promise from God and built an altar for sacrifice there, calling on the name of the Lord (Genesis 26:24-25). It was probably at this very place Israel sacrificed, *remembering what God had done before*.
> >
> > iii. "It was, therefore, a memorable spot in the history of his family, and it was just then a turning-point in his own career, and therefore it called for special waiting upon the Lord. He was to break new ground, and enter upon a way which he had not trodden heretofore; and so we read that he offered sacrifices to the God of his father Isaac." (Spurgeon)

b. **God spoke to Israel in the visions of the night**: More than 40 years before, when Jacob was about to leave the Promised Land, God spoke to him in a dream (Genesis 28:12-17). Now, when he was about to leave the land again, God again brought assurance through a dream (**visions of the night**).

c. **Do not fear to go down to Egypt**: This strongly suggests that Israel was afraid to go to Egypt. Jacob may have remembered that Abraham had gone to Egypt in a time of famine once before, and it was an expression of his unbelief, and much evil eventually came from it (Genesis 12:10-20). He also may have remembered God told his father Isaac *not* to go down to Egypt (Genesis 26:2).

i. Also, Jacob knew God told Abraham that his descendants would *be strangers in a land that is not theirs, and will serve them, and they will afflict them four hundred years* (Genesis 15:13). As Jacob led his family into this foreign land, he did not know what the future held. At the same time, he knew the future was in God's hands.

ii. As Israel connected with what God did in the past (by sacrificing at Beersheba), he was assured of God's plan for the future.

iii. "Hesitate, my dear friend, while you are not sure that it is God's will; but when once you are certain that it is according to the Lord's mind, it will be unfaithfulness to God to have any kind of fear. Steam straight ahead, for that way lies your haven." (Spurgeon)

d. **I will make of you a great nation there**: God told Israel what His purpose was in bringing this large family or clan down to Egypt. Because of the exclusive, segregated nature of Egyptian life, Israel's descendants could grow as a large, distinct nation there. Egypt became like a mother's womb to Israel as a nation, where they grew from something small to something to full size.

e. **I will also surely bring you up again**: The great reason Jacob did not need to fear the journey to Egypt was that God promised to **bring** him back to the Promised Land. This would be fulfilled after Jacob's death, but it would be fulfilled – Egypt would never be the *permanent* home for Israel and his children.

f. **And Joseph will put his hand on your eyes**: The final assurance was for *God Himself* to tell Jacob that **Joseph** lived and would care for him until his dying day. This was sweet assurance.

2. (5-27) Listing of Jacob's family who came with him to Egypt.

Then Jacob arose from Beersheba; and the sons of Israel carried their father Jacob, their little ones, and their wives, in the carts which

Pharaoh had sent to carry him. So they took their livestock and their goods, which they had acquired in the land of Canaan, and went to Egypt, Jacob and all his descendants with him. His sons and his sons' sons, his daughters and his sons' daughters, and all his descendants he brought with him to Egypt. Now these *were* the names of the children of Israel, Jacob and his sons, who went to Egypt: Reuben *was* Jacob's firstborn. The sons of Reuben *were* Hanoch, Pallu, Hezron, and Carmi. The sons of Simeon *were* Jemuel, Jamin, Ohad, Jachin, Zohar, and Shaul, the son of a Canaanite woman. The sons of Levi *were* Gershon, Kohath, and Merari. The sons of Judah *were* Er, Onan, Shelah, Perez, and Zerah (but Er and Onan died in the land of Canaan). The sons of Perez were Hezron and Hamul. The sons of Issachar *were* Tola, Puvah, Job, and Shimron. The sons of Zebulun *were* Sered, Elon, and Jahleel. These *were* the sons of Leah, whom she bore to Jacob in Padan Aram, with his daughter Dinah. All the persons, his sons and his daughters, were thirty-three. The sons of Gad *were* Ziphion, Haggi, Shuni, Ezbon, Eri, Arodi, and Areli. The sons of Asher *were* Jimnah, Ishuah, Isui, Beriah, and Serah, their sister. And the sons of Beriah *were* Heber and Malchiel. These *were* the sons of Zilpah, whom Laban gave to Leah his daughter; and these she bore to Jacob: sixteen persons. The sons of Rachel, Jacob's wife, *were* Joseph and Benjamin. And to Joseph in the land of Egypt were born Manasseh and Ephraim, whom Asenath, the daughter of Poti-Pherah priest of On, bore to him. The sons of Benjamin *were* Belah, Becher, Ashbel, Gera, Naaman, Ehi, Rosh, Muppim, Huppim, and Ard. These *were* the sons of Rachel, who were born to Jacob: fourteen persons in all. The son of Dan *was* Hushim. The sons of Naphtali *were* Jahzeel, Guni, Jezer, and Shillem. These *were* the sons of Bilhah, whom Laban gave to Rachel his daughter, and she bore these to Jacob: seven persons in all. All the persons who went with Jacob to Egypt, who came from his body, besides Jacob's sons' wives, *were* sixty-six persons in all. And the sons of Joseph who were born to him in Egypt *were* two persons. All the persons of the house of Jacob who went to Egypt were seventy.

    a. **In the carts which Pharaoh had sent to carry him**: In Genesis 45:27, we saw how important these **carts** were to Jacob. His spirit revived when he saw this impressive wealth and technology from Egypt.

    b. **All his descendants he brought with him to Egypt**: This shows the great faith Israel had. He brought the *entire* family down to Egypt. No one was left behind to continue a presence in Canaan. Jacob was both all in, and he *knew* they would be back.

c. **The sons of Judah were**: The sons of Judah are of special note because this is the Messianic lineage. The line of descent to this point went like this: Abraham to Isaac to Jacob to **Judah** to **Perez** to **Hezron** (Luke 3:33-34).

d. **All the persons of the house of Jacob who went to Egypt were seventy**: The total number of males of this clan was 70. There were 66, plus Jacob himself, Joseph, and his two sons. This large family would become a nation of perhaps more than two million over the next 400 years.

> i. Like many great works of God, Israel had a slow beginning.
>
> - From the time God called Abraham, it took at least 25 years to add one son – Isaac.
> - It took Isaac 60 years to add another son of Israel – Jacob.
> - It took 50 or 60 years for Jacob to add 12 sons and one daughter.
> - But in 430 years, Israel would leave Egypt with 600,000 men.
> - It took this family 215 years to grow from one to 70, but in another 430 years they grew to two million or more.
>
> ii. In Acts 7:14, Stephen said that there were 75 who went into Egypt. This is because Stephen quoted from the Septuagint version of the Old Testament, which says 75. The number in the Septuagint is not wrong, just arrived at in a different way, specifically adding five more sons (or grandsons) of Joseph born in Egypt.

B. The family settles in the land of Goshen.

1. (28-30) The emotional meeting between Joseph and his father.

Then he sent Judah before him to Joseph, to point out before him *the way* to Goshen. And they came to the land of Goshen. So Joseph made ready his chariot and went up to Goshen to meet his father Israel; and he presented himself to him, and fell on his neck and wept on his neck a good while. And Israel said to Joseph, "Now let me die, since I have seen your face, because you *are* still alive."

> a. **He sent Judah before him to Joseph, to point out before him the way**: It was fitting for Judah, of the Messianic line, to do this. He demonstrated the true spirit of repentance and change of heart among Joseph's brothers.
>
> b. **Now let me die, since I have seen your face, because you are still alive**: This reunion of Israel with Joseph was more than he ever before dreamed. He had heard the news that the favored son lived; now it was fulfilled. This was a dramatic change from the attitude that said before, *all things are against me* (Genesis 42:36).

2. (31-34) Joseph tells his family of the plan to ask for the area of Goshen.

Then Joseph said to his brothers and to his father's household, "I will go up and tell Pharaoh, and say to him, 'My brothers and those of my father's house, who *were* in the land of Canaan, have come to me. And the men *are* shepherds, for their occupation has been to feed livestock; and they have brought their flocks, their herds, and all that they have.' So it shall be, when Pharaoh calls you and says, 'What is your occupation?' that you shall say, 'Your servants' occupation has been with livestock from our youth even till now, both we *and* also our fathers,' that you may dwell in the land of Goshen; for every shepherd is an abomination to the Egyptians."

a. **I will go up and tell Pharaoh**: Joseph became the representative and the advocate for the whole family. They came to safety in Egypt, but needed Joseph to represent them. In the same pattern, the believer needs Jesus Christ to represent him or her.

i. Indeed, the pharaohs after Joseph's death forgot about Joseph and made the people of Israel slaves (Exodus 1:8-10). This shows what would happen (in theory) if we had *no* representative or advocate before God. But Jesus – not Mary, not saints – is our eternal representative and advocate, being the same yesterday, today, and forever.

b. **That you may dwell in the land of Goshen**: *God had a place for His people*. He didn't bring them to Egypt and give them no home. It wasn't enough for Joseph to provide for their needs in Canaan; he had to bring them to the place he prepared for them.

i. We see Jesus in both aspects – He takes care of us in the present, but has gone to heaven to prepare a place for us – and *will* receive us to Himself.

c. **Every shepherd is an abomination to the Egyptians**: The Egyptians were agricultural in the sense of farming crops. They considered sheep unclean, and therefore detested shepherds. God had a place for His people, but it was a different place and a sometimes-despised place.

Genesis 47 – Jacob Meets Pharaoh; the Family Settles in Egypt

A. Jacob meets Pharaoh.

1. (1-4) The brothers ask for the land of Goshen.

Then Joseph went and told Pharaoh, and said, "My father and my brothers, their flocks and their herds and all that they possess, have come from the land of Canaan; and indeed they *are* in the land of Goshen." And he took five men from among his brothers and presented them to Pharaoh. Then Pharaoh said to his brothers, "What is your occupation?" And they said to Pharaoh, "Your servants are shepherds, both we *and* also our fathers." And they said to Pharaoh, "We have come to dwell in the land, because your servants have no pasture for their flocks, for the famine is severe in the land of Canaan. Now therefore, please let your servants dwell in the land of Goshen."

a. **My father and my brothers... have come from the land of Canaan**: When Joseph spoke those words to Pharaoh, it was the fulfillment of both God's plan and Joseph's desire. Joseph was again with his **father** and **brothers** and all their families.

b. **Please let your servants dwell in the land of Goshen**: Joseph had remarkably high status in the government of Egypt. Yet the family still had to ask permission to **dwell in the land of Goshen**.

2. (5-6) Pharaoh gives them the best of the land.

Then Pharaoh spoke to Joseph, saying, "Your father and your brothers have come to you. The land of Egypt is before you. Have your father and brothers dwell in the best of the land; let them dwell in the land of Goshen. And if you know *any* competent men among them, then make them chief herdsmen over my livestock."

a. **Dwell in the best of the land**: This blessing was all because of Joseph. He saved Egypt – and much of the world – from terrible famine, and now the whole family of Israel was blessed and received an inheritance because of Joseph.

b. **If you know any competent men among them**: We can assume that at least some of Joseph's brothers and their families were **competent** as **herdsmen**.

3. (7-10) Jacob blesses Pharaoh.

Then Joseph brought in his father Jacob and set him before Pharaoh; and Jacob blessed Pharaoh. Pharaoh said to Jacob, "How old are you?" And Jacob said to Pharaoh, "The days of the years of my pilgrimage are one hundred and thirty years; few and evil have been the days of the years of my life, and they have not attained to the days of the years of the life of my fathers in the days of their pilgrimage." So Jacob blessed Pharaoh, and went out from before Pharaoh.

a. **The days of the years of my pilgrimage are one hundred and thirty years**: Jacob explained that he was on a **pilgrimage**. He knew that his real home was somewhere else – heaven.

b. **Few and evil have been the days of the years of my life**: This was not a cynical statement by Jacob. He recognized that the general character of his life (lived in the flesh) and the length of his life did not compare either to eternity or to the lives of his ancestors.

c. **So Jacob blessed Pharaoh**: Pharaoh acknowledged Jacob was a man of God by accepting his blessing. In the Egyptian religion, Pharaoh himself was thought to be a god. They considered Pharaoh the human embodiment of Ra, the sun god. This means that it was remarkable that he allowed Israel to bestow a blessing on him.

4. (11-12) Israel takes the best of the land.

And Joseph situated his father and his brothers, and gave them a possession in the land of Egypt, in the best of the land, in the land of Rameses, as Pharaoh had commanded. Then Joseph provided his father, his brothers, and all his father's household with bread, according to the number in *their* families.

a. **Joseph situated his father and his brothers**: The family of Israel looked to Joseph, and Joseph only, as their source of provision and supply.

b. **Then Joseph provided his father, his brothers, and all his father's household with bread**: Though there was a great famine in that entire region, God's wise preparation meant there was **bread** for Joseph's family and countless others.

B. Joseph deals with the famine.

1. (13-14) In the early years of the famine, money pours into the treasury of Egypt, because it was the only place to buy food.

Now *there was* no bread in all the land; for the famine *was* very severe, so that the land of Egypt and the land of Canaan languished because of the famine. And Joseph gathered up all the money that was found in the land of Egypt and in the land of Canaan, for the grain which they bought; and Joseph brought the money into Pharaoh's house.

   a. **There was no bread in all the land**: The famine went far beyond Egypt, and it was **very severe**.

   b. **Joseph brought the money into Pharaoh's house**: Joseph was not only a hard worker and a brilliant administrator, he was also an honest worker. He did not cheat the Pharaoh; as a loyal employee he **brought the money into Pharaoh's house**.

2. (15-26) In the later years of the famine, Joseph arranged ways for the people to purchase food with whatever they had to give.

So when the money failed in the land of Egypt and in the land of Canaan, all the Egyptians came to Joseph and said, "Give us bread, for why should we die in your presence? For the money has failed." Then Joseph said, "Give your livestock, and I will give you *bread* for your livestock, if the money is gone." So they brought their livestock to Joseph, and Joseph gave them bread in *exchange* for the horses, the flocks, the cattle of the herds, and for the donkeys. Thus he fed them with bread in exchange for all their livestock that year. When that year had ended, they came to him the next year and said to him, "We will not hide from my lord that our money is gone; my lord also has our herds of livestock. There is nothing left in the sight of my lord but our bodies and our lands. Why should we die before your eyes, both we and our land? Buy us and our land for bread, and we and our land will be servants of Pharaoh; give *us* seed, that we may live and not die, that the land may not be desolate." Then Joseph bought all the land of Egypt for Pharaoh; for every man of the Egyptians sold his field, because the famine was severe upon them. So the land became Pharaoh's. And as for the people, he moved them into the cities, from one end of the borders of Egypt to the other end. Only the land of the priests he did not buy; for the priests had rations *allotted to them* by Pharaoh, and they ate their rations which Pharaoh gave them; therefore they did not sell their lands. Then

Joseph said to the people, "Indeed I have bought you and your land this day for Pharaoh. Look, *here is* seed for you, and you shall sow the land. And it shall come to pass in the harvest that you shall give one-fifth to Pharaoh. Four-fifths shall be your own, as seed for the field and for your food, for those of your households and as food for your little ones." So they said, "You have saved our lives; let us find favor in the sight of my lord, and we will be Pharaoh's servants." And Joseph made it a law over the land of Egypt to this day, *that* Pharaoh should have one-fifth, except for the land of the priests only, *which* did not become Pharaoh's.

a. **When the money failed in the land of Egypt and the land of Canaan**: Food was available in Egypt, but at a price. Because the famine lasted so long – seven years in total – eventually people ran out of money to buy more grain. When the money first **failed**, Joseph received their **livestock** as payment. When the livestock was gone, then Joseph received their **land** as payment.

b. **So the land became Pharaoh's**: In the process, the power and wealth of Pharaoh was multiplied greatly. In times of national crisis, the power of central government often increases. Under Joseph's administration, Pharaoh owned the land and the people worked it for the price of one-fifth of the produce of the land.

c. **In the harvest that you shall give one-fifth to Pharaoh**: Joseph wasn't unfair. He fed the people when they would have starved, and in return asked for one-fifth (20%) annually from the produce of the land. Many people today would be happy with only 20% in total taxes.

C. Israel anticipates his death.

1. (27) The multiplication of the family of Israel.

So Israel dwelt in the land of Egypt, in the country of Goshen; and they had possessions there and grew and multiplied exceedingly.

a. **Grew and multiplied exceedingly**: This was certainly true. In some 400 years, they became a nation of some two million or more people.

b. **Multiplied exceedingly**: Henry Morris calculated the initial group of five (Jacob and his four wives) grew into a clan of about 100 in 50 years (the 100 includes the 70 of Genesis 46:27 plus a few wives of the sons not mentioned and grandchildren). That is a growth rate of just over 6% per year. At that rate, there would be several million descendants by the time of the Exodus 430 years later.

2. (28-31) Israel requires Joseph vow to bury him in Canaan.

And Jacob lived in the land of Egypt seventeen years. So the length of Jacob's life was one hundred and forty-seven years. When the time drew near that Israel must die, he called his son Joseph and said to him, "Now if I have found favor in your sight, please put your hand under my thigh, and deal kindly and truly with me. Please do not bury me in Egypt, but let me lie with my fathers; you shall carry me out of Egypt and bury me in their burial place." And he said, "I will do as you have said." Then he said, "Swear to me." And he swore to him. So Israel bowed himself on the head of the bed.

a. **Jacob lived in the land of Egypt seventeen years**: Jacob's life lasted 147 years. As he knew his death drew near, he made Joseph take a solemn oath after the pattern of the oath Abraham made his servant make in Genesis 24:1-9.

b. **Please do not bury me in Egypt, but let me lie with my fathers**: This was the oath Israel required from Joseph. Israel knew Egypt was not his home. He belonged in the land promised to he and his descendants. He clearly believed and understood he was the inheritor of Abraham's covenant.

Genesis 48 – Jacob Blesses Joseph's Sons

A. Jacob calls for his sons.

1. (1-4) Jacob remembers God's promise.

Now it came to pass after these things that Joseph was told, "Indeed your father is sick"; and he took with him his two sons, Manasseh and Ephraim. And Jacob was told, "Look, your son Joseph is coming to you"; and Israel strengthened himself and sat up on the bed. Then Jacob said to Joseph: "God Almighty appeared to me at Luz in the land of Canaan and blessed me, and said to me, 'Behold, I will make you fruitful and multiply you, and I will make of you a multitude of people, and give this land to your descendants after you as an everlasting possession.'

a. **God Almighty appeared to me at Luz**: *Luz* is another name for Bethel (Genesis 28:19, 35:6), where Jacob first met God. Jacob vividly remembered this outstanding encounter with the LORD.

b. **Behold, I will make you fruitful and multiply you**: Jacob's phrasing is reminiscent of exact promises God made to Abraham in Genesis 17 (see Genesis 17:2, 17:6, and 17:8). Abraham was careful to pass down the exact words of God's covenant with him to the inheritors of the covenant, because the exact words of God were important.

2. (5-6) Jacob adopts Joseph's sons as his own.

"And now your two sons, Ephraim and Manasseh, who were born to you in the land of Egypt before I came to you in Egypt, are mine; as Reuben and Simeon, they shall be mine. Your offspring whom you beget after them shall be yours; they will be called by the name of their brothers in their inheritance.

a. **As Reuben and Simeon, they shall be mine**: Reuben and Simeon were the first and second born of Israel. Jacob received the two sons of Joseph as adopted into the family at the highest level (as if they were his own first and second born).

>i. And, perhaps, they were something similar to replacements for Reuben and Simeon, who were in a sense disqualified from positions of status and leadership in Israel's family because of their sin (Genesis 34:25, 35:22).

b. **They shall be mine**: Jacob's adoption of Manasseh and Ephraim explains why there are 12 tribes often listed in different combinations. Because of this adoption, there were actually 13 sons of Israel. The 12 were born, but Joseph was divided into two tribes.

>i. Therefore as the tribes are listed through the Old Testament, they can be arranged different ways and still remain 12 tribes. There are more than 20 different ways of listing the tribes in the Old Testament.

>ii. As a number, 12 is often associated with government or administration in God's eyes. There are 12 tribes; 12 apostles; 12 princes of Ishmael; 12 pillars on Moses' altar; 12 stones on the high priest's breastplate; 12 cakes of showbread; 12 silver platters; silver bowls; and gold pans for the service of the tabernacle; 12 spies to search out the land; 12 memorial stones; 12 governors under Solomon; 12 stones in Elijah's altar; 12 in each group of musicians and singers for Israel's worship; 12 hours in a day; 12 months in a year; 12 Ephesian men filled with the Holy Spirit; 12;000 from 12 tribes sealed and preserved through the tribulation; 12 gates of 12 pearls in heaven, and 12 angels at the gates; 12 foundations in the New Jerusalem, each with the names of the 12 apostles of the Lamb; it's length, breadth, and height are all 12,000 furlongs; and the tree of life in heaven has 12 fruits. The number 12 is special to God.

3. (7) Jacob concludes his testimony with consideration of his soon death.

"But as for me, when I came from Padan, Rachel died beside me in the land of Canaan on the way, when *there was* but a little distance to go to Ephrath; and I buried her there on the way to Ephrath (that is, Bethlehem)."

a. **Rachel died beside me in the land of Canaan**: With lingering grief, Israel remembered the tragic death of his beloved wife Rachel at the birth of their son Benjamin (Genesis 35:16-18).

b. **I buried her there**: Rachel's burial is described in Genesis 35:19-20.

B. Jacob blesses Manasseh and Ephraim.

1. (8-12) Jacob calls for Joseph's sons, to bless them.

Then Israel saw Joseph's sons, and said, "Who *are* these?" And Joseph said to his father, "They *are* my sons, whom God has given me in this *place*." And he said, "Please bring them to me, and I will bless them." Now the eyes of Israel were dim with age, *so that* he could not see. Then Joseph brought them near him, and he kissed them and embraced them. And Israel said to Joseph, "I had not thought to see your face; but in fact, God has also shown me your offspring!" So Joseph brought them from beside his knees, and he bowed down with his face to the earth.

a. **These are my sons, whom God has given me in this place**: We remember that the names of Joseph's sons were *Manasseh* (the firstborn) and *Ephraim* (the younger). The name *Manasseh* means *forgetfulness*, and the name *Ephraim* means *fruitfulness* (Genesis 41:51-52).

b. **He bowed down with his face to the earth**: Joseph lived as a high official of Egypt for many years, and had no contact with his father during that time. Yet it did not diminish the reverence he had towards his father.

2. (13-14) Jacob puts the favored hand on the second-born, despite Joseph's efforts.

And Joseph took them both, Ephraim with his right hand toward Israel's left hand, and Manasseh with his left hand toward Israel's right hand, and brought *them* near him. Then Israel stretched out his right hand and laid *it* on Ephraim's head, who *was* the younger, and his left hand on Manasseh's head, guiding his hands knowingly, for Manasseh *was* the firstborn.

a. **Ephraim with his right hand toward Israel's left hand**: The **right hand** in the Bible always has the idea of the *favored* position, because generally speaking, the right hand is the hand of strength and skill.

i. The right hand is associated with God's strength (Exodus 15:6), favor (Psalm 16:11), and help (Psalm 20:6). This is why Jesus is described as sitting at the *right hand* of God the Father (Mark 14:62).

b. **Guiding his hands knowingly**: Israel knew exactly what he intended to do. By placing **his right hand** on **Ephraim's head**, he intended to grant a greater blessing to **the younger**. This was against normal custom and expectation.

3. (15-16) The blessing of Jacob upon Manasseh and Ephraim.

And he blessed Joseph, and said:

"God, before whom my fathers Abraham and Isaac walked,
The God who has fed me all my life long to this day,
The Angel who has redeemed me from all evil,

Bless the lads;
Let my name be named upon them,
And the name of my fathers Abraham and Isaac;
And let them grow into a multitude in the midst of the earth."

a. **God, before whom my fathers Abraham and Isaac walked**: Israel granted the blessing in deep awareness of the covenant that came from God's promise to his grandfather **Abraham** and his father **Isaac**.

b. **And he blessed Joseph**: In blessing Joseph's sons, it could be rightly said that Israel **blessed Joseph**. Israel gave the same blessing to both sons, but the son of the right hand received a greater proportion of the blessing.

> i. "Our text tells us that Jacob blessed Joseph, and we perceive that *he blessed him through blessing his children*; which leads us to the next remark, that no choicer favor could fall upon ourselves than to see our children favored of the Lord. Joseph is doubly blessed by seeing Ephraim and Manasseh blessed." (Spurgeon)
>
> ii. This was fulfilled in Israel's history. Both tribes were blessed, but Ephraim was greater as a tribe, even to the point where the name *Ephraim* was used to refer to the whole northern nation of Israel (see examples in Isaiah 7:8, 7:17, and 11:13).

c. **The God who has fed me all my life long to this day**: Jacob's testimony was a testimony of grace, not personal merit. He did not say how faithful he was to God, but how faithful God was to him.

> i. The phrase, "**the God who has fed me**" is literally, "The God who has shepherded me." This is the first mention in the Bible of God as a *shepherd* to His people.
>
> ii. "The old man's voice faltered as he said, 'The God which fed me all my life long.' The translation would be better if it ran, 'The God which shepherded me all my life long.'" (Spurgeon)

4. (17-20) Jacob answers Joseph's objection about the order of blessing.

Now when Joseph saw that his father laid his right hand on the head of Ephraim, it displeased him; so he took hold of his father's hand to remove it from Ephraim's head to Manasseh's head. And Joseph said to his father, "Not so, my father, for this *one* is the firstborn; put your right hand on his head." But his father refused and said, "I know, my son, I know. He also shall become a people, and he also shall be great; but truly his younger brother shall be greater than he, and his descendants shall become a multitude of nations." So he blessed them that day, saying, "By you Israel will bless, saying, 'May God make you as Ephraim and as Manasseh!'" And thus he set Ephraim before Manasseh.

a. **This one is the firstborn; put your right hand on his head**: As the two sons of Joseph stood before Israel, the older (**Manasseh**) was before Israel's right hand, and the younger (**Ephraim**) was before Israel's left hand. Joseph positioned them intentionally so the older could receive the right-hand blessing, according to custom. Yet Isaac deliberately crossed his hands and put his right hand on Ephraim's head and his left hand on Manasseh's head.

b. **For this one is the firstborn... truly his younger brother shall be greater than he**: Ephraim was not the **firstborn**, but God chose him to take the *position* of firstborn. Jeremiah 31:9 described this: *For I am a Father to Israel, and Ephraim is My firstborn* (Jeremiah 31:9).

i. This shows how the idea of *firstborn* in the Bible is often a position of pre-eminence, not necessarily meaning "first out of the womb."

ii. David had the position of firstborn, even though he was the youngest son (1 Samuel 16:11 and Psalm 89:27).

iii. Jesus has the pre-eminent position of firstborn (Colossians 1:15), though this does not mean Jesus was literally the first "born" creature of God, because Jesus was not created.

5. (21-22) Jacob makes a personal bequest to Joseph.

Then Israel said to Joseph, "Behold, I am dying, but God will be with you and bring you back to the land of your fathers. Moreover I have given to you one portion above your brothers, which I took from the hand of the Amorite with my sword and my bow."

a. **Behold, I am dying**: This was truly a passing of the torch from Israel to Joseph. Israel was the last of the three great patriarchs to pass from the scene.

i. "If Abraham dies, there is Isaac; and if Isaac dies, there is Jacob; and if Jacob dies, there is Joseph; and if Joseph dies, Ephraim and Manasseh survive. The Lord shall never lack a champion to bear his standard high among the sons of men. Only let us pray God to raise up more faithful ministers day and night. We have plenty of a sort, but, oh, for more that will weigh out sixteen ounces to the pound of gospel in such a way that people will receive it. We have too much of fine language, too much of florid eloquence, and little full and plain gospel preaching, but God will keep up the apostolic succession, never fear of that. When Stephen is dying, Paul is not far off. When Elijah is taken up, he leaves his mantle behind him." (Spurgeon)

b. **One portion above your brothers**: This referred to Joseph being father of two tribes, while each of his brothers only fathered one each.

c. **Which I took from the hand of the Amorite**: Apparently, while still in Canaan, Jacob battled for control of a portion of land from the Amorites, and he deeded the land to Joseph and his descendants. The descendants of Joseph would take this land some 400 years later.

d. **God will be with you and bring you back to the land of your fathers**: This completed a wonderful work regarding Jacob's recognition of God's presence in his life.

- *I am with you* (Genesis 28:15): God gives the young believer every possible assurance of His presence and grace.
- *I will be with you* (Genesis 31:3): God expects the growing believer to trust He will be with him, even when he only has the promise of His presence.
- *God… has been with me* (Genesis 31:5): God gives a glorious testimony to the mature believer, able to say how God has been with him, even when he hasn't felt His presence in the way he wished.
- **God will be with you** (Genesis 48:21): God gives the mature believer the opportunity to encourage others with the promise of God's presence.

Joseph as a Picture of Jesus

Joseph is one of the most remarkable portraits of Jesus, the Messiah, in all the Bible. In many ways, his life illustrated the future life and work of Jesus. Here are a few ways in which Joseph and Jesus are alike.

"There is scarcely any personal type in the Old Testament which is more clearly and fully a portrait of our Lord Jesus Christ than is the type of Joseph." (Charles Spurgeon)

1. Was a shepherd.
2. Loved by his father.
3. Sent unto his brethren.
4. Hated by his brothers.
5. Prophesied his coming glory.
6. Rejected by his brothers.
7. Endured unjust punishment from his brothers.
8. Sentenced to the pit.
9. Condemned to the pit, though a leader knew he should go free.
10. Sold for pieces of silver.
11. Handed over to the Gentiles.

12. Regarded as dead but raised out of the pit.
13. Went to Egypt.
14. Made a servant.
15. Tempted severely but did not sin.
16. Falsely accused.
17. Made no defense.
18. Cast into prison and numbered with sinners and criminals.
19. Endured unjust punishment from Gentiles.
20. Associated with two other criminals; one was pardoned, and one was not.
21. Showed compassion.
22. Brought a message of deliverance in prison.
23. Wanted to be remembered.
24. Shown to have divine wisdom.
25. Recognized as having the Spirit of God.
26. Betrayed by friends.
27. Glorified after his humility.
28. Honored among Gentiles while still despised or forgotten by his brethren.
29. Given a Gentile bride.
30. Was 30 years old when he began his life's work.
31. Blessed the world with bread.
32. Became the only source of bread for the world.
33. The world was instructed to go to him and do whatever he said to do.
34. Was given the name "God Speaks and He Lives."
35. His brethren were driven out of their own land.
36. In his second appearing, he did not first go to his brothers; they came to him.
37. He knew his brethren even while unknown and unrecognized by them.
38. He blessed his brethren without their knowledge.
39. He wanted *all* of his brethren to come to him.
40. There was a significant time gap between his initial relationship with his brothers and his second relationship to his brothers.
41. He gave his brothers a way of deliverance through substitution.

42. His "second coming" to his brothers had two appearances. He made himself known to his brethren at his second appearing to them.

43. He was revealed as a man of compassion.

44. His brothers repented of rejecting him, with great amazement and tears.

45. He allowed no fellowship (as in eating together) until his brothers repented and he revealed himself.

46. His brethren went forth to proclaim his glory.

47. He made provision for his brethren.

48. He prepared a place for his brethren, and he received them into it.

49. He brought Jew and Gentile together in the land.

Genesis 49 – The Blessing of the Sons of Jacob

A. The prophetic blessings upon the Sons of Israel.

1. (1-2) What will **befall** the sons of Jacob in the **last days**.

And Jacob called his sons and said, "Gather together, that I may tell you what shall befall you in the last days:

**"Gather together and hear, you sons of Jacob,
And listen to Israel your father.**

> a. **Jacob called his sons**: This was Jacob's last significant act as a patriarch and as the heir to Abraham and Isaac. Here, he prophesied blessings upon each son, one-by-one.
>
> b. **What shall befall you in the last days**: Some of what follows are not so much *blessings* as they are prophecies regarding what God will do with these tribes in the future.
>
>> i. This is the first conscious prophecy spoken by a man in the Bible. There were many prophecies announced by God (such as the promise of the triumph of the seed of the woman in Genesis 3:15), and other veiled prophecies by men, but this is the first *declared* prophecy through a man in the Bible.
>>
>> ii. Jewish traditions tell us that as Jacob was about to bless his sons, he was ready to tell them the "great secret concerning the end of time." But at that moment, the glory of God visited and left just as quickly, taking all trace of the knowledge of the great mystery, so he couldn't tell them. Again, we regard this as just an interesting legend.
>
> c. **You sons of Jacob, and listen to Israel your father**: At the very beginning of the blessing, Jacob realized he was both **Jacob** and **Israel**, and his sons are sons of each. This was a place of spiritual maturity, realizing both what God made him (**Israel**) and what he had to battle against (**Jacob**).

2. (3-4) Reuben: **You shall not excel**.

"Reuben, you are my firstborn,
My might and the beginning of my strength,
The excellency of dignity and the excellency of power.
Unstable as water, you shall not excel,
Because you went up to your father's bed;
Then you defiled *it*—
He went up to my couch.

> a. **You are my firstborn**: As the firstborn of the family, Reuben had claim to the inheritance rights of the firstborn, but he forfeited it through pride (**the excellency of dignity**) and through immorality (**you defiled it**).
>
>> i. Reuben's immorality with his father's concubine Bilhah (the mother of his brothers Dan and Naphtali) is recorded in Genesis 35:22.
>
> b. **Unstable as water, you shall not excel**: Because of Reuben's instability, the birthright was divided. Usually the firstborn was the spiritual and social leader of the clan; but among the sons of Israel, the rights of *blessing*, *priesthood*, and *ruling authority* were divided among brothers rather than being centralized in one.
>
>> i. Though we see the great wisdom of God in decentralizing authority among the sons of Israel, Reuben paid a high price for his instability. As much as anything, God looks for stable character in those who will lead His people.
>
> c. **You shall not excel**: The tribe of Reuben never did excel. No prophet, no judge, or no king that we know of came from the tribe of Reuben. Reuben is an example of how the first can be last (Matthew 19:30).
>
>> i. "So a man may have great opportunities, and yet lose them. Uncontrolled passions may make him very little who otherwise might have been great." (Spurgeon)

3. (5-7) Simeon and Levi: **I will… scatter them in Israel**.

"Simeon and Levi *are* **brothers;**
Instruments of cruelty *are in* **their dwelling place.**
Let not my soul enter their council;
Let not my honor be united to their assembly;
For in their anger they slew a man,
And in their self-will they hamstrung an ox.
Cursed *be* **their anger, for** *it is* **fierce;**
And their wrath, for it is cruel!
I will divide them in Jacob
And scatter them in Israel.

a. **Simeon and Levi are brothers**: The second-born son Simeon and the third-born son Levi received the same words for the same evil deed. They were **instruments of cruelty** when they wiped out all the men of Shechem in retaliation for the rape of their sister Dinah (Genesis 34:25-29).

    i. Jacob, perhaps in weakness, did nothing at the time except register a small, self-centered complaint (Genesis 34:30). Yet he (and the Lord) remembered this event. This illustrates the principle that the sins of our past can come back and haunt us. Even when forgiven, they may carry consequences we must face for a lifetime.

b. **Cursed be their anger, for it is fierce**: The real problem with Simeon and Levi was their **anger (in their anger they slew a man)**. Their anger was sin because it was rooted in **self-will (in their self-will they hamstrung an ox)**.

    i. The Bible speaks of a godly anger (*Be angry and do not sin*, Ephesians 4:26) and an ungodly anger (*Let all bitterness, wrath, anger...be put away from you*, Ephesians 4:31). Often, the difference between a godly, righteous anger and an ungodly anger is *self-will*.

c. **I will divide them in Jacob and scatter them in Israel**: The prophecy of dividing and scattering turned out to be a *curse* for Simeon. The tribe of Simeon was the weakest numerically of the 12 (Numbers 26:14) and shared an allotment of land with Judah (Joshua 19:1).

    i. The tribe of Simeon became small during the wilderness wanderings. They started out from Egypt being the third largest tribe (Numbers 1:23), but some 35 years later, at the second wilderness census of Israel, 63% of the tribe perished and they became the smallest tribe (Numbers 26:14).

d. **I will divide them in Jacob and scatter them in Israel**: The prophecy of dividing and scattering became a *blessing* for Levi. Because of the faithfulness of this tribe during the rebellion of the golden calf (Exodus 32:26-28), it was scattered as a blessing throughout the whole nation of Israel. They received no large tract of land, for the Lord was their inheritance, not land (Joshua 13:33).

    i. So both Simeon and Levi were scattered, but one as a blessing and the other as a curse. "Happy is that man who, though he begins with a dark shadow resting upon him, so lives as to turn even that shadow into bright sunlight. Levi gained a blessing at the hands of Moses, one of the richest blessings of any of the tribes" (Spurgeon).

    ii. The American author Washington Irving said: "It lightens the stroke to draw near to him who handles the rod." When we suffer from our sin, we should draw near to God and anticipate that in mercy He will turn suffering into blessing.

4. (8-12) Judah: **The scepter shall not depart from Judah**.

"Judah, you *are he* **whom your brothers shall praise;**
Your hand *shall be* **on the neck of your enemies;**
Your father's children shall bow down before you.
Judah is a lion's whelp;
From the prey, my son, you have gone up.
He bows down, he lies down as a lion;
And as a lion, who shall rouse him?
The scepter shall not depart from Judah,
Nor a lawgiver from between his feet,
Until Shiloh comes;
And to Him *shall be* **the obedience of the people.**
Binding his donkey to the vine,
And his donkey's colt to the choice vine,
He washed his garments in wine,
And his clothes in the blood of grapes.
His eyes *are* **darker than wine,**
And his teeth whiter than milk.

a. **Judah, you are he whom your brothers shall praise**: Judah wasn't a completely exemplary character. He suggested a profit motive in getting rid of Joseph (Genesis 37:26). He did not deal faithfully with his daughter-in-law Tamar (Genesis 38:26), and he had sex with her as a prostitute (Genesis 38:18). But he showed good character when he interceded and offered himself as a substitute for Joseph (Genesis 44:18-34). Overall, this blessing is an example of the richness of God's grace to the undeserving.

i. In a powerful way, this prophecy over Judah is a description of Judah's greatest descendant: Jesus Christ. "The dying patriarch was speaking of his own son Judah; but while speaking of Judah he had a special eye to our Lord, who sprang from the tribe of Judah. Everything therefore which he says of Judah, the type, he means with regard to our greater Judah, the antitype, our Lord Jesus Christ" (Spurgeon).

b. **You are he whom your brothers shall praise…as a lion…the scepter shall not depart from Judah, nor a lawgiver from between his feet…to Him shall be the obedience of the people**: Each of these refer to the *ruling* position Judah will have among his brethren. He inherited the leadership aspect of the firstborn's inheritance. This leadership position among his brothers meant that the eventual kings of Israel would come from Judah and that the Messiah – God's ultimate leader – would eventually come from the tribe of Judah.

> i. In Revelation 5:5, Jesus is called *the Lion of the tribe of Judah*.

> ii. "The firstborn normally had two rights. First, he became the leader of the family, the new patriarch. Second, he was entitled to a double share of the inheritance, receiving twice as much as any of the other brothers." (Boice)

c. **Until Shiloh comes**: The leadership prophecy took some 640 years to fulfill *in part* with the reign of David, first of Judah's dynasty of kings. The prophecy took some 1600 years to *completely* fulfill in Jesus. Jesus is referred to as **Shiloh**, the name meaning, *He whose right it is* or *to Whom it belongs* and a title anciently understood to speak of the Messiah.

> i. From David until the Herods, a prince of Judah was head over Israel (even Daniel in captivity). The promise was that Israel would keep this **scepter** until **Shiloh comes**. Even under their foreign masters during this period, Israel had a limited right to self-rule, until A.D. 7. At that time, under Herod and the Romans, their right to capital punishment – a small but remaining element of their self-governance – was taken away.

> ii. At the time, the rabbis considered it a disaster of unfulfilled Scripture. Seemingly, the last vestige of the **scepter** had passed from Judah, and they did not see the Messiah. Reportedly, rabbis walked the streets of Jerusalem and said, "Woe unto us, for the scepter has been taken away from Judah, and Shiloh has not come." Yet God's word had not been broken.

> iii. Certainly, Jesus was alive then. Perhaps this was the very year He was 12 years old and discussed God's Word in the temple with the scholars of His day. Perhaps He impressed them with His understanding of this very issue.

d. **Binding his donkey to the vine**: This blessing also contained a description of Judah's material abundance (**the vine… the choice vine**). Judah's land was great wine-growing country.

5. (13) Zebulun: **A haven for ships**.

"**Zebulun shall dwell by the haven of the sea;**
He *shall become* a haven for ships,
And his border shall adjoin Sidon."

a. **Zebulun**: Jacob now skipped the birth order, moving to the tenth-born and ninth-born sons, but keeping his focus on the sons born of Leah.

> i. The tribe of Zebulun was noted for its faithfulness to David, supplying the largest number of soldiers to David's army of any single tribe: *Of Zebulun there were fifty thousand who went out to battle, expert in war with all weapons of war, stouthearted men who could keep ranks* (1 Chronicles 12:33).

b. **He shall become a haven for ships**: The tribe of Zebulun seems to have settled the piece of land sitting between the Mediterranean Sea and the Sea of Galilee. Literally, **shall dwell by the haven of the sea** can be translated *looking towards the sea*. Zebulun did look to the sea, both to the east and west.

6. (14-15) Issachar: **A strong donkey**.

"Issachar is a strong donkey,
Lying down between two burdens;
He saw that rest *was* **good,**
And that the land *was* **pleasant;**
He bowed his shoulder to bear *a burden*,
And became a band of slaves.

a. **Issachar is a strong donkey**: Issachar was a large tribe – third in size according to the Numbers 26 census.

b. **And became a band of slaves**: Because of their size and abundance, they were often targets of oppressive foreign armies who put them into servitude. Thus, they **became a band of slaves**.

> i. "The meaning seems to be that Issachar was strong, but docile and lazy. He would enjoy the good land assigned him but would not strive for it. Therefore, eventually he would be pressed into servitude and the mere bearing of burdens for his masters." (Leupold)

7. (16-18) Dan: **A serpent by the way**.

"Dan shall judge his people
As one of the tribes of Israel.
Dan shall be a serpent by the way,
A viper by the path,
That bites the horse's heels
So that its rider shall fall backward.
I have waited for your salvation, O LORD!

a. **Dan shall judge his people**: The tribe of Dan did **judge his people**. They supplied one of the most prominent of the Judges, Samson (Judges 13:2).

b. **Dan shall be a serpent by the way**: Dan was a troublesome tribe. They introduced idolatry into Israel (Judges 18:30). Jeroboam set up one of his idolatrous golden calves in Dan (1 Kings 12:26-30), and later Dan became a center of idol worship in Israel (Amos 8:14).

> i. Some think the **serpent by the way** refers to the idea that the Antichrist would come from the tribe of Dan (based on Daniel 11:37 and Jeremiah 8:16).

> ii. Dan is left *out* of the listing of tribes regarding the 144,000 in Revelation 7:5-8. But Dan is the *first* tribe listed in Ezekiel's millennial roll call of the tribes (Ezekiel 48). This is a remarkable sign of God's redemption.

c. **I have waited for your salvation, O LORD**: The Hebrew word for **salvation** is *"yeshuwah."* At this point in the prophecy, when Jacob was near death, he called out for God's salvation. Knowingly or not, Jacob called out for Jesus.

> i. "What a happy breathing-space is this! When you and I also are near our journey's end, may we be able to say, as Jacob did, 'I have waited for thy salvation, O Lord.'" (Spurgeon)

8. (19) Gad: **He shall triumph at last**.

"**Gad, a troop shall tramp upon him,
But he shall triumph at last.**

a. **Gad:** The tribe of Gad supplied many fine troops for the later king of Israel, David (1 Chronicles 12:14).

b. **A troop shall tramp upon him**: In the days of Jeremiah (among other times), foreign armies oppressed Gad (Jeremiah 49:1). Yet victory would be his in the end (**he shall triumph at last**).

> i. **He shall triumph at last**: "This has been the blessing of many a child of God – to fight, and apparently to lose the battle, yet to win it at the end" (Spurgeon).

9. (20) Asher: **He shall yield royal dainties**.

"**Bread from Asher** *shall be* **rich,
And he shall yield royal dainties.**

a. **Bread from Asher shall be rich**: In Deuteronomy 33:24, Moses again took up this prophecy regarding Asher: *Asher is most blessed of sons; let him be favored by his brothers, and let him dip his foot in oil.*

b. **He shall yield royal dainties**: Apparently, the land eventually occupied by Asher was good enough to bring not only necessities, but also luxuries.

10. (21) Naphtali: **He gives goodly words**.

"Naphtali *is* **a deer let loose;**
He uses beautiful words.

> a. **Naphtali**: Naphtali's land was in a key portion near the Sea of Galilee, the region where Jesus did much of His teaching and ministry.
>
>> i. *Now when Jesus heard that John had been put in prison, He departed to Galilee. And leaving Nazareth, He came and dwelt in Capernaum, which is by the sea, in the regions of Zebulun and Naphtali, that it might be fulfilled which was spoken by Isaiah the prophet, saying: "The land of Zebulun and the land of Naphtali, by the way of the sea, beyond the Jordan, Galilee of the Gentiles: The people who sat in darkness have seen a great light, and upon those who sat in the region and shadow of death light has dawned."* (Matthew 4:12-16)
>
> b. **He uses beautiful words**: Because so much of the ministry of Jesus took place in the region of **Naphtali**, this was fittingly said of him.

11. (22-26) Joseph: **A fruitful bough**.

"Joseph *is* **a fruitful bough,**
A fruitful bough by a well;
His branches run over the wall.
The archers have bitterly grieved him,
Shot *at him* **and hated him.**
But his bow remained in strength,
And the arms of his hands were made strong
By the hands of the Mighty *God* **of Jacob**
(From there *is* **the Shepherd, the Stone of Israel),**
By the God of your father who will help you,
And by the Almighty who will bless you
With **blessings of heaven above,**
Blessings of the deep that lies beneath,
Blessings of the breasts and of the womb.
The blessings of your father
Have excelled the blessings of my ancestors,
Up to the utmost bound of the everlasting hills.
They shall be on the head of Joseph,
And on the crown of the head of him who was separate from his brothers.

> a. **Joseph is a fruitful bough**: This was both a description of Joseph's life and a personal blessing concerning his descendants. In a sense, Joseph's

tribes were already blessed when his sons received their blessing in Genesis 48.

> i. This description of Joseph – as **a fruitful bough by a well** – speaks of his being well-watered and provided for in his deep and real relationship with God. "The main point in Joseph's character was that he was in clear and constant fellowship with God, and therefore God blessed him greatly. He lived to God, and was God's servant; he lived with God, and was God's child" (Spurgeon).

b. **The archers have bitterly grieved him**: Though Joseph was **shot at** and **hated**, he was still **a fruitful** bough. This was because **the arms of his hands were made strong by the hands of the Mighty God of Jacob**. The idea is that God's hands were on Joseph's hands, giving him strength and skill to work the bow expertly. God was there, even when Joseph did not know it.

c. **The Almighty who will bless you**: Joseph was certainly blessed in his posterity. His tribes were some of the most populous. In this sense, he received the *material* blessing, the double portion aspect of the inheritance of the firstborn.

d. **The blessings of your father have excelled the blessings of my ancestors**: Jacob could say this because he was, for much of his life, a scoundrel. Now at the end of his days, he saw just how good God was to him. He was forgiven much and loved much (Luke 7:47).

e. **The Mighty God of Jacob**: In his words about Joseph, Jacob listed five great titles for God. These titles show that Jacob did come to an understanding of who God is.

- **The Mighty God of Jacob**.
- **The Shepherd**.
- **The Stone of Israel**.
- **The God of your father**.
- **The Almighty**.

> i. This is much better than when Jacob referred to God as *the God of Abraham* or *the Fear of his father Isaac* (Genesis 31:53). Now he knew who God was for *himself*.

12. (27) Benjamin: **a ravenous wolf**.

"Benjamin is a ravenous wolf;
In the morning he shall devour the prey,
And at night he shall divide the spoil."

a. **Benjamin is a ravenous wolf**: This was the tribe with a reputation for fierceness.

b. **He shall devour the prey**: To see the great extent of this, look at Ehud (Judges 3:15-23), Saul (1 Samuel 9:1, 14:47-52), and Paul (Acts 8:1-3). The cruelty of the tribe in general is seen in Judges 19 and 20.

13. (28) Jacob concludes his blessing of the sons.

All these *are* the twelve tribes of Israel, and this is what their father spoke to them. And he blessed them; he blessed each one according to his own blessing.

a. **And he blessed them**: Some of the things mentioned regarding these tribes may seem a bit cloudy, but only because we may not know their exact fulfillment until the age to come.

b. **Each one according to his own blessing**: Each son and each tribe that would come from them had their own calling and destiny. Yet the remarkable promise remained – that they each would survive and grow into significant tribes, without one perishing during the centuries to come in Egypt.

B. Jacob's death.

1. (29-32) Jacob makes his sons promise to bury him in Canaan.

Then he charged them and said to them: "I am to be gathered to my people; bury me with my fathers in the cave that is in the field of Ephron the Hittite, in the cave that is in the field of Machpelah, which is before Mamre in the land of Canaan, which Abraham bought with the field of Ephron the Hittite as a possession for a burial place. There they buried Abraham and Sarah his wife, there they buried Isaac and Rebekah his wife, and there I buried Leah. The field and the cave that is there *were* purchased from the sons of Heth."

a. **I am to be gathered to my people**: Jacob was confident that his father Isaac and his grandfather Abraham continued to live in the eternal state, and that he would be **gathered** to them.

b. **Bury me with my fathers**: Though Jacob was now in Egypt, he knew he was not an Egyptian. He was a son of the promise, an heir of God's covenant with Abraham, and he asked to be buried in the land promised to Abraham, Isaac, and Jacob by covenant.

c. **In the cave that is in the field of Machpelah**: Egypt was filled with magnificent tombs, and because of the respect Jacob had, he could have been buried like a Pharaoh. But he wanted to be buried in an obscure cave in Canaan, because Canaan was the land of promise.

2. (33) The death of Jacob.

And when Jacob had finished commanding his sons, he drew his feet up into the bed and breathed his last, and was gathered to his people.

   a. **Breathed his last**: This ends the life of the last of the great patriarchs, of Abraham, Isaac, and Jacob. Yet the work and plan of God did not end. It continued through men and generations to come.

      i. **When Jacob had finished commanding his sons**: "Jacob did not yield up the ghost until he had delivered the last sentence of admonition and benediction to his twelve sons. He was immortal till his work was done. So long as God had another sentence to speak by him, death could not paralyze his tongue" (Spurgeon).

   b. **And was gathered to his people**: There are said to be three basic attitudes towards death. Among the ancient Greeks, they held to what can be called the *death-accepting* view. Our modern world is sold out to a *death-denying* approach. The Biblical approach is the *death-defying* attitude.

Genesis 50 – The Burial of Jacob; the Death of Joseph

A. Jacob is buried in Canaan.

1. (1-3) Jacob is embalmed and mourned.

Then Joseph fell on his father's face, and wept over him, and kissed him. And Joseph commanded his servants the physicians to embalm his father. So the physicians embalmed Israel. Forty days were required for him, for such are the days required for those who are embalmed; and the Egyptians mourned for him seventy days.

> a. **Joseph fell on his father's face, and wept over him, and kissed him**: The passing of Jacob in the presence of his sons was a deeply moving and dramatic scene.
>
> b. **The Egyptians mourned him seventy days**: Jacob was mourned for 70 days among the whole nation of Egypt. A *royal* mourning period in Egypt was 72 days. Jacob was obviously a greatly honored man.

2. (4-6) Joseph asks Pharaoh for permission to bury his father in Canaan.

And when the days of his mourning were past, Joseph spoke to the household of Pharaoh, saying, "If now I have found favor in your eyes, please speak in the hearing of Pharaoh, saying, 'My father made me swear, saying, "Behold, I am dying; in my grave which I dug for myself in the land of Canaan, there you shall bury me." Now therefore, please let me go up and bury my father, and I will come back.'" And Pharaoh said, "Go up and bury your father, as he made you swear."

> a. **Joseph spoke to the household of Pharaoh**: The fact that Joseph made his initial request, not directly to the ruler of Egypt, but **spoke to the household of Pharaoh**, is the kind of detail that would be noted by true witness of the events, and not made up by a storyteller.

b. **My father made me swear**: Joseph explained the solemn promise his father required of him, and Pharaoh gave him the liberty to keep the promise and **bury** Israel in Canaan.

3. (7-11) Jacob's body is brought to Canaan.

So Joseph went up to bury his father; and with him went up all the servants of Pharaoh, the elders of his house, and all the elders of the land of Egypt, as well as all the house of Joseph, his brothers, and his father's house. Only their little ones, their flocks, and their herds they left in the land of Goshen. And there went up with him both chariots and horsemen, and it was a very great gathering. Then they came to the threshing floor of Atad, which *is* beyond the Jordan, and they mourned there with a great and very solemn lamentation. He observed seven days of mourning for his father. And when the inhabitants of the land, the Canaanites, saw the mourning at the threshing floor of Atad, they said, "This *is* a deep mourning of the Egyptians." Therefore its name was called Abel Mizraim, which *is* beyond the Jordan.

a. **Joseph went up to bury his father**: This was a dramatic burial. The entire clan gathered together to pay tribute to the man who was the last link with the patriarchs. The life of this man's grandfather overlapped with the sons of Noah.

i. "Luther remarks that there is no burial recorded in the Scriptures quite as honorable as this or with such wealth of detail." (Leupold)

b. **They mourned there with a great and very solemn lamentation**: This was, no doubt, a day of rededication of the sons of Israel to the God of Israel, the God of the great covenant made to Abraham, Isaac, and Jacob. Their dedication to the God of Israel would be tested over the next many hundred years, but would survive.

4. (12-14) Jacob's burial in the cave of the field of Machpelah.

So his sons did for him just as he had commanded them. For his sons carried him to the land of Canaan, and buried him in the cave of the field of Machpelah, before Mamre, which Abraham bought with the field from Ephron the Hittite as property for a burial place. And after he had buried his father, Joseph returned to Egypt, he and his brothers and all who went up with him to bury his father.

a. **His sons did for him just as he had commanded them**: Jacob's sons had often opposed or disappointed him in life. They were careful to honor him in his death.

b. **Buried him in the cave of the field of Machpelah**: This was the cave purchased by Abraham (Genesis 23:9), the only part of the land of Canaan that Abraham held deed to (Genesis 23:17). This was the burial place of Sarah (Genesis 23:19), of Abraham (Genesis 25:9), and of Isaac, Rebekah, and Leah (Genesis 49:31).

B. Joseph comforts his brothers' fears.

1. (15) The fears of Joseph's brothers.

When Joseph's brothers saw that their father was dead, they said, "Perhaps Joseph will hate us, and may actually repay us for all the evil which we did to him."

> a. **Perhaps Joseph will hate us**: The brothers feared that perhaps Joseph would turn on them after Jacob's death. Knowing human nature, this was certainly possible.
>
> b. **And may actually repay us for all the evil which we did to him**: Here, they freely acknowledged **all the evil which they did**. What they worried about was *justice*. They feared *righteous* retribution. Joseph, with his high status and prestige in Egypt, was certainly capable of bringing this retribution.

2. (16-18) The unlikely story of Joseph's brothers.

So they sent *messengers* to Joseph, saying, "Before your father died he commanded, saying, 'Thus you shall say to Joseph: "I beg you, please forgive the trespass of your brothers and their sin; for they did evil to you." ' Now, please, forgive the trespass of the servants of the God of your father." And Joseph wept when they spoke to him. Then his brothers also went and fell down before his face, and they said, "Behold, we *are* your servants."

> a. **Before your father died he commanded**: This story was probably made up. They didn't feel they had the moral right to ask Joseph for mercy, since they sinned against him so greatly. So they put the request for mercy in the mouth of their honored and dead father.
>
> b. **Joseph wept when they spoke to him**: Joseph probably wept because it seemed that his brothers thought so little of him and they doubted his character so greatly.
>
> c. **Fell down before his face, and they said, "Behold, we are your servants"**: They backed up their plea for mercy with a genuine display of humility.

3. (19-21) Joseph comforts his brothers.

Joseph said to them, "Do not be afraid, for *am* I in the place of God? But as for you, you meant evil against me; *but* God meant it for good, in order to bring it about as it is this day, to save many people alive. Now

therefore, do not be afraid; I will provide for you and your little ones." And he comforted them and spoke kindly to them.

    a. **Am I in the place of God**: Joseph first understood he was not **in the place of God**. It wasn't his job to bring retribution upon his brothers. If the LORD chose to punish them, He would have to find an instrument other than Joseph.

        i. From a human perspective, Joseph had the right and the ability to bring retribution upon his brothers, but he knew God was God and he was not. Such retribution was God's **place**, not Joseph's.

    b. **As for you, you meant evil against me; but God meant it for good**: Joseph did not romanticize the wrong his brothers did. He plainly said, "**You meant evil against me**." Although this was true, it was not the *greatest* truth. The greatest truth was "**God meant it for good**."

        i. Every Christian should be able to see the overarching and overruling hand of God in their life; to know that no matter what **evil** man brings against us, God can use it for **good**.

        ii. Joseph did not have the text of Romans 8:28, but he had the truth of it: *And we know that all things work together for good to those who love God, to those who are the called according to His purpose.* Sadly, many of us who have the text do not have the truth.

        iii. Ultimately, our lives are not in the hands of men, but in the hands of God, who overrules all things for His glory.

        iv. There was an old minister who had a unique gift to minister to the distressed and discouraged. In his Bible, he carried an old bookmark woven of silk threads into a motto. The back of it, where the threads were knotted and tied, was a hopeless tangle. He would take the bookmark out and show the troubled person this side of the bookmark and ask them to make sense of it. They never could. Then the pastor would turn it over, and on the front were white letters against a solid background saying, "God is love." When events in our life seem tangled and meaningless, it is because we can see only one side of the tapestry.

    c. **To save many people alive**: This was the *immediate* good in the situation. If this large family did not come to Egypt and live, it would have perished in the famine. Had the family barely survived, it would have assimilated into the Canaanite tribes surrounding it. Only by coming to Egypt could they be preserved and grow into a distinct nation.

        i. As said before, if Joseph's brothers never sold him to the Midianites, then Joseph would never have gone to Egypt.

- If Joseph never went to Egypt, he would never have been sold to Potiphar.
- If Joseph was never sold to Potiphar, Potiphar's wife would never have falsely accused him of rape.
- If Potiphar's wife never falsely accused Joseph of rape, then Joseph would never have been put in prison.
- If Joseph was never put in prison, he would have never met the baker and butler of Pharaoh.
- If Joseph never met the baker and butler of Pharaoh, he would have never interpreted their dreams.
- If Joseph never interpreted their dreams, he would have never interpreted Pharaoh's dream.
- If Joseph never interpreted Pharaoh's dream, he never would have become prime minister, second in Egypt only to Pharaoh.
- If Joseph never became prime minister, he never would have wisely prepared for the terrible famine to come.
- If Joseph never wisely prepared for the terrible famine, then his family back in Canaan would have died in the famine.
- If Joseph's family back in Canaan died in the famine, then the Messiah could not have come from a dead family.
- If the Messiah did not come forth, then Jesus never came.
- If Jesus never came, then we are all dead in our sins and without hope in this world.
- *We are grateful for God's great and wise plan.*

d. **And he comforted them and spoke kindly to them**: Because Joseph trusted the overarching hand of God, even in all the evil that came upon him through his brothers, he showed the love and compassion to them he did.

i. Often, the problem we have in loving others and in freeing ourselves from bitterness we may have towards them is really a problem of not knowing who *God is* and trusting Him to be who He says He is.

e. **I will provide for you and your little ones**: Joseph's love for his brothers was shown not only in feelings and words, but also in practical action. He actually *did* provide for his brothers and their families.

C. The death of Joseph.

1. (22-24) Joseph is still in Egypt, but his heart is in Canaan.

So Joseph dwelt in Egypt, he and his father's household. And Joseph lived one hundred and ten years. Joseph saw Ephraim's children to the third *generation*. **The children of Machir, the son of Manasseh, were also brought up on Joseph's knees. And Joseph said to his brethren, "I am dying; but God will surely visit you, and bring you out of this land to the land of which He swore to Abraham, to Isaac, and to Jacob."**

a. **Joseph lived one hundred and ten years**: His long life was further evidence of God's blessing on Joseph's life, as was seeing **Ephraim's children to the third generation**. The hardships of his life did not diminish God's ultimate blessing upon him.

b. **God will surely visit you and bring you out of this land to the land which He swore to Abraham, to Isaac, and to Jacob**: Joseph was the human agent most responsible for bringing this family to Egypt. Yet he knew that because of the covenant God had made with Abraham, Isaac, and Jacob, this would not be their resting place. They were headed – eventually – back to Canaan.

2. (25-26) The death and embalming of Joseph.

Then Joseph took an oath from the children of Israel, saying, "God will surely visit you, and you shall carry up my bones from here." So Joseph died, *being* **one hundred and ten years old; and they embalmed him, and he was put in a coffin in Egypt.**

a. **He was put in a coffin in Egypt**: According to this passage and Hebrews 11:22, Joseph was never buried. His coffin laid above ground for the 400 or so years until it was taken back to Canaan. It was a silent witness for all those years that Israel *was* going back to the Promised Land, just as God said.

i. Joseph lived a life of dramatic faith. Yet in the end, this is how he was remembered in the Hebrews 11 Museum of Faith: *By faith Joseph, when he was dying, made mention of the departure of the children of Israel, and gave instructions concerning his bones* (Hebrews 11:22).

- This was faith, because it trusted God's promise to His people.
- This was faith, because it knew where God's people belonged.
- This was faith, because it looked to the future.
- This was faith, because it proclaimed God's faithful promise in any way possible – even through a dead man's bones!

b. **You shall carry up my bones from here**: This promise was fulfilled some 400 years later, when Israel left Egypt (Exodus 13:19). This command showed that Joseph's heart was in the Promised Land. It also proved him to be a man of great faith, trusting in things not yet seen (Hebrews 11:22).

i. All during that time, when a child of Israel saw Joseph's coffin and asked what it was there for and why it was not buried, they could be answered, "Because the great man Joseph did not want to be buried in Egypt, but in the Promised Land God will one day lead us to."

ii. Some promises of God take a long time to fulfill, and we must persevere in trusting God. George Mueller was a remarkable man of faith who ran orphanages in England. In a sermon preached when he was 75 years old, he said 30,000 times in his 54 years as a Christian he received the answer to prayer on the same day he prayed it. But not all his prayers were answered so quickly. He told of one prayer that he brought to God about 20,000 times over more than 11 years, and he still trusted God for the answer: "I hope in God, I pray on, and look for the answer. Therefore, beloved brethren and sisters, go on waiting upon God, go on praying."

iii. Joseph died looking forward to God's unfolding plan of redemption, and that is where the Book of Genesis – the Book of Beginnings – ends. It concludes looking forward to the continuation of God's eternal, loving, wise plan.

Genesis – Bibliography

Barnhouse, Donald Grey *Genesis, A Devotional Exposition*, Volumes 1 and 2 (Grand Rapids, Michigan: Zondervan, 1973)

Boice, James Montgomery *Genesis, An Expositional Commentary, Volumes 1, 2, and 3* (Grand Rapids, Michigan: Zondervan, 1987)

Clarke, Adam *The Holy Bible, Containing the Old and New Testaments, with A Commentary and Critical Notes* (New York: Eaton and Mains, 1826)

Ginzberg, Louis *The Legends of the Jews, Volumes 1-7* (Philadelphia: The Jewish Publication Society of America, 1968)

Johnson, Philip *Darwin on Trial* (Downer's Grove, Illinois: InterVarsity Press, 1993)

Kidner, Derek *Genesis, An Introduction and Commentary* (Leicester, England, Inter-Varsity Press, 1967)

Leupold, H.C. *Exposition of Genesis, Volumes 1 and 2* (Grand Rapids, Michigan: Baker Book House, 1976)

Maclaren, Alexander *Expostions of Holy Scripture, Volume 1* (Grand Rapids, Michigan: Baker Book House, 1984)

McMillen, S.I. *None of These Diseases* (Old Tappan, New Jersey: Fleming H. Revell Company, 1968)

Meyer, F.B. *Our Daily Homily* (Westwood, New Jersey: Revell, 1966)

Morgan, G. Campbell *An Exposition of the Whole Bible* (Old Tappan, New Jersey: Revell, 1959)

Morgan, G. Campbell *Searchlights from the Word* (New York, Revell: 1936)

Morris, Henry M. *The Genesis Record* (Grand Rapids, Michigan: Baker Book House, 1976)

Poole, Matthew *A Commentary on the Holy Bible, Volume 1* (London, Banner of Truth Trust, 1968)

Ross, Hugh *The Fingerprint of God* (Santa Ana, California, Promise Publishing, 1991)

Sailhamer, John H. "Genesis," *The Expositor's Bible Commentary, Volume 1* (Grand Rapids, Michigan: Zondervan, 1990)

Spurgeon, Charles Haddon *The New Park Street Pulpit, Volumes 1-6 and The Metropolitan Tabernacle Pulpit, Volumes 7-63* (Pasadena, Texas: Pilgrim Publications, 1990)

Trapp, John *A Commentary on the Old and New Testaments, Volume One* (Eureka, California: Tanski Publications, 1997)

As the years pass I love the work of studying, learning, and teaching the Bible more than ever. I'm so grateful that God is faithful to meet me in His Word.

Two proofreaders gave their time and skill to this book and made it much better. Thanks to Ruth Gordon and Debbie Pollaccia, especially for your patience with my many repeated mistakes!

The first edition of my Genesis commentary was published in 1998. After 20 years it was more than time for an update and a new cover. Thanks to Brian Procedo for the cover design and all the graphics work.

Most especially, thanks to my wife Inga-Lill. She is my loved and valued partner in life and in service to God and His people.

David Guzik

David Guzik's Bible commentary is regularly used and trusted by many thousands who want to know the Bible better. Pastors, teachers, class leaders, and everyday Christians find his commentary helpful for their own understanding and explanation of the Bible. David and his wife Inga-Lill live in Santa Barbara, California.

You can email David at david@enduringword.com

For more resources by David Guzik, go to www.enduringword.com

www.ingramcontent.com/pod-product-compliance
Lightning Source LLC
Chambersburg PA
CBHW020346170426
43200CB00005B/61